THE WORLD COUNCIL OF CHURCHES
IN INTERNATIONAL AFFAIRS

The Institute and its Research Committee are grateful for the comments and suggestions made by the Reverend Alan R. Booth, Professor Geoffrey Goodwin and the late Mr Noël Salter, who were asked to review the manuscript of this book.

The World Council of Churches in International Affairs

Darril Hudson

Published for
THE ROYAL INSTITUTE OF
INTERNATIONAL AFFAIRS

by
THE FAITH PRESS
1977

First published in 1977 by The Faith Press Ltd.,
Leighton Buzzard, Beds. LU7 7NQ

© Royal Institute of International Affairs 1977

ISBN 0 7164 0465 6

PRINTED IN GREAT BRITAIN
BY THE FAITH PRESS LTD.
LEIGHTON BUZZARD LU7 7NQ

TO EMMA LEE VAN METER, MY MOTHER,
AND LLOYD E. VAN METER

CONTENTS

FIGURES

TABLES

ACKNOWLEDGEMENTS

GRATEFUL acknowledgement is made to the Royal Institute of International Affairs for supporting my belief that a study of the activities of the World Council of Churches in international affairs should be undertaken, and for providing financial help from the Wren Bequest.

Inevitably an author's debts pile up. The writing of this book would have been immeasurably more difficult without the co-operation of the Reverend Alan Booth, who has recently retired as Director of Christian Aid and was formerly London Secretary of the Commission of the Churches on International Affairs. I am grateful for help from Dr A. J. van der Bent, of the World Council of Churches Library at Geneva. The staffs of the Library and Press Library of Chatham House are warmly thanked for their most useful services. I wish also to thank Miss Rena Fenteman, Chatham House editor, who went through the tribulations of editing by post, with an author travelling in Asia and Africa. The Research Committee of California State University, Hayward, made available student assistance for the compilation of financial and other quantifiable data.

Dr Roger Morgan, Deputy Director of Studies at Chatham House while this book was being written and now Professor of European Studies at Loughborough University of Technology, followed and guided the long and laborious process of research and writing with a mixture of cajolery and discipline. His comments and criticisms were invaluable. Professor Geoffrey Goodwin, Montague Burton Professor of International Relations at the London School of Economics and Political Science, provided critical observations which have enormously improved the work. The fact that it did not attain the height of Dr Morgan's and Professor Goodwin's expectations is entirely the responsibility of the author.

D.H.

ABBREVIATIONS

AACC	All Africa Conference of Churches
ACTS	Advisory Committee on Technical Services
ANC	African National Council (Rhodesia, Zimbabwe)
BCC	British Council of Churches
BOSS	Bureau of State Security
CCA	Commission on Conventional Armaments
CCD	Conference of the Committee on Disarmament, formerly ENDC
CCIA	Commission of the Churches on International Affairs
CCPD	Commission on the Churches' Participation in Development
CICARWS	Commission on Inter-Church Aid, Refugee and World Service
CMC	Christian Medical Commission
CMSGBI	Conference of Mission Societies in Great Britain and Ireland
CWME	Commission on World Mission and Evangelism
DICARWS	Division of Inter-Church Aid, Refugee and World Service. In 1971 this became CICARWS
DICASR	Division of Inter-Church Aid and Service to Refugees. In 1961 this became DICARWS
DWME	Division of World Mission and Evangelism
EABC	European American Banking Corporation

EACC	East Asia Christian Conference, later the Christian Conference of Asia
ECA	Economic Commission for Africa
ECOSOC	(United Nations) Economic and Social Council
EKD	Evangelische Kirche in Deutschland
ENDC	Eighteen Nation Disarmament Committee, later the CCD
EPEAA	Ecumenical Programme for Emergency Action in Africa
EPTA	(United Nations) Expanded Programme of Technical Assistance
FAO	Food and Agriculture Organization of the United Nations
Frelimo	Mozambique Liberation Front (Fronte de Libertação de Moçambique)
GRAE	Revolutionary Government of Angola in Exile (Governo Revolucionario de Angola no Exil)
HNP	Herstigte Nasionale Party
IAEA	International Atomic Energy Agency
IBRD	International Bank for Reconstruction and Development
ICAO	International Civil Aviation Organization
ICFTU	International Confederation of Free Trade Unions
IDA	International Development Association
IFC	International Finance Corporation
IGO	Intergovernmental Organization
ILO	International Labour Organization
IMC	International Missionary Council

IMCO	Intergovernmental Maritime Consultative Organization
IRO	International Refugee Organization
ITU	International Telecommunication Union
JWG	Joint Working Group between the Roman Catholic Church and the World Council of Churches
MPLA	People's Movement for the Liberation of Angola (Movimento Popular de Libertação de Angola)
NCCCUSA	National Council of the Churches of Christ in the USA
NGO	Non-governmental Organization
OAU	Organization of African Unity
PAC	Pan-Africanist Congress
PAIGC	African Independence Party of Guinea and Cape Verde Islands (Partido Africano da Independencia da Guiné e Cabo Verde)
PCR	Programme to Combat Racism
PDL	Poverty Datum Line
RCC	Roman Catholic Church
SACC	South African Council of Churches
SALT	Strategic Arms Limitation Talks
SASP	Specialized Assistance for Social Projects
SODEPAX	Committee on Society, Development and Peace
SSLM	South Sudan Liberation Movement
SUNFED	Special United Nations Fund for Economic Development
SWANU	South West African National Union

SWAPO	South West African People's Organization
TAB	Technical Assistance Board
TAC	Technical Assistance Committee
UNAEC	United Nations Atomic Energy Commission
UNCTAD	United Nations Conference on Trade and Development
UNDC	United Nations Disarmament Commission
UNDP	United Nations Development Programme
UNESCO	United Nations Educational, Scientific and Cultural Organization
UNITA	National Union for the Total Independence of Angola (União Nacional para a Independencia Total de Angola)
UNRRA	United Nations Relief and Rehabilitation Administration
UNTDB	United Nations Trade and Development Board
UPU	Universal Postal Union
WCC	World Council of Churches
WCCE	World Council of Christian Education
WHO	World Health Organization
WMO	World Meteorological Organization
WSCF	World Student Christian Federation
YMCA	Young Men's Christian Association
YWCA	Young Women's Christian Association
ZANU	Zimbabwe African National Union
ZAPU	Zimbabwe African People's Union

Introduction

THE World Council of Churches is a unique institution. Some would even say it had a divine mission: to create Christian unity. Those faithful who fervently believe that its otherworldliness is its most important aspect will be disappointed in this study. And yet if the ecumenical movement is to speak to those in the world who are not of the World Council, they must be able to understand its functioning in worldly terms. Its believers, too, must be aware of this side of the World Council; they must realize that it exists also as a non-spiritual entity, a very practical organization in the perceptions of many, Christians and non-Christians alike, who come in contact with it through its multifaceted activities in the world. For United Nations officials, for example, it is one of a class of international entities known as international non-governmental organizations (NGOs). The role of these NGOs in the international system is analogous to that of interest groups at the national level. Through representations, objective information (available only through Christian bodies), subjective information (the Christian ethical judgement regarding the objective conditions), and through ministration to the needs of refugees and victims of catastrophe in co-operation with governmental and intergovernmental agencies, the World Council, like other NGOs, participates directly and indirectly in international deliberations.

The lack of a great amount of empirical data concerning the NGOs, their activities, and the results of their efforts leaves their participation largely unevaluated. Their role in international integrative and functional processes has been surmised on an inadequate basis; the intuitive evaluation is that non-state, voluntary entities have 'minimal'[1] or 'mediocre'[2] effects in international decision-making. Scholars admit the lack of a basis for evaluating them while continuing to do so.[3] There is, however, a group of scholars who are delving into the transnational nature of these NGOs and their interactions. A pioneer body in this study has been the Union of International Associations (UIA), itself an NGO comprising a federation of NGOs! With headquarters in Brussels, it was founded to look after the interests of the private international associations which multiplied with the creation of the League of Nations. In interpreting its mission, UIA leadership has attempted to guide, to encourage, and to conduct studies of the role of its constituents in international affairs.[4] Since the founding

17

B

of the United Nations, the minimal resources available for studies of the world's non-official agencies have contributed to the lack of scholarly interest in them when contrasted with the more highly subsidized research concerning their romantic and glamorous stepsisters, the intergovernmental organizations (IGOs).[5] In addition to the UIA, a group of scholars in the United States has begun an attempt systematically to collect data on the activities of NGOs and other non-governmental actors on the international scene.[6] It is as a contribution to this badly needed data bank that it is hoped this study will prove useful.

The World Council, like other NGOs, is basically a federation of national members; therefore, the process of arriving at a World Council position on an issue can also be instructive in the more general study of these bodies. International politics is dynamic, a World Council position must be so, too, and evidence of the evolution of its thought will be given in the statements, pronouncements, studies, and reports here summarized or quoted in order to put at the disposal of the reader information otherwise obtainable only from divers sources. In successive statements, the influence of world events on World Council opinion can be followed, as well as any effect these statements might have had on others.

The subjective rationalizations for ecumenical international concerns are couched in theological language in the discussions among its officers, delegates, and participants, the particular terminology and rationalization varying with the ecclesiastical tradition of the speaker. However, this is not a theological study and no attempt is made to evaluate the theological positions taken by individuals or by the World Council in its statements. Where opposing theological stands have been a factor in action taken or avoided, that has been noted. In order to make a manageable study, three cases from among the wide range of ecumenical activities have been chosen; in each the World Council used a different approach in trying to achieve its goal.

To understand better the present role of the World Council in international affairs, a brief background on the beginning of international interest and activities in world affairs of the ecumenical movement is provided in the first chapter. This is followed by an explanation of the organization of the World Council as it applies to international concerns, particularly the Commission of the Churches on International Affairs (CCIA), which in the first twenty-five years of World Council existence acted as its primary arm in world affairs. The form of organization has a great deal to do with the manner in which a task is executed; it may limit initiative, allow it, or actively encourage it. In the formative years the leeway given to CCIA officers was such that it was they who chose the direction it followed, and their judgements which determined the priorities set and the topics concentrated upon (within the broad limits imposed by the World Council Assemblies). The centralization of World Council activities, especially in foreign affairs, conducted under Dr Eugene Carson Blake's tenure as General Secretary and coinciding with the resignation of the 'rugged individualists' who had organized and conducted the World Council's international affairs since 1946, Sir Kenneth Grubb and Professor O. F. Nolde, radically altered the influence of the CCIA as an arm of the World Council of Churches.

The first of the case studies deals with the quest for equality among men, for though the church has ever preached the equality of men before God, it has condoned inequality. Since its foundation, the World Council has inveighed and struggled against racism, primarily but not exclusively in the form of apartheid as practised in the Republic of South Africa. In this instance it faced an incompatibility of goals: it felt obliged to protest against a governmental policy it regarded as an absolute evil, while at the same time trying to preserve the Christian unity thus far achieved. Some of its members actively supported this racist policy, justifying it in theological language. Unable to reconcile these goals, it chose to bear witness to what its leadership regarded as its moral imperative. It sought primarily to influence one government's policy, that of the Republic of South Africa, though it spoke out against racial discrimination wherever it occurred. Through representations and pronouncements and in its work through the United Nations, it helped to create new international standards of behaviour which the General Assembly, with overwhelming world consensus, has brought into being. By actively collaborating with those who are victims of racism, it has gone a step further than speaking. It has acted by providing funds to groups of racism's victims throughout the world, receiving great notoriety on account of the few groups in Southern Africa which received grants for educational and humanitarian work while fighting for their independence.

In another area of concern, the World Council was moved to attempt to free man from the slavery of poverty and ignorance, so that he might achieve his fullest potential. This second case study analyses the programme which developed from post-war emergency service for European churches into recognition of the need to continue similar efforts throughout the world in order to ameliorate natural and man-made emergencies. This view in turn led to a realization of the need to combat endemic starvation as well as famine. To achieve results, the World Council had to interest a disinterested world in action rather than to overcome active opposition; to this end it joined forces with the Roman Catholic Church, following the Vatican Ecumenical Council, in actively formulating an economic development policy for the Third World.

It practised its preaching when, after the Uppsala Assembly in 1968, the churches of the industrialized states were encouraged to tax themselves and to give this sum as development aid through the World Council. More than simply funding projects as in its first quarter-century, the new Commission on the Churches' Participation in Development is trying to develop a pattern of giving and administering aid in a programme to maximize the effectiveness of the aid effort. The outcome of this experiment could be of use to governments and to international organizations.

The final case study deals with the traditional Christian opposition to man's killing of man, manifested in the encouragement of arms control and disarmament. Having come to terms with combating the ideological images of East and West, the World Council has been accused simultaneously by critics on both sides of being a communist stooge and a capitalist lackey. It has, nevertheless, borne Christian witness as its officials have perceived this duty. It acted through pronouncements, through representations to the governments of great powers, and by conducting in Geneva disarmament consultations in which the ambassadors of the superpowers participated. The educational programme of the World Council throughout this period encouraged its constituents in the Western democracies to accept as desirable the cessation of atmospheric testing and varying degrees of control on nuclear weapons. Although it is impossible to substantiate the claim of direct influence upon decision-makers, there is no doubt that many of the disarmament goals sought by the Christian community have been achieved during a period of twenty-five years.

In the fifth chapter, the international activities of the World Council are analysed as those of a political interest group whose main method of approach depends on the clear presentation of moral argument and the supply of information. A comparison is made between a national political interest group and an international one in considering the qualities which make such a group capable of sustaining the attention of those whose decisions will hinder, alter, maintain, or initiate policies as the group feels necessary. A consideration of the World Council role in society and of the acceptability of its élite by the political and economic élites at the national and international levels and the interaction of these élites, is made in some detail, since such interaction has been a major mode of World Council activity. Evidence of this societal and élite role is adduced by citing the many newspapers, communist and capitalist, which follow the operations of the World Council. Finally, an attempt is made to understand its role in the international decision-making process in communicating values, goals, and information.

Placing the World Council and NGOs into the traditional concept of international relations—if that concept sees international relations as being solely a struggle for power—does not account for their continued activity in international affairs, nor for the institutionalization of their relationships with intergovernmental organizations. A theory which allows for mutually influential relationships between governments, intergovernmental organizations, and non-governmental bodies, interprets the World Council relationship as that of a social institution, the church, transposed to the international level where it retains its function as a norm-creating institution in society and whose opinions are valued by those in power simply because they accept the basic ordering of their society.[7] It appeals to their reason, to their ethics, to their intellect. As an institution which has recaptured its original essence of universality, the World Council of Churches feels an obligation to act as spokesman for the poor and powerless of all religions throughout the world.

1. An International Witness

THE World Council of Churches is to most people's minds an international ecclesiastical body concerned with Christian unity; to some people's minds this ought to be its sole concern. But its Protestant-Orthodox character is catholic in its interests; it is concerned with the problems of men as well as of churches. When one looks at the background to the formation of the World Council, one sees that out of the multitudinous interactions which gave it birth, it could not be otherwise. For its concern has been with Christian service as well as Christian unity; the concept of service has grown to include all spheres of activity and has expanded to include all mankind. The World Council, with its far-reaching concerns, was not something created suddenly by fiat of religious czars but resulted from four decades of growing experience of committed Christian leaders.

The early twentieth century witnessed the beginning of a phenomenon which came to be called 'the ecumenical movement'; it has been regarded by some Christians as the working of the Holy Spirit and by some dissident believers as, at best, an act of misguided souls or, at worst, as a work of the Devil. Sociologists have seen this movement for Christian unity as a religious reaction to the increasing secularization of society in the late nineteenth and twentieth centuries,[1] and disgruntled ecclesiastics have regarded it as a simple canonical power play. When religion was a central institution of society—whether church, temple, or mosque—throughout the world, the viewpoint of its spokesmen both through its role as a socializing factor and as representing one of society's élites was of great importance. In the West, secular institutions multiplied and gained power as a result of the Industrial Revolution, and the pre-eminence which religion had held in what were predominantly agrarian societies was gradually eroded in these new industrial ones. The divided voices with which the religious establishment spoke and gave its often contradictory viewpoints were weakened by this division and could all the more easily be ignored or outshouted. So sociologists may be right in attributing this trend towards unity to an institutional reaction to secularization, though, in spite of a perhaps accurate sociological explanation, many Christians still claim to see the working of the Holy Spirit in this matter.

It would be helpful in understanding the World Council of Churches as an international organization of secular as well as religious interest (dichotomous terms of which many modern Christians deny the validity) to look briefly at the twentieth-century background to its founding. To appreciate its particular role in world affairs better, the creation of its specialist organ in this area, the Commission of the Churches on International Affairs, will be described. Its organization and workings in detail, along with those of other World Council bodies active in international problems, will then be delineated. In the final part of this chapter these specialist organs will be placed in perspective, with a description of the general organization of the World Council and the changes effected in it since 1948 in order to meet new concerns in new times.

The effect of the ecumenical movement's first action in international affairs was that it attached significance not to church unity itself but to unified Christian action to relieve suffering in the world for the love of Christ. Thus the primary imprint of the ecumenical movement on world affairs was one of service to man. This action was performed by an *ad hoc* Christian body in Great Britain which eventually included Roman Catholic, Protestant, and Jewish leaders from that country, the United States, and several European states.[2] It may have been that the *Zeitgeist,* one of increasing internationalism, affected these Christian gentlemen; it is certain that this particular ecumenical action was a reaction to the secular world. But it should be no shame that these religious leaders were stirred, like others throughout the world, by the hopes for a continued peace evoked by the calling of the Second Hague Peace Conference for 1907.

It was a small action which these British Christians initiated: they prepared memorials to be presented to the Peace Conference. In them they urged not only the general admonition one might expect of churchmen, to work for peace; they also specifically called for an end to the arms race and acceptance of the principle of arbitration in international disputes.[3] Although today this would be regarded as a rather commonplace and timid action, for those church leaders, some of established national churches, publicly and unitedly to exhort statesmen to act was in itself a bold move for that time and place.

Joseph Allen Baker, British Member of Parliament and Canadian Quaker who gave leadership in this action, also developed with Baron Eduard de Neufville, a noted peaceworker of Frankfurt-am-Main, a programme of exchange visits between German and British ecclesiastical and lay leaders, Protestant and Roman Catholic, in 1908 and 1909.[4] These visits in turn led to the creation of the first twentieth-century international and ecumenical organization, called *The Associated Councils of Churches of the British and German*

Empires for Fostering Friendly Relations between the Two Peoples.

Some historians of the ecumenical movement have ignored these beginnings and have credited the World Missionary Conference at Edinburgh in 1910 with the seminal action which led to the ever-increasing international Christian awareness. It has often happened that an invention has occurred in two widely separated places at about the same time without the possibility of the one drawing upon the other; such was the case with the telescope, the camera, and the telephone. J. Allen Baker and his colleagues, not at all influenced by the members of European, British, and American mission societies preparing for their meeting in Edinburgh in 1910, acted entirely on their own initiative before the missionary efforts. Indeed the Continuation Committee of the World Missionary Conference and the Associated Councils paid little attention to each other, and each continued its own way, pursuing its own mission. It can truly be said that there were these two distinct, separate, and parallel beginnings of the modern ecumenical movement.

The mission societies, not unexpectedly, saw as their sole task the conversion of the heathen. To this end all other actions were to be subordinated. But the desires of men do not always coincide with the possibilities offered by circumstances. As an integral part of operating in foreign lands, the principles governing the relations between missions and governments were discussed at Edinburgh and put into practical use soon afterwards by the Continuation Committee and its constituent bodies, the mission societies. An example of the overlapping of mission interests and international affairs soon occurred in Korea under Japanese domination. A danger to further conversions was perceived by missionary leaders when some prominent Korean Christians were arrested and tried for sedition, acts in which missionaries were implicated in confessions obtained through torture. Representations were made to the Japanese government and to the foreign offices of the mission societies' home governments.[5] In the end the publicity resulted in acquittal on appeal for most, and a small sentence for a few. In other unjust situations the mission societies went their own way, intervening only where they felt their own interests directly threatened, with no thought of general service to mankind which concerned the Associated Councils.

The work for international reconciliation of the British and German empires through the efforts of the Associated Councils inspired the American churches to convene an international meeting of representatives of Christian churches on the very eve of war in August 1914 in Konstanz, Germany. Although meeting in the last hectic days of mobilization under the express protection of the Kaiser—whose assistant court chaplain, Friedrich Siegmund-

Schultze, had been a key figure in preparations for the meeting—the foreigners had to hurry out of Germany on the last trains to cross the German frontier; but they did not do so before founding the World Alliance for Promoting International Friendship through the Churches.[6] Ironic though the name may be for an organization created while Europe prepared its sons for ritual slaughter, it was the only ecumenical body which remained active as a representative of international, inter-denominational Christendom during that war. The Continuation Committee of the World Missionary Conference purposely did not convene during the war so as not to seem unfair and put at a disadvantage the German mission societies whose representatives could not meet the others.

The Associated Councils, consisting of ecclesiastical and lay leaders of the various British and German churches, died in giving birth to the World Alliance; the latter, originally planned as an organization of churches, found that due to the war it could function only if individual Christians were members, albeit prominent clerical and lay leaders. This new organization was concerned with united Christian action promoting peace rather than with Christian unity through doctrinal discussion. It took actions on this belief throughout the war and tried to maintain a voice of reason in a sea of hysteria. The neutral church leaders of America (until 1917) and Scandinavia attempted to mediate between the warring sides; as contact became more and more difficult and the efforts bore no fruit, World Alliance groups contributed to movements on behalf of a post-war organization to prevent future wars.[7] They were especially active and effective in the United States and Great Britain, but they were not silent in France and Germany.

In the immediate post-war period the World Alliance acted as an instrument to reconcile those churchmen whose nationalism and feeling of self-righteousness indicated the extent to which they were children of their times. It furthered the acceptability of the role of international organization and world order, and it particularly concerned itself with the minorities left by the peace treaties.[8]

The World Missionary Conference Continuation Committee, which had been dormant throughout the war, was reactivated—primarily through the Conference of Mission Societies in Great Britain and Ireland (CMSGBI) and the Foreign Missions Conference of North America—to participate in the deliberations at the Paris Peace Conference. The representatives of the mission societies kept the cause of missions constantly before the Allied leaders, especially Lloyd George and Woodrow Wilson, to whom they had unique access. Their activities managed to save much German mission property from the general confiscation clauses of the Versailles Treaty. The desire for a more permanent body led to the creation in 1921 of the International Missionary Council

(IMC) whose purpose was again single-minded: to contribute only to the spread of the Gospel in non-Christian lands. It found, however, that even a single purpose has many ramifications. In order to provide proper witness in foreign mission fields, the IMC also had to strive for reconciliation between the vanquished and the victorious; it helped retrieve the missionaries' own savings which had been confiscated as German private property in accordance with peace treaty provisions. It found itself called upon to do social work as well. How could it proselytize if it did not help to remove bad practices encouraged by European governments, such as the opium trade, when called upon to do so by the League of Nations? It did its duty with the League, but it felt little need to co-operate with the World Alliance.

The parallel development of the non-missionary movement was both more enthusiastic and wider in range and effort. In addition to the international reconciliation efforts of the World Alliance, its existence provided the machinery by which Archbishop Nathan Söderblom, Primate of Sweden, sought to create an international organization of Christian churches (to fulfil the original intention of the World Alliance), with a wider mandate than the Alliance itself. The new body would apply 'the principles of Christianity to social, industrial and international affairs' and its ultimate goal would be Christian 'unity . . . without waiting for community in doctrine and Church Government'.[9]

Much preparatory work culminated in the Universal Christian Conference on Life and Work, held at Stockholm in August 1925 and attended by Orthodox, Protestant and Anglican, established churches and free, from all parts of the globe (though primarily European and North American). Christians had been actively propounding a Christian view on international conflict since 1907; from 1925 onwards representatives of various churches would be considering and acting on all aspects of social, political, and economic world problems. Although agreement had been reached on the principle of this action at Stockholm,[10] when these church leaders of varying traditions of church-state relationships returned home, all were not equally fervent in carrying out their newly agreed duties. Nevertheless, organizations once created maintain a certain life of their own; this was true of the Continuation Committee resulting from Stockholm, which, in 1930, became the permanent Universal Christian Council on Life and Work. Mention has already been made of the sociological interpretation of the increased activity of the churches—an attempt by the clergy to remain relevant to society when secularization has diminished the overall importance of the social function of religion; it must also be pointed out that it was not only churches which became interested in international affairs, but that many other groups in the pluralist societies developed an international organization and concern, e.g., the trade union movement. The spirit of the times moved men of all interests.

'Dogma divides, service unites' had been the motto of the Stockholm Conference. Nevertheless, it soon became necessary to create a Theological Commission to provide doctrinal justification for Life and Work actions. Meanwhile, in 1927, several years of preparation culminated in the World Conference on Faith and Order, convened at Lausanne; dogma might divide, but at this conference eminent divines (many of whom had attended Stockholm and were imbued with its spirit) attempted to achieve Christian unity through forthright discussion of doctrinal points of division.

Thus there were four international Christian organizations in the inter-war period, three of which were concerned in varying degrees with action in the world of men and one of which was solely interested in harmonizing Christian doctrine. Archbishop Söderblom and his colleagues believed that Christian unity could come about through Christian service to those in need, but many of the actions required justification in theological terms for those Christians primarily interested in preserving the *status quo*; this was especially so when action required defiance of public authorities. To many Christians the state had been ordained by God and its right to command unquestioning obedience was assumed as part of the natural order of things. With the rise of the totalitarian state and its sometimes inhuman commands, basic Christian doctrine regarding church-state and individual-state relations was called into question.

The still, small, separate voices of the divided ecumenical organizations were too small and still for an increasingly secularized world where the state was being made into a god. The ecumenical leaders conceived of uniting as many as possible into one international council of Christian churches able to speak out authoritatively (though not necessarily unanimously) for Protestant-Orthodox Christendom on matters of doctrine, political principle, or social ethic. The preparations for Life and Work's World Conference on Church, Community and State, at Oxford, and for the World Conference on Faith and Order, at Edinburgh, in 1937 included a plan for their union; both conferences overwhelmingly endorsed it.[11] The IMC, which had begun to co-operate with Life and Work in the critical years of the early Thirties, considered joining the new organization but could only bring itself to be 'in association with' it.

A conference of church representatives meeting at Utrecht on 9 May 1938 approved the proposed constitution and created the Provisional (executive) Committee of the 'World Council of Churches (in process of formation)'. At this same meeting the Administration Committee of Life and Work transferred its responsibilities to the provisional World Council. The Second World War, which prevented the First Assembly of the World Council of Churches from taking place in 1940, also prevented Faith and Order from completing its constitutional amalgamation until 1948. There was, nevertheless, an embryonic World Council with headquarters in neutral Switzerland from 1938. During the war, the new body provided a focal point for the co-ordination of international Christian co-operation. Working with the World Alliance, the YMCA, YWCA, and other Christian bodies, it helped to organize a chaplaincy service to prisoners of war and emergency care for displaced civilians.[12] In the immediate post-war years the infant World Council became a dispenser of aid, provided by religious and secular authorities in North America, to Christian bodies and refugees.

The World Council Provisional Committee also spoke out on international affairs in the first years of peace, making headlines with its criticisms of Allied policy in defeated Germany. Learning from the reticence of their predecessors in failing to make known the reservations of reasonable men regarding the Versailles peace settlement, the Christian leaders—through the Archbishop of Canterbury, Dr Geoffrey Fisher—declared the Allied policies to be 'confused and inconsistent . . . directed towards such an extreme limitation of German industry and exports as cannot be enforced except by long military occupation'. Such a policy, the Committee held, condemned millions of Germans to charity or starvation. The Provisional Committee further commented on the settlement of refugees and displaced persons, and on transfers of populations, and it urged a policy of mercy towards the vanquished.

Given this tradition of activity and the perceived need for a Christian voice to participate in the formation of the post-war world, World Council and international missionary leadership discussed the need for some organ devoted solely to international affairs. An internal World Council department and an independent organ responsible to both the WCC and the IMC were mooted as possible forms it might take. To arrive at a final decision, it was decided to convene a Christian conference on international affairs in August 1946 at Cambridge, England. There Christian leaders, ecclesiastical and lay, would consider the best means for an effective Christian witness in world affairs. The American Commission on a Just and Durable Peace, having the most resources, took the initiative and invited all churches to send experts to the Conference and carried out a large part of the preparatory work.

The Foundation Stone

Dr W. A. Visser 't Hooft opened the Conference on International Affairs on 4 August 1946, with a speech of praise for the Peace Aims Group in England and the Commission on a Just and Durable Peace. He drew attention to the work on a post-war order that had been going on under incredibly difficult conditions both in Germany and the occupied countries during the war. This present conference, he asserted, followed in the tradition of activity of the churches in international affairs, an activity and concern of ever-increasing importance. He concluded by presenting the proposal of the Administrative Committee of the World Council and of leaders of the IMC that Mr John Foster Dulles of the United States be Chairman of the conference, that Pastor Marc Boegner of France, Mr (later Sir) Kenneth G. Grubb of the United Kingdom, and Dr Francis Wei of China be Vice-Chairmen, and that Dr Walter Van Kirk (Secretary of the Commission on A Just and Durable Peace) and Dr W. A. Visser 't Hooft be the Secretaries.

The Anglo-American predominance in the preparations for the conference was apparent. To obviate this imbalance, Dr Van Kirk had sent out questionnaires on the role of the churches in international affairs to church leaders in forty-four countries. In the chaotic post-war conditions, only fourteen replies had been received and those primarily from English-speaking countries.[13] Finally as representative a group as it was possible to gather together in the world of 1946—a world of occupation armies, hunger, poverty, and dislocation—some sixty lay and ecclesiastical leaders, with interest and experience in international affairs from seventeen countries, convened to discuss the function of the churches in international affairs and to create an organization that would guide their future activities in this sphere. The predominance of Anglo-American delegates must not give the impression that they themselves viewed the possibilities and characteristics of such an organization in the same light. The Americans felt that the Commission should be a 'high-powered' group ready to present its views forcefully wherever possible. With some exceptions, the European and British view tended towards an unpretentious, cautious body, one which could do no one any harm. With a transcendent view of the Church, they preferred to depend on divine intervention rather than be 'considered simply another power bloc'.[14]

The meetings of the Conference had to be held in private because the British Home Office, in order to allow German delegates entry to the United Kingdom, set the condition that no German might make public statements.[15] Immediately upon election as Chairman, John Foster Dulles, American corporation lawyer and leading Presbyterian layman, delivered his opening statement. As the son of a Presbyterian clergyman, strictly raised,

Mr Dulles perceived the world in terms of the moral and the immoral. The Allies had won, he asserted in his opening statement, because the Axis leaders had been contemptuous of moral forces and Christianity.[16] One might ask, as no one at the meeting did, if the Soviet Union, too, was not a victor, and if its leaders, too, were not contemptuous of Christianity. He saw the very existence of the United Nations as a result of Christianity in the United Kingdom and the United States. The character with which it emerged from the San Francisco Conference was 'very largely determined by organized Christian forces which worked at San Francisco'.[17] These forces were not the World Council of Churches, of course, but the Federal Council of the Churches of Christ in America. It had happened before that the main national Christian force of the hegemonial world power had acted as the *alter ego* of the international Christian body when it was either in a nascent state or impotent. Thus the Conference of Missionary Societies of Great Britain and Ireland had acted for the Continuation Committee of the World Missionary Conference during the First World War, and later for the International Missionary Council, in order to urge upon the British government from time to time various international missionary policies;[18] in a similar role the Federal Council, through its Commission on a Just and Durable Peace, had observers at the earliest meetings of the Security Council, the Economic and Social Council, and other United Nations organs and agencies. It can be considered to have acted for, or at least in the interests of, the provisional World Council, which had still to gather its full forces after the long, hard war.

The Cambridge Conference had been convened because men with strong Christian convictions felt that the churches had a calling to make known a Christian morality in international deliberations. Its leaders were the Anglo-Americans, who had undertaken the groundwork for the conference and prepared the papers and problems to be considered. Of course, the chair was not closed to suggestions or alterations in the agenda, but the advantage always lies with those who are able to present their ideas and plans completely, thoroughly, and first. A nine-point Charter was drawn up to guide the future body. The primary responsibility of the Commission of the Churches on International Affairs, which it was decided to establish, was to serve the two parent bodies (the WCC and the IMC) 'as a source of stimulus and knowledge in their approach to international problems, as a medium of common counsel and action, and as their organ in formulating the Christian mind on world issues and in bringing that mind effectively to bear upon such issues.'

31

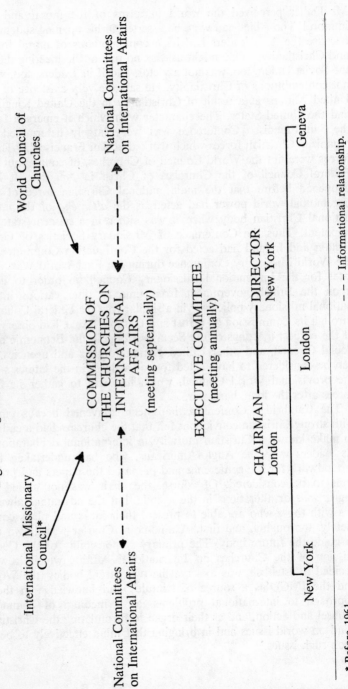

Fig. 1. *Organization of the CCIA 1947–1968*

International Missionary Council*

National Committees on International Affairs

World Council of Churches

National Committees on International Affairs

COMMISSION OF THE CHURCHES ON INTERNATIONAL AFFAIRS
(meeting septennially)

EXECUTIVE COMMITTEE
(meeting annually)

DIRECTOR
New York

CHAIRMAN
London

New York   London   Geneva

* Before 1961.

– – – Informational relationship.

This Commission, as just stated, would be an organ of both the World Council and the IMC. When the Continuation Committee of the World Missionary Council (predecessor to the IMC) was considering from 1910 to 1912 how best to deal with governmental problems for its member missionary societies, it was suggested by a subcommittee that a committee dealing only with the relations between missions and governments be established.[19] This was not done, however, because the Continuation Committee's executive committee judged itself competent to handle this important work in addition to its other responsibilities. The IMC was never the strong force in international affairs that it might have been, and this organizational factor was one reason for its relative weakness. Now, over thirty years later, a separate body dealing with international political, social, and economic problems was created to serve the missionary interest in this manner.

Apparently those preparing the Cambridge Conference were not certain how forceful such a Commission would be. One of the preparatory papers noted that the World Council and the IMC were the two organizations through which contact of the churches with the United Nations could 'be best established and maintained. From the standpoint of effective contact with the United Nations, these Councils of the churches are in the stage of infancy. If developments take their normal course, neither the two Councils separately, *nor the two Councils in co-operation, will be able to achieve well-defined and established policies and procedures* in this field for a considerable time.'[20] What this 'normal course' might be was not elaborated upon, but this Christian diffidence coupled with realism seemed in this instance salutary.

The Commission would consist of Commissioners nominated by the CCIA Executive Committee and appointed by either the World Council or the IMC for three-year periods. Geographical and denominational factors were to be considered in the appointment, but the primary criterion was the individual's knowledge and experience of world affairs. These individuals were not appointed by church committees, though such had been consulted, and were not, therefore, delegates of the churches. Provision was later made for the world confessional bodies and ecumenical organizations to be represented on the Commission and at the meetings of the Executive Committee. Nevertheless the structure indicates some independence of the CCIA from national and denominational hierarchies.

There was in the first year of creation some confusion over the designation of the various officers. Finally Baron Frederick van Asbeck, Professor at the University of Leiden, was chosen President (on his resignation, due to failing health, this office was abolished); Mr K. G. Grubb became the Chairman with general supervisory

33

functions, resident in London; Professor O. Frederick Nolde served as Director, resident in New York at the seat of the United Nations. After the conference had adjourned with the feeling of a job well done, the tedious but necessary work involved in the formation of the Commission devolved upon Grubb and Nolde. Their preliminary organizational efforts were crowned on 1 January 1947 when the Commission was declared in existence in New York; its sponsorship by the World Council was not formally approved until the following April when the Provisional Committee met in Buck Hill Falls, Pennsylvania.

Pragmatic Development

Organization with limited resources must perforce take longer than when resources are plentiful or at least generously given. The budget of the CCIA from the Amsterdam Assembly in 1948 to the Evanston Assembly in 1954 averaged $38,000. (By way of comparison, from 1955 until the New Delhi Assembly in 1961, it averaged $86,000; from 1962 until the Uppsala Assembly in 1968, its average was $114,000; from 1969 until the Nairobi Assembly it was $171,503.)

The first evaluation of the CCIA's work was conducted by the Preparatory Commission on International Affairs in its pre-Evanston survey,[21] in which the paucity of CCIA resources was called to the attention of the Assembly. The natural result of the lack of resources, it was pointed out, had to be the limitation of its interests to a few problems or a superficial survey of many. The CCIA had chosen the former alternative; consultative relations with some Specialized Agencies had been deferred. Its thoroughness in dealing with the problems which it did tackle, the evaluation continued, had won it an enviable reputation among the intergovernmental organizations. In its choice of problems, it had acted on the basis of criteria empirically developed: (1) An inherently urgent problem (2) of clear Christian concern (3) about which there was substantial world-wide Christian consensus (4) which could be competently handled by a CCIA officer (5) and for which there was a reasonable possibility that a contribution might be effective, or for which there was an overriding imperative for Christian witness.

TABLE I

Expenditure of the CCIA 1947–1975
(US $)

Year	Amount	Year	Amount	Year	Amount
1948	21,085*	1958	81,811	1968	120,746
1949	34,454	1959	88,674	1969	121,182
1950	36,531	1960	87,691	1970	141,720
1951	46,614	1961	98,727	1971	147,379
1952	48,378	1962	107,405	1972	169,457
1953	46,675	1963	112,684	1973	194,894
1954	52,453	1964	119,003	1974	254,387
1955	79,915	1965	109,700	1975	257,405
1956	91,897	1966	112,903		
1957	82,576	1967	121,984		

* Covers the period 1 Jan. 1947–30 June 1948. Thereafter amounts relate to fiscal years beginning on 1 July.
Sources: WCC, yearly *Financial Statement;* CCIA, *Annual Report* for the years shown.

The Evanston Assembly adopted the report of the Committee on the CCIA which called for substantially increased resources, urging the Central Committee to give the work of the CCIA the highest priority in its financial planning. Specifically it recommended that resources be expended to employ a continental European and an Asian with special responsibilities for Europe and Asia, in order to redress the predominantly Anglo-Saxon composition of the CCIA. In addition to the Chairman and Director, Dr Richard M. Fagley, an American, worked in the New York office with Dr Nolde. Dr Elfan Rees—although as a Welshman he might dispute the label 'Anglo-Saxon'—had responsibility in Geneva for liaison with international organizations there, representing DICARWS as well as the CCIA. The Reverend Dominique Micheli, a European, was appointed in 1955 to work in New York with particular reference to human rights work and not to the European continent. Although the Reverend Alan Booth replaced the Reverend E. Philip Eastman in London in 1956, Mr Micheli was the only addition to the officers, and the CCIA remained predominantly a European-American affair.

The merger of the IMC with the World Council at New Delhi in 1961 meant that the CCIA would no longer serve two masters. A new constitution (formerly called Regulations) of the CCIA was submitted to, and approved by, the New Delhi Assembly. The semi-autonomy enjoyed by the CCIA was maintained. The report of the Committee of the CCIA adopted by the Assembly again called for the expansion of the CCIA staff by appointments of an African, an Asian, and a Latin American. This had not been accomplished before the Uppsala Assembly, but Mr M. M. Thomas of India had been designated as the East Asian Christian Conference consultant to the CCIA; he was followed in this position by U Kyaw Than of Burma. Soon after arrangements had been made for Mr Henry Makulu of Zambia to serve as CCIA Representative in Africa he was called by his government to an important post; Samuel Amissah was the All Africa Conference of Churches consultant to the CCIA.

In 1970 Canon Burgess Carr of Liberia moved from his position as Africa Secretary for CICARWS to the CCIA to become its first African staff member. He had hardly had time to become orientated to his new position when he accepted a call to be the General Secretary of the All Africa Conference of Churches, leaving the CCIA in December 1970. Anglo-Saxonism reared its head again in 1971, with the appointment of the capable Reverend Dwain C. Epps from the United States to the Geneva Office, although Dr Rees' retirement in June 1971 diminished it somewhat. (Dr Rees has been retained as a part-time consultant on Middle East and United Nations affairs.) In February 1972 another African, the Reverend Eduardo Bodipo-Malumba from Equatorial Guinea, interrupted his doctoral studies and teaching in the United States to go to Geneva. In November 1973 he decided to return to his teaching duties in California. In mid-1974 the first Asian on the staff, Professor Ninan Koshy, assumed a CCIA post in Geneva. In a period of increasing secularization, able Africans and Asians find the opportunities to serve their countries and international society so numerous that positions in church organizations seem less rewarding personally, and usually monetarily.

In order to achieve maximum results from the resources poured into the World Council, the New Delhi Assembly called for the creation of a Committee on the Re-Examination of the Structure of the World Council. In co-operation with this body, the CCIA Executive Committee conducted a searching self-analysis. Sir Kenneth Grubb and Dr Nolde summarized the opinion of the Executive Committee in a memorandum to the Committee on Structure. It had been felt that the CCIA should maintain its semi-autonomy. Its staff should remain technically competent in the affairs of the world; the issues with which they dealt should remain selective, in order to allow the most efficient use of resources. Continuing contact with the United Nations and its Specialized Agencies was recommended. Again, correction of the European-American predominance among the staff officers was urged. It was also noted that the budget would have to be increased to make up for resources which the Chairman and Director had drawn from other sources for CCIA expenses.

The Committee on Structure, reporting to the Central Committee in January 1965, accepted many of these recommendations. It, too, felt that the measure of autonomy which the CCIA retained as a Commission (rather than becoming a department of the World Council) was necessary for maximum effectiveness. However, it recommended that relationships between the CCIA and the Secretariat and Divisions of the World Council be made as close-knit as possible to compensate for the autonomy! It also suggested better liaison between the CCIA and the constituency of the World Council. Naturally the perennial recommendation for more African and Asian staff members was made. Greater resources were also recognized as a necessity for adequate functioning. It further suggested that a representative consultation should be held to select the officers to replace the retiring Sir Kenneth Grubb and Dr Nolde, and to conduct an inquiry into the future work of the Commission.

The Hague Consultation, meeting 12–17 April 1967, fulfilled this request. As a result, a new constitution of the CCIA was drafted to be later adopted by the Uppsala Assembly. This constitution spelt out explicitly many CCIA practices, and provided more controls for the Commission, while still allowing it its autonomous status.

The Committee of the CCIA reporting to the Uppsala Assembly concerned itself with the future; it listed the points which would be the recurring political issues of special interest to the Christian community; it noted the areas in which special study was needed by the CCIA. It felt that 70 per cent of the CCIA function would be representation, 20 per cent long-range study, and only 10 per cent educative and advisory functions. It had detailed recommendations on the relationships of CCIA with other World Council units (more co-operation and co-ordination), with related Christian agencies (increased consultation and collaboration), and with the Roman Catholic Church (encouragement for Christian co-operation.)

All this reordering of the CCIA may have been premature, for the new World Council organization provided by the Central Committee, meeting in Addis Ababa in January 1971, in fact made the CCIA less autonomous.

Fig. 2. *Organization of the CCIA 1977*

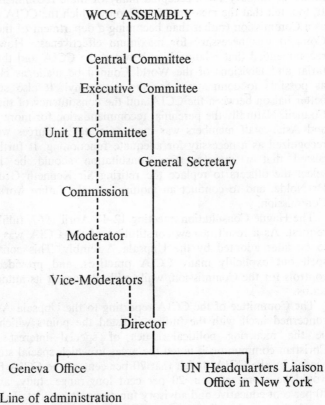

WCC ASSEMBLY

Central Committee

Executive Committee

Unit II Committee

General Secretary

Commission

Moderator

Vice-Moderators

Director

Geneva Office   UN Headquarters Liaison
                                        Office in New York

———— Line of administration
– – – Line of policy development

The new CCIA constitution approved at Uppsala was replaced at Nairobi by mere By-Laws which subordinated the CCIA to the Central Committee, as a sub-unit of Programme Unit II on Justice and Service. This revision by succeeding Assemblies, combined with a major change in leadership, has provoked several years of uncertainty, and the path of the CCIA is no longer the clearly marked one of its first twenty-five years. Perhaps the most striking event has been the retirement of the two men who had guided this body and directed its work for twenty-two years. Both coming from an Anglo-Saxon heritage, they represented, nevertheless, two different streams of experience; they provided each other with the tension naturally existing between the exuberant and the restrained which resulted in the great productivity of those years. Dr O. F. Nolde came from the American activist tradition which always wanted 'to do something' about a problem; and he did. Sir Kenneth Grubb, trained in the British tradition of acting after careful deliberation, kept the reins just tight enough to check, but not to thwart, the ardour of his North American colleague. Sir Kenneth describes this creative relationship with humour and affection in his autobiography *Crypts of Power*. During their tenure the CCIA became a respected institution at the UN, in the Specialized Agencies where it was active, and in the countries with strong Christian constituencies.

Professor Ulrich Scheuner of Germany was elected to succeed Sir Kenneth as Chairman,[22] but held his office only slightly more than two years before resigning in 1971. Mr Olle Dahlén took office after Professor Scheuner's resignation. He had had extensive diplomatic experience, both as a delegate to the United Nations General Assembly and to the Conference of the Committee on Disarmament in Geneva. On his assumption of the chairmanship of the CCIA he was a member of the Swedish Parliament and Vice-Chairman of its Foreign Relations Committee; in 1974 he was appointed Ambassador within the Swedish Foreign Office with special responsibility for relations with non-governmental organizations. Immediately on his appointment to the CCIA Mr Dahlén showed great initiative in planning its future role. The new By-Laws transform the Chairman into the President of the CCIA.

Mr Leopoldo Niilus succeeded Dr Nolde as Director of the Commission. Here the World Council has a citizen of the Third World, from Argentina (though Mr Niilus came originally from the Baltic area) as the new Director of its foreign office. During the CCIA's period of turmoil, already described, no clear leadership emerged from the Geneva office. The removal to Geneva of CCIA headquarters (from New York) and of its second most important office (from London) has deprived the CCIA staff, including the Director, of day-to-day opportunities for interaction and contact with government and other officials. Perhaps this suits Mr Niilus well, for he seems to like working on his own—not in an authoritarian manner but in order to produce work of consequence.

The effect of the chief administrative officer of the World Council, its General Secretary, on the whole organization, but especially on its primary political voice to the outside world, is important. He, after all, sets the tone of the international work of the organization. Dr Visser 't Hooft had 'graduated' from leading the World Student Christian Federation to be the first occupant of the major office of the embryonic World Council in 1939. The appointment of the youthful Dutchman greatly disappointed the Reverend Henry-Louis Henriod, the Swiss General Secretary of the World Alliance for International Friendship Through the Churches, who had hoped to serve the new body. Dr Visser 't Hooft's ecumenical enthusiasm and leadership skills were already legend. As the World Council grew, after the Second World War, he demonstrated that he knew how to delegate responsibility; this was especially obvious in regard to the CCIA. With its own Chairman and Director, the CCIA developed its own methodology and personality. Of course, it was aided by being technically an autonomous unit serving both the International Missionary Council and the World Council; it was always more closely associated with the latter, whose interests in world affairs were broader and better organized than the missionaries', but the General Secretary made no 'imperialistic' moves towards its authority. He did not try to dominate the CCIA nor any other part of the Council; he chose to lead it. Nearly three decades of serving the Council (many more in ecumenical affairs) indicate the affection in which he was, and still is, held by the world's ecclesiastical leaders and his own bureaucracy. Upon his retirement, he was elected by acclamation as Honorary President for life of the World Council. He still maintains an office at the Ecumenical Center, where he works on his memoirs with his door open to those who seek his advice and help.

When Dr Eugene Carson Blake, the American Presbyterian and Civil Rights leader, was chosen as the World Council's General Secretary in 1967, a dynamic, energetic, self-confident individual, conscious of the prerogatives of political eminence, undertook the world leadership of Protestant-Orthodox Christendom. At first there was some friction with church leadership in Western Europe, but as the two sides became accustomed to each other, it diminished. Under Dr Blake's administration a centralizing tendency was visible within the World Council, especially with regard to the CCIA, with its experience of autonomy. Although this independence was already declining due to the amalgamation of the IMC and the World Council, the actual contraction of CCIA offices and the removal of its headquarters and principal seats of activity to Geneva were due to the powerful personality of Dr Blake. This change took place with the retirement of Sir Kenneth and Dr Nolde, making the transition less tense. Only one person, Dr Richard Fagley, was left at the United Nations in New York where major international activity of interest to the World Council still takes place. Dr Fagley retired at the end of 1975, and, in spite of the World Council orientation towards the problems of the developing world, CCIA representation at the UN has remained in abeyance, awaiting a suitable Third World candidate. Centralization, originally begun to satisfy one person's desire for direct control of all activities, has been continued due to inertia and fiscal realities.

Not only was the New York office diminished in personnel and activities, but the London one was completely eliminated as a seat of CCIA activities. London is certainly more important in world politics than Geneva; as an old imperial capital, it finds itself still a major communications centre and a political influence in its former colonies and in world politics generally. The Commonwealth Secretariat is located there, and many African political negotiations still take place in Whitehall or under its aegis. It was surely false economy to close the London office of the CCIA, where Sir Kenneth Grubb had carried out his Chairmanship so ably. The personal commitment and wide experience of both Sir Kenneth and his Executive Secretary, the Reverend Alan Booth, were lost. Mr Booth had for so long brought British (Irish!) finesse to bear in the joining of ecclesiastical and international politics.

Dr Philip Potter succeeded Dr Blake as General Secretary in 1972. Already many years in the World Council bureaucracy, first in the Youth Section and then as head of the Commission on World Mission and Evangelism, he understands the peculiarities of ecumenical leadership and conducts a more collegial management in Geneva. With a British education, this black pastor from Dominica represents the commitment of the World Council to its constituents of the Third World; no longer daughter churches, they are now equals in the international meetings of the churches. He framed his commitment thus: 'We cannot speak of unity of the Church without speaking of the unity of mankind. We cannot speak of the church's mission to proclaim the gospel of Jesus Christ without seeing that that gospel has political implications.'[23] In his earlier days he had already given an indication of similar thinking when he pointed out that so long as missionaries built schools and hospitals no one felt threatened; when, however, they preached the Gospel as hope for freedom and justice, everyone wrung his hands. His commitment both to the gospel and to justice will give the Council's supporters, and its critics as well, much food for thought and argument in the future.

No matter how collectively the World Council is administered henceforth, the damage to the CCIA is done. The old organization, respected and specialized in the carrying out of foreign affairs with authority on behalf of the General Secretary, is no more. In an interview on assuming office, Dr Potter described the CCIA personnel as ecclesiastical diplomats who were on a first-name basis with world politicians and moved freely within the United Nations headquarters. The world, he stated, had changed; the task has become bigger and more complex and the CCIA cannot work on its own any longer.[24] Apparently he sees the CCIA as only one body of many conducting the World Council's foreign relations. Yet whether or not the General Secretary acts as his own foreign secretary, surely good organization calls for a united voice in world affairs, even if several departments have an interest in the outside world. In the case of a state, many government departments are interested in certain aspects of foreign affairs, yet its Foreign Office co-ordinates those interests to ensure that they are consistent with overall policy. It is the present writer's opinion that, if conditions remain as they are, with no move to breathe new life into the CCIA, it cannot escape becoming a mere preparer of background material for a General Secretary acting as his own foreign secretary or a simple information-passing agency, much as the Department of Social and Industrial Research of the IMC was in the 1930s, and that organ quickly sank into oblivion.

It is unfortunate that the period of reorganization and soul-searching in regard to the purposes and duties of the CCIA in 1967 preceded the restructuring of the World Council at the same time as its key personnel changed. This coincided with an increase of revolutionary secularism in the world which regards the churches as part of the Establishment, a part of a closed system with no possibilities of change. Ironically enough, many of the greater financial supporters of the churches, looking upon the churches as too revolutionary, have decreased their support.

Whether the new structure of the World Council of Churches (described below) adopted by the Central Committee at Addis Ababa will drastically change things, only the passage of time will reveal. In evaluating the work of the CCIA and the World Council in its first quarter of a century, it will be useful to consider the CCIA organizational basis: the usefulness of a Commission which rarely meets, of Commissioners who seldom communicate with the Executive Committee, of national and regional commissions or departments of international affairs which have no regular inter-action with the CCIA, and of its documentation and representation services. Other organs of the World Council also act in, and speak out on, international affairs; they, too, will be discussed.

Organization of the CCIA

COMMISSIONERS AND THE COMMISSION. A Commission of some thirty individuals, plus officers of the World Council and the CCIA *ex officio,* was intended to be the guiding voice and mind of the ecumenical movement in actions in the international political field. With the increase in World Council membership this number became nearly eighty after Uppsala. Originally they were nominated by the CCIA Executive Committee and appointed (changed to elected in 1968) by the WCC (and until 1961 also by the IMC) for a period of three years. The Nairobi By-Laws provide again for thirty Commissioners, elected by the Central Committee out of nominations by the Commission. The Commissioners have been, as intended, primarily laymen active in international affairs. They have also been, as required, representative of geographical and denominational interests, and to this end the Executive Committee is obliged to consult with the appropriate confessional and national Christian bodies. Other ecumenical organizations were each asked to nominate a Commissioner, a means, it was hoped, to achieve concerted Christian international action. After the Evanston Assembly, the concept of Commissioner-at-Large was adopted to allow the inclusion of members whose skill, knowledge, or experience was valuable to the CCIA apart from geographical origins. The balance sought after the Uppsala Assembly, as stated in the new constitution, adds race, age, and culture as additional criteria in the selection of Commissioners. Nairobi provided for up to forty Corresponding Commissioners with all the rights of elected Commissioners except the vote.

The tasks of the commissioners have changed little since the inception of the CCIA. As at present stated, they are: '(1) to correspond with the officers of the Commission, drawing their attention to matters which . . . should occupy their attention; (2) to co-operate with recognised councils and church agencies . . . in educating public opinion or in making representations to authorities on matters in the international sphere of concern to the Christian conscience; and (3) to attend meetings of the Commission.' [25]

The idea of Commissioners actively guiding the actions of the officers by means of correspondence as envisaged at Cambridge in 1946 was never realized; as the officers gained experience, it became a staff operation—as indeed it had to be in order to be effective. Diverse and diffuse opinions coming by airmail from the various parts of the globe, from individuals with other responsibilities in their homeland and more immediate demands on their time, would not seem to offer the best possibilities for well-reasoned, fully considered, timely action.

Nor have the Commissioners been convoked to offer their views and advice except just prior to World Council Assemblies. These septennial meetings have been able to do little more than discuss in broad generalities the actions taken by the officers. It is true that Commissioners were extended a general invitation to attend Executive Committee meetings, but those not Committee members who accepted varied between three and five before 1960 and between four and eight after that year. A record eighteen attended the 1974 meeting. The lack of opportunity to meet together has been primarily due to lack of resources; the CCIA could not pay the annual transportation and other expenses for the Commissioners, and most of them, although acceptable to, were not necessarily close to, their church leadership and budgets. In order to ensure that the churches, the Commissioners, and the Commission should work more closely together, the Committee on Structure recommended in 1965 that church leaders, as well as those experienced in international affairs, be included among the Commissioners.

In the absence of an aggressive Commission, the real guidance has been carried on by the Executive Committee, a self-perpetuating body consisting of the officers of the CCIA, the General Secretary of the World Council (originally the General Secretary of the IMC also), and such other World Council officers as he may decide, and 'not more than fifteen' Commissioners (until 1968 ten), a small coterie indeed. The Executive Committee has met annually; led by able officers, it has carried out its duties competently. For those with Anglo-Saxon political values, the concept of Commissioners and a Commission represented the ideal of popular participation in, and control of, responsibilities of the Church at the action level. But this structure did not achieve the active, world-wide participation that had been predicted; many cultures in which the Church exists do not hold these values and prefer the work of duly appointed professionals. The new By-Laws require the Commission to meet annually and they make no provision for an Executive Committee.

NATIONAL COMMITTEES. To further the Anglo-Saxon concept of participatory democracy, the creation of national, and later regional, Christian committees on international affairs was encouraged from the very beginning of the CCIA. Whether as an independent national CCIA or merely a department of international affairs of the national Christian council (that is, council of churches of individual countries) was immaterial, for these were not to be bodies subordinate to the CCIA nor in any other way an integral part of its organization; nevertheless, it was expected that many CCIA activities would benefit from their co-operation. A national committee's duties are to further the aims of the CCIA in its own state, to interest the churches there in the work of the CCIA, and to communicate with the national government on matters of concern to the CCIA. If for any reason a national committee feels that representation to its government is undesirable, it is not obliged to take action, and, in fact, the CCIA would itself make representations in such cases only on matters of 'extreme urgency'.

The use of national committees has not been without its hazards. These bodies tended to use in their own titles the name of the CCIA modified only by an adjective of nationality. In 1955 there was apparent confusion over the origin of a letter concerning Japanese-Korean relations from the Executive Committee of the Korean CCIA. The unfortunately belligerent tone of the missive embarrassed the international CCIA; the CCIA Executive Committee urged that the national bodies should plainly distinguish their names from that of the international body.

The primary means of communication of the CCIA with the

national committees has been through the documentation information service provided since 1947. A typical year might see some fifteen communications sent out to the national committees. These have always included a CCIA-prepared memorandum concerning items of the provisional agenda of the General Assembly of interest to the churches; this memorandum has been followed at the end of the session with a summary of General Assembly activity on matters of Christian concern. Other correspondence would include minutes of the Executive Committee, and statements by CCIA officers, the Central Committee, or World Council officers on international politics. There would also be sent to each World Council member summaries of activities of the various United Nations organs and Specialized Agencies of particular interest to the churches, e.g., the Trusteeship Council or the United Nations Development Programme.

Originally communication was to be a two-way flow of information; indeed, one of the functions of the national committees was to provide CCIA officers with reliable information on local matters of international importance. However, about the only information which has been supplied to the CCIA has been the annual reports of national committee activities. There is no indication of any reciprocal influence from the national committees, and the absence of evidence must lead to the conclusion that it has been minimal.

The extent to which institutions maintain structures which have, in point of fact, served them poorly, is a constant source of amazement. The number of national committees in the 1949/50 annual report of the CCIA was listed as sixteen; in the 1970/71 report it was twenty-five. This is not a startling increase, especially when compared to the huge increase in membership. What is astounding is the paucity of activities the national bodies have to report to the CCIA. Except for the Anglo-Saxon countries, there seems to be no leadership at the national level. In periodic moments of verbal self-flagellation, the CCIA officers asked themselves if they had done enough to stimulate the national committees to action. Surely the original intention was that the national committees would constantly goad, stimulate, and direct the international commission. Part of this lack of initiative is due to the fact that most of the national committees have in reality been subcommittees of a national ecumenical council in which the churches in membership come together for a wide range of ecumenical business. These church leaders are not concerned solely with international political, social, and economic affairs; a multitude of matters competes for their attention. In addition, the subcommittee is often the foreign office of one of the large state churches, dealing primarily with international ecclesiastical relations and only secondarily with world political matters.

An inquiry conducted by the CCIA in 1966 on the usefulness of national committees elicited only twenty-four replies from member churches in seventeen countries out of a World Council membership of over 200 in more than sixty countries. Among these replies there was unanimous agreement to keep the national committees and to strengthen them, though there was not always agreement on the roles they should play. Mr Nöel Salter of the United Kingdom stressed their importance and suggested that the CCIA be based on national representation; that, he felt, would strengthen national participation in, and control over, the CCIA as well as co-ordinate the national follow-up of CCIA decisions.

The concept of national committees also indicates the predominance of Anglo-American Protestantism, not only in the running of the CCIA but also in the thinking of its founders. The Wilsonian idea of participatory democracy working in the realm of foreign affairs is embodied in this concept. In addition, the ecclesiastical polity of the Nonconformist churches is quite evident. Although the usefulness of some contact-body at the national level cannot be gainsaid, this concept of popular participation need not follow. A full-time, national expert in international affairs could as well provide the contact. Another Anglo-American value is evident in the oft-repeated derogatory references to a bureaucracy, which the CCIA and World Council strive to avoid (without success). Political thought in other cultures does not automatically condemn out of hand the concept of bureaucracy. For prompt, full attention, the amateur with other interests and the necessity to earn a living is nearly always less capable of accomplishment than the paid bureaucrat whose *raison d'être* is to produce results.

Various nostrums have been suggested to increase participation of the national committees: that their annual reports should be more detailed; that the CCIA should provide a better documentation service; that the CCIA staff should be expanded in order to permit closer co-operation with the committees; and that concerted efforts should be made to create committees in Latin America, Africa, and Asia. Alternatively, it has been suggested that participation by the Third World would be more immediate and effective if use were made of the regional ecumenical bodies, such as the Christian Conference of Asia, the All-Africa Conference of Churches and the Latin American *Junta*. Not one of these suggestions has been put into practice except the last. One might deduce that national participation is not high on the list of CCIA priorities nor in the desires of the national bodies.

The fact remains that the strongest national committees are in those countries of Anglo-American political thought and in continental European states where the church has traditionally been a state church or had a central position in the social structure.

Although this has provided an imbalance in CCIA thought and action, it has proved useful. Since the overwhelming international political influence exercised in the world emanates from the Anglo-American-European states, this same predominance in the CCIA helps to ensure maximum influence on the part of the churches in international affairs through the normal, close relationship of state-church co-operation.

It was inevitable that an unwieldy organization should give way to a more pragmatic one. The Commissioners, a noble idea, the national committee, a useful idea, were in fact inappropriate to the work of the churches in international affairs as it developed. This was recognized in regard to the Commissioners by the Structure Committee reporting to the Central Committee at Addis Ababa, when it proposed a Commission slightly larger than the present Executive Committee. With bureaucratic timidity, however, it recommended keeping the present Commissioners as well 'for the two-way flow of information', which, as pointed out above, it has not accomplished. It further recommended a deepened relationship with regional and national committees;[26] such recommendation has no basis in reality.

The pragmatic development of an effective agency in international affairs has been directed towards an activist policy for which expert knowledge and quick reaction, coupled with personal relationships at the centres of power, are a *sine qua non* of effectiveness. Thus the work of the CCIA, of necessity, became primarily staff work. The overseeing of the operations fell, more or less by default, to the Executive Committee. The retirement at the Uppsala Assembly of the faithful leaders of the CCIA staff for twenty years, Sir Kenneth Grubb and Dr Nolde, reduced its Anglo-Saxon, though not its white European, predominance. It remains to be seen whether new personnel bring new life to the body of Commissioners and to the national committees or whether the bulk of the work continues to be staff work by experts.

Other Bodies, Other Voices

It must not be forgotten that, although the CCIA has been the principal organ of the ecumenical movement in international affairs, created to co-ordinate the policies of the World Council and the IMC, it was not the sole organ so involved. Indeed, at its foundation, it will be remembered, its existence was not meant to preclude, and did not, either parent-body speaking out on matters of especial concern to it. As specific departments or agencies within the World Council had need to participate in international interactions, they did so. The Department of Reconstruction, later DICARWS, was the first into the breach of international suffering; it worked actively with UNRRA, the International Refugee Organization, the United Nations High Commissioner for Refugees, and other international organizations and governments to bring emergency aid to those in need.

The Department on Church and Society initiated and carried out the Rapid Social Change Study which had such influence in shaping international Christian thought and later action on the problems of developing countries. This study led to the 1966 World Conference on Church and Society, which in turn generated intensive study in the field of economic development and the Third World. The extent of the Rapid Social Change project and the range of DICARWS activities in the field of economic development (as distinct from emergency relief measures) and the increasing importance of the Commission on the Churches' Participation in Development will be discussed in chapter 3 below. A more recent spin-off of the Department on Church and Society has been the Programme to Combat Racism; its extensive foray into international affairs in an area formerly within the competence of the CCIA is discussed in chapter 2 below.

The CCIA has been the ecumenical movement's principal agency in dealing with international affairs and has co-ordinated—or where that has been impossible—has at least taken note of, the actions of other World Council organs in this sphere. Upon amalgamation of the World Council and the IMC, the CCIA maintained its autonomous status within the World Council organization until 1969 rather than immediately taking its place alongside the other departments. Although the foreign affairs adviser of the Council, its advice has not always been sought by officers making pronouncements on behalf of the World Council concerning international crises. In regard to the statements of its official bodies, such as the Central Committee, the CCIA usually prepares the position papers which result in resolutions or messages.

A revised constitution of the WCC, approved by the Central Committee in 1972, was presented to, and ratified with modifications by, the Fifth Assembly in 1975. The new constitution provides that the Assembly is 'the supreme legislative body'[27] of the World Council. The Rules authorize the Assembly to publish statements upon issues of concern to the World Council or to any of its constituents. Such pronouncements dealing with world affairs are usually prepared by the CCIA and presented to the Assembly. The delegates then debate, discuss, probably change, and finally pass this statement of concern. The Uppsala Assembly, for example, issued statements on Nigeria and Vietnam. These are the headline-makers in world newspapers. The more detailed reports, results of months or years of study and decades of experience, are rarely reported at all. These reports are usually prepared by the World

Council staff for the Committee of the Assembly on the particular Sub-unit within whose jurisdiction the topic falls. This report is debated first in committee, where its recommendations may be changed or a postulated fact challenged. Finally the report is put before the full Assembly which may again debate it before 'receiving' it as a report of the Assembly. These documents set the policy to be followed by the various organs until the next Assembly and provide the basis for World Council advice to intergovernmental organizations and action in the world.

At the end of each Assembly, a Message is issued to the churches and the world, in which the spiritual and physical state of the world and its inhabitants, collectively or particularly, is discussed. It is a message of consolation and general advice; the detailed advice is found in the reports mentioned above or is delegated to be developed by subordinate bodies in the coming years. Throughout this study the Message, the statements, and especially the reports, are cited as evidence of the consensus achieved in Christian thought on a particular subject.

The Central Committee, elected by the Assembly, is in a much more prominent position (owing to the regularity of its annual meetings, publicized in the newspapers of the Western world and sometimes the Eastern) than the latter. Though its membership of 155 (including *ex-officio* and co-opted members) makes it considerably more unwieldy than a cabinet, it is a more flexible body than the Assembly. While its primary function is to carry out the policies established by the previous Assembly, it is authorized to take action and make decisions, where necessary, in the intervals between Assemblies. It is also authorized to publish statements on matters of concern to the World Council or its constituents.[28] The Rules explicitly state, however, that neither the Central Committee nor the Assembly has the authority to speak *for* the member churches. The Central Committee has not been reticent in declaring for itself the Christian position on current world issues.

The Central Committee meets annually and has an Executive Committee, consisting of 14-16 elected and *ex-officio* members, to carry out its functions between meetings. It is specifically forbidden to make policy except in circumstances of 'special urgency', though policy proposals for the Central Committee emanate more easily from its guiding body than from its own larger membership.

Before the revised Rules came into force, this body could also make statements 'in circumstances of immediate urgency'. The Executive Committee had acted with great restraint, yet this opportunity to serve in urgent situations was taken from it. Dr Ernest A. Payne of Great Britain, a President of the World Council, went on record as dissenting [29] from this removal of emergency authority from the Executive Committee. The Nairobi Rules restored it.

The new Rules seem to ease the making of statements by subordinate bodies and officers. A Programme Unit or Sub-unit which previously would have had to comply with the 'immediate urgency' rule, may now issue a statement without Assembly or Central Committee approval if, in its judgement, such a statement 'should be issued' before approval can be obtained, provided the matter is within the competence of the Unit or Sub-unit and has received the approval of the Moderator (formerly Chairman) of the Central Committee and the General Secretary.[30] Any statement issued under these circumstances must be accompanied by a disclaimer that neither the World Council 'nor any of its member churches is committed by the statement'.

It is a great temptation for men in the spotlight to feel that they can accomplish more than the capabilities of their office in fact allow. The temptation for elected and appointed officials of the World Council to speak *for* it, is tremendous. The new Rules provide that the Moderator of the Central Committee or the General Secretary each on his own authority, or the Moderator and the Vice-Moderators and the General Secretary together may issue a statement not contrary to established World Council policy 'when in their judgement the situation requires' it. The previous Rules provided this authority only 'in cases of exceptional emergency' [31] and not to these specific combinations of officials.

Mention has been made of the major full-time officer of the WCC, the General Secretary; one equally as important, and more influential than the ceremonially more significant Presidium, is the Moderator (formerly Chairman) of the Central Committee. Elected by that body, he is a full-time church leader in his own country and church. Although his office lacks the continual influence of the General Secretary, he is a powerful ecclesiastical politician in his own right, one who knows his peers and who can 'get things done'. The first Chairman of the Central Committee elected at Amsterdam was the Right Reverend George K. A. Bell, Bishop of Chichester. His interest in the ecumenical movement was an early one, and he served as the Archbishop of Canterbury's representative to its meetings. The second Chairman was the President of the United Lutheran Church in America, Dr Franklin Clark Fry, a clerical powerhouse who had served as Vice-Chairman under Bishop Bell since Amsterdam and succeeded Bell on his death. On Dr Fry's untimely death in 1968 the Central Committee's first non-Western Chairman, Dr M. M. Thomas of India, took office. The new Rules explicitly recognize the pre-eminence of the Moderator of the Central Committee by enabling him to make a statement on his own authority. The Most Reverend E. W. Scott, Primate of the Anglican Church in Canada, was elected Moderator at Nairobi.

During Bishop Bell's chairmanship, an attempt was made to

introduce an informal means of letting the world and its statesmen know Christian opinion on matters of the moment. He devised the method of writing in his personal capacity (which he stressed in his letters) to the Editor of *The Times*. This was effective because the cleric was eminent and British, but it would not necessarily be a suitable means for his successors. There has been little concern over the abuse of power in making statements. One of the most controversial pronouncements by World Council officers was occasioned by the Cuban Missile Crisis of 1962 when several officers collectively spoke out, without the advice of their 'foreign office', the CCIA, criticizing President Kennedy's actions. Although their concern was not shared by many Western church leaders, it was felt unwise on the basis of this one precedent to restrict their capacity to speak out when the world is confronted by an issue requiring immediate ethical judgement.

When one considers the restrictions placed by the Constitution and Rules on each organ and official wishing to speak for the World Council, it seems as though ecumenical pronouncements can be made only with difficulty. Yet for the public-at-large, for world statesmen, for the group the World Council is trying to reach, the statements of any officer, appointed or elected, acting in either a personal or an official capacity, are thoughts and opinions of 'the World Council of Churches'. For the world watching, whoever made the news by sending a telegram to a statesman, a letter to an editor, or a petition to the United Nations, represented the whole constituency of the World Council. This is certainly not in accord with its Constitution nor with the wishes of some of its members; nevertheless, the perception of the onlooker tends to be that as long as an official is not dismissed from his office, he can be considered to be carrying out the wishes of the majority of his constituents. According to the value placed on the World Council and on the societal role of religion in general, each individual statesman or parishioner will be suitably impressed or indifferent. As the Rules themselves aptly note, statements issued by or in the name of the World Council will have only the authority they bear in themselves 'by their own truth and wisdom'.[32]

The ecumenical experience of the previous half century had provided much of the internal organization created after the World Council's formal institution in 1948. The departments and bodies that were set up are shown in Fig. 3. The first six years' experience led to reorganization at the Evanston Assembly in 1954 when the primary unit became three divisions with subordinate departments: Studies, Ecumenical Action, Inter-Church Aid and Service to Refugees, as shown in Fig. 4. With the amalgamation of the World Council and the International Missionary Council in 1961, a separate Commission on World Mission and Evangelism

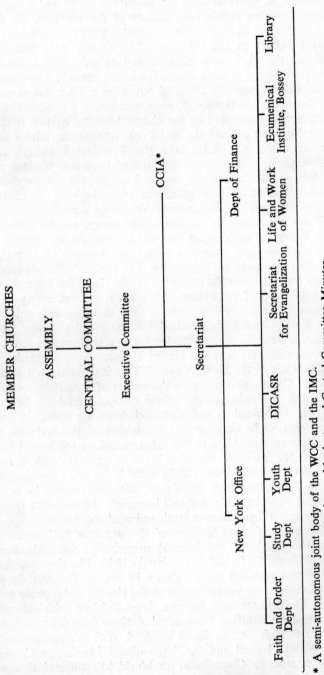

Fig. 3. *Organization of the WCC 1948–1954*

MEMBER CHURCHES

ASSEMBLY

CENTRAL COMMITTEE

Executive Committee

Secretariat

CCIA*

| Faith and Order Dept | Study Dept | Youth Dept | DICASR | New York Office | Secretariat for Evangelization | Life and Work of Women | Dept of Finance | Ecumenical Institute, Bossey | Library |

* A semi-autonomous joint body of the WCC and the IMC.
Source: Based on WCC constitution and budgets and Central Committee *Minutes:*

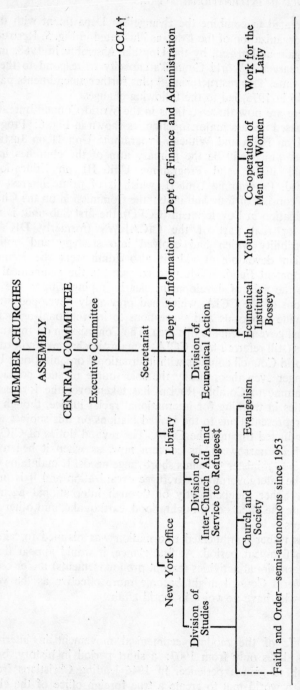

Fig. 4. *Organization of the WCC 1954–1961**

MEMBER CHURCHES

ASSEMBLY

CENTRAL COMMITTEE

Executive Committee

Secretariat

CCIA†

Division of Studies	Division of Inter-Church Aid and Service to Refugees‡	Library	New York Office	Division of Ecumenical Action	Dept of Information	Dept of Finance and Administration

Faith and Order—semi-autonomous since 1953

Church and Society

Evangelism

Ecumenical Institute, Bossey

Youth

Co-operation of Men and Women

Work for the Laity

* Shown in simplified form.

† A semi-autonomous joint body of the WCC and the IMC.

‡ During these years this body also dispensed aid for the IMC.

– – – Line of co-ordination.

Source: Based on WCC, 4th Assembly, *Assembly Work Book* (Geneva, WCC, 1954), p. 51.

was created to combine the Evangelism Department with the previous organization of the IMC, as illustrated in Fig. 5. Restructuring was again authorized, by the Uppsala Assembly in 1968, in order to increase the World Council's capacity to respond to the needs of the time. This restructuring,[33] plus further amendments passed at Nairobi in 1975, led to the following changes

There are now three sections in the World Council bureaucracy, each based upon a major function, as shown in Fig. 6: Programme Unit I on Faith and Witness, Programme Unit II on Justice and Service, which will be the primary arm of the churches in international affairs, and Programme Unit III on Education and Renewal. Programme Unit II, which is of prime interest to this study, consists of four Sub-units: the Commission on the Churches' Participation in Development (CCPD), the first Sub-unit, is responsible for that part of the CICARWS (formerly DICARWS) responsibility which had evolved into strategy and policy for Christian development aid; it also administers the Ecumenical Development Fund. Its duty to co-ordinate the ecumenical activities in the field of development clearly impinges upon the former functions of the CCIA, which had previously developed strategies and made proposals and suggestions to international agencies and national governments in this area. The Commission on International Affairs (still referred to as CCIA) remains in charge of co-ordinating all World Council contacts with international organizations; but it is no longer even theoretically the sole source of such contact. The Programme to Combat Racism has taken over the former CCIA activities in working for international racial justice, though apparently representations to the United Nations on this subject will still be conducted through the CCIA. The revised duties of CICARWS have been narrowed: its concern now, as when it began life in 1945, is to minister to man's short-range needs. It maintains contact with the intergovernmental refugee organization and it is prepared to act either independently or through international agencies to alleviate the effects of drought, flood, earthquake, and other natural disasters.

This rather complicated reformation was planned to take place over a five-year period. At first glance, it would appear that with all international activities (except pronouncements) under one roof, the World Council might become more effective as the voice of those who have no voice in world affairs.

The life of the modern ecumenical movement in international affairs dates only from 1907: a short period in history, but long enough to gain experience. In 1946 leading Christians from the Western world met to create a true foreign office of the churches

Fig. 5. *Organization of the WCC, after Amalgamation with the International Missionary Council, 1961–1971*[*]

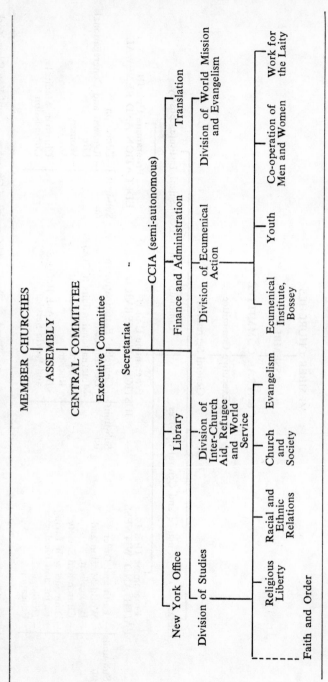

[*] Shown in simplified form.
Source: Based on WCC constitution and budgets and Central Committee *Minutes*.

– – – Line of co-ordination.

Fig. 6. *Organization of the WCC since 1976**

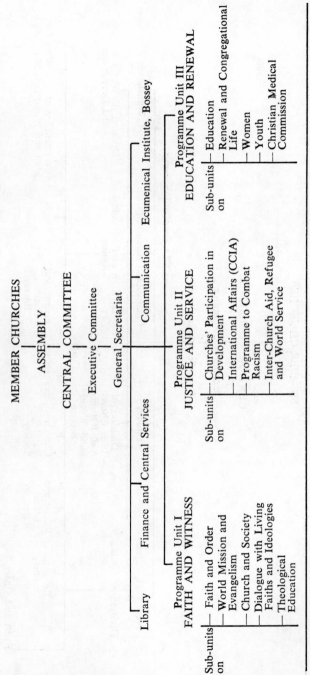

MEMBER CHURCHES

ASSEMBLY

CENTRAL COMMITTEE

Executive Committee

General Secretariat

Library   Finance and Central Services   Communication   Ecumenical Institute, Bossey

**Programme Unit I
FAITH AND WITNESS**

Sub-units
on
— Faith and Order
— World Mission and
  Evangelism
— Church and Society
— Dialogue with Living
  Faiths and Ideologies
— Theological
  Education

**Programme Unit II
JUSTICE AND SERVICE**

Sub-units
on
— Churches' Participation in
  Development
— International Affairs (CCIA)
— Programme to Combat
  Racism
— Inter-Church Aid, Refugee
  and World Service

**Programme Unit III
EDUCATION AND RENEWAL**

Sub-units
on
— Education
— Renewal and Congregational
  Life
— Women
— Youth
— Christian Medical
  Commission

Source: Based on *The World Council of Churches . . . and You* [New York, WCC US Office, 1977].

* Shown in simplified form.

in international affairs. Stringent budgets and a lingering hesitancy to become completely engaged in the affairs of this world—anyway to the extent of offering solutions—limited the potential of CCIA officials. Yet every new institution has to work and feel its way with deliberation, if it is to grow with strength.

By the twentieth anniversary of the CCIA in 1966, a moderate-sized foreign office received praise from ecclesiastical and lay leaders. Its leadership had been strong, its actions generally careful and wise. The organization was based on Anglo-Saxon Protestant concepts of self-government; however, the Commissioners came from all ecclesiastical traditions. Needless to say, the Western ones, understanding the rules of the game best, were most active. With the amalgamation of the IMC and the World Council, the reason for an independent foreign office grew less, and the CCIA came more under the direct control of Geneva, culminating in the centralization of its activities there under General Secretary Blake.

Concurrently World Council restructuring created new bodies, for example, CCPD and the Programme to Combat Racism, with jurisdiction over problem areas formerly dealt with exclusively by the CCIA. The Christian Medical Commission received its own consultative status with the World Health Organization thereby taking from the CCIA one of its more successful areas of activity, population control. This diffusion of authority over foreign affairs has further weakened the position of the CCIA, and possibly that of the World Council as a single body speaking on behalf of Protestant-Orthodox Christendom to world statesmen.

Nevertheless, the World Council continues to examine the ethical rightness or wrongness of international actions. Its effectiveness as an international remembrancer may be disputed, but its role as an international upholder of moral integrity is less equivocal. The following three studies offer the reader the opportunity to judge the extent and effectiveness of its activities in international affairs.

2. White Devils

THE ecumenical organizations preached the equality of man before God. Christians of all races came together in the ecumenical meetings of the Universal Christian Council on Life and Work and of the World Alliance, but the Asians and Africans were always outnumbered by their occidental counterparts. Even in the International Missionary Council, the non-whites were in a minority, depending as they did on the munificence of the mission societies. The churches in the colonial areas and other mission fields were considered 'daughter' churches of those providing the missionaries and were under their tutelage. The few independent non-European churches were of such ancient origin as the Coptic Church of Asia Minor and North Africa, reaching southwards to Ethiopia, and the Mar Thoma Church of India.

The mission leaders believed not only in equality before God but also before men, as many of their struggles with the secular authorities attest. The fact that a majority of the ecclesiastical administrators were European meant only that the non-white races were not yet equal to the whites in their administrative capabilities! With appropriate tutoring the white Christians felt they would reach the goal of self-governance. As one African in Zanzibar noted, before independence 'we were told that it was too early to grant us independence or to make advancement in other fields including the Church, because of the short contact we had with what was described as "white civilization" '.[1] He further observed that, in South Africa, contact with this civilization had been continuous for three hundred years. Nevertheless the Christian leaders did believe in the educability of the non-whites; some secular groups held that no amount of tutoring could develop an innate inferiority. The mission societies acted on their beliefs and made great efforts to bring education, health services, and agricultural technology to these peoples, showing faith in their inherent ability to become capable administrators, pastors, priests, doctors and nurses, farmers, and workers.

Records of international conferences and of the League of Nations provide evidence that the mission leaders protested against the ill-treatment of the blacks of the Congo and of several East African colonies, of the Assyrian Christians, of the Armenians, indeed of all human beings who were treated by their fellow men as less than human. Where this maltreatment was more psycho-

59

logical than physical, as in the United States, the churchmen were not so observant, nor did they protest it frequently. The blatantly racist doctrine of Adolf Hitler's Nazi party in Germany led to the open consideration of racism as an issue by Life and Work at its Oxford Conference on Church, Community, and State in 1937. One of the conference reports 'The Church and Community' included a section on 'The Church and Race', in which not only the Nazi attempt to set the Jews apart but also the greater world-wide racial situation were discussed. 'Against racial pride, racial hatreds and persecutions, and the exploitation of other races in all their forms, the Church is called by God to set its face implacably and to utter its word unequivocally . . .'[2]

The work of the World Council of Churches in this area of human concern followed upon the heels of the Oxford Conference, beginning with the formation of its Provisional Committee in 1938. In 1939 eleven German pastors—Christians—issued the 'Declaration of Godesberg', in which they supported the racist doctrines of Nazism. Dr William Temple, Archbishop of York and later of Canterbury and Chairman of the Administrative Committee, Dr W. A. Visser 't Hooft, General Secretary, and Dr William Paton, Secretary of the International Missionary Council, issued a statement affirming the 'spiritual unity of all those who are in Christ irrespective of race, nation or sex . . .'[3]

Through this auspicious beginning in inauspicious times, the World Council came to devote much time and effort to the equality of man. Its efforts to overcome racism in general among members of 'Christian' civilization began with its fight against apartheid in South Africa; for this reason the particular effort of the churches in regard to South Africa as well as their efforts to alleviate the more general, all-pervasive racism in the world will be considered together in some detail along with the issue of South West Africa. In the latter case the motivation for Christian and world reaction was the extension of apartheid to this area, though the problem was more often discussed as part of the legal issue of the duties towards a League mandate. The role of the churches in preventing a South African situation from developing in Central Africa will be observed and analysed in this chapter. Finally consideration will be given to the summary actions of the ecumenical movement in regard to other racial situations throughout the world, where apparently no real effort at influence was attempted.

A word on the concept of race as used here will be useful. Anthropologists and biologists themselves differ on definitions and criteria of race.[4] It is not a scientific concept that is the bane (or in some cases the blessing) of race transmuted into racism. UNESCO defined the phenomenon thus:

Racism, namely anti-social beliefs and acts which are based on the fallacy

that discriminatory inter-group relations are justifiable on biological grounds
. . . Racism falsely claims that there is a scientific basis for arranging groups
hierarchically in terms of psychological and cultural characteristics that are
immutable and innate.[5]

In inter-group relations, it is the perception of those involved. In
international politics it is the perception by one group of stimuli
which it considers racial, therefore different, therefore inferior. The
stimulus is generally colour but may also be whatever race symbol is
important to those concerned. Thus a given situation becomes a
'racial situation' when the tension of the groups is based on perception of qualities considered racial. Tensions also exist within
homogeneous groups and may be based on class, caste, economic
status, or any number of artificial divisions. The problems considered by the World Council as racial are those in which the groups
involved perceive the problem, or the basis of it, as racial, and this
has been exclusively in terms of white and non-white.

At first the World Council's attention in the matter of race was
directed mainly at its own constituents. Its aims were twofold:
firstly to reform the practice of erring white Christians who worshipped in predominantly white congregations. How could the
Church witness to human equality, if in practice its own members
of different colours worshipped in segregated congregations, no
matter how informal the separation was? And secondly, to form
(or reform) the general attitudes of white Christian thinking, and
indeed the thinking of non-Christians, for many of its messages and
statements were addressed to all mankind. It called upon its own
constituent churches and their members to recognize racism as an
evil against the teaching of the Holy Scripture. It sent public and
private statements of comfort to those oppressed and admonished
the oppressors. Finally it attempted to get the churches to act—
both to correct their own practices and to help in making representations to their governments on behalf of the international
actions of the World Council.

The Council also directed its attention to international organizations; but, at the United Nations itself, it preferred to take no
action in regard to any of the apartheid resolutions. One explanation given at the CCIA meetings was that nothing which might
disrupt the inter-church talks (which took place over a period of
years) was desirable. The officers stated that they kept before delegates to the United Nations the official World Council position
against any manifestation of racism. A former official of the CCIA
described the inhibition as being due to the extremely partisan and
somewhat irresponsible activities of the Special Committee of
Twenty-Four, which made it difficult for the representatives of the
churches to present a moderate viewpoint. When this was possible,

as in the various stages of the Convention on the Elimination of All Forms of Racial Discrimination, the CCIA supported the efforts of the United Nations in this area.

At a third level, the World Council attempted to reach governments directly in its fight against racism. It addressed itself publicly and privately to those governments which practised racial discrimination officially, principally but not exclusively to South Africa. Those governments which were non-committal in their approach to human rights so far as racial discrimination was concerned, primarily in states of white European background, were approached to support international movements against racial discrimination.

The Fight Against Apartheid

Unlike the Covenant of the League, which stressed states' rights, the Charter of the United Nations gives prominence to human rights, i.e., rights of individuals not dependent on a grant by the state. Man has been inordinately cruel to his own kind throughout history, but the scale on which modern technology allows him to carry out his sadistic desires so horrified the world that its leaders meeting at San Francisco in 1945 authorized the United Nations to promote and encourage 'respect for human rights and for fundamental freedoms for all without distinction as to race, sex, language, or religion'. A Commission on Human Rights was established by the Economic and Social Council in February 1946, which began work on a draft Declaration of Human Rights in which the CCIA participated.

Thus, when the First Assembly of the World Council of Churches met in 1948 at Amsterdam, it was not without knowledge of, and some concern for, racial discrimination and tension in the world. The Amsterdam Assembly had representatives from all parts of the world, yet predominantly it was a European-American Assembly. Its concern was to relieve the suffering and destruction caused by the war and to ease the tension which its delegates perceived as the greatest at that time, the potential conflict between two great white powers: the United States and the Union of Soviet Socialist Republics.

Nevertheless, the topic of race entered into three of the section reports, the youth report, and the Assembly's Message. The report of Section I, appropriately entitled 'The Glory of the Church and the Shame of the Churches', stated that 'there exist churches segregated by race and colour, a scandal within the Body of Christ. We are in danger of being salt that has lost its savour and is fit for nothing.'[6] Section III followed this with the categorical statement:

'It is here that the Church has failed most lamentably, where it has reflected and then by its example sanctified the racial prejudice that is rampant in the world.'[7] It went on to cite the duty of the Church to call society away from prejudice, but acknowledged that, to carry out its duty convincingly, the Church must first eliminate practices of racism within its own community. The Youth Report of the same section condemned any church which upheld segregation in its own life based on race, class, or other distinctions. Section IV expressed concern for discrimination on whatever grounds, but it particularly urged: 'With all the resources at their [the churches'] disposal they should oppose enforced segregation on grounds of race or colour, working for the progressive recognition and application of this principle in every country.'[8]

The pattern of definite but rather diffuse shots at the evil of racial discrimination as one evil among many was repeated in the 'Message' where 'pride of nation, class and race' and 'economic or national or racial interests' as well as 'terror, cruelty and race discrimination' were evils considered equally reprehensible. Dr Visser 't Hooft in his report on the Assembly felt that insufficient emphasis had been given to the race question. Although the concern had been there, a well-planned programme to combat it was not only absent but not even considered.

The Declaration of Human Rights was adopted by the UN General Assembly three months after Amsterdam's adjournment. Although the CCIA (as a Category B organization, in relationship with the Economic and Social Council) had been active in the formulation of the Declaration, its primary interest in human rights had been in the realm of religious liberty. The International Convention on the Prevention and Punishment of the Crime of Genocide was drafted without exciting much concern on the part of the churches or the CCIA. Adopted by the General Assembly on 9 December 1948, the Convention made it a crime 'to destroy, in whole or in part, a national, ethnical, racial or religious group'. There was no great rush to deposit instruments of ratification and a year and half later only ten of the twenty ratifications required for it to come into force had been communicated to the Secretary General. On 18 January 1950 the officers of the CCIA wrote to national church leaders urging their support for its ratification. The Convention finally came into force on 12 January 1951. CCIA officers continued measures to stimulate ratification. A notable exception to the seventy-seven ratifications and accessions to 1976 is still the United States.

Although legal separation of the races in South Africa had long been practised, the year of the Amsterdam Assembly saw the election of the National Party of South Africa on a platform of apartheid, an ill-defined doctrine understood to require more rigorous separation of the races than theretofore practised. In spite of the poor definition of this doctrine as an overall concept and the basis of policy, the Malan government passed further racially restrictive legislation. The first was the Prohibition of Mixed Marriages Act which forbad inter-racial marriages, voided those that existed, and provided fines for clergymen knowingly performing such marriages; final parliamentary approval was given on 30 June 1949 to an act opposed by Roman Catholic, Anglican, and all other Christian churches. This was accompanied by an amendment of the Asiatic Land Tenure Act further restricting Indians (as well as other Asiatics) from acquiring land.

Under the pall of this newly enunciated policy of the Afrikaners and its embodiment in two racially discriminatory acts, the CCIA Executive Committee and the Central Committee met in the summer of 1949. In both bodies the Christian representatives were divided in their discussions of racism, specifically the appropriate ecumenical reaction to the new South African racial policy. One view was that the World Council must speak out as the conscience of Christendom, the other was that it had to work quietly and attempt to influence the churches of South Africa without the added difficulty of the alienation which a denunciation of South Africa and South Africans would cause. Influencing the churches, it was felt, would in turn transform society and government.

Strangely enough, or perhaps not so strangely, those who counselled moderation were the Europeans, especially the Anglo-Saxons and their Dutch cousins. Mr M. M. Thomas of India, however, took the member churches to task for not speaking out; he cited the need for these very same churches to educate their consciences on race; they should make representations to governments. Professor Josef Hromadka of Czechoslovakia supported Mr Thomas, urging that the Central Committee utter the 'words of guidance and of warning about what is going on in South Africa and elsewhere'. Dr H. Kraemer of Holland and Dr Visser 't Hooft both advised against causing a rupture with the South African Dutch Reformed Churches, most of which were not yet trustful enough of the World Council to have become members.[9] Sir Kenneth Grubb stated that he had been advised by Christian liberals in South Africa that the best action the churches could take was not to protest about the situation there.[10] In proper English fashion, therefore, he proposed a resolution which condemned no one. Citing the request of the Bossey Conference on International Affairs of April of the same year (that churches in areas of racial tension provide information to the World Council, along with suggestions as to how the Council could best help in solving the problems), he proposed the CCIA develop a study on racial questions with particular reference to South Africa. The Central Committee approved this and reaffirmed the findings of the Amsterdam Assembly against racism.

Ecclesiastical organization often follows the political and social divisions of the world. As South African white society was divided by language, so the churches were, too, in order to make their message understood. The Christian Council of South Africa consisted of English-speaking Protestant churches. The Afrikaans-speaking churches were joined in the Federal Council of Dutch Reformed Churches in South Africa. The Christian Council of South Africa at the Rosettenville Conference of 1949 spoke out clearly and firmly against apartheid. 'The real need of South Africa is not *apartheid* but *eendrag*' (concord). In trying to influence social and political action, statements of platitude and condemnation are less effective than showing that some thought has been put into a problem; the Rosettenville Conference proposed that apartheid should be replaced by the principle that those who progressed from a primitive social structure to an advanced one should share in the rights and responsibilities of the new status. Citizenship should mean participation in responsible government, with the franchise open to all. For those who had not yet progressed, the principle of trusteeship on the part of the whites and the more advanced blacks should prevail. This was certainly the opinion and sincerely held belief of the church leaders, but it was not that of the man in the pew who was not eager to welcome more competition at the workbench.

The Dutch Reformed Churches were isolated from the rest of Christianity not only by geography—an isolation which the English-speaking churches had overcome—but also by language and by a feeling of being misunderstood by their co-religionists. These churches identified themselves closely with the Afrikaner nation. When the Afrikaners had lost their political independence to the British, and when commercially Afrikaans had been replaced by English, it was the churches which had preserved the language and the culture. This close identification with the group, Dr Visser 't Hooft thought, had led to the churches' accepting uncritically the policies proposed by the Afrikaner leaders.

Early in 1950 the Federal Council of Dutch Reformed Churches in South Africa convened the Bloemfontein Conference to discuss the question of apartheid which had so raised the hackles of the brethren abroad. They met not only to counter criticism but to search their own consciences to ascertain the Christianness of this new political policy. The leaders at this conference stated that apartheid was necessary; they defined the still vague concept as total territorial separation, with self-government for each people, thus giving each the fullest possibility for self-development. These Christian leaders noted that apartheid, as they defined it, would

65

end migratory labour; this called for sacrifice on the part of the European South Africans, who would no longer be able to exploit native labour. Needless to say, this idea did not appeal to the South African government which repudiated this understanding of its still cloudy concept of apartheid. In an odd way, then, neither the English-speaking nor the Dutch-speaking church leaders spoke for their followers. Dr Visser 't Hooft at that time interpreted the goals of both groups as being the same, except that the English-speaking churches believed they could be achieved in a multi-racial society, whereas the Dutch Reformed Churches stated they must be carried out by the creation of separate uni-racial societies.[11]

While the Afrikaner Christian leaders were holding discussions to arrive at the principle of total separation, the political leaders were grinding out legislation to assure this. Perhaps because in spring a gentleman's fancy turns to spring-like activities, the Immorality Amendment Act—making intercourse between whites and Coloureds illegal—was shepherded through Parliament. The original Act of 1927 had already regulated similar activities between whites and 'natives' (Africans). In addition, the Population Registration Act was introduced into Parliament, as had been promised. Every person in the Union was to be registered, and all pertinent facts about him noted, a condition not in keeping with Anglo-Saxon practice but quite common in the parliamentary democracies of western Europe. However, this was more than a simple registration of the whole population and provision of identity cards as, for example, in France. The Minister of the Interior, Dr T. E. Dönges, told the House of Assembly, in recommending its passage, 'I may perhaps mention one more example. The determination of a person's race is of the greatest importance in the enforcement of any existing or future laws in connection with separate residential areas . . .'[12] By 9 June 1950 it had made its way through both Houses of Parliament. In retrospect, it can be seen that this Act was the first small step towards the complete destruction of parliamentary democracy and the rule of law in South Africa; the Group Areas Act followed two steps behind and became law on 7 July 1950. Now the ruling élite could designate areas of the country as the homeland of various non-white groups, an area to which they would have to repair when ordered and in which they would be confined by law, and compulsory registration would identify them. The floodtide of segregation seemed unable to be contained.

On 11 July 1950 the International Court of Justice, in response to a request by the General Assembly, rendered an Advisory Opinion on the international status of South West Africa. The issue of South West Africa, while technically a legal one over the status of the mandate granted by the Allied and Associated Powers through the League, was in reality the rallying point of that part of the international community appalled by apartheid. Everyone including the World Council of Churches, feared that the hated policy would be implanted in this international territory which South Africa held in trust for the inhabitants, since the mandate system was to be a prelude to independence (at least as the League envisaged it), a time of tuition for dependent peoples in the arts of European governance. The status of a Class C Mandate (of which South West Africa was one) was granted to those territories which seemed least likely to develop into self-governing entities in the near future; the administering authority was authorized to administer such a mandate as an integral part of its own territory—but it was not a part of that territory nor was it ever intended to become so. The United Nations Charter provided for a trusteeship system very similar to the mandate system in concept; and it was expected that, with the dissolution of the League, the mandated territories (except the A mandates scheduled for independence) would be converted into trust territories. This occurred with all B and C mandates except South West Africa. In the 1950 Opinion, the Court advised the United Nations General Assembly that South Africa is still bound by Article 22 of the League Covenant and the mandate agreement. South Africa, it was held, had still to carry out the duties of that Article under the supervision of the United Nations as successor to the League. The status of South West Africa could be modified by South Africa only with the consent of the United Nations. South Africa had the option, but not the duty, to place the mandate under the trusteeship system.

The supervision of the administering authorities under the United Nations system was more stringent, and the rights of the people of such areas were greater in matters of petitioning in writing and orally. United Nations teams were allowed to visit the territories, an unthinkable infringement of the sovereignty of the administrator in Covenant days. And it was just this guarantee of individual rights which South Africa wished to avoid. It seemed to the churches that one way to assure the rights of everyone was for South West Africa to be under United Nations supervision. Although some may have regarded this as a question of the legal rights of the international organization and the Union, to South Africa it was a political question of high importance. Nevertheless, if international society could use international legal procedures to achieve a political end, it was worthy use of such means. The CCIA Executive Committee authorized its officers at the 1949 meeting to support reference of this issue to the International Court of Justice, if in their judgement that became desirable.

The CCIA officers made representations to the Fifth and Sixth Sessions of the General Assembly that it give effect to the finding of the Court, but without prescribing the particular means to achieve that goal. The Director of the CCIA also transmitted to the United Nations delegates the statement of the Standing Committee of the Conference of Missionary Societies of Great Britain and Ireland supporting a United Nations hearing for the tribal representatives from South West Africa. So that other members of the CCIA would not be implicated, and reprisals taken, the Director called special attention to the source of the resolution. South West African affairs became a perennial subject of discussion before the General Assembly. As South Africa applied its laws more and more to that territory, the two facets of the same problem became inseparable in ecumenical affairs and no further indication of it as an independent item on the World Council agenda appeared.

These further actions not unnaturally kept the racial problem before the Central Committee meeting in the summer of 1950. The same division of opinion as to the usefulness of action or inaction on the part of the World Council remained. Dr B. J. Marais, a professor of theology from South Africa, interpreted for the Central Committee the viewpoint of the Dutch Reformed Church in the Transvaal and opined that any announcement by the World Council would only increase existing tensions. Christian unity, ever a fragile flower among the Protestants and Orthodox, was being shielded at the expense of Christian justice by the acquiescence of the Northern European and American representatives—until Dr Benjamin E. Mays, Negro leader in the National Baptist Convention in the USA, spoke up, as he stated, in spite of the American racial situation which he deplored, for eight million Bantus whose voices were not being heard in the ecumenical movement. He held the opinion that a clear word on race relations could not possibly make the situation any worse for them. And if, as Dr. Marais suggested, Communists alone were against apartheid, it was the shame of the Christian churches which should also be against it. In the end a resolution was agreed upon which did not condemn South Africa. (And it must be questioned why this country, only one area of racism among many in the world, should be singled out for explicit criticism.) The resolution made clear the position of the World Council against racism and prescribed certain aids, including a multi-racial delegation from the World Council to South Africa.[13]

The Natives' Representative Council, the South African government's condescension on democratic opinion within and without South Africa, was convened in Pretoria on 5 December 1950 and presented with an agenda by the Minister of Native Affairs, Dr H. Verwoerd, who stated that they might discuss only the agenda and no political matters. Professor Zachariah K. Matthews, African ecumenical leader, challenged this limitation of the already limited powers of the Council. The move for adjournment on 8 December was regarded by the chairman (the white Secretary for Native Affairs) as a vote of no confidence and the Council was disbanded. This was a prelude to the introduction in June 1951 of the Bantu Authorities Bill, creating new native governmental bodies based on government-appointed chiefs, which was passed that same month.

It was not as a surprise, therefore, that the Central Committee meeting in 1951 heard the news that the Afrikaans-speaking churches considered that a multi-racial delegation would not be useful at that time. The English-speaking churches welcomed one in principle, but rhetorically asked if it would be practicable in the circumstances. The Christian Council of South Africa indicated that the way for such a delegation should be prepared by the visit of officials of the World Council and the IMC, thus setting the stage for the 1952 visit of Dr Visser 't Hooft. The Central Committee regretted the lack of an invitation for a multi-racial delegation but held itself ready for the time when one should come.

The South African policy of apartheid at least had the dubious quality of being unjust, albeit in varying degrees, to all non-whites, including Indians. In the strange wonderland of international relations, the black Africans had no outside power to champion their cause, therefore they were a 'domestic' matter. It is true that Liberia and Ethiopia were independent governments which might have raised the question of the treatment of Africans in the councils of the mighty but without legal foundation in international law. However, their governments were not renowned for rocking any boats, and the rest of Africa south of the Sahara still suffered the indignity of European rule. (In 1960, emboldened by the surprisingly quick decolonization of Africa, these two states instituted proceedings in the International Court of Justice regarding South West Africa. After six years of consideration, the Court found that they had no legal right or interest in the subject matter. The case was decided by the President of the Court casting a second vote to break a tie.) The Indians of South Africa, however, had a champion in the government of their homeland even before its independence; the matter of their treatment was brought before the General Assembly as early as 1946 and remained a perennial subject until it joined with the general question of apartheid in 1962.

India and Pakistan had instituted an embargo on trade with the Union of South Africa in 1949; Pakistan lifted its embargo in February 1950, but India did not and indicated that it would not negotiate on any matter with South Africa until racial segregation was ended. When the Group Areas Act was passed Pakistan requested a delay in its enforcement until a conference between Pakistan, India, and South Africa could be held. In spite of the passing of the second amendment to the Asian Land Tenure Act in March 1950, Prime Minister Malan asked India to reconsider its aloofness; the Transvaal Indian Congress, however, urged the Commonwealth to expel South Africa. The General Assembly adopted a resolution on 2 December 1950 recommending that the three states hold a conference on the treatment of the Indian minority. The CCIA made no formal representations, but informally expressed concern at the failure of these states to find a solution and encouraged the holding of such a conference.

The Group Areas Act became effective on 30 March 1951. South Africa rejected categorically any round-table conference. In November of that year the General Assembly voted to consider charges of South African discrimination against Indians, but this international action was to no avail. Further repressions occurred in 1952. The Supreme Court ruled that the placing of Coloured voters on a separate electoral roll, as required by the Separate Representation of Voters Act, had been passed unconstitutionally. The day after this verdict, Prime Minister Malan announced governmental plans to curb the Court's power. Anti-government rallies followed, but the government bill to create a High Court of Parliament to overrule the Supreme Court on constitutional issues was nevertheless introduced in the House of Assembly. By 15 May it had passed the House and by 29 May the Senate. On 3 June, barely six weeks after its introduction, this far-reaching constitutional change was signed into law. Non-white groups, supported by some whites, began massive, non-violent campaigns of disobedience of the segregation laws. By the time the CCIA Executive Committee met in the summer of 1952 more than 1,500 had been arrested.

Dr R. B. Manikam of India regretted that the churches had been unable to take direct action regarding the treatment of the Indian minority in South Africa. The Reverend A. W. Blaxall of South Africa pointed out that since this was a political problem the churches could really take no initiative; the CCIA would make better use of itself, he advised, in undertaking large projects of a general nature such as the Covenant on Human Rights. Mr Blaxall was right, apartheid was a political problem, one which his government perceived as political, one it perceived as vital to its national interests. From past ecumenical experience, it could not be expected that on a matter which a state regarded as vital to its existence, it would pay attention to, or be influenced by, exhortations of Christian groups. And naturally, if the churches or their agencies should limit themselves to broad projects sufficiently vague in concept, they would be of little trouble to anyone. Could this be the role of the Church?

But time does not wait for indecisive churchmen to make up

their minds: by October rioting had broken out. Although leaders of the African National Congress condemned the riots, the government linked them to the civil disobedience campaign and to communist subversion. During the first fortnight in November the riots spread to Johannesburg, Kimberly, and East London. On 13 November the South African Supreme Court held the High Court of Parliament Act illegal, due to the manner in which it had been passed. The following day Dr Malan announced that he would abide by the Court's decision, and the next election would be held with the Cape Coloured on the common electoral roll. That election would then decide what other actions the government would take. In spite of this concession, rioting and civil disobedience continued; political right of assembly was suspended on 28 November. The total arrests in the civil disobedience campaign by the end of 1952 numbered 7,544.

The 1952 session of the General Assembly saw apartheid raised as a major issue. Although the CCIA, in consultation with United Nations delegations, made it clear that the churches opposed segregation, it was felt advisable not to take a stand in regard to specific resolutions or devices by which the United Nations sought to erase the problem. The ostensible reason for this discretion was to avoid jeopardizing the conversations within the churches.[14] CCIA officials also judged that it would weaken the United Nations if there were an attempt to enforce that which it had not yet authority and strength to do.

Meeting at the turn of the year (31 December 1952–9 January 1953), the Central Committee was faced by an increasingly explosive South African situation and more vociferous United Nations action. Dr Visser 't Hooft reported to the Central Committee on his visit to South Africa the previous April and May. After having met political, industrial, and educational leaders as well as ecclesiastical, and after having reviewed the whole situation, he made specific recommendations designed to integrate the churches of South Africa, isolated by geography and by language, more closely into the life of Christendom.[15]

Although the Central Committee approved these recommendations, Dr Z. K. Matthews, then Visiting Professor at Union Theological Seminary and President of the African National Congress of Cape Province, characterized the report as 'pussyfooting all the way through'. Africans, he warned, would not be pleased with the attitude of appeasement evident throughout the report.[16] The ensuing discussion again illustrated that opinion on the attitude which the World Council should take was divided. One might describe the desire not to disrupt the delicate relationships with the South African churches as a pragmatic policy decision rather than a matter of principle. Other voices, however, might characterize this as the racism inherent in white society, subconsciously present in the attitudes of the most well-meaning Christian. Without designating the individual leaders who have shown their concern for all people, it might be noted that studies on the American racial problem have shown unconscious racist attitudes in everything from the characters portrayed in children's readers to the exclusive use of white models in advertisements. It is instructive to note that those who urged a strong moral stand against racism, not only in regard to South Africa but throughout the world, were overwhelmingly the non-white Christians: Rajah Maharaj Singh of India, U Maung U of Burma, and Bishop W. J. Walls, an American black. Advocating moderation were Pastor Marc Boegner of France, Bishop Hans Lilje of Germany, and Dr Edwin T. Dahlberg of the United States; they were joined by the Indian Dr Devadutt, who felt that the World Council should assist in reconciliation among races and governments and therefore should do nothing that might break its contacts with each party.

Speaking for the action agency of the World Council in international affairs, Sir Kenneth Grubb stated that the CCIA could act only if its resources were increased. In the manner of *Realpolitik*, he suggested that rather than attempt to correct South Africa through the United Nations or the Commonwealth, it might be better to devote Christian resources to preventing similar situations arising in other parts of Africa.

The resolution that was finally adopted condemned not South Africa but rather the phenomenon of racism which many other states in the world practised: 'The Central Committee, holding strongly the convictions expressed by the First Assembly, affirms that all political, social, economic discriminations based on the grounds of race, wherever they may exist, are contrary to the Will of God as expressed in the Christian Gospel. Recognizing that existing racial discriminations are increasing bitterness and tension in various parts of the world, the Committee calls upon the member Churches to engage in the Christian ministry of reconciliation and do all in their power to end such discrimination wherever it exists.' [17]

In South Africa the General Election was only three months away. The National Party ran on a policy of curbing the power of the Supreme Court, and it won a decisive majority of 94 seats to a total of 62 in opposition. On 2 July the government introduced a bill to make legal all previously disputed segregation laws; it did this according to the procedure required to amend the 'entrenched clauses', a procedure insisted upon by the Supreme Court in its interpretation of previous statutes. The two-thirds votes of both Houses of Parliament sitting together was, however, still not achieved.

The CCIA Executive Committee meeting in August heard a report from Mr Maurice Webb, an Englishman who had emigrated to South Africa after World War I, a leading Quaker, and a distinguished member of the South African Institute of Race Relations. His statement to the Committee was generally pessimistic: the only ray of hope he saw was that more than half the total population of South Africa expressed allegiance to the Christian church. This, he felt, would preclude a blood-bath and lead to eventual solution of the problem by reason. Hindsight tells us this was a poor prophecy.

On 18 September 1953 a new bill was introduced into Parliament to increase the number of judges in the Supreme Court (and thus to enable new appointments to be made); its opponents condemned it as a court-packing bill. It was soon withdrawn, for disagreements within the opposition United Party made the two-thirds majority that was necessary to change the entrenched clauses seem a possibility; therefore, the Supreme Court would need no packing. On 2 October a joint session of Parliament approved the introduction of a new bill validating the disputed Separate Representation of Voters Act. It was immediately referred to a Select Committee and passed from the news until the following April.

The months August to October saw the enactment of still more laws to repress the non-whites: the Immigrants Regulation Amendment Act, unilaterally abrogating the Smuts-Gandhi Agreement of 1913—which allowed Indian wives and children to enter South Africa to join their husbands—the Native Labour (Settlement of Disputes) Act forbidding strikes by non-whites, the Reservation of Separate Amenities Act to strengthen segregation in public places, and the Bantu Education Act, which was eventually to end the educational mission of the churches. On 26 October 1953 the Anglican bishops of the Church of the Province of South Africa issued a statement condemning apartheid, though deprecating the singling-out of South Africa for world opprobrium, since the evil existed elsewhere in the world as well. Three days later the Methodist Church of South Africa unanimously condemned apartheid, for its 'mass differentiation of colour alone' made injustice inevitable by ignoring 'the sacredness of personality and the potentiality of men and women as individuals'.

The Federal Missionary Council of the Dutch Reformed Churches convened in November 1953 a conference at Pretoria on 'The application of Christian principles in our multi-racial land, with special reference to the extension of the Kingdom of God amongst the non-European people of South Africa', an attempt to discuss the theological foundations of apartheid. Of the 150 participants about 50 were leaders and theologians from English-speaking churches. The keynote paper by Professor B. B. Keet, an

Afrikaner theologian, came out against the policy of apartheid. To Dr Norman Goodall, representing the World Council, the reception of this talk and the willingness to discuss its basis were in themselves cause for optimism. It must be admitted that nationalistic religious fanaticism was also a viewpoint often presented; nevertheless, a decision to adjourn without attempting to record a conclusion and emphasize any split was a momentous one, all the more since the English-speaking churches at their synods the previous month had publicly condemned the policy adhered to by the Afrikaner segment of the population. Dr Goodall has written that the problem in South Africa was made more complex by the lack of racial integration at the parish level in other parts of the world; not unnaturally, the Afrikaners felt unjustly singled out as the scapegoat for a universal sin. Dr Goodall foresaw the urgency of a Christian decision on the theological basis for segregation; East and Central Africa (an Africa where independence, for many so close, seemed yet remote), it appeared to him, were rapidly approaching the condition of South Africa.[18]

Dr Malan's Christmas gift to the nation was a declaration ending the co-education of white and non-white at Cape Town and Witwatersrand universities. The students of these universities voiced their objections; as with so many objections in South Africa, however, they had no influence on this national obsession. The General Assembly's annual discussion of apartheid, accompanied by meaningless resolutions, continued despite South Africa's objection.

March's autumnal colours in South Africa were barely beginning when Dr Verwoerd introduced the Natives Resettlement Bill, to move Africans from the Sophiatown section of Johannesburg to an area some ten miles away. Ostensibly this was a matter of slum clearance, but opponents of the bill pointed to governmental embarrassment caused by the existence of a poor black section surrounded by affluent white suburbs. However, appeals based on the injustice of dispossessing freeholders of their land, as well as tenants of their dwellings, did nothing to halt the inexorable march of legislation.

Ever since Dr Visser 't Hooft's visit to South Africa in 1952 Afrikaner theologians had been co-operating in the preparatory work of the Section of Inter-Group Relations for the Evanston Assembly. For the first time, a major ecumenical conference devoted the full attention of one of its sections to a discussion of the world's racial ills. Post-Evanston comment on this report described it as 'the most dynamic, forthright and uncompromising of all the reports . . .' [19] The Assembly was held in a country which professed the equality of all men, and yet in part of which the Negro was legally discriminated against. The first judicial blow at this whole system of legalized inferiority was dealt shortly before the Assembly, on 17 May 1954, when the Supreme Court of the United States declared that the segregation laws requiring separate state schools for whites and Negroes violated the Constitution. Upon this precedent would be shattered all legislative discrimination in the United States.

Thus, undoubtedly encouraged by the situation in his own land, Dr Benjamin E. Mays, American black president of Morehouse College, a segregated institution in Atlanta, Georgia, presented to the Assembly the report of the Section on Inter-Group Relations. In doing so, he gave a moving historical compendium of the absence of racial discrimination in biblical history. Dr Ben J. Marais, white, South African, professor of historical theology at the University of Pretoria and fellow member of the section, proffered to the Assembly the Dutch Reformed churches' viewpoint on the scriptural validity of apartheid, while dissociating himself from that interpretation; apartheid was wrong, he felt, but it might *in certain situations* be the less of two evils.[20] Other members of the Section included Alan Paton, South African author (*Cry, the Beloved Country*) and later political party leader, and Dr Brink, moderator of the Dutch Reformed Church of the Transvaal. The report, received by the Assembly and commended to the churches for their study and action, did not deal with the issue of international racism. Finding this too broad a subject, the mandate of the Section was to focus its attention on the problem of racial tensions within the Church.

The Section spent some time formulating the theological and biblical foundations of the Christian approach to races and ethnic groups. The result, not satisfactory to all, was a Christocentric statement with sin held to be the root of all inter-group tensions. It then stated that the intrinsic duty of the Church was not to conform to the world's demands unquestioningly; its task was to obey God rather than society, and, in doing so, to challenge the conscience of society. To those who are obedient to God and suffer the world's consequences, the Church must be a comforter. The Church itself must even contemplate reluctantly disobeying a law which is unjust to certain human beings; those who disobey such laws must, however, be made aware of the possible consequences of their action.

The result of the speeches, reports, and discussions were four resolutions on the racial situation. In the first, the Assembly forthrightly declared 'its conviction that any form of segregation based on race, colour, or ethnic origin is contrary to the gospel, and is incompatible with the Christian doctrine of man and with the nature of the Church of Christ'. The Assembly urged the churches within its membership to renounce 'all forms of segregation or discrimination and to work for their abolition within their own life and within society'.[21]

The delegates from the Dutch Reformed churches took exception to this resolution in a statement to the Assembly. Although realizing that no resolution bound any member church, these ecclesiastical representatives voiced their fear that such a resolution as this might jeopardize the conversations between the churches then under way. The temptation is always to regard these 'conversations', sometimes going on for some years, as excuses for a do-nothing attitude. As long as dialogue can continue, however, there is the chance that moderation will reign. Often a dialogue hinders the ultimate step-of-no-return from being taken. If a wall is built between two contending parties, there is no chance for understanding; every move becomes a threat from the unknowable. Political leaders have indicated this in their establishment of 'hot lines', communications routes always open and unused until a crisis arises.

The close identification of the Dutch Reformed churches with the Afrikaner nation made it particularly desirable to maintain open communications between the leaders of the Dutch Reformed churches and of the World Council. Afrikaner delegates at Evanston vouched for the Christian goodwill evidenced there towards the people and churches of South Africa: the Bantu Presbyterian Church of South Africa, run entirely by Africans, and the Dutch Reformed Church of South Africa in the Cape Province were both admitted to membership and fellowship of the World Council by this Assembly. The delegates pledged themselves to urge their churches to study and reply to the Section's report.

The other three resolutions were more practical in their intent and were meant to set the stage for further work on this overwhelming problem. The most important of these [22] recommended that a department be established within the World Council of Churches to devote its full efforts to a solution for racism, particularly by study and exchange of information among the churches. Unfortunately for the progress of Christian study and action, this resolution was not put into effect for several years, and then only with the barest financial support for several more.

The Message from the Assembly was addressed 'To all our fellow Christians, and to our fellow men everywhere'. The other-directedness of the World Council, the concern for non-Christians as persons, as individuals, rather than merely as potential converts, became visible in this assertion in the Message: 'It is not enough that Christians should seek peace for themselves. They must seek justice for others . . . Millions of men and women are suffering segregation and discrimination on the ground of race. Is your church willing to declare, as this Assembly has declared, that this is contrary to the will of God and to act on that declaration? Do you pray regularly for those who suffer unjust discrimination on grounds of race, religion or political conviction?' [23]

Comments on the Section report from church leaders were that this was 'the most forthright statement on segregation yet made by any ecumenical gathering', and that although 'eleven o'clock on Sunday morning is the most segregated hour of the week', one must not try 'to force desegregation too rapidly on a society of sinful men'.[24] While many seemed to stress the need for gradualism, it was felt that the World Council had the responsibility of keeping this issue before the Christian conscience. One refreshing note of originality in the masochism of self-flagellation was the urging by the Bishop of Bombay, The Right Reverend W. Q. Lash, for everyone to get away from the obsession 'with the problem of the relations between Black and White in America and Africa, and to make a study of racial tensions in which no white race was involved'. After all, the white races do not have 'a monopoly of sin' as far as racism goes. Although there was already enough evidence of this elsewhere in the world, under white domination of the world it had been nearly hidden. Soon, as power came into the hands of non-white races, so racism of black against brown in Kenya and Uganda, brown against yellow in Malaya and Indonesia would indeed show that hate is no monopoly of the white man.

Even as Christians debated and discussed, racism marched inexorably forward in South Africa. An official circular of 3 September 1954 provided that no sites might be leased for mission purposes in Native Areas without ministerial approval; such leases could be cancelled if activities were such as to encourage 'deterioration in relations between Natives and Government'. This action was condemned by the Anglican, Roman Catholic, and Free churches, while the Dutch Reformed churches approved. Prime Minister Malan announced his retirement on 11 October 1954. At eighty years of age, he stated that he would not be persuaded to stay on; that it was best for a politician to go voluntarily, before failing physical or mental faculties forced his retirement. Mr J. G. Strydom, at the young age of sixty-one, was elected leader of the National Party. At the United Nations, the annual condemnation of apartheid and a walk-out by the South African representative, protesting against interference in domestic affairs, was accompanied by a reprimand to the churches in the General Assembly debate for their complacency about racism. For its previously stated reasons, the CCIA did not endorse the apartheid resolutions, but by personal consultation it attempted to give a truer picture of the churches' attitude about racial discrimination, especially since the strong statement of the Evanston Assembly.

Another inter-racial church conference was held in Johannesburg from 7 to 10 December. Of the 172 delegates, 56 were non-Europeans, seated separately; the conference only emphasized the division between the Dutch Reformed and the rest of the Protestant churches. In spite of a partiality towards apartheid, the Dutch Reformed churches joined with the others in appealing to the government to allot another £10 million for the development of non-Europeans.

The change in leadership of the National Party did not even cause a stop for breath in the oppression of a people. In February the residents of Sophiatown were forcibly removed in accordance with the law passed the previous year. Nor was a step lost in the march to the abolition of constitutional government, government based on respect for the law and the rights of dissenters. On 5 May 1955 the Appeal Court Quorum Act was approved by Parliament. This increased the number of judges in the Appellate Division of the Supreme Court from six to eleven, making it necessary for the government to appoint additional judges. All eleven are required to hear an appeal on the validity of an Act of Parliament; the judgment depends on a simple majority. With careful selection of the new appointees the government expected its viewpoint to prevail. A government spokesman (Mr Swart) stated that 'the Government will not rest until Parliament is supreme and the courts have no right to test its legislation'. When asked by Senator Rubin whether the government would accept an adverse judgment of eleven judges, he replied, 'if the steps we take are found to be illegal, we will take other steps—we must have certainty'. Immediately thereafter the government introduced a bill to increase the membership of the Senate from 48 to 89 and to change the method of senatorial election in order to give the government the necessary two-thirds majority to amend the South Africa Act. This bill became law on 20 June 1955 and the election held under it took place on 25 November following. The final results gave the government 77 of the 89 seats. Their object was accomplished.

The act of apartheid which most affected the churches was the full implementation of the Bantu Education Act. Government sophistry explained that the Africans would have more and better education under central government control with a standard curriculum. All opponents of the bill recognized these as the hypocritical arguments they were. Dr Verwoerd, then Minister of Native Affairs, in the 1953 debate on the bill stated that the wrong type of education was instilling false expectations into native minds. The natives must be made to feel they are part of the Bantu community only and not a wider one. Therefore, those who believed in equality, he stated, were not desirable teachers. Academic subjects for natives were a waste of time; they should be taught what was most useful to them, and the Department of Native Affairs knew this best.

The churches and missions had not expected that the harshness of the law would be applied to its fullest; the slow beginning had lulled them into a false feeling of security. The year 1955 brought complete withdrawal of grants to mission schools which did not accept governmental control; even those which agreed found that their subsidy was reduced by 25 per cent. By 1 April 1955 about 5,000 mission schools had been taken over by the government. With the exception of individual leaders, the Dutch Reformed churches approved of the action; all other mission societies and churches strongly opposed the government's policy. The Roman Catholic Church refused to co-operate with the government and stated that it would try to fund its programme from general revenues. The Anglican bishops, on the other hand, decided that, rather than take even this limited opportunity for education from the African, they would lease Anglican mission schools to the government. Of the Anglican leaders only the Bishop of Johannesburg, the Right Reverend Ambrose Reeves, refused to participate in a scheme which would perpetuate the African in a subordinate position, and all mission schools in his diocese were ordered closed.

The following year found the Bantu Education Amendment Act —giving the Minister for Native Affairs still more arbitrary and uncontrolled power over all schools for Africans—being put through the legislative process. It prohibited the charging of fees and stipulated that all curricula must conform to those set by the government. Although this had not yet become law, on 7 February 1956 the Minister ordered the closing of the Christ the King School (Anglican) in Johannesburg, because fees were being charged (the Amendment Act was to protect the Bantu against 'exploitation' in this regard). The real reason was also cited by the Minister: there was an 'undesirable spirit' in the school. The new Act's far-reaching effects were such that, in its report to the Tenth Session of the United Nations General Assembly, the Commission on Apartheid declared the Bantu Education Amendment Act to be 'a negation of the principles of human rights'.

In the midst of the implementation of the Bantu Education Amendment Act, in July 1955, the CCIA Executive Committee met. Although this was a matter of great principle for missions, for example, the right to proselytize and freedom of religion, no action was taken other than discussion of the Act as presented by Mr Maurice Webb to the Committee. Nostalgically one might long for a man of strong vision, a J. H. Oldham, to arise and smite the mighty. But the political situation which existed in the period prior to 1940, when Mr Oldham was active, has undergone enormous change. Another factor to be considered is the degree to which control of religion in South Africa is regarded as vital to the national survival. And any matter involving 'natives' in South Africa had become a matter of saving 'Christian civilisation'.

The South Africa Act Amendment Act was passed by a two-thirds majority of the Parliament sitting in joint session on 27 February 1956, with, be it remembered, a Senate specially constituted for the purpose. In May the Act was upheld in the Supreme Court, also packed to achieve that result. The Federal Council of Dutch Reformed Churches in South Africa had established an *ad hoc* Commission for Race Relations which produced a report already adopted by two of the member churches. It traced the development of separate racial churches in South Africa on a historical basis. It noted that Christianity did recognize nations or races as desirable characteristics, and it denied that Christians could be separated on the basis of colour alone. However, it felt that in the present historical context, it was wiser not to attempt to force any amalgamation. Closer communion between the separate churches should, however, be encouraged. Meanwhile repression continued and laws were passed either to implement further the policy of apartheid or simply to restrict the freedom of the Africans to a still greater extent, for instance, as far as labour union membership was concerned.

The government implemented the legislation relentlessly. With an eye to drama, or simply following the practices of other totalitarian police systems, early in the morning of 5 December 1956, 156 persons (103 Africans, 23 Europeans, 22 Indians, and 8 Coloureds) were arrested, many prominent Christians, including Professor Z. K. Matthews, among them. The charges were treason under the Suppression of Communism Act. The preliminary hearing began on 19 December 1956 and continued until 30 January 1958, although on 17 December 1957 the charges against sixty-one of the accused were withdrawn. One might hail that as proof of the rule of law. But only governments are rich enough to make the legal process drag out interminably. Men have families to support: who would house them? Women have children to nourish: who would care for them? The answer was not the government, but men and women round the world who contributed to the South African Defence Fund.

The churches were still fumbling. The World Council, owing to lack of funds, had not filled the special post on racism authorized by the Evanston Assembly. The National Council of the Churches of Christ in the USA seconded Dr Oscar Lee for three months to prepare a proposal in the field of race relations for World Council action. The Division of Ecumenical Action, then responsible for implementing the racial mandate, attempted without success to find funds for the authorized consultant. In 1959 a private donation finally allowed the temporary retention of the Reverend Daisuke Kitagawa to study the American churches and racial tension to ascertain the applicability of their techniques in other areas.

The Native Laws Amendment Bill began its legislative process in February 1957; the purpose of the bill was to make it illegal for Africans to attend church services, go to schools, hospitals, clubs, or other meetings outside the native areas. The churches of South Africa, with the understood exception of the Dutch Reformed churches, regarded this as an unacceptable limitation of the freedom of religion. The Archbishop of Cape Town, the Most Reverend Geoffrey Clayton, signed the official protest of the Church of the Province of South Africa shortly before he died, unexpectedly, on 7 March 1957. Writing for all his bishops, he stated that the clergy could not obey this law. Dr Owen McCann, the Roman Catholic Archbishop of Cape Town, and the Cape Town Presbytery also protested against the bill. In order to avert the opprobrium of the churches—though it is difficult to believe it was sincerely felt that this would overcome objections—the bill was amended so that it did not become a crime to attend church services unless the Minister of Native Affairs directed that such attendance was a public nuisance. In this case the native became liable to punishment, not the churches, as the original bill had provided. This was an additional weapon against the individual.

Bishop Reeves complained that the amended law still gave a politician the right to determine who might and who might not worship in a particular place, though the Dutch Reformed churches found the revised version quite satisfactory. The bill became law on 17 May 1957. All the English-speaking churches, in company with the Roman Catholic, reaffirmed their opposition to the new law. A pastoral letter read in all the Anglican churches on 14 July 1957 called upon the laity and the clergy to ignore the 'church clause'. The following Sunday a similar letter was read in the Roman Catholic churches, in which Dr McCann declared that the 'Catholic churches must and shall remain open to all without regard to their racial origin'. The Roman Catholic bishops meeting that same month condemned apartheid as 'blasphemous'.

At the 1957 meetings of the CCIA Executive Committee and of the Central Committee, resolutions took note of the treason trials and this violation of human rights. The CCIA resolution condemned, by inference rather than directly, the early-morning arrests. The Central Committee recognized 'the further deterioration in race relations in some parts of the world' and reaffirmed the resolutions of the Evanston Assembly on racism. It further re-emphasized 'the task of the churches in challenging the conscience of the societies in which they are set'. As a result of the

81

Oscar Lee report, the services of a consultant on racial affairs, one trained in both theology and sociology, was approved. His services would be available to any member church or national Christian council as well as to World Council departments. The financial support, unfortunately, would have to come from outside normal sources of World Council income.

The sincerity of the Central Committee cannot be doubted, but this action was terribly reminiscent of the funding of the Department of Social and Industrial Research of the International Missionary Council in the early 1930s. It was a department not really desired by a powerful, conservative part of the IMC; the concession made by Oldham and those who felt that the mandate of the Jerusalem meeting (due to the initiative of the mission churches) ought to be followed, was that its funding would not come from sources normally contributing to the missionary enterprise. And though it might seem unreasonable to the white churches, and to whites of the industrial North in general, the African, as Mrs Rena Karefa-Smart noted, insisted 'upon thinking in terms of colour as the dominant fact of human relations', when others might see the issue as an economic or colonial or political one.[25] And did the African not look at the white churches and their lack of vigour in this instance and wonder?

On 23 January 1958 the Most Reverend Joost de Blank, elected Archbishop of Cape Town on 7 May 1957 as successor to Dr Clayton, spoke out against apartheid in the following words: 'Here [man] sees that the working out of apartheid is not a working policy of fair and just separation of races in different areas, as conceived and explained by bodies like the South African Bureau of Racial Affairs and the Dutch Reformed Church, but is rather the maintenance and consolidation of White domination and White privilege.' And later that year, on 2 September 1958, Dr Verwoerd, former Minister of Native Affairs, was elected National Party leader. His statement on assuming the Prime Ministership clearly let all know that there would be no change in the policy the government had pursued over the last decade. His words were proved correct early the next year when his government introduced the Separate Universities Education Bill. Originally introduced in 1957, it had been withdrawn twice on technicalities (the letter of the law must be upheld). Such was the opposition that the government invoked guillotine procedures and the bill was finally passed on 30 April 1959. It provided that no non-whites might be registered at Cape Town and Witwatersrand universities. A companion bill closed the famous non-white Fort Hare College to all but members of the Xhosa tribe. An indignant academic world watched with impotence as their colleagues in South Africa protested in vain. Dr Verwoerd stated during the Fort Hare Bill debate that all telegrams of protest received from university and political leaders all over the world would go 'straight into the wastepaper basket'.

The Thessalonica Conference on Rapid Social Change, meeting in July 1959, with 140 delegates from 34 countries, over half of whom were from the Third World, including a considerable number of Africans, noted that rapid social change accentuated racial tensions. Increasing education and rising standards of living provoked new hopes where previously an under-privileged status was accepted as destiny. The Evanston Assembly's judgement on racism was approvingly quoted, and the duty of the church and individual Christians to take positive steps to end racism was reiterated. No specific steps were recommended, however;[26] this was rather like a request to untie the Gordian knot without providing instructions. And there was no Alexander to hand. The International Confederation of Free Trade Unions at a meeting on 11 September 1959 provided what it considered to be a means of at least loosening the knot to the point where the Africans could breathe. Since African labour was exploited, a boycott of South African goods and products was proposed with the aim of encouraging national and international capital to exert pressure on the South African government to change its racial policy. Many national labour unions and political parties joined in support, and on 5 April 1960 the ICFTU called for a two-month boycott. According to a survey reported in the *New York Times,* the boycott had caused a $1 million loss to South African exporters. The idea of boycotts was taken up by the United Nations General Assembly, but resolutions calling for boycotts have attracted participation only by Third World states. They have proved of little detriment to the South African economy and of no effect in lessening the hardships of apartheid. This has been due primarily to the fact that South Africa's main trading partners, the United Kingdom, the United States, and France have opposed the resolutions passed and refused to abide by them.

The black South Africans did not remain inactive. 'Sharpeville' became a name of infamy throughout the world when white South African policemen fired on black Africans protesting against apartheid by peacefully violating the pass laws. The African National Congress and the Pan Africanist Congress had chosen 21 March 1960 as a day for civil disobedience. All were to leave their passes at home and then go to the police station and give themselves up. Who can say what really happened that day? Who can deny that 2,000 blacks assembled even peacefully would not strike fear in the hearts of those whose daily job was to continue their oppression? But since the crowd was unarmed and the police had armoured cars, the sudden use of guns can surely be questioned. The shooting left 67 Africans dead and 186 wounded. A smaller but similar shooting occurred at Langa. On 23 March, Archbishops de Blank and McCann, the Congregationalist Union of South Africa, and the Chief Rabbi of Cape Town, Professor I. Abrahams, condemned apartheid and deplored the shootings to which it had led. On 28 March a strike by African workers began. On 30 March a state of emergency was declared and more than 1,900 people, including 94 whites, were arrested.

On 1 April 1960 the Dutch Reformed churches issued a statement that attributed the crisis to irresponsible statements by church leaders in South Africa and abroad. They continued, 'We appeal to the authorities as we have always done in the past, to do everything possible in their efforts to restore human relationships in the Union. The improvement of the wage structure deserves the fullest attention of the authorities . . . We assure the authorities . . . of our faith in them.' Archbishop de Blank stated that his church could no longer be associated with the Dutch Reformed churches, in any organization, including the World Council of Churches, unless they repudiated apartheid. He appealed to the World Council to send a fact-finding team. The *Guardian* (London) considered that there was real danger of a split within the ranks of the World Council. The South African newspapers gave great prominence to the controversy. The *Johannesburg Star* reported that, although Archbishop Fisher publicly stated that the Church of England had 'constantly, for many years past, denounced the evils and injustices of the policy of apartheid', he did so only after pressure by the British press publicly to condemn apartheid.[27]

Dr Visser 't Hooft had already been considering the possibility of an independent inquiry as suggested by Archbishop de Blank, and when assured that such a mission would be welcomed, he sent Dr Robert S. Bilheimer, Associate General Secretary, to South Africa in mid-April. His tasks were not easy: to find a way to achieve Christian unity—or, at the very least, ecumenical co-operation—and to discuss race relations. It is not clear what could actually be achieved by the latter task; however, should ecumenical co-operation be the result, a united stand on the part of all South African churches would indicate the possibility of greater pressure on the government. The very fact that the World Council sent a representative was a witness to its concern for this race-torn country; its position on racial discrimination was well known from the Evanston statement. However, the unity desired was not achieved, and it was proposed that the World Council arrange a meeting of South African member churches with its own leaders. The World Council concurred and issued a letter of invitation.

In addition to the World Council of Churches' action, a group of twenty-nine Afro-Asian states called for a meeting of the

Security Council to discuss the situation 'arising out of large-scale killings of unarmed and peaceful demonstrators against racial discrimination and segregation' in South Africa. Although, at the 30 March meeting, the United Kingdom, France, and Italy voted in favour of hearing the item, they considered that it was a matter falling within the domestic jurisdiction of South Africa. Mr B. Fourie, representing South Africa, protested that the Council had no right to discuss the matter and then withdrew from the Council table. This was the first time that the Security Council had had before it a motion on apartheid. In spite of this and of the absence of South Africa, the Security Council adopted on 1 April a resolution deploring the policies of the South African government and calling upon it to abandon apartheid. It went even further than might have been thought conceivable and recognized the situation in South Africa as one 'likely to endanger international peace and security'. South Africa continued its own way.

Meanwhile the earlier interference with parliamentary procedure to give a semblance of the rule of law was admitted by Mr J. F. Naude, Minister of the Interior, in the debate on the second Senate Reorganization Bill. Basically this restored the organization of the Senate to that existing before the Senate-packing Act of 1955. Mr Naude candidly stated that the changes had been made in order to assure the government of the two-thirds vote in joint session necessary for the Separate Registration of Voters Bill. The Senate could now return to its original form! In October 1960 a referendum was held on whether the white population would favour South Africa's becoming a republic. On the basis of the narrow franchise, 52 per cent favoured a republic and 47.5 per cent were against it. There was no doubt that the disfranchised part of the population favoured maintaining its ties with the British Crown.

A great deal of attention was devoted to Africa at the 1960 CCIA Executive Committee meeting. Ghana had become independent in 1957, Guinea in 1958, and 1960 saw the dissolution of the French empire in Africa (except for Algeria) and of British rule in most of West Africa. Sir Francis Akanu Ibiam (also known as Dr Akanu Ibiam) of Nigeria challenged the churches to more substantial action on behalf of the black man in South Africa. As at previous meetings, the north Europeans temporized. Sir Kenneth Grubb suggested that it would be wiser to await the results of the December consultation in South Africa before making further statements. Dr Visser 't Hooft suggested, and it was agreed, that a general statement on Africa might be appropriate. A minute on Africa was drafted, which, in addition to dealing with the economic development of Africa and the duty of the ex-colonial powers to assist their former wards, also noted the opportunity Africa offered to the Christian churches as an area of service. Christians, it averred, wherever foreign rule or minority rule with discrimination existed, had the duty to strive for a social order based on the dignity of man.[28] The Central Committee meeting that same summer sent a 'Message to the Churches in Africa' in which it rejoiced that some colonies had already achieved independence and that others would soon do so. Reaffirming the Evanston Assembly's statement against segregation, it asserted the principle that those areas with minority rule should be prepared for self-government in which all races should share.

The preparations for the December consultation with the South African churches on apartheid went nearly for naught when Bishop Reeves, returning to his see in Johannesburg in September, was deported by the government. On the night of 1 April he had fled to Swaziland, having been warned of his impending arrest; receiving no assurances from the South African government for his safety and feeling that he would be of more use in London than held incommunicado in a South African jail, he had proceeded to England, where he remained until September when he returned and was deported. Archbishop de Blank urged that, because a key delegate could not attend, the consultation be held outside the Union or not at all. The World Council requested a full report on the deportation from the churches in South Africa. A Commission of Dutch Reformed churches described this as interference in South Africa's political affairs and stated that the Dutch Reformed churches would not attend if the consultation were held outside South Africa. The largest Dutch Reformed churches requested the government to allow Bishop Reeves into the country for the purpose of attending the consultation, but this compromise was refused. The solidarity of the churches, up to a point, had been demonstrated. The Planning Committee, judging that the consultation would have a greater impact upon the situation if held in South Africa, prevailed upon the Church in the Province of South Africa to agree to participate as planned.

The Cottesloe Consultation was convened on 7 December 1960, with delegations of ten each from the eight churches in South Africa. All but two were inter-racial; non-whites comprised about one-quarter of the delegates. (Sir Francis Akanu Ibiam of the World Council delegation was unable to attend because of new duties imposed upon him by his election as Governor of the Eastern Province of Nigeria.) Frankness was the keynote of the consultation. Memoranda so open they were not made public were circulated beforehand; the views exchanged at Cottesloe remained plainspoken throughout. Although no statement had been planned, the desire for such a means of expressing unity grew. A draft was debated, sentence by sentence, and voted on, paragraph by paragraph. It was decided that an 80 per cent majority would

be required for passage, thus ensuring the widest possible acceptance.

As there was lack of agreement on a definition of the policy of
apartheid, the statement made no judgement of it as a policy of
the South African government. The unity of all Christians regardless of colour was stressed and accepted. The conditions of non-
whites in South Africa were criticized by mentioning such practices
as the migrant labour of men and the low wages paid to non-whites.
The delegation of the Nederduitse Gereformeerde Kerk of the Cape
and Transvaal issued a statement confirming that 'a policy of
differentiation can be defended from the Christian point of view,
that it provides the only realistic solution to the problems of race
relations and is therefore in the best interests of the various population groups'. The Nederduitse Hervormde Kerk van Afrika noted
that 'separate development is the only just solution of our racial
problems'. As a result of the consultation, these latter two churches
withdrew from the World Council.[29] The Council was feeling the
strain of divided loyalties, of loyalty to the nation, and of loyalty
and fidelity to scripture.

Even if it cannot be claimed that a policy advocated by the
World Council was adopted by a government, in this case it
appears that the Cottesloe Consultation acted as a catalyst and
forced action. *Die Burger,* the influential Afrikaner newspaper,
came out against the no-compromise stand on apartheid by the
Verwoerd government. Its basis for reaching this conclusion was
the statement issued by the Consultation.[30] Less surprising was the
Johannesburg Star's support in editorials before, during, and after
the consultation: 'This is the authentic voice of the Christian
conscience. . . . The majority statement does not ignore racial
differences but it insists that these differences must and can be
adjusted by mutual consultation and without injustice to any
section.'[31] *Die Vaderland* implicitly recognized this catalytic role
and the dissenting voices within the Afrikaner churches [32] when it
wrote that the controversy over apartheid had reached such proportions that intervention by 'the highest lay authority' was necessary to prevent further confusion.

At the beginning of the new year 1961 Dag Hammarskjöld, Secretary General of the United Nations, visited South Africa in
pursuance of a United Nations resolution. Although he could report
no success in persuading South Africa to abide by the United
Nations resolutions, he described the exchange of views as useful.
The General Assembly in April passed the usual annual resolution
regarding apartheid. A new effort to insert teeth into the old
resolutions by calling for diplomatic and economic sanctions failed
for lack of the necessary two-thirds majority.

The Commonwealth Prime Ministers' conference held in March

1961 was the first since the South African referendum on the proclamation of a republic. South Africa had made it clear that she wished to remain in the Commonwealth and that she considered that the Indian precedent of a republic in the Commonwealth ensured no problems for a republican South Africa. Reaction from Commonwealth capitals had indicated that South Africa would be expected to apply for readmission; Dr Verwoerd did so at this conference. Restricted sessions were held at which views on South Africa's application and on conditions within the country were exchanged; on 15 March 1961 Dr Verwoerd announced that South Africa would withdraw from the Commonwealth on 31 May 1961, when the Republic of South Africa would be proclaimed.

The new status was not, alas, a new beginning for South Africa. The largest mass arrests ever undertaken in the Union were carried out from 3 May to forestall strikes threatened by Africans in protest at the new Republic. So effective was the police action that only in Johannesburg did the three-day strike materialize, when 40 to 50 per cent of the work force stayed at home. On 4 May the General Law Amendment Bill was introduced giving the Minister of Justice discretionary powers in regard to bail and trial by jury in certain cases, and otherwise eroding the procedural rights normally available where the rule of law prevails. It became law within two weeks. A general election was called for 18 October and the government was returned by a larger majority than ever before.

Amid such news the Third Assembly of the World Council of Churches met in New Delhi, a non-white land, and not unnaturally devoted attention to this emotional topic. The Section on Service, responsible for the report on racism, noted that the race issue had been exacerbated since Evanston and reaffirmed that Assembly's strong stand against racism in any form. In addition to a condemnation, it further called upon the churches to strive actively for racial justice by all means short of violence. It did not, however, offer a programme to guide the churches and the World Council other than by urging Christians to identify themselves with the oppressed race and be ready to lead in its struggle for justice. As an example, local churches were urged to end segregation, and to assign pastors without regard to race. Finally, and unmistakably, 'separate development' (apartheid) was condemned.

As well as receiving the above report, the Assembly passed the resolution proposed by the Committee on Church and Society. This resolution noted that rapid social change in the world had made confrontation between the races more acute than ever before. It affirmed that the unity of Christians transcended racial divisions and welcomed the establishment of a Secretariat on Racial and Ethnic Relations within the World Council. Dr F. C. Fry, who had been at the Cottesloe Consultation, proposed to the Assembly a 'Message to Christians in South Africa'. This message reiterated the Cottesloe statements on racial equality and assured those in South Africa that they were not forgotten.[33] The New Delhi Assembly saw that the racial issue remained of concern to the World Council, but nothing startling was proposed which it could offer as a programme to international organizations or to individual states.

This interest, however, did not retard the continued implementation of the abhorrent policy. Under the General Law Amendment Act, known also as the Sabotage Act, a list of 102 persons was published on 30 July 1962 who were prohibited from attending gatherings; the fact that they were so named also made illegal the dissemination of statements by them, including books they had written. This led to the ridiculous exclusion of two pages from T. Hopkinson's book *In the Fiery Continent,* which quoted ex-Chief Albert Luthuli, Nobel Peace Prize winner and one of the proscribed persons. House arrest restrictions were imposed on still others. But fear did not prevent riots, actions of violence, and assassinations in the Transkei, organized by Poqo, successor to the banned Pan-Africanist Congress.

The General Assembly at the Seventeenth Session that December passed its annual apartheid resolution, this time calling for the rupture of diplomatic relations, the closure of seaports to South African vessels, prohibition of airspace to South African planes, and a boycott of South African goods. The Addis Ababa Conference of African Heads of State and Government the following May (1963), also urged African states to break off diplomatic relations. This occurred, as did an economic boycott joined in by many smaller Asian states as well. These actions perhaps hardened South Africa's attitude, for new laws on internal security were passed as well as others reinforcing and continuing apartheid, thereby making necessary still more stringent internal security laws to maintain the government in power. The rule of law was further eroded by an act providing for the indefinite detention of persons who had served their sentence for sabotage or similar crimes, and detention in solitary confinement for 90 days, renewable for further 90-day periods, at the discretion of the police with no court having authority to order release. This Act was supported by the opposition parties 'with great regret'. The Bantu Laws Amendment Act provided more complete control over Bantu labour, and The Coloured Persons Education Act arrogated to the central government the education of Coloured persons. And sabotage trials continued.

But South Africa was not the only country fermenting with the leaven of equality. The Reverend Martin Luther King and civil rights groups in the United States led the March on Washington to witness against racial discrimination in that country in August 1963, as the Central Committee met in Rochester, New York. Its attention could not help but be drawn to the drama unfolding in the capital of the richest and most powerful state on earth. In the discussion preceding the adoption of a 'Statement on Racial and Ethnic Tension', the Reverend Jean Kotto of Cameroun attacked the church discipline exercised by many churches in Africa regarding polygamy. 'The big copper magnate who exploits 40,000 underpaid, badly housed labourers is a good church member, but the polygamist who remains faithful, all working peacefully together for the good of the family, is not allowed to go in church.' [34] These words exemplify the African feeling that European values were being imposed under the guise of Christianity. The Statement recognized that the American and South African struggles were part of the same international problem of racism and condemned it wherever it appeared. It called upon the churches in the United States to change society and their own life; it asked the South African churches to repudiate their government's policy.

The Security Council debate held on 31 July 1963, deploring apartheid and calling upon states to cease the selling of arms and munitions to South Africa, followed the boycotting of the International Labour Conference in Geneva on 14 June by African and Arab states and Israel to protest against the presence of South Africa. The Eighteenth Session of the General Assembly beginning in the autumn of 1963 was dominated by the apartheid debate, which included a discussion of the status of South West Africa. In addition to its usual condemnation, the resolution called for the abandonment of arbitrary trials and the release of all political prisoners. The Security Council again became seized of the subject and passed a resolution calling for compliance with its resolution of 31 July and further widening the embargo to include all military supplies, and equipment and materials with which to manufacture and maintain arms. The United Nations Group of Experts (on apartheid) who had been instructed to study the problem of apartheid attempted to carry out their task in South Africa, but they were refused admittance by the government.

A major piece of apartheid legislation was passed on 7 April 1964 in the form of the Bantu Laws Amendment Act. It provided that Bantu were no longer protected against legal removal to a Native Area by right of residence, and the African wife or child could no longer claim permanent residence with the husband or father by virtue of his long service in a particular area. The Christian Council of South Africa spoke out against the infringement of certain basic Christian concepts regarding family life and the freedom and dignity of the individual. It was joined in this condemnation by the Conference of Roman Catholic Bishops of South Africa.

The Department of Church and Society in conjunction with the South African Institute of Race Relations and the Mindolo Ecumenical Centre in Kitwe, Northern Rhodesia (to become Zambia in September), convened a 'Consultation on Christian Practice and Desirable Action in Social Change and Race Relations in Southern Africa', from 25 May to 2 June 1964, in order to consider what plans the churches could offer in respect of this intractable problem.[35] The participants acted personally and not as official representatives of their churches, which included several Protestant denominations in Northern and Southern Rhodesia, Malawi, Tanganyika, the Congo, South Africa, and the then High Commission Territories.

Alan Booth, attending for the CCIA, first made a four-day trip to South Africa to visit National Party leaders, as a demonstration of World Council willingness to hear both sides. His conversations with the Minister for External Affairs Dr Muller, and the Minister for Information Mr Frank Waring, the leader of the Opposition Sir de Villiers Graaf, and the editors of two important Afrikaans newspapers, *Die Burger* and *Die Huisgenoot,* as well as with church leaders, offered an opportunity to sound out the leadership on possible solutions and to understand the fervency with which opinions were held.

The Consultation addressed itself to the churches and all Christians, even though its report concerned only Southern Africa. In reviewing the role of the churches in Africa, their development of the educational system was cited; but it was also admitted that they had not recognized early enough the right of the African to determine his own life, nor the need to help him maintain his dignity and to oppose the white attitude of racial superiority. The Consultation emphasized the commitment of the Christians of Southern Africa and their churches to social justice and equity between peoples of differing races, to the maintenance of the ministry, and training of the laity in concern for the whole Christian community regardless of race. The Consultation stated there was no scriptural basis for the segregation of Christians. Further the Church had too often declared itself in purely Western terms, both in what it valued and in ignoring Africa's own specific problems, for example, circumcision and other initiation rites, polygamy, worship of ancestral spirits, etc.

The Protestant ethic, by distorting the role of individualism and moralism, had also ignored Africa's peculiar characteristics. If Christianity offered nothing more than this to a communal society, if it offered no guidance in the new industrialization and urbanization of Africa, then rival ideologies which purported to offer a solution would be seized upon by the Africans. In order to teach, preach, and counsel all races in Africa with a relevance that was striking, the churchmen needed scientific knowledge of the basis of racial prejudice and discrimination.

In surveying the extent to which justice entered into the political life of Southern Africa, the Consultation unanimously agreed that all adults should participate in policy-making decisions through the franchise. The attainment of majority rule in Northern Rhodesia and Malawi was felt to be an encouraging counterweight to the slow whittling away of political rights in South Africa and Southern Rhodesia. The principle of gradualism, so revered by northern Europeans, was recognized, but it was noted that those with power had not begun the process of political education early enough, and, the longer the delay, the greater the chance that political rights would be demanded all at once. It recommended that a Bill of Rights secured by an independent judiciary should accompany the granting of political rights. Surely, however, in view of the demise of judicially protected rights in South Africa and the foreseeable Southern Rhodesian unilateral declaration of independence, this was a pious hope rather than a viable programme to be seriously considered by those reading the report.

The urgency of the situation, it continued, was evidenced by the training of 'freedom fighters' in different parts of Africa and the increasing defence measures of the governments threatened by them. When the privileged groups in Southern Africa trusted to military power alone to prolong the *status quo* indefinitely, they were enjoying the complacency of those in the eye of the storm. Peaceful measures had been tried and had resulted in further repression; the trend towards violence was therefore not surprising because it was, unhappily, inevitable. Many African leaders maintained that if modes of negotiation remained open, there would be no violence. But in fact on certain issues, for example, the status of South West Africa, the policy of apartheid in South Africa, or the question of majority rule in Rhodesia, no real communication was possible.

In considering international responsibility for the two most critical racial situations, the Consultation urged the British government not to shirk its responsibilities but to make it clear to Southern Rhodesia that it would not condone a unilateral declaration of independence. Meanwhile the churches in both countries should work to create the climate of opinion which would allow a constitutional conference of Africans and Europeans. As for South Africa, the other critical situation, the Consultation proposed that the international community should be prepared not only to condemn but also to offer alternative solutions, perhaps even to the extent of guaranteeing the security of the minority groups. This was a radical proposal which would most certainly not be readily accepted by the independent African states, but one which might be the only suitable response to the paranoia of the Afrikaners.

The dissatisfactions of dual standards of living based entirely on race were recounted and the practice was condemned. The pattern of South Africa—in land ownership and the control of vocational and technical education by legislation designed to limit the rights of the non-white—was rapidly being approached in Southern Rhodesia. The end result could only be economic upheaval. The duty of the Church in this situation was to discover how to reverse the outmoded attitudes which perpetuated the problem. This situation which kept individuals, a whole race of individuals, from realizing their full capabilities as human beings was condemned as repugnant to Christian doctrine.

Christians and the Church could help relieve the sufferings inherent in the system by working towards its elimination. Secondly, the churches should formulate and support schemes aimed at providing full employment to thwart the exploitation of Africans' labour. In disregard of the South African government's closing of mission schools, it was recommended that further efforts be made by the churches to supplement the government education system. Protestant individualism crept in by way of the suggestion to Christian businessmen that they should train Africans for executive positions while the Church persuaded government to provide the capital and credit facilities for entrepreneurial activity. The churches themselves, through their agriculture missions, would help relieve rural poverty by teaching Africans how to grow enough to change from a subsistence to a cash economy.

Consideration was given to the moral implications of the use of violence, a problem which was to recur as this solution appeared to be more and more the only practicable means of bringing about political change. Although some members dissociated themselves from the majority viewpoint, the Consultation conceded that after all lawful means to attain economic equality had been tried, then Christians would be justified in supporting boycotts, general strikes, and—as a last resort—planned industrial disruption to achieve justice.

The Consultation recognized the guilt of the churches in not speaking out earlier—a failure that might have been occasioned by lack of identification with the suffering, or by indifference to the suffering, or by an unwillingness to become involved. Now the church was involved, and its task was fourfold: (1) to act as prophet and conscience; (2) to aid in legal resistance; (3) to join in disobedience of unjust laws, being ready to suffer the consequences; and (4) not to encourage violence but neither to condemn it, only to ask of those embarking upon it whether they had exhausted all other possibilities. When violence was the method chosen, the Church should be there, trying to limit it to the extent that negotiation would always be possible.

African issues continued to be of ecumenical concern in 1964. At the late June meeting of the CCIA Executive Committee, Alan Booth reported on his trip to South Africa and on the Mindolo Consultation.[36] Maurice Webb, of South Africa, considered that the South African Christians were so convinced of their rightness that outside pressure would only solidify them. He envisaged two tasks for the CCIA-WCC: (1) to convince the white Christians that world concern included them too, and (2) to help the South African government and ecclesiastical leaders to make contact with African national and church leaders. Dr Visser 't Hooft took issue with the evaluation of the attitude of the South Africans. From personal conversations, he doubted that the Afrikaner leadership was acting with good conscience in its repressive actions. He also rejected the idea that the World Council could think in terms of solutions requiring unlimited time: the arming of Freedom Fighters indicated that the time for action was short indeed. Mr Henry Makulu of Zambia stressed that Africans were more interested in freedom than in economic progress; they would gladly suffer economic regression due to sanctions, if to do so led to better conditions later. He felt that the churches in countries from which South Africa received most financial benefit had especial responsibilities in this matter.

In the ensuing discussion the importance was stressed of CCIA-WCC initiatives in establishing a dialogue with leaders, Christian and political, in South Africa in order to remove the sense of isolation their language and geography gave them. The self-sufficiency of South Africa in everything except oil would, it was noted, make sanctions less than effective. All actions thus far taken by the United Nations in regard to South Africa had been negative; no one had offered a plan to end the discrimination and yet preserve the position of whites in a biracial republic. Dr Visser 't Hooft proposed a special minute on South Africa which the Committee approved. The minute noted the similarity between the report of the United Nations Group of Experts and the Mindolo Conference report, in that both cited the urgency of the present situation if future violence were to be averted. The officers of the CCIA were instructed to continue their study of possible ways of arriving at a peaceful settlement.

The World Council Executive Committee meeting in late July of that same summer adopted a resolution dealing with the racial situation in both South Africa and the United States. It urged those living in uniracial societies not to feel superior, since the absence of obvious racial prejudice might only be due to lack of opportunity to express it. The findings of the Mindolo Consultation were commended to the churches for their study and to elicit suggestions for possible solutions to this world-wide problem. Arbitrary detention and expulsion were condemned as interfering with freedom of worship!

In South Africa the Coloured Representative Council Bill was enacted, further institutionalizing apartheid and subordinating a non-white group. It provided for a Coloured Representative Council, consisting of 30 elected and 16 nominated (by the government) members, to advise the government on matters affecting the Coloured population, when it was asked to do so. It could be empowered to legislate on certain matters involving Coloureds, but each piece of legislation would still require (white) ministerial approval. The United Nations did not pass its usual resolution condemning apartheid during the Nineteenth Session, because the United Nations financial crisis of that year prevented any votes being taken.

The city of Enugu, Eastern Nigeria, was the site chosen for the Central Committee meeting in January 1965. It was preceded by a Consultation of the All African Conference of Churches in conjunction with the Division of Inter-Church Aid, Refugee and World Service, the Department of Church and Society, and the Commission of the Churches on International Affairs. Not unnaturally, the problem of human rights and apartheid was broached by the Consultation, which endorsed previous Central Committee stands against apartheid; it further urged the Dutch Reformed churches and all churches in South Africa to struggle for human and racial rights in South Africa and against the enforced 'separate development'.[37]

The Reverend E. A. Adegbola, Nigeria's leading Methodist theologian, criticized the ethnocentrism of European Christianity for not allowing African churches to adapt Christianity to African customs. The European theologians considered that the churches of their denominations in Africa should follow traditional Christian moral principles as interpreted by European theologians. When a Nigerian reporter asked Archbishop Ramsey if his church could bring itself to accept an African with more than one wife, he replied, 'Certainly not!' Both Mr Adegbola and Mr Samuel Amissah, Methodist layman and General Secretary of the All Africa Conference of Churches, disagreed with this attitude.[38] However, the Central Committee did not consider this cultural aspect of racism, but in the 'Statement on Current International Issues of Peace, Justice and Freedom' condemned the evils of racial discrimination whether they existed illegally as in the United States or legally as in South Africa. It supported the Consultation's appeal to the Dutch Reformed churches in South Africa to declare themselves against apartheid. It praised the courageous minority within those churches that was beginning to speak out. The Committee expressed sympathy with the victims of political and racial laws and supported an appeal for funds to be used on their behalf. 'In order that recourse to violence may be found unnecessary, we are convinced that international and national efforts must continue until nations and men, now subject to domination or discrimination, are indeed independent and free.'[39]

As the collectivity of states—over a period of twenty years—had had no success in inhibiting a government bent on a racist policy, it was not surprising that the collectivity of churches, whose only power was moral suasion, should have exercised no notable influence on the South African government. Indeed, on 12 February 1965, a proclamation extended segregation to all public places of recreation, such as concerts and sporting events; whites could not attend such functions in non-white areas, nor non-whites in white areas. On 30 April 1965 the Indians' Education Act took education of Indians out of the jurisdiction of the provinces and placed it in the hands of the central government. On 13 May 1965 the Official Secrets Act was amended to make it an offence to publish information about any military or police matter, no matter how trivial. On 7 June the Police Amendment Act empowered the police to search without warrant anyone within one mile of South Africa's borders. On 22 June the Suppression of Communism Amendment Act widened the powers of the government in banning publications, and renewed for another year the authority for continued detention of persons whose sentences had been served. But the most ominous of all was the Criminal Procedure Amendment Bill, which would empower the Attorney General to order a court not to grant bail and to arrest and detain for up to 180 days state witnesses. The Christian Council of South Africa protested against its enactment to no avail.

Faced with twenty years of *faits accomplis,* that summer's meeting of the CCIA Executive Committee wandered in purposeless discussion. What could be the solution to the nigh-insurmountable problems of Southern Africa? No one had the answer in this small group, but a statement was prepared and adopted on the general situation in Southern Africa.[40] It deplored the intensification of South Africa's policies of apartheid and the 'increasingly ruthless' repression which accompanied it. The Committee believed that contact with churches, organizations, and individuals in the countries of Southern Africa should be continued and that communications between white governments and African leaders should be encouraged. Those countries which were sources of technically proficient immigrants to South Africa should make known in their countries the extent to which immigration was responsible for continued African poverty and repression. To ease the fear of the unknown, the new African leaders should indicate the place they foresaw for the white community in future Africa. Ending with praise for the intellectual, technical, and commercial capabilities of the South African whites, it urged an end to apartheid.

In December 1965 B. J. Vorster, Minister of Justice, Police and Prisons, announced that, between 1 February 1963 and 31 December 1964, 2,436 persons had been charged under the Sabotage Act. Of this number 1,308 had been found guilty, and no sabotage had been committed since July 1964. At its Twentieth Session, the General Assembly set up a United Nations Trust Fund to help victims of apartheid and their families, both within and outside South Africa. It would help provide support for the families of those whose breadwinner had been imprisoned officially or was unofficially known to be imprisoned. It also passed its 28th resolution in 20 years condemning apartheid.

On 18 March 1966 the South African government declared the South African Defence and Aid Fund—to which millions of people throughout the world, but especially in Great Britain, had contributed—an unlawful organization under the Suppression of Communism Act. At the General Election on 30 March 1966 the National Party was returned with a larger majority than ever before, having gained support among the English-speaking voters. The United Party, the principal opposition party, had throughout the years gradually moved nearer to the political position of the National Party. During this election it, too, called for support of the Smith régime in Rhodesia (which, as Southern Rhodesia, had unilaterally declared its independence on 11 November 1965) but opposed apartheid, not on principle but on the basis that independent Bantustans would be open to Communist influence. Only the Progressive Party with its lone parliamentary representative, Mrs Helen Suzman, urged that the rights of man do not depend on race.

Half the participants in the World Conference on Church and Society, convened in Geneva on 12 July 1966, were from non-white countries; it was not surprising, then, that the Conference devoted a large part of its programme to racial issues. The problem of racism was brought forcefully home to the Conference when Dr Martin Luther King, scheduled to preach at the ecumenical service of the Conference, was unable to leave for Geneva because of a massive racial confrontation in Chicago. The Conference participants sat before an empty pulpit in St Peter's Cathedral in the old quarter of Geneva and with all Europe, via Eurovision, heard and saw on television sets placed in the church, a sermon recorded by Dr King in the United States and flown to Geneva for a waiting continent.

As with all such meetings, lengthy studies and planning shaped the format of the Conference, yet the events in the world—in South Africa and in the United States—could not help but give a greater immediacy to the problems as they were studied and discussed in the Sections. The report of Section III on world economic development examined the problem of racism as an example of economic self-interest on the part of whites.[41] The support which international capital investment lends to régimes which discriminate against non-whites was decried. The churches, it was recommended, should urge a curriculum upon secular and religious educational systems which stresses the oneness of humanity and respect for unfamiliar cultures. The churches should urge upon their governments the ratification and enforcements of the United Nations Covenants on Human Rights and of the Convention on the Elimination of All Forms of Racial Discrimination. And they should encourage the creation of a United Nations High Commissioner on Human Rights to oversee the implementation of all international treaties concerning human rights.

The report of Section IV on Man and Community in Changing Societies also urged pressure at the governmental level upon the churches: they should actively attempt to change 'the structure of society through legislation, social planning and corporate action' in order to assure the participation of all groups in a pluralistic society. It also endorsed further World Council dialogues with churches which persisted in segregation, while calling upon the rest of the churches to eliminate it from their daily activities.[42] Thus, although the Conference had specific suggestions to help alleviate this problem, it had no detailed or comprehensive plan; undoubtedly it was a well-considered plan that statesmen needed. And not only the leaders of those countries where the government was trying to end racial discrimination, but also leaders of countries like South Africa and Rhodesia. If a viable alternative were placed before them, one which would assure them that the traditions and customs which they treasured would be preserved, there would at least be one less excuse for this behaviour.

As it was, the government of South Africa continued its charted course. This was briefly and tragically interrupted when Prime Minister Verwoerd, who had previously recovered from an assassin's bullets, fell to the knifeblows of a Portuguese national, Tsafendas, a messenger in the Parliament buildings, on 6 September 1966. A week later the National Party elected Mr B. J. Vorster,

Minister of Justice, Police and Prisons, as its leader and he of course became Prime Minister. The following month the General Law Amendment Bill was enacted, further tightening the government's grip upon individuals. Any police officer above the rank of lieutenant-colonel was authorized to detain for up to fourteen days anyone suspected of security offences, and no court had authority to intervene. Further, any person on trial for sabotage would be presumed guilty of the crime if he had ever left South Africa illegally.

The Twenty-first Session of the General Assembly adopted its usual resolution on apartheid on 16 December. In addition to condemning apartheid, it was designated as a crime against humanity. The resolution also 'deplored the attitude of South Africa's main trading partners', the United States, the United Kingdom, and France, for their non-co-operation in regard to former Assembly resolutions. It called upon the Security Council to apply mandatory economic sanctions to end apartheid. Among the thirteen abstentions were the United States, the United Kingdom, and France. A UNESCO report condemning apartheid, published on 18 January 1967, was denounced the following month by South Africa as 'a carefully slanted, preconceived political attack'.

In spite of a general boycott of South Africa by African states, some co-operated with that country. Chief Jonathan of Lesotho visited South Africa in January 1967 and negotiated with Prime Minister Vorster an economic assistance agreement. On 13 March a trade agreement between South Africa and Malawi was signed. Dr Hastings Banda, President of Malawi, to offset criticism from other African states, announced he was not afraid to trade openly with South Africa in spite of possible expulsion from the Organization of African Unity, for many others were doing so secretly.

The possibility of normalization of relations with black states did not deflect governmental policy from its appointed route. On 15 February a law to eliminate 'Communists' from the legal profession was passed, which in effect disbarred lawyers in disfavour with the government. On 5 May the Population Registration Amendment Act set aside court judgments of race classification by empowering the President to make final decisions on race classification—a decision from which there was no appeal. But the most extreme legislation of the year was the 'Terrorism Bill' (General Law Amendment Bill of 1967), enacted on 21 June 1967. It made terrorism an offence equated with treason. It provided that persons suspected of terrorism could be arrested without warrant, could be detained indefinitely, and held in solitary confinement; this included any persons suspected of withholding information about terrorists or acts of terrorism. There was to be no bail. A summary trial by a judge without a jury would take place, and mass trials of persons charged with different offences could be held. The bill specifically extended its provisions to South West Africa. In addition to the elimination of the above procedural safeguards, the Act was made retroactive to 27 June 1962. On the basis of this retroactivity, thirty-seven South West African Ovambo leaders were charged with crimes six days after the bill was enacted.

'The Obligation of Christians in the Present World Racial Crisis' was a statement adopted by the Central Committee at its meeting in August 1967. It expressed the World Council's concern over continuing racial injustice in the world as evidenced by growing disorders in the United States, by tribal conflict in the new nations of Africa, and by the racial tension in South East Africa, as well as the continuing problems in Southern Africa. Reiterating its previous statement at Rochester and quoting the report of the World Conference on Church and Society, the Committee requested member churches to examine their efforts at eliminating racial discrimination and to report their findings to the Central Committee. The Committee urged the churches to re-examine their priorities, reminding them that no real progress could be made without governmental programmes to eliminate discrimination and the related problem of poverty; to this end it urged representations be made to their respective governments.

The trial of the Ovambo leaders charged under the retroactive Terrorism Act began in late 1967 and continued well into 1968, designated 'Human Rights' Year' by the United Nations. The trial awakened world-wide interest: *Le Monde* reported the evaluation of Professor Arthur Larson, Vice-President of the American National Council of Churches, who was sent jointly by the CCIA and the Lutheran World Federation to observe the Pretoria trial during the final period and sentencing. He characterized the trial as a 'monstrous parody of justice', because proof came from the 180 witnesses subject to limitless detention, from evidence obtained by torture, and from declarations made by the police which were manifestly false.[43] The World Council Executive Committee, meeting in February 1968, issued a statement condemning South Africa for violating the United Nations Declaration of Human Rights by passing a law retroactively, by torturing the prisoners, and by placing them in solitary confinement for periods of up to eighteen months. It called for the immediate release and repatriation of the prisoners. This was certainly one of the strongest condemnations of a state yet undertaken by the World Council. Needless to say, its words were ignored.

With an overwhelming majority in Parliament, the government nevertheless felt it necessary to weaken the Progressive Party and to further its own policy of total separation by passing the Prohibition of Improper Interference Act which prohibited multi-racial political parties, or participation by any individual in the affairs of political parties of another group or acceptance by any political party of funds from abroad. At the same time the Coloured Persons' Representative Council had its membership increased in anticipation of the ending of representation of Coloureds (by white persons) in the South African Parliament in 1971.

Race consciousness in the world was growing; it was not surprising, then, that the Fourth Assembly of the World Council of Churches meeting in Uppsala, Sweden, from 4–20 July found itself dealing extensively with this problem. One plenary session of the Assembly was devoted to a discussion of 'White Racism or World Community?' Mr James Baldwin, American black writer, made world headlines with his accusation: 'I address you as one of God's creatures whom the Christian Church has most betrayed.' He recited a litany of charges perpetrated by white society, equating it, perhaps not unjustly, with Christendom. After all, during this period of black suffering, the white man claimed a monopoly of Christianity, and the Church was a powerful social and political institution. His simplistic charge was rhetorical rather than scientific: 'The Christian Church still rules this world, it still has the power to change the structure of South Africa. It has the power, if it will, to prevent the death of another Martin Luther King junior. It has the power, if it will, to force my Government to cease dropping bombs in South-East Asia.'[44] If indeed the Christian Church were so powerful, there would be cause to worry about power corrupting the worldly institution of the church. It is, in reality, only one of many institutions in an increasingly secularized, pluralistic society, not entirely without power, but not with overwhelming power.

Lord Caradon (formerly Sir Hugh Foot), Permanent Representative of the United Kingdom to the United Nations, more sedate than excitable, more analytical than rhetorical, acknowledged that 'Coupled as it is with the world problems of poverty and population and youth . . . race is the most explosive and most dangerous issue which the world must face'.[45] He found the risk of a present racial confrontation grave, especially in regard to the white-supremecist nations of Southern Africa. However, he placed hope in the youth of the world, who are impatient with the racial problem; mobilizing the enthusiastic support of youth in all states, he suggested, was the key to racial harmony. 'In such an international campaign we have a right to look for courageous leadership to the World Council of Churches.' Indeed the world looked.

And the Council responded. Racism was considered in four reports. That on 'World Economic and Social Development' called to the churches' attention the fact that white racism often impedes economic development.[46] 'Towards Justice and Peace in International Affairs' noted that racism robbed the concept of human rights of all meaning and that it was a danger to world peace. It, too, affirmed that 'Racism is linked with economic and political exploitation'. It urged that the duty of the churches in such cases was to make extra resources available to the underprivileged so that they might fully develop their own potentialities. It called upon the churches to act as pressure groups, when it exhorted them to try to change political institutions which prevent members of particular races from participating in the governmental process. The churches must end racism in their own lives; and, through the mass media and education, attempt to change the values which perpetuate racism.[47] The report on 'Worship' stated that Christians must refuse all efforts to segregate religious services.[48] And 'Towards New Styles of Living' alluded again to the relationship between poverty and race. Going further than either the CCIA or World Council had gone previously, it urged that 'the churches . . . continue to rebuke those churches which tolerate racism . . .'[49]

A further plenary session was devoted to a discussion of human rights. A message of greeting from U Thant, Secretary General of the United Nations, pointed out the moral guidance which the World Council of Churches could give to secular organizations such as the United Nations in the field of human rights. Dr Robert K. A. Gardiner, African diplomat and Executive Secretary of the UN Economic Commission for Africa, spoke on the role of Christianity and Christian missions in making the peoples of Africa and Asia aware of the possibilities open to them in the twentieth century. As a religion which did not emphasize a fatalistic acceptance of one's lot, Christianity had played a major role in Africa's rebellion. In spite of this, the non-white world generally regarded the white missionary as one with the white merchant and administrator. Dr Gardiner admitted that today's racial confrontation is not between white and non-white only, but between various peoples throughout the world. He held that the Church could help forestall racial wars by urging its members not to conform to communal pressures directed towards racial hatred; on the contrary Christians must question societal attitudes. They must act as a pressure group to do away with segregation laws; they must even go further and take positive steps to introduce legislation to protect human rights.

Thus stimulated, the Assembly was ready to adopt a statement on racism, and such a statement did come before Policy Committee II for consideration. Objection was made by Dr D. T. Niles, of the Methodist Church in Ceylon, who found the statement too general and moved that it be referred to the Central Committee at its 1969 meeting. The Committee so voted.[50] Nevertheless in its 'Message', the Assembly noted ' . . . we Christians will manifest our unity in Christ by entering into full fellowship with those of other races, classes, age, religious and political convictions, in the place where we live. Especially we shall seek to overcome racism wherever it appears . . .'[51] And racism appeared, according to twenty-five American blacks, at Uppsala where not one black American delegate was nominated for election to the Central Committee. The Reverend Edler G. Hawkins of the Bronx Presbyterian Church, the Reverend Roy C. Nichols of the Harlem Methodist Church, and Miss Jean Fairfax of the National Association for the Advancement of Coloured People replaced three white nominees, two of whom willingly ceded their seats.[52] Martin Luther King had been unable to preach before the World Conference on Church and Society in Geneva in 1966 because he considered it his duty to remain with his brethren in trouble in Chicago; instead, a video-tape was made for presentation to that body. Neither a video-tape nor Martin Luther King himself was able to keep his preaching appointment before the Assembly, for he fell victim to a racist's bullet as he again went to his people in trouble in Memphis, Tennessee, three months before the Assembly, on 5 April 1968. Racism appeared; it had not yet been overcome. James Baldwin voiced the scepticism of many non-whites when he commented on the Message: 'I don't care what you say here. I shall watch what you do when you get home.'[53]

Perhaps emboldened by the Uppsala show of solidarity, a commission of the South African Council of Churches (formerly South African Christian Council) issued a report condemning apartheid as a 'false faith hostile to Christian belief'. This began a public dialogue with the government. Mr Vorster declared on 27 September that there were some who wished to disturb order in South Africa 'under the cloak of religion'. And rather ominously he ended with the warning that clerical garb would be no protection. On 21 October twelve of the leading Protestant clergy of South Africa, including Archbishop R. Selby Taylor who had replaced Archbishop de Blank, declared that the Church could not cease all political utterances, for it had responsibility for proclaiming God's word. Prime Minister Vorster replied on 26 October that if the pulpits were to be used to attack the government and the National Party, the clergy should not be sensitive about his and others' reactions. Cardinal Owen McCann published a statement on 7 November that 'the Church . . . has the mandate and the obligation to speak on moral matters. Politics also include moral matters.' Of course, in the long run, the government had the last word. For in the two years 1967 and 1968, several foreign-born clergy who had been critical of South Africa's racial policies had been expelled.

On Human Rights Day, 10 December, of Human Rights Year,

1968, the Presidents of the World Council proclaimed in a Message their dedication to securing human rights for all peoples. 'Yet violations of the basic rights of man continue not only through racial discrimination, apartheid, arbitrary arrests, detention without trial . . . but also through violence, terror, slavery, starvation, even massacre. We therefore ask you to press forward the struggle against apathy and not to rest until governments have indeed ratified such instruments on human rights, and we urge you to find ways to put into practice the standards set forth in these instruments.'

As the result of the arrest and charging of the editor-in-chief of the *Rand Daily Mail* and his senior reporter for publishing false information about the South African prisons the United Nations General Assembly adopted a resolution on 19 December calling upon South Africa to investigate prison conditions as well as to abolish the laws under which opponents of apartheid were prosecuted and to release all political prisoners. The following June Mr M. I. Botha, South African representative to the United Nations, stated that his government had no intention of complying with the resolution, but submitted voluntarily a monograph on South African prisons.

The most significant action in the long run by the United Nations, however, may prove to be the Convention on the Elimination of All Forms of Racial Discrimination, which came into force on 4 January 1969 after the ratification of Poland, the twenty-seventh state to do so. Of the forty-six ratifications that had been made by January 1971, the majority were by East European and Third World states. France, Portugal, and South Africa (among others) had not even signed it. By January 1976 eighty-seven states had ratified or acceded to it. The only major one not to have done so was the United States of America. The Convention had been four years gaining the first twenty-seven ratifications; it had been adopted with 106 in favour and none against with one abstention in December 1965. Throughout the three-year drafting stage (the General Assembly requested the Commission on Human Rights in 1962 to draft such a convention), the CCIA expressed its general support and kept the position of the World Council of Churches on racial intolerance before the United Nations delegates.[54]

A convention is only as strong as the will to enforce it, no matter how many ratifications and adherences it receives. In any case, a multilateral treaty applies only to those states which indicate their willingness to abide by it. As the treaty was entering into force, the South African Prime Minister Vorster was able to announce that actual territorial separation of the races was growing. In order to speed development of the Native Areas, it was announced, white entrepreneurs would be given long-term contracts in them. Five native universities were established further to consolidate the gains in apartheid at that level. A new Population Registration Amendment Act was passed trying to legislate for all possible combinations of racial mixture for generations back. As Sir de Villiers Graaf, South African opposition leader, characterized it, 'trying to classify the unclassifiable'.

The most threatening part of the policy of apartheid was the ever tighter control over the rights of all parts of the population. The fact that individuals could be detained after they had served their terms of punishment, and that still others could be detained by ministerial fiat, meant that judicial punishment was less common than executive imprisonment. It was therefore a logical step to promulgate the Abolition of Juries Act; jury trials had become superfluous. The Community Development Amendment Act provided that the Minister of Community Development could exercise the powers of local authorities in a proclaimed racial group area if in his opinion such authorities had failed to act. This really meant, of course, having failed to act as directed by the central government. Censorship was carried to the extent of banning future editions of any South African periodical whose contents had been declared undesirable. The euphemistically named Public Service Amendment Act established the Bureau of State Security (BOSS), answerable only to a minister: there would be neither judicial nor parliamentary control in this case. In establishing BOSS, the government had been supported by the opposition United Party, which now, however, joined the South African Bar and Bench in opposing the General Law Amendment Bill, which greatly increased executive discretion at trials and further weakened the courts while increasing the area of uncertainty of citizens, by defining 'security' matters in very broad terms. The courts were prohibited from requiring the testimony of any witness if a minister sent a statement to court that evidence disclosure 'would be prejudicial to the interest of the public or state security'.

The Department on Church and Society had been charged with the primary responsibility for fulfilling the mandate of the Uppsala Assembly in regard to racism. In its efforts to find a solution which would obviate the necessity for the harsh and repressive legislation characteristic of such racist societies as South Africa, it convened an International Consultation on Racism in London, in the area called Notting Hill—where the first English race riot had taken place in 1958. Some 65 representatives from 26 countries were called to order by United States Senator George McGovern, Methodist layman and church leader, on 19 May 1969. The presence of American militant black leaders as well as Roy Sawh, Guyanese student and black power advocate in England, guaranteed that the proceedings of the consultation were not the smooth, efficient, bland meeting so usual in ecumenical circles.[55] Their white counterparts, jeering members of the extremist, and un-English, National Front Party, saw that a public meeting organized by the Consultation at which Bishop Trevor Huddleston spoke was not the pious talking of converted to converted it would otherwise most likely have been.

Black militants (never precisely identified as representing any organization) staged a disorderly interruption of a meeting of the Consultation on the eve of its adjournment, requesting £60 million in 'reparations' to be paid by the following morning at eleven o'clock. This ultimatum was not met, but it was treated as worthy of serious reply. After much debate, the Consultation accepted the principle of reparations by the churches, with no strings attached. It further proposed a programme of action for the World Council of Churches to undertake in the elimination of racism.[56] It proposed structural change within the World Council and action by the member churches outside it. Only as a last resort did it recommend support of revolutionary movements.

The Programme to Combat Racism

The Central Committee meeting in August 1969 at Canterbury, England, received the report of the Consulation. However, the programme to fight racism derived from it, which was presented for approval, had been greatly modified by the ecumenical 'curia', an action deplored by the non-white members of the Committee. The discrepancy between the Consultation's programme and that proposed for approval arose partly, according to highly placed sources, from the fact that those who had a major share in formulating policy at the Consultation in no way bore responsibility for the World Council of Churches and the relationships of its many constituents. Due to the vociferous protests of the non-whites, a Reference Committee undertook to produce a more activist programme for the World Council, one which did not reflect its white wealth. It was not surprising, therefore, that 'The Ecumenical Programme to Combat Racism' appeared still too radical to some white ecclesiastics. The Reverend Dr Robert J. Marshall, President of the Lutheran Church in America, proposed that the entire section on a rationale for reparations (which involved approval in principle only, without specifications for payments) be deleted. This motion was defeated primarily by the American blacks who caucused with the Asians and Africans and convinced the Asians to help them seek reparation. In accepting this section of the Report, the Central Committee went on record as recognizing the economic benefit to the churches of structural racism in the past and approved the transfer of an economic power-base to non-white institutions. It declared, however, that reparations alone were not enough; without compassion, brotherhood, and community they would have little effect.

The five-year programme that was adopted focused on white racism as the most dangerous form of racism, based as it is on the overwhelming economic, political, and military power of white states. Teams of inquiry would nevertheless investigate selected racial problems around the world, and consultations would be held to consider specific problems common to all geographical areas of racism. Studies would examine all possible means for promoting political action in order to bring about racial justice. Member churches would be assisted in developing strategies for combating racial injustice in their own countries. The best studies and analyses on racism suitable for educational use by member churches would be circulated by the World Council. Its budget and structure would be examined with a view to increasing support of efforts for racial justice. Specific recommendations were made for additions to the World Council staff and for the creation of an International Advisory Committee (later the Commission of the Programme to Combat Racism) from among members of the Central Committee. A total annual budget of $150,000 was requested from the three basic budgets of the World Council, and a supplementary budget request was authorized for projects developed by the new staff. A special fund was created—with $200,000 from World Council reserves and $300,000 from an appeal to member churches—for distribution to organizations of oppressed racial groups and for the support of victims of racial injustice, upon advice of the Advisory and Executive Committees. An attempt was made to delete this provision by Dr E. A. Payne of England, supported by Dr Marshall and Dr Adolf Wischmann of Germany, but it was resoundingly defeated by 62 to 7, with 11 abstentions, which indicated the determined attitude of the World Council members.[57] Editorial opinion in the *Guardian* was against the World Council using any of its money for American racial problems and against any aid to the guerrilla organizations of oppressed racial groups.[58] Another north European editorial opinion, that of K. A. Odin of the *Frankfurter Allgemeine Zeitung*, criticized the World Council action for relying too strongly on the American experience and for impatience.[59] Such white demands for moderation indicate yet again that those favoured by the *status quo* find those attempting to correct it are always too impatient.

This programme was by far the most radical move made by the World Council of Churches to combat racism since it had first considered the problem. To have provided a budget, even a modest one of $150,000, from its *regular* budgets was an earnest act of good faith. The fiasco of non-establishment of the Secretariat on Racism, authorized by the Evanston Assembly, was caused by the need for that proposed body to find its own budget, outside World Council sources. One can only wonder what progress might have been made in the fourteen years since Evanston if the mandate had been taken seriously—and speculate whether it was the increasing racial tension visible throughout the world or additional non-white members of the World Council which had forced it to act.

One final testimony to the purging of unconscious, structural racism from the World Council was the admittance of the 'Church of Christ on Earth by the Prophet Simon Kimbangu', with headquarters in Zaïre. This indigenous African church, with an estimated following of more than a million, is one of some 5,000 independent African churches which are regarded uneasily by European churches because of their disregard for traditional European liturgy and polity. 'We've always said we were for indigenous religion; now we have it,' said the Reverend W. Henry Crance, African specialist of the World Council.[60] By this action, the white man (and we must remember that the financial power of the World Council is still white) recognized that there were other forms of Christianity which might be regarded as equally authentic.

The founding of the Programme to Combat Racism created the problem of delineating responsibility between it and the CCIA in this field. The CCIA Executive Committee, in attempting to develop a criterion of distinction at its 1969 meeting, was divided between those who saw the CCIA effort as primarily one of action (leaving study to the PCR) and those who envisaged the role of the CCIA as primarily one of providing information. In this capacity it would evaluate and interpret the news coming from South Africa for the benefit of the churches; at the same time it could to good effect address itself to the study of political structures offering viable alternatives to apartheid. This latter suggestion was especially appropriate, since one cause of the continued hardening of the white position in South Africa has been the lack of any conception of how this minority would preserve itself under any other system. In the report finally adopted, the Executive Committee recommended that the CCIA should follow the suggestion of the Notting Hill Consultation and increase its past efforts to secure ratification and implementation of international declarations, conventions, and covenants on human rights. It tempered its anti-racist enthusiasm by noting that, to follow the advice of the Consultation and mobilize all its efforts to eliminate racism, would lead to neglect of its total mission which embraces more than race alone.

Racial and security policy in South Africa in 1969–70 continued to go hand-in-hand: the acquittal of Africans tried on security charges was soon followed by their detention or subjection to banning orders under the Terrorism Act of 1967 (charges not being required under that Act). The homelands policy was continued, but with modifications in favour of African labour in the homelands. This seeming liberalization prompted Dr Albert Hertzog to found the right-wing Herstigte Nasionale Party (Reconstituted National Party). Apartheid was extended to South West Africa where a homelands policy began to be implemented, a policy opposed by independent African states, by the Africans in South West Africa, and by the opposition United Party in South Africa. At the general election in 1970 the National Party lost nine seats and the United Party gained eight, but political commentators did not interpret this as a turn against apartheid.

Finding no relaxation of apartheid, the World Council continued the action and policy it had planned for the international struggle against racism, a policy publicly decided upon at the Uppsala Assembly of 1968 and the Central Committee of 1969. As clearly as the policy had been stated, as openly as it had been worked upon, the simple press release of 3 September 1970 shocked the World Council's more vociferous white-élite supporters in the industrialized countries with the announcement that it was disbursing $200,000 to nineteen organizations combating racism throughout the world. Those too close to the daily activities of planning and policy failed to consider that many of the faithful, and most of those with only a modicum of interest in the Council's activities, had long forgotten the reports of the heated ecumenical debates and the resulting statements on a programme to combat racism; therefore, there was no preparation of the public mind for this announcement.

Undoubtedly the Council staff had a right to feel that these grants were a natural outcome of World Council policy over the last decade of study and consultations on racism. In fact, aid had already been collected and disbursed since 1965 for the legal defence of victims of discriminatory laws in South Africa and Rhodesia and for maintenance of their helpless dependants. These funds were funnelled through white liberal organizations which disbursed the legal fees and passed on the subsistence money to the white and non-white families who were suffering in the struggle for equality. Perhaps this seemed natural: whites making decisions and dispensing largesse to non-whites. But all the legal defence funds and all the white legal organizations changed not at all the racial situation in Southern Africa. During that period of trial the non-white membership of the World Council increased as the political independence of African and Asian states occurred, and the indigenization of the ecclesiastical leadership soon followed.

The white liberals upon whom the Africans had at first relied heavily seemed to accomplish nothing for them. Africans took matters into their own hands and organized resistance, and they were pushed in that direction by the increasing demands of apartheid and other systems of racial discrimination. On the World Council, Africans and Asians resented the preachings for patience by their white brethren, who were losing nothing and whose families were not suffering. Many of the Africans active in the Council had also been leaders in struggles for political independence. During this period of ferment Dr Eugene Carson Blake, who had been in the forefront of the American struggle for civil rights, became General Secretary, bringing an activist leadership combined with a commitment to the equality of men. All these circumstances played upon the World Council, bringing forth a strong programme.

The apparently sudden policy move expressed in the press release was primarily a public relations *faux pas*. Some supporters of the World Council expressed the idea that General Secretary Blake could have prepared the ground better and that he could have elaborated on the grants, in public, at the time when the information was released. One British ecumenist, Bishop Oliver Tomkins, later told a Central Committee meeting that he had been 'taken aback' by the off-hand nature of the announcement.[61] To be just, it should be noted that the press release, for the careful and even the not-so-careful reader, clearly stated the authority for the grants and their objectives: to raise the level of awareness in the world to the existence of suffering of racially oppressed people and to strengthen the organization of the groups combating racism.

These grants were used to support militant groups rather than welfare organizations; the latter simply alleviate symptoms (e.g., the hunger of a family whose breadwinner has beeen arrested or executed), while the former prepare society for change. 'Militant' should be understood as referring to the activist programmes of those bodies around the world which received grants: they actively sought to change the consciousness of their societies or engage in constitutional activities for change (e.g., registering voters). Some, it is true, also took up arms. In the abstract, there would probably have been little controversy surrounding the grants. In the concrete, rage and fear in the white establishment arose out of the priority given to Southern Africa; a total of $120,000 went to militant organizations called 'liberation movements' or 'guerrilla rebels', depending on the political orientation of the speaker.

The grants to Southern African groups were given expressly for humanitarian and educational purposes. The People's Movement for the Liberation of Angola (MPLA) and its rivals the Revolutionary Government of Angola in Exile (GRAE) and the National Union for the Total Independence of Angola (UNITA), as well as the Mozambique Liberation Front (Frelimo) and the African Independence Party of Guinea and Cape Verde Islands (PAIGC), all claim to control territory. All attempt to carry out educational and health programmes among their peoples, and there is good evidence that they do so. These, as well as the Zimbabwe African National Union (ZANU) and the Zimbabwe African People's Union (ZAPU), both of Rhodesia, and the African National Congress and the Pan Africanist Congress, both of South Africa, and the South West African People's Organization (SWAPO) have refugees in neighbouring states which they try to support. In Rhodesia and South Africa, where there are government fee-charging schools, these groups wish to pay the fees for the education of as many of their people as possible. Appendix II below lists the groups which received grants during the period 1970-6.

The public debate that followed the announcement of the grants was carried on entirely within the frame of reference enunciated by the white minority régimes, especially that of South Africa's Prime Minister Vorster, who accused the churches of 'subsidising murder in the name of God'.[62] It was continued in terms of aiding 'terrorism' and 'terrorists' rather than in terms of aiding the victims of racism. Indeed, the Religion Editor of the *New York Times* stated that the verbal outburst by Mr Vorster was part of a political offensive brought about by his own domestic political problems in South Africa, primarily a labour shortage and the inability to achieve genuine economic progress along racially separate lines.[63]

The controversy raised a bogus issue of whether the Christian churches by this act supported violence or not. In fact, there was explicitly no intention to support violence; the Central Committee at Canterbury had specifically rejected the part of the recommendation of the Notting Hill Consultation which spoke of the necessity of violence in certain cases. So there was not even an implication of any official approval of violence. It is true that the grants had been given with no controls, but the World Council had been assured that the grants would be used only for humanitarian and educational measures. It was a calculated risk to give the money without strict control; it was a calculated act of faith in black groups.

The question of violence and non-violence had not previously been studied by the World Council. There had been no explicit pronouncements against civil violence, but there had been encouragement and praise for the non-violent civil disobedience of Dr Martin Luther King, and his example had been urged on others. The topic of violence, however, had been broached at several international gatherings of the World Council. The Mindolo Consultation of 1964 (mentioned earlier) noted that, as avenues of peaceful

111

change were slowly closed, there would eventually remain only the way of violence for effecting social change. This consultation consisted of private individuals and in no way bound the World Council. The World Conference on Church and Society in 1966 spoke to the World Council in its Conclusions: 'There is need for reflection on the character of Christian responsible action in situations of violence where existing institutions directly or indirectly exert violent pressures on men, and where some Christians are resorting to force as the only way to bring about change.' [64]

It further stated: 'It cannot be said that the only possible position for the Christian is one of absolute nonviolence. There are situations where Christians may become involved in violence. Whenever it is used, however, it must be seen as an "ultimate recourse" which is justified only in extreme situations . . . The use of violence requires a rigorous definition of the needs for which it is used and a clear recognition of the evils which are inherent in it, and it should always be tempered by mercy.' [65] This and other references to the possibility of violence, it should again be emphasized, were not World Council of Churches' findings or recommendations; they were made *to* the World Council.

The reactions to these grants brought the importance of a Christian study of violence to the attention of the Central Committee at its Addis Ababa meeting in 1971, when it requested the Department on Church and Society to undertake a two-year programme aimed at '(a) furthering the churches' reflection on the ethical dilemmas posed by violence and nonviolence in the struggles for justice and peace; and (b) contributing to the search for strategies of action which will minimize the sum total of violence in conflict situations'.[66] The question under discussion really becomes one of the Pauline doctrine of being 'subject to the powers that be'; this involves a discussion of the legitimacy of rulers and governments in Southern Africa, a discussion completely avoided by those disturbed by the possibility of black violence against whites. A similar outcry was not raised by the same groups when the churches supported humanitarian aid for a black group fighting against a black government, as they did when the Biafrans were revolting against the Nigerian government. Nor has there been any outcry by those same groups at the violence done by white governments to black peoples. At Addis Ababa the Central Committee itself called attention 'to the fact that violence is in many cases inherent in the maintenance of the *status quo*'.[67] Such violence does not attract similarly vociferous condemnations from the same groups.

The righteous indignation which was the automatic reaction of many conservative white church members and Christians was not necessarily due to hypocrisy. Many works have been written on the structural racism in white society—racism built into the organization of society and unconsciously perpetuated in attitudes formed, for example, by passive but continuous observation of the kind of work most blacks do in Europe or the United States. Mr Garfield Todd, Prime Minister of Southern Rhodesia from 1953 to 1958, an astute politician well versed in the amount of violence innate in the situation in Southern Africa, characterized the shock in western Europe and white Southern Africa as 'a wave of pious hysteria'.[68] He noted that it was white leaders of white churches, not the black leaders of black churches, who protested. Since they had learnt their theology in European-run seminaries, if such outrage were based on a travesty of unchallenged Christian doctrine, then one could have expected equal vehemence. In fact, the Executive Committee of the All Africa Conference of Churches meeting in Lomé, Togo, on 23 September 1970, unanimously supported the World Council action and welcomed 'the revolution in the thinking of donors, in being prepared to trust people who are taking radical action against racism'.[69] In the debate within the British Council of Churches, which this action caused, Mr R. A. Tsehlana, African president of the Student Christian Movement, stated that the churches no longer had a message for the black people: 'The black people of South Africa don't want your blessings. You have no blessings to give. What you are being asked to do is to redeem Christianity.' [70]

The reaction of Prime Minister Vorster at first was simply that the action was 'to put it mildly, shocking'.[71] It was only when he perceived the disarray among the church bodies in Europe and the shock among the more conservative laity that he intensified his verbal attacks. Editorials in *The Times, Guardian, Daily Telegraph* and *Sunday Times* and in *Die Zeit* and the *Frankfurter Allgemeine Zeitung* took positions for and against the action, much as one would expect from their political orientations. It is immaterial which supported it and which did not, for the attacks as well as the defences emanated from a subconsciously preconceived white image of violence and justice. For example, both sides in the debate used the terminology of the South African premier and spoke of aiding terrorists and buying weapons to carry on warfare, not (as in the terminology of the gift), of helping the victims of racist terror or of buying medicines, food, or books. European perceptions of African liberation groups have led many to conclude that the humanitarian aid would enable more arms to be bought; in fact, in the absence

113

H

of aid, the extreme poverty of most African refugees and those living in liberated areas means that education, medicines, and other 'luxuries' would simply be foregone.

The uncomprehending attitude of Africans in this situation can be more readily understood when it is remembered that at the same time a controversy was going on in Great Britain over the sale of arms to the South African government. Of course, the British churches and the World Council General Secretary condemned such trade. Dr Blake, in a press release of 24 July 1970, held that it was 'clearly unacceptable to Christian moral convictions [and that it would] further entrench the government of South Africa rather than put pressure on it to change its policy of apartheid'.[72] It would confirm, Blake continued, that the African liberation movements can 'rely on very little sympathy or support from the Western world'. This indeed it did confirm, coupled as it was with outcries against the *humanitarian* aid the World Council was offering groups suffering from racial discrimination and white tyranny.

It is to the credit of World Council officials that they did not let the threat of withdrawal of funds and of some churches from membership affect their decision. In fact, although the Executive Committee decided which groups were to receive aid, and in what amounts, the money for the first grants was the gift of three churches for this specific purpose and not from the general World Council budget, although $200,000 was transferred from WCC reserves to the Special Fund to Combat Racism. 'In the two hundred years in which force was practised by whites, no one interested himself in this theme', Dr Blake told critical German church officials.[73]

In contrast to the World Council's posture of confrontation, a voice of conciliation was heard from black Africa. President Félix Houphouet-Boigny of the Ivory Coast proposed that the confrontation between Africa and South Africa be replaced by a dialogue. Leaders in Gabon, Dahomey, and Ghana supported him, and criticism from other black African leaders did not prevent him from reiterating his proposal in April 1971. Although dialogue as a policy for black Africa was rejected by the OAU at its June 1971 meeting, President Houphouet-Boigny has continued his policy of conciliation.

Ecclesiastical blood was still boiling when the Central Committee met in Addis Ababa in January 1971. Dr M. M. Thomas, the Indian layman who was chairman of the Committee, defended the action publicly at the opening meeting as 'nothing more or less than the protest of the World Council of Churches against the *status quo* ideology of violence and an attempt to break the moral and religious sanctions behind it'.[74] Dr Blake defended it, although he noted that certain ecumenical programmes had been harmed by the controversy. On the other hand, he continued, it had caused widespread and serious discussion of racism.[75] Surely this was the understatement of the meeting. The Central Committee approved the grants made by the Executive Committee and voted for the continuation of the Programme to Combat Racism.

The German churches had been divided by the controversy engendered by the grants. The immediate reaction of the leaders of the Evangelische Kirche in Deutschland (EKD), a federation of churches, was denunciation of the action. Individual churches of the federation such as the Evangelische Kirche in Hessen-Nassau disagreed with this sharp reaction and made a donation to the Special Fund. At Addis Ababa the German church leaders prevailed on the Central Committee to devise alternative action to the grants.[76] A projects list was one result—projects drawn up by the PCR provided for study (Racism in Education), training (Maori Community Organization Training), consultation (International Conference of Indigenous Peoples), and for encouraging support for the PCR administrative budget. Donations for these projects came especially from churches which did not wish to appear to condone violence by giving to the PCR Special Fund.

The Central Committee, in a resolution which should have made clear to all 'the *status quo* ideology of violence', unanimously called on the United Kingdom not to resume arms sales to South Africa. Prime Minister Heath announced resumption of these sales the following month. They were continued until 1974, when suspended by the Labour government. The French churches were asked to request President Pompidou to cease French arms sales to South Africa. Their success was no greater than the Central Committee's.

The Archbishop of Canterbury (who was not at the Central Committee meeting) denounced the grants in an address to the General Synod of the Church of England the following month, urging that the Programme to Combat Racism be not limited to white racism. His African colleagues, meeting in the Anglican Consultative Assembly in Kenya, in March, were of a contrary opinion. Mr S. H. Amissah of the All Africa Conference of Churches pointed out that Africans regarded these grants as recognition of their sense of responsibility.[77] At the same meeting the Right Reverend Paul Burrough, Bishop of Mashonaland (in Rhodesia), vehemently opposed the grants for 'sending men to their death' and encouraging 'a resistance movement which does not exist'. He walked out in protest at the Anglican approval.[78] Further support came from an announcement that Queen Juliana of the Netherlands had given from her privy purse an unspecified amount to the World Council's Special Fund, perhaps as much as £83,000. Causing caustic comment in the Afrikaans newspapers, it indicated to the world that there were members of the European élites who not only approved this action but also emulated it.

In South Africa balkanization as an official policy was further endorsed in the Bantu Homelands Constitution Act of March 1971, which empowered the government to grant by proclamation self-government to any Bantu area on its request. The self-governing units would not be able to maintain any military organization, manufacture arms or explosives, conduct diplomatic relations with other states, or legislate on posts, communications, transport, the entry of non-citizens, or on any other subject reserved by the South African government. For the first time, during the debate on the Bill, Mr Botha mentioned the eventual independence of the homelands. Taking the South African government at its word on self-government, the Chief Minister of the Transkei, Kaiser D. Mantanzima, called for the immediate transfer of all departments of state to the homeland. This request was rejected by Pretoria.

On 21 June the International Court of Justice issued the Advisory Opinion requested by the Security Council, holding that the presence of South Africa in South West Africa was illegal. States were under an obligation to recognize this illegality and to refrain from acts implying recognition of South African occupation of the territory. This decision was debated at several Security Council meetings between 27 September and 20 October 1971. For the first time a South African Minister of Foreign Affairs, Dr Hilgard Muller, took part in a Security Council debate on this topic. Dr Muller declared that there was no threat to international peace unless such a threat was 'artificially' created. He renewed an invitation to the Secretary General to visit South Africa and South West Africa. He also agreed to submit to his government any Security Council decisions for a plebiscite in South West Africa.

Seldom responding to specific acts of racism, the World Council continued to implement its own programme against racism. The WCC Executive Committee, sitting in September 1971, authorized the PCR to grant a further $200,000 to twenty-four organizations combating racism in various parts of the world. These included nine groups active in Southern Africa, which received more than half the total grant.[79] A policy once embarked upon attracts less attention than a more open situation—one in which critics see the possibility of preventing a single action from becoming a policy. These second grants, in fact, caused almost no comment in the world press and no denunciation by white élites except in Southern Africa.

In December 1971 the first major illegal strike by Africans in

South West Africa for a time paralyzed sections of the economy and caused modifications in the contract labour system in use for forty-two years. As a result of pastoral care for the strikers and an outspoken desire for justice, the Right Reverend Colin O'Brien Winter, Anglican Bishop of Damaraland, had his permit to enter Ovamboland—where 90 per cent of his flock lived—withdrawn. He denounced this as a 'culmination of deliberate attempts to curb and weaken the Anglican Church'. On 26 February he and three other church workers were ordered to leave the territory, with no reason given; an appeal was rejected. Dr Kurt Waldheim, Secretary-General of the United Nations, visited South Africa and South West Africa from 6 to 10 March 1972. In Ovamboland he received petitions for independence; in Windhoek he met leaders of the Namibia National Convention who also requested independence. In addition, pro-South African black leaders made representations to him.

At the Central Committee meeting in August 1972 at Utrecht the Programme to Combat Racism was discussed in fairly heated but less acrimonious tones than it had been at Addis Ababa. A report presented to the Central Committee claimed that the World Council grants had encouraged four governments, those of the Netherlands, Sweden, Denmark and Norway, to make grants for humanitarian purposes to liberation movements. In the wake of World Council action, the Joseph Rowntree Trust of the United Kingdom also gave grants to these bodies, as did the Lutheran World Federation-World Service; the World Council Commission on Inter-Church Aid, Refugee and World Service; and the Commission on the Churches' Participation in Development (CCPD).[80]

Evaluating results in terms of objectives was more difficult, but several groups provided voluntary reports to the Programme. Many of the organizations got in touch with World Council Sub-units to discuss their programmes and it became evident that the money was used for humanitarian or educational purposes. Some examples: the Africa 2000 project in Zambia conducted educational campaigns in its high schools regarding racism in Southern Africa. This resulted in support of the liberation groups operating outside Zambia. The Mozambique Institute of FRELIMO increased agricultural production in areas under its control, purchasing seeds and tools. It is beginning to print textbooks for its schools, a means to create identity among the diverse groups of Mozambique. The South West African People's Organization (SWAPO) has increased care for refugees in Zambia and Botswana, as well as opening 'bush-schools' in Namibia, an illegal act under South African laws.[81]

In spite of these positive reports, the German church leadership still stood aloof from grants to guerrilla groups. Nevertheless, the

Committee increased the Special Fund from $500,000 to $1 million. Except for the first year, when funds were taken from World Council reserves, the grants had been financed by gifts from individuals, church groups, and other interested bodies. The President of the German Federal Republic, Dr Gustav Heinemann, made a personal donation to the WCC Special Fund in December 1972. The WCC Executive Committee, meeting in January 1973, made a third grant of $200,000 to 25 groups of which $101,000 went to groups in Southern Africa. Although the newspapers had tired of the sensation they had created in 1970, it must be admitted that the debate they engendered, though muted, still goes on within the churches—no longer the debate on whether aiding liberation groups is a proper activity for the World Council but the more general debate to which, however falsely, it gave rise: the extent to which violence may be consonant with Christian principles in promoting social change.

The results of this attempt to clarify what has been an ongoing discussion ever since Christians had to decide whether they could serve in the Roman army or not, were presented to the Central Committee meeting in Geneva in August 1973. Church and Society conducted the study and in a summarizing statement noted that its distinctive role was in 'helping white affluent Christians take seriously the perspectives of other parts of the Church'.[82] The two contrasting viewpoints presented in the study were a condemnation of violence by theologians in the industrialized states (except for a few who may be the precursors of change, such as Richard Shaull of the United States and Jürgen Moltmann of Germany)[83] and that represented primarily by non-white theologians who more intimately understood violence to be present in the unjust social order of racist societies. 'The Third World is compelled to take its destiny into its own hands just as the Christians of Europe did when fighting Hitler',[84] is how Dr Philip Potter understood the violence which is erupting in areas where non-white peoples struggle for their freedom.

The Central Committee adopted the report *Violence, Non-violence and the Struggle for Social Justice* as its 'statement' on the subject and commended it 'to the churches for study, comment and action'. It noted that the Christian discussion of earlier centuries had been concerned almost exclusively with the use of violence by sovereign states against each other, but that now the discussion was much wider and included the use of violence in the struggle for social justice.

The statement sought to help those who looked to the Church for guidance when faced with the dilemma of choosing between violent change or acceptance of, and responsibility for, continuing injustice. Because of this duty to guide, Christians and the Church must not simply succour those who suffer but must attack that which causes the suffering. Divisions of thought regarding the theological basis of the use of violence were clearly stated, yet all could agree—whether or not they held non-violence to be the only permissible means—that Christians had the duty to help attain justice and freedom for all people. All agreed, whether accepting violence or not, that 'governments have a legitimate function in restraining private power in the interests of justice for all, to assure human rights and to serve public welfare'. Some forms of private power, economic and technological, seem to be inadequately controlled, it noted, and Christians must stand with those oppressed by the unjust use of power. All agreed that the object of resistance was not to destroy an enemy but to create a just social order.

Regarding the methods of resistance to injustice there were three viewpoints. Some believed that non-violence was the only means of action open to a Christian. Others considered that in 'extreme circumstances' violent resistance was acceptable. The criteria to be satisfied were that (1) the cause be just; (2) all other possibilities be exhausted; (3) there be a reasonable expectation that the desired ends will be attained; (4) the methods be just; and (5) there be a positive concept of the ensuing order. A third group thought that those who find themselves in situations of violence cannot help but react with violence; non-violence is not an option to them unless they retire from the world and the struggle for justice. The Christian duty is to humanize the means of conflict and to build just structures for peace.

All agreed that certain types of violence are condemned and that Christians may not participate in them: conquest of a people, deliberate oppression of a class or race, torture, the taking of hostages, and killing of non-combatants. The statement warned Christians far from areas of conflict against glibly prescribing the strategies to be used by those living in different social situations and conflicts. Especially ought the wealthy Christians of the industrial North to forego giving their moral advice to others throughout the world.

It must be stressed and reiterated that this report was commended to the churches for their study. The World Council did not endorse the use of violence but neither did it condemn it. Further, a Central Committee motion specifically encouraged the study of non-violent action in bringing about social justice. Church and Society was requested to continue the study, reconsidering especially the concept of a just war in relation to contemporary violent change and how frequently the law has been used to hinder social change.

Interestingly enough, the World Council policy which caught world headlines, in spite of continued grants to guerrilla groups, was the attitude and future policy towards investment in companies operating in Southern Africa. The Uppsala Assembly had already recommended withdrawal of investments 'from institutions that perpetuate racism'. The PCR report on this subject caused some controversy at the Central Committee meeting in 1972. The German churches, which had few investments but subsisted on 'church tax', presented a statement to the meeting urging that nothing be done which would increase racial tensions. They proposed reform by talks and pressure on firms operating in Southern Africa.[85] Bishop Alphaeus Zulu of South Africa and one of the Presidents of the World Council, warned the Central Committee that pressing for withdrawal would embarrass South African churches; furthermore, he did not think that the withdrawal would help black South Africans very much.[86] The PCR presented its three alternative policies in a report to the Central Committee: increased investment, reform through attendance at stockholders' meetings, and withdrawal of investment. It concluded that standard-of-living statistics invalidated the primary argument for increased investment i.e., that technology would raise standards of living and that higher standards, in turn, would break down apartheid. Given the statistics used, that conclusion seemed better founded than the argument for reforming apartheid by influencing the policies of the multinational corporations. This latter alternative was denied validity not on the basis of statistics but solely on the basis of the alleged failure of the Polaroid Corporation's experiment in South Africa.[87] This American Corporation manufactures cameras which take and develop pictures instantly; its machines were being used to make passbooks for black South Africans. Polaroid's American black employees objected to the company's involvement in apartheid. Rather than leave the market, Polaroid undertook to raise the pay of its African workers more nearly to that of whites, provide greater opportunity for advancement, and pay for the education of workers' children. Polaroid has claimed certain results which are challenged by the Programme to Combat Racism. Whichever opinion is in fact right, it seems to be a questionable argument to dismiss one alternative to alleviate apartheid based on one experiment.

Further it was held that the white community would not allow corporation policies which would overturn their way of life. Again, this assumes no liberal thought in South Africa that would accept gradual change. Surely this is the only kind of change acceptable to whites, liberal or conservative. It appears that the Programme was arguing for confrontation policies. The only alternative, it held, was the total withdrawal of foreign capital in order to force the white South Africans to accept change. One observer has ably argued that change, however slight, is in fact taking place as the Afrikaner government responds to outside political pressure and internal economic realities.[88] The Programme apparently assumed that if the World Council, all churches, and other sympathetic groups sold shares in corporations giving support to Southern African régimes (Portuguese and Rhodesian, as well as South African) through investment, those corporations would be forced to withdraw. It may not have occurred to the PCR that the corporations were unlikely to withdraw, except *in extremis,* because they would lose more by withdrawing and leaving capital investment behind than by staying and experiencing a possible fall in the value of their shares.

At the Utrecht meeting there was disagreement between the Finance Committee and Policy Reference Committee II, which latter body supported the PCR proposal. The Central Committee resolution instructed the Finance Committee 'to sell forthwith' holdings of companies 'directly involved in investment in or trade with' Southern Africa. The Finance Committee pointed out that this sweeping reference even to trade with any of those countries might make it difficult to find investment managers willing to undertake the responsibilities. (In effect the World Council investment managers later resigned.) There was also the possibility of loss of income to consider. The Finance Committee, 'On the basis of their knowledge of corporation management', considered that stockholder action would be a more effective course than to withdraw the rather insignificant WCC investments. Corporations might well be relieved by the sale and the riddance of potential troublemakers. Sale, the Finance Committee felt, was the easy way out. The Central Committee nevertheless held to its original resolution.[89]

A second part of the resolution urged 'all members churches, Christian agencies and individual Christians outside Southern Africa to use all their influence, including stockholder action and disinvestment, to press corporations to withdraw investments from and cease trading with' Southern Africa. The Reverend George Balls, Church of Scotland, attempted to amend the resolution, in order to make it more flexible, by adding after 'to press corporations' the words 'either to operate policies which will promote inter-racial social justice or'.[90] This attempt failed and the Council continued in its uncompromising line.

In any event, no impact on the stock market was observed after adoption of the Central Committee's resolution ordering the Finance Committee to sell WCC holdings. Nor did the actual sale of $1.5 million worth of stocks, as announced at an Executive Committee meeting in January 1973, cause a ripple in capitalist waters.[91]

A report to the Central Committee in August 1973[92] summarized the attitudes of churches in several countries to this problem. It indicated that, despite no observable stock market fluctuations, the corporate executives of American firms had been busy defending, explaining, or hiding their policies in Southern Africa. A report to the British Council of Churches did not accept total withdrawal of funds as a solution except in circumstances where boards of directors remain aloof from the pressures for information and change. Church bodies in Canada, the Netherlands, Norway, Denmark, Sweden, Belgium, France, Switzerland, and Japan are studying and acting on church investments. The Evangelische Kirche in Deutschland reported that talks with German firms on the improvement of working conditions in their South African affiliates had made progress. It dissociated itself from publication of the list of firms whose stocks the World Council recommended selling:[93] as 127 German firms were on this list, publicity might hinder further talks.

One example of effective publicity, publicity which the World Council could regularly create, was a *Guardian* article on the low wages paid by British firms in South Africa, following upon the World Council divestment in March 1973. This article may have prompted the British government to publish guide-lines for such firms, pointing out that there was no fixed minimum wage and that, in any case, fringe benefits could be provided.[94] A House of Commons sub-committee proposed an investigation into wages and conditions of employment in United Kingdom firms in South Africa. Many British firms stated they did not know the wages their South African subsidiaries were paying, and raised them after the publicity given to the Poverty Datum Line (PDL), an amount calculated by South African researchers (favourable to blacks) as the absolute minimum amount necessary for a family of five to live on.

Even the South African Council of Churches is making inquiries into the pay policies of South African firms. Some 150 foreign corporations have indicated their willingness to contribute to black-initiated projects of economic development. The SACC recognized the danger of 'conscience money' being paid in order to continue unjust employment practices. If pressure can be maintained on the corporations throughout the industrialized world, through publicity and stockholders' vigilance, more defensive actions may be taken —such as bettering conditions, especially pay, for black South African workers. In March 1973 the United Kingdom South Africa Trade Association urged its members 'to pay at least subsistence wages to blacks employed by their South African subsidiaries'.[95] The World Council and its members are one source of unending pressure and propaganda.

As apartheid continued, so the World Council Executive Committee continued its grants to groups that were victims of racism, including guerrilla groups. At its meeting in February 1974 at Bad Saarow in the German Democratic Republic it made grants totalling $450,000, a larger amount than usual, due to a Dutch government donation of $179,000 to the PCR through the Interchurch Peace Council of the Netherlands the previous December. Again the lion's share went to organizations in Southern Africa. In May 1974 Canon Burgess Carr, speaking to the AACC Assembly, urged African Christians to support liberation movements.[96] He criticized the compromising attitude of many Protestants towards apartheid. The AACC contributed £2,083 for freedom fighters in Southern Africa.[97]

Dr Lukas Vischer, Swiss director of the World Council's Faith and Order Unit, visited South Africa the following month. On his departure, on 14 March 1974 after a press conference at which he had answered questions on the grants to guerrilla groups, he was told that he would not be permitted to re-enter South Africa. On 19 March Dr Connie Mulder announced that, as long as the WCC supported 'terrorist activity', all its leading members would be banned from entering South Africa.[98]

The South African government continued implementing its homelands policy, with the creation in 1972 and 1973 of four new ones. Homeland leaders, however, were gaining confidence and began using their limited autonomy to speak out against South African policy and to think of federating, the antithesis of the Balkanization intended by the Afrikaner government. This new feeling of black identity, coupled with increasing prosperity due to the rise in the price of gold and the effects of world-wide inflation, led to a great deal of industrial unrest between 1972 and 1974. To limit even peaceful resistance to official racial policies, two new pieces of security legislation were passed. The Affected Organizations Act empowers the government to declare an organization 'affected' if three magistrates decide that it has been engaging in politics with aid from an organization or person abroad. Such a finding allows premises to be entered and assets to be frozen. The Christian Institute of South Africa, which has conducted studies and generally fought against apartheid, came under this ban in 1975. In addition, the Riotous Assemblies Amendment Act empowers the authorities to prohibit any public or private gathering of two or more people if it is thought to pose a threat to law and order.

The Central Committee met in West Berlin in August 1974. The Programme to Combat Racism remained one of its more emotional topics. The Programme had originally been given a five-year mandate at Canterbury in 1969. Some pressed for no Central Committee action until the Assembly could vote on it; however, if that were to happen, the programme would expire. As it was, the original draft resolution renewing the life of the PCR raised such sharp criticism—that it was too polemical, too much against whites, the West, and industrialized states—that the Central Committee Preparatory Committee changed the draft before it was submitted to the Central Committee, a rare occurrence.[99] The German churches, continual critics of the programme, had been joined by others in criticism of this draft. The Central Committee resolved to continue the PCR as part of the WCC and set a minimum target of $300,000 to be raised and dispensed in grants each year. One of the five West German church delegates, Dr Richard von Weizsächer cast the sole vote against the resolution.

The Utrecht resolution on corporations in Southern Africa also included a clause that the WCC 'deposit none of its funds in banks which maintain direct banking operations in those countries'. This was interpreted to mean banks with branches in Southern Africa. The WCC Executive Committee, meeting in Bangalore in January 1973, directed the staff to develop a formula for identifying those banks more involved than others in supporting the Southern African minority régimes. Account had to be taken of the world-wide activities of the World Council, especially its relief and rehabilitation programmes in areas as widely separated as the Sahara and Southeast Asia. Clearly the WCC needs an international banking system: if it uses small banks—in an attempt to avoid banks active in Southern Africa—they must in turn employ the big international ones to transfer WCC funds across the world.

In June and July 1973 a letter with questionnaire was sent to each of the ten banks holding WCC accounts on the extent of their involvement in activities in Southern Africa. Nine replied: while stating that they had no branches in Southern Africa, they refused to answer questions concerning deposits from, or loans to, governments in that area or their holding of government bonds or accounts of corporations of those countries. The PCR published information about the European American Banking Corporation (EABC) which provided $210 million to the South African government, roughly 20 per cent of its loans from external sources. The Corporation is owned by six major European banks: Deutsche Bank, West Germany; the Société Générale, France; Midland Bank, United Kingdom; Amsterdam-Rotterdam Bank, The Netherlands; Société Générale de Banque, Belgium; and the Creditanstalt-Bankverein of Austria.[100] The Central Committee meeting in August 1974 instructed its Finance Department to communicate with the named banks to solicit assurances that they would stop loans to South Africa. It further 'urged all member churches, Christian agencies and individual Christians, to use all their influence to press these . . . banks and the other banks participating in the loans to cease granting loans to the South African government and its agencies'. [101] It was reported to the WCC Executive

Committee meeting in Geneva in April 1975 that replies had still not been received from all EABC banks. The Committee directed that, if satisfaction had not been obtained by October 1975, World Council funds must be withdrawn from banks in that organization.

As drops of water falling continuously may break a stone, so the constant seemingly useless drops of action by the WCC and others may have created a more receptive attitude on the part of the South African government. There was of course the Portuguese coup d'état in April 1974 which assured eventual black rule on two of South Africa's borders. In March 1974 the British Labour government cancelled further arms deliveries. In August 1974 in South West Africa leaders of the Roman Catholic, Lutheran, Anglican, and Baptist churches published a memorandum criticizing conditions in South West Africa, unequal wages, segregated education, oppressive police powers, flogging, torture, etc. In September 1974 Mr A. H. du Plessis, leader of the National Party of SWA, announced that he would try to reach agreement with Africans. Mr Vorster proposed consultations with the SWA Advisory Council, a move rejected by some but conditionally accepted by Clemens Kapuuo, a SWAPO leader. A combination of all these and other international pressures over the years may have helped persuade Mr Vorster to make his secret visit to the Ivory Coast to meet President Houphouet-Boigny and President Senghor of Senegal on 29 September 1974. In November secret talks took place in Lusaka between the South African Prime Minister and Presidents Kaunda, Nyerere, and Seretse Khama (of Botswana), Dr Gabellah of the ANC, and Mr Joshua Nkomo of ZAPU who had been released on parole for the meetings. On 11 December 1974 Mr Smith announced a cease-fire with the guerrillas and the release of detainees (some 300 to 500 it was estimated); he was caught up in Mr Vorster's détente policy with black Africa. The next several months saw Mr Smith teetering back and forth in his treatment of released and rearrested leaders, in allowing them to leave the country for consultation, and in his agreement to hold talks with them. Mr Vorster himself did not go full speed ahead. Some say he could not take his conservative electorate with him. In his talks with Indian, Coloured, and homeland leaders in January 1975 he conceded nothing to the Africans and little to the others. But throughout 1975 he has attempted to keep dialogue with black Africa open. The Organization for African Unity, meeting in April 1975, voted in the Dar Es Salaam Declaration to continue to respond favourably to South Africa's overtures.

In April 1975 the World Council Executive Committee allocated a record $479,000 to twenty-seven organizations of racially oppressed people and their support groups. This large amount was made possible by donations from the governments of the Netherlands, Sweden, and Norway. Over half of it, $257,000, went to groups in Rhodesia, South Africa, and South West Africa. Those in Mozambique and Angola no longer qualified for such grants, though they would still be aided through CICAWRS and the CCPD. Since some churches had felt unable, in good conscience, to contribute funds to guerrilla groups, alternative means of helping to end racism had been sought. These alternatives—which included the special project list, and stockholder action rather than dis-investment—came to be called 'multiple strategies' to combat racism. They had never won more than faint praise from PCR officials. A paper on multiple strategies presented by the PCR to the 1975 WCC Executive Committee questioned whether 'change through investment' would bring 'radical transformation of systems based on racist ideologies'. The Executive Committee asked the PCR to survey the ways in which member churches understood and practised multiple strategies, and to advise them on how effective these strategies had been. A new record sum of $560,000 was awarded in August 1976, with $275,000 for Southern Africa. The total of grants made since 1970 now stands at $2,110,000.

It appears that WCC officials have moved from a policy of bending over backwards in order not to offend white South Africans to one of stiff-necked resistance to compromise with them, at least as reflected in the policies of the Programme to Combat Racism. The World Council has seemed less conciliatory and less willing to compromise than Prime Minister Vorster. It is difficult to see the ultimate goal to which this posture will lead except to awesome and bloody confrontation of the races. It may be that without any action by the World Council, that will take place; nevertheless, the unique Christian voice in world affairs seems to be blending in with the uncompromising demands for blood by those with no spiritual reason to restrain their hatred.

A policy of positive action may develop into a policy of confrontation without an awareness on the part of those who initiate the action, for example giving aid to groups of victims of racism to carry out campaigns to change the structures which perpetuate oppression. The Mindolo Consultation in 1964 noted the possibility of Christian support for violence on the part of those reacting to injustice, but it constantly reiterated the Christian duty to restrain violence to the point of accomplishing the desired end and to the extent that negotiation would always remain a possibility. In other words, reconciliation was the ultimate duty of the Christian even if he were participating in violent action. In a more recent World Council publication[102] it appears to the outsider, unfortunately, that dialogue is no longer perceived as an alternative of the ecumenical movement to violence in the Southern African context. In an internally contradictory section of this publication, it is stated that where preconditions for dialogue do not exist—defined as 'ability and willingness to learn from the other'—the churches have 'to wait, actively, constructively and intelligently'. In comparing the Sudan situation with that of Southern Africa, it states, 'The white régimes of South Africa or Rhodesia have never demonstrated their willingness to enter into an open conversation. . . . Unless those in political power are willing to build bridges and demonstrate respect for the other, no amount of outside assistance can help.' It is apparently rejecting the use of the Sudan as a model for the Christian churches' action in South Africa. However, the precondition of willingness to learn did not appear to exist in the Sudan in 1966 when Pastor Jean Kotto of Cameroun, as noted below, accused the Sudanese government of massacring Southern Sudanese, and the Prime Minister of the Sudan replied, 'This is yet another red herring; professional religionists prey on man's distress everywhere.' [103] Yet thereafter a convergence of events over which the World Council had no control: the power of the guerrilla group Anya Nya, the mediatory efforts of Emperor Haile Selassie, coupled with the interest of the All Africa Conference of Churches under a dynamic African leader, may have led the Sudanese government to be approachable in dialogue.

Indications within South Africa are that it is not yet too late there either; a research survey undertaken in 1971 by Dr Melville L. Edelstein, a South African sociologist, gives reason to believe that it is not. The survey was carried out among young Africans in Soweto, a black African suburb of Johannesburg. The response to the question which way of life they preferred was that 68 per cent chose Western and 31.1 per cent chose Tribal or Mixed. When asked what kind of government they preferred, 70 per cent chose a multi-racial government, while 13 per cent chose tribal, and 17 per cent white government.[104] These were pupils in the sixth form, young African leaders of tomorrow. Their bitterness was not yet irreconcilable; it may become so.

Is it hubristic, during a period of turmoil in Southern Africa—when even the Organization of African Unity at its meeting of 11 April 1975 agreed to continue dialogue with the Vorster government—for the World Council of Churches to turn its efforts resolutely away from the possibility of reconciliation? These Christian officials could surely maintain the need for change in Southern Africa, and still afford humanitarian help to guerrilla groups, without declaring that dialogue is impossible with those at fault in Southern Africa. A re-evaluation of the overall Programme to

Combat Racism to stress conciliation rather than confrontation would seem to be needed.

Central Africa

In 1953 a British Conservative government forced the colonies of Northern Rhodesia and Nyasaland into a federation dominated by white-ruled Southern Rhodesia. Nyasaland, because of its lack of exploitable wealth, had almost no white settlers; Northern Rhodesia, because of its copper, had a small minority; while Southern Rhodesia, with experience of internal autonomy since 1923, had a sizable white minority firmly entrenched in power. Not surprisingly, African nationalists opposed this disposition of their future to the graces of a people which had shown little concern for their poverty, well-being, or development theretofore. The British Council of Churches, working closely with the Conference of Missionary Societies in Great Britain and Northern Ireland which had many member-societies active in Central Africa, recommended to the African Christians the acceptance of the new proposals as a true attempt at the creation of a multi-racial state. Having thus induced African acquiescence, the churches felt a continuing responsibility in the never fully accepted federal system. Especially because in 1957 changes in the Federal parliament effectively reduced African representation and in 1958 electoral reforms were proposed which would work to the disadvantage of the African, did the British Council of Churches (BCC) maintain interest and pressure on the British government.

In July 1958 Dr Hastings (later Kamuzu) Banda returned to Nyasaland from Britain as leader of the African National Congress, dedicated to take Nyasaland out of the Federation. In spite of opposition by the British Council of Churches, the United Kingdom parliament passed the Constitution Amendment Bill detrimental to the Africans; the BCC then urged that the Electoral Reform Bill be passed only if it could be accompanied by official assurance of the ultimate development towards enfranchisement of African majorities. The British Council of Churches was supported by the officers of the CCIA in presenting to the British government the extent of African suspicion to the new proposals.[105]

Early 1959 saw further disturbances in the form of intermittent rioting in Nyasaland. White troops from Southern Rhodesia were called in to quell the disturbances. African political organizations were banned; Dr Banda was placed under arrest. The British Council of Churches met the Colonial and Commonwealth Secretaries and presented a programme which called for greater African participation, honouring earlier British commitments to Northern Rhodesia and Nyasaland. In fact a major share of the resources of the International Department of the BCC was devoted to the Central African Federation during this period. The summer of 1959 saw stepped-up negotiations between opponents and proponents of federation, and Sir Roy Welensky, Premier of the Federation, visited London to participate, receiving BCC representatives. When Mr Iain Macleod took office as Colonial Secretary in the autumn, a small group of churchmen expressed concern over the general situation and the detention without trial of a large number of people in Nyasaland. The BCC gave both written and oral testimony before the Monckton Commission, appointed by the British government to advise on constitutional changes for the Federation.

Although the issue remained on the CCIA Executive Committee agenda at its 1958 meetings, it was not until 1960 that the Reverend Alan Booth could report concrete actions taken.[106] He described the CCIA-sponsored Consultation held in the Federation between African and European leaders, both ecclesiastical and political, and representatives of the World Council and the IMC. The names of those attending had been kept confidential so that all would feel free to communicate frankly in the privacy of the Christian community, and the openness and understanding of the participants exceeded the expectations of the organizers. The insights gained had been communicated to certain prominent persons in the Federation, but it was not known what effect this had had; in any case private channels for future contacts had been made. In the ensuing discussion, certain members suggested that the CCIA take similar initiatives over the next twelve months, but Sir Kenneth Grubb pointed out that the small number of CCIA staff made this an impossibility.

The British Council of Churches meeting in October 1960 passed a series of resolutions urging governmental acceptance of a report by its Advisory Commission which advocated a federation with protection for the African against the white minority. To gain African acceptance for an economically viable state, it urged extension of the franchise in Southern Rhodesia and complete constitutional reform in Northern Rhodesia. A deputation led by Dr E. A. Payne, a Vice-President of the British Council of Churches and future President of the World Council, discussed these factors with the Colonial and Commonwealth Secretaries. When the Conference for Review of the Constitution of the Federation met in London in late 1960, the churches continued to manifest their interest through a reception presided over by the Archbishop of Canterbury at Lambeth Palace.

By early 1961 it became apparent to all that the Africans would not peacefully accept the Federation as envisaged by the British; constitutional reform would first have to take place in Northern

Rhodesia. The British Council of Churches urged again in March that the constitution for Northern Rhodesia should grant the franchise to the Africans. Unrest and violence there led the Executive Committee of the BCC to urge the British government to remove the cause of the unrest by announcing in definite terms what it had previously mouthed in generalities.

The absence of a white minority in Nyasaland facilitated negotiations and a constitution was granted in 1961. Elections held in August of that same year brought Dr Banda to the premiership. The richer mines in the protectorate of Northern Rhodesia in the hands of an entrenched white economic élite and a small white population, not nearly so great as that of Southern Rhodesia, complicated the situation and made negotiations more difficult. However, it could only delay the inevitable, and an African majority in the legislature was finally achieved in 1963. The Federation was dissolved at the end of 1963 as a prelude to the granting of independence to Malawi (ex-Nyasaland) in July 1964, and Zambia (ex-Northern Rhodesia) in September.

The contribution of the Christian churches—national and international—to the attainment of African rule in Malawi and Zambia cannot be ascertained. It is known, however, that the churches in the three territories and in Great Britain kept each other informed both directly and through the CCIA. They offered statements in public concerning the norms they felt the British government ought to follow; they organized private consultations at which those in power in Great Britain, in the territories, and in the churches could exchange ideas and offer solutions to the tensions in this part of Africa.

Two-thirds of the Central African Federation had achieved independence, but the problem was by no means two-thirds solved. There still remained the white-dominated government of Southern Rhodesia. The 1963 meeting of the CCIA Executive Committee directed its attention to Southern Rhodesia and its attempts to break the last vestige of ties with Great Britain; independence for Southern Rhodesia would mean that there would no longer be any restraint on the white government of that country. Sir Francis Akanu Ibiam of Nigeria urged the CCIA officers to press upon Britain its duty not to grant independence so long as a white minority denied Africans a substantial share in government. The question was again raised at the CCIA Executive Committee meeting in 1964, but neither it nor any other group was able to produce a solution.

A more thorough discussion of the issue and some realistic if difficult proposals for its solution took place at the 'Consultation on Christian Practice and Desirable Action in Social Change and Race Relations in Southern Africa' from 25 May to 2 June 1964 at Kitwe, Northern Rhodesia (discussed above in relation to South Africa). After a general consideration of the problem of race in Southern Africa, the two most critical situations, Southern Rhodesia and South Africa, were discussed. It urged the British government not to shirk its responsibilities but to make clear to Southern Rhodesia that it would not condone a unilateral declaration of independence. The churches in both countries would attempt to create the climate of opinion necessary to allow a constitutional conference of Africans and Europeans to take place. It was realized that Rhodesian society was rapidly approaching the racial conditions of South Africa. It offered general but definite suggestions regarding the economic and educational activities of the churches and the financial responsibilities of the government and businessmen in ameliorating the present trend.

The government of Southern Rhodesia continued resisting the blandishments of the British government to institute a constitution to assure that the majority population would one day achieve majority rule. The CCIA Executive Committee meeting in the summer of 1965 continued its fruitless discussions. The Chairman and Director of the CCIA issued a statement expressing their opinion about the catastrophic results which would issue from a seizure of independence. The primary responsibility for preventing this, they noted, lay with the United Kingdom, but they called upon the international community to offer to support the British government in any collective action necessary.

The British Council of Churches, meeting on 26 October 1965, adopted a statement calling for the sharing of government by 219,000 Europeans with 4,020,000 Africans. In the event of a unilateral declaration of independence, it urged upon the British government its responsibility to govern the colony directly until there was justice for all the people in Rhodesia. During the debate the Archbishop of Canterbury even noted that non-pacifist Christians would support the use of force by the British government in carrying out its obligations. The International Department of the British Council of Churches urged the early release of African political leaders, provision of compensation for any Rhodesians who felt it necessary to emigrate, and active support with personnel and money for a crash programme in education and technical and administrative training for Africans.

All the activity, all the blandishments, all the queen's men could not deflect the will of the Rhodesian whites as stated by their Prime Minister Ian Smith in a unilateral declaration of independence on 11 November 1965 for the new state of Rhodesia (the adjective 'Southern' had been dropped). Upon receipt of the news, the CCIA immediately cabled its constituent national councils to urge their governments to take firm stands against the new state.[107]

The Central Committee meeting the following February (1966) issued a statement on the Rhodesian situation, deploring 'the attempt to prolong indefinitely the political domination of the minority white community over the black majority'.[108] In order that violence need not be used, the Committee urged non-co-operation with the rebel government by governments and companies normally doing business with it. Majority rule, racial co-operation, and civic equality should be the platform of all Rhodesian political parties, it stated. The heads of African states were urged to use their influence to find a peaceful solution to the problem.

Economic sanctions were instituted by the United Kingdom and the United Nations. It did not go unnoticed in Africa that while Britain had been ready to use force against blacks in Kenya, Nyasaland, and Northern Rhodesia, none was now used against whites in Southern Rhodesia. The economic sanctions did not prove so successful because of the lack of co-operation on the part of South Africa and Portugal, to say nothing of 'blockade runners'. In 1967 Great Britain increased the economic sanctions and challenged other states to share the burden it was causing her. Sanctions were at best a long-range policy.

Short-range violence had begun before the declaration of independence. On 30 April 1967 Peter Mtandwa of the Zimbabwe African National Union (ZANU) declared the first anniversary of the armed struggle in Rhodesia. In November the first guerrillas were sentenced to death. The General Secretary of the WCC, Dr Visser 't Hooft, after consultation with CCIA officers, cabled the Rhodesian Christian Council:

Apart from the moral issue of capital punishment as General Secretary of the World Council of Churches I reflect to you the widespread concern and protests within our constituency at the executions in Rhodesia. This concern is intensified by our fear that similar measures may be extended to those tried for political offences. Authorities are reminded of the rule of law and of the civilized traditions of sparing the lives of political opponents and reprieving those who have suffered a long uncertainty under a pending sentence of death.[109]

Nevertheless the executions were carried out after unsuccessful challenges of the legality of the government which imposed them. These appeals brought about a *de facto* break of the tenuous relationships with the British crown. The *de jure* break, from the Rhodesian point of view, came with a referendum on the question of republican status in the summer of 1969 and proclamation of the republic on 28 February 1970.

The Consultation on Racism held at Notting Hill, London, in May 1969, called upon Rhodesia and its white electorate to seek a just settlement to the problem of majority rule. It called upon governments and churches to urge the United Kingdom: (1) to reaffirm that independence for Rhodesia would depend upon majority rule; (2) to intensify sanctions in consultation with the United Nations; (3) to withdraw the assurance that force would not be used against the Rhodesian government; and (4) to refuse to veto stronger measures than those already taken if proposed in the Security Council. The United Nations was pressed to ensure that guerrilla forces captured in Rhodesia would be treated as prisoners of war.

In November 1970, the British government began exploratory talks with the Rhodesian government in an attempt to 'find a sensible and just solution' in accordance with a Conservative Party pledge. By 23 June 1971, these had become 'official' talks held in Salisbury, lasting until 7 July and based, according to Sir Alec Douglas-Home, Foreign and Commonwealth Secretary, on the 'Five Principles'. Worked out in 1964 when Sir Alec was Prime Minister, these principles were taken over by the succeeding Labour government and publicly enunciated in 1965 as Southern Rhodesia prepared for its unilateral declaration of independence.[110] While taking part in the exploratory talks with the United Kingdom, the Rhodesian government continued to implement its policies of racial segregation. In late 1970 and early 1971 it ended the existence of the Cold Comfort Farm Society, a multiracial co-operative farm—purchased with money from the World Council of Churches and other interested groups—in an area designated exclusively for Europeans. After confiscation of the farm, the World Council asked that its investment of £15,000 be returned by the Rhodesian government. The latter requested suggestions for use of the money within Rhodesia. Also in late 1970 the Tangwena tribe was evicted from tribal lands recently declared a European area. In October 1971 the government removed Africans from the Methodist Epworth Mission and the Roman Catholic mission at Chiphawasha. Racial restrictions on pupils enrolled in church schools in European areas were accepted under protest by five Roman Catholic bishops.

Sir Alec Douglas-Home flew to Salisbury on 14 November 1971 and signed a draft settlement with the Smith régime on 24 November. Although he had met African leaders, except for some in detention, he negotiated solely with the white minority government. Since repression was occurring simultaneously with the negotiations, it is little wonder that African comment within and without Rhodesia was negative and that Africans had little faith that the outcome would be to their benefit.

In order to abide by the fifth principle, the United Kingdom government established a commission, headed by Lord Pearce, to ascertain the views of all Rhodesians, black and white, on the acceptability of the proposals. This Commission sat in London and Salisbury from 12 January to 22 March 1972. White opinion was overwhelmingly in favour of the agreement. Rhodesian Christians were divided. The Anglican bishops of Matabeleland and Mashonaland urged acceptance. The Christian Council of Rhodesia —after a debate in which Mr Garfield Todd urged rejection (he and his daughter were arrested under the Emergency Regulations on 18 January 1972), and the Right Reverend Paul Burrough, Bishop of Mashonaland, strongly favoured acceptance—voted to recommend rejection. The Roman Catholic bishops urged the same action. Bishop Abel Muzorewa of the United Methodist Church in Rhodesia formed the African National Council to work for rejection of the proposals. Testifying before the Pearce Commission he objected to the proposals on the basis (1) that three separate voters' rolls would further entrench racism; (2) that the higher qualifications for Africans would still leave most teachers, pastors, policemen, and nurses off the rolls; and (3) that Africans had not been involved in the negotiations determining their future.

In spite of the Rhodesian government's refusal to allow political meetings, which resulted in riots, the Pearce Commission felt able to report on 23 May 1972 that Rhodesians as a whole did not find the proposals acceptable. Sir Alec accepted the finding gracefully; Mr Smith rejected it as 'naïve'. The ANC welcomed the finding and called for a national convention where all Rhodesians could discuss their future. Mr Smith refused to participate in such a 'circus'.

The WCC Executive Committee, meeting in Auckland in February 1972 during the Pearce Commission hearings, issued a 'Statement on Rhodesia' in which it urged the United Kingdom to continue to exercise its responsibility until all Rhodesians had full political rights. It also requested all member churches to press their governments for more efficient sanctions. The Central Committee meeting in August endorsed the Executive Committee 'Statement' and itself supported the call of the ANC for a national convention. It deplored the American decision to violate the United Nations sanctions by importing chrome from Rhodesia.[111]

The World Council no longer separates the Rhodesian problem from that of South Africa. Its grants to guerrilla groups have included Rhodesian liberation movements. Firms active economically in Rhodesia come in for the same treatment as those with economic ties to South Africa: the selling of shares by the World Council and organizations co-operating with it. With the liberation of Mozambique and Angola, pressure has increased on the Smith régime for settlement. Internally Bishop Abel Muzorewa has united the Rhodesian liberation movements into his own African National Council and pressed for a national constitutional convention of all Rhodesians. Externally independent black Africa, especially the neighbouring states of Zambia and Tanzania as well as the former

Portuguese territories, is pressing for a settlement. But the greatest blow and the most irresistible pressure come from South Africa. Prime Minister Vorster appears ready to sacrifice an independent white Rhodesia for *détente*—and a breathing period—with the rest of Africa, as recounted above.

The Sudan

Another area of racial concern deserves to be mentioned if for no other reason than that it has had a more successful consummation than the other, sadder areas already discussed. This felicitous experience occurred in the Sudan, which, unlike many other African states, existed long before the arrival of the European powers. Arab influence entered the Sudan in the eighth century and an 'arabized Negro' state arose whose remnants existed until the late eighteenth century. In the early nineteenth century, Egypt, as a part of the Ottoman Empire, conquered and gained control of the Sudan. When the British and the Egyptians established a condominium over the Sudan in 1898 to thwart encroaching French interests, firm borders were established with Ethiopia, Kenya and Uganda.

Until after World War II British policy was to administer separately the Arabic North and the Negroid South which were not only racially but also religiously divided: the North was predominantly Muslim and the South animistic with some Christians. The latter area provided a more fruitful vineyard for the labour of British missionaries than that faithful to the Prophet. The British considered uniting (even as late as 1945) the southern Sudan with Uganda because of racial and cultural similarities. But the experiences of the Second World War caused a consciousness among colonial peoples, which, in its aftermath, led the Europeans to question their own previous views on colonialism; in the Sudan the Colonial Office suddenly implemented a new policy directly opposed to that of the preceding period: the unification of the North and the South. Whereas previously Northerners had to obtain special permission to enter the South, now they were actively recruited by the British to administer it.

The Sudan achieved independence in 1956. The problems of the newly independent country were aggravated by the existence of these two disparate groups, especially since the Arabs were primarily in administrative and economic control. As any new state wishes to have internal unity, an arabization programme was begun, a programme felt by Christians to discriminate against them, especially as the mission schools and their missionary teachers came under government control and attack for promoting an alien doctrine. In 1964 all foreign missionaries were expelled, further causing a feeling of isolation on the part of the Southerners. In addition, economic development projects were concentrated in the North, and that produced resentment in the already impoverished South. All these difficulties came to a head in 1963, when the Anya-Nya armed resistance group began operating, helped by certain Christian bodies in neighbouring countries.

The CCIA Executive Committee from 1964 onwards discussed the religious and racial troubles in the Sudan. Though no active role for that body was recommended, CCIA officers kept the Sudan under observation and reported annually to the Executive Committee. In 1965 the Christian churches of the Sudan formed the Sudan Council of Churches and sought association with the All Africa Conference of Churches (AACC) and the World Council of Churches. The World Council sent a representative to the Sudan to investigate the kind of service the churches could offer to the entire Sudanese people. The immediate need was help for the suffering, especially for refugees outside the Sudan and for displaced Southerners in other parts of the Sudan.

The Central Committee, in consultation with the All Africa Conference of Churches, at its 1966 meeting expressed concern for the Sudanese in a resolution and urged the CCIA 'to continue to take all appropriate steps, including approaches to governments so that an end may be put to the suffering of the population in the Southern Sudan and the exercise of religious freedom ensured'. The concept of religious freedom, coupled in the Northern Sudanese mind with European missionaries, made for a cold reception to this resolution in Khartoum. However, the AACC after eight months of negotiations and preparations through the Sudanese ambassadors in Kenya, sent a goodwill mission to the Sudan which conferred with government leaders and Southern church leaders. The ensuing conciliatory report was not well received in all missionary quarters, but it provided a beacon for future negotiations. Prompt follow-up to this auspicious beginning was hindered by a coup in the Sudan, a difficult change in the World Council leadership, and structural changes in both the World Council and AACC organization. It was June 1970 before a second AACC mission ventured into the Sudan. This successful visit resulted in a repeal of the Missionary Expulsion Order to allow African missionaries to enter the Sudan to aid the churches there.

One prominent African churchman has written that the World Council as well as the AACC had produced sentimental clichés regarding the Sudan.[112] He believed there was no clear and coherent policy as to how the World Council (and the AACC) could actively promote a settlement. This provides an excellent illustration of the necessity for the churches to make proposals as well as condemnations and exhortations, to provide, if not *the* answer, at least alternative solutions which statesmen might otherwise fear to try. World Council officers carefully reflected and arrived at a policy for ending the conflict in the Sudan. The World Council, it was considered, should view the problem as a political one to be solved through political means: the WCC/AACC should take the initiative in bringing this matter to the attention of African leaders who might influence the Sudanese government and the dissidents. In spite of the initiatives, the Christian bodies would remain politically neutral, speaking out against both sides when the necessity arose.

With this policy in mind, the WCC-AACC mission in May 1971 effectively sought to provide good offices between the government and the Anya-Nya and its political arm, the South Sudan Liberation Movement (SSLM). It also requested permission to furnish a relief programme within the Sudan. The Sudanese government agreed to both requests. The AACC immediately began making contacts with SSLM leaders in Africa, and the World Council followed suit in London, where exiled SSLM leaders had their headquarters. With positive answers, the World Council paid for the SSLM European-based leaders, Mr E. M. de Garang and Dr Lawrence Wol Wol, to travel to Africa to confer with their Movement's leaders in the field. In late August Mr Garang and Dr Wol Wol reported to the World Council and the CCIA that the SSLM was ready to negotiate. In October another WCC-AACC mission went to Khartoum to report this readiness, and President Jaafar al Nemery's government agreed to hold preliminary discussions in Addis Ababa.

These 'informal discussions' led to 'official negotiations', which were concluded in February 1972.[113] The agreements provided for a cease-fire and for regional autonomy in the South. Article 6 of the Cease-Fire Agreement provides for members of the Joint Supervisory Commission to include representatives of the World Council of Churches and the AACC as well as the International Committee of the Red Cross.[114] Leopoldo Niilus and Kodwo E. Ankrah as representatives of the World Council, and Burgess Carr as General Secretary of the AACC, signed the agreements as witnesses, along with a delegate of the Emperor of Ethiopia.

Here is an example of positive World Council/CCIA action. Six years of observations and platitudes led to no action to solve the problem; two years of definite policy and its implementation, coupled with a desire of the parties to end the dispute, led to its solution—or at least to the beginning of its solution. This may provide a model for the solution of other racial disputes. In spite of nine years of guerrilla warfare, the fund of goodwill and good faith was not exhausted. The establishment of a positive policy and the encouragement of negotiations which fulfilled some goals of both parties without reversing the power situation immediately illustrate that perhaps it is not yet too late to consider possible non-violent alternatives to the present situation in Southern Africa.

Other Voices, Other Groups

Some Christian churches, acting as apologists for apartheid, caused early involvement of the World Council of Churches in the racial problem of South Africa. In fact, it seemed to concentrate on apartheid to the near-exclusion of other racial issues. The United States did not escape criticism, but the US government's attempts to 'de-racialize' American society from 1954 onwards perhaps softened any reference to the United States. In 1956 and 1959 the CCIA Executive Committee heard reports on the progress of desegregation in the United States, but took no action. The Central Committee, meeting in Rochester, New York, as Dr Martin Luther King led the March on Washington in the summer of 1963, issued a 'Statement on Racial and Ethnic Tensions'. Again putting emphasis on the Southern African problem, it did note the movement for equal rights in the United States, placing it as 'an integral part of world-wide racial tension'. It called upon the American churches 'to intensify efforts to eliminate all forms of racial discrimination from every aspect of life in their country'.[115]

The World Council Central Committee, meeting at Canterbury in 1969, made it clear that the Programme to Combat Racism would be concerned with world-wide racism; it would be a world programme. However, it was to concentrate on white racism, since that form was based on the preponderant economic power of the white states, As already mentioned above, grants have been made to groups combating racism all over the world. On the question of grants the United States has come in for more attention, not only because of the continuing black problem, but also in the context of American Indians and Spanish-speaking Americans of Mexican and Puerto Rican descent.

The Commission of the PCR issued a communiqué after its meeting in May 1973 condemning the 'policy of extermination, ethnocide, and exploitation of the Indian people continuously practised in the United States'.[116] This excited tone was occasioned by the Indian occupation of Wounded Knee, North Dakota, during which the Indians used the publicity to make known their demands against the American government. American Indian and Eskimo groups in Canada have been aided. In Latin America the problems of the American Indian have been studied and groups helping them aided. Symposia on their problems have been held in co-operation with regional Latin American Christian bodies. In Colombia and the Caribbean black workers have been helped. The rights of Australian Aborigines and New Zealand Maoris have been the object of attention.[117]

The Australian representative at the 1972 Central Committee meeting requested a resolution on Aboriginal land rights in his country to help the Australian Council of Churches. There was no time for the Committee to consider this, but the Chairman and Vice-Chairman of the Central Committee and the General Secretary wrote to the Australian Council of Churches urging that the Australian government should take 'positive and immediate' steps to grant land titles to Aborigines in the Northern Territory as well as to institute a comprehensive programme to meet their representation and employment needs.[118] The Australian representative the following year stated that this had helped, and that the new government was more inclined to consider the problem. From West Indians in the United Kingdom and migrant workers in Europe to Koreans in Japan, the Programme to Combat Racism has carried out its mandate.

Until the PCR was established, the World Council paid little attention to the issue of racism in Portuguese Africa. The Secretariat for Racial and Ethnic Tensions had few resources and did not spread its interest so far; Protestant mission churches in Portuguese colonies were not strong. In 1970 Frelimo and the three independence movements of Angola and the PAIGC of Guinea-Bissau were among the first to receive grants. These bodies were recipients until independence. In fulfilling its educational informational function of making white Christians aware of racial problems the PCR published booklets on Frelimo, PAIGC and Portugal's relationship with the European Community.[119] It also published information about the Cunene Dam in Angola and the Cabora Bassa Dam in Mozambique, condemning the enterprises as strengthening white rule in Southern Africa.[120] In 1973 the Central Committee approved the establishment of a five-year programme to help deserters from the Portuguese armed forces and other conscientious objectors to colonial rule fighting in Portuguese Africa, providing for the raising of $100,000 a year. There were already church groups in Europe helping these young men, and work would be continued through them.

The coup d'état in Portugal occurred on 25 April 1974 when General Antonio Spínola overthrew the government of Dr Marcello Caetano. Liberation groups welcomed the change but continued fighting until, on 27 July, General Spínola stated that Portugal recognized 'the right of the populations . . . to take their destinies in their own hands'. In August 1974 an agreement was signed with the PAIGC granting independence to Guinea-Bissau on 10 September 1974. The Lusaka agreement between Portugal and Frelimo, signed on 6 September 1974, provided for a transitional government to complete arrangements for independence in July 1975. The problem between black and white and black and black in Mozambique and Angola is not finished; there is room still for the reconciling mission of the World Council, which, due to its controversial grants, ought to enjoy some confidence from the liberation movements.

The World Council announced that it was concentrating on white racism and gave its reasons for doing so. As the Central Committee was meeting in Utrecht in August 1972, President Idi Amin began a campaign against Asians (mostly Indians and Pakistanis) in Uganda. First it was applied only to non-citizens of Asian origin, then to citizens, then erratically once more only to non-citizens, finally depending on an interpretation of who was a citizen. In any case several thousand people had to leave their homes within three months and were allowed to take out only a fraction of their possessions. Could the World Council deal equably with non-white racism? The first draft resolution was so vague as not to mention Uganda, and it was sent back to Committee for revision—to be made more specific and to address the Ugandan government. Mr P. T. Odumosu of Nigeria, the Right Reverend Janani Luwum of Uganda, and Canon Burgess Carr of Liberia (and General Secretary of the AACC), with the Very Reverend K. M. Simon of the United States were requested to prepare a resolution. As finally approved, it expressed the Central Committee's 'deep concern' over the situation as reported in the news from Uganda. The Central Committee called upon the government of Uganda to refrain from any actions which impaired or denied the 'citizenship of Ugandans of Asian origin'.[121] Later in August the WCC made £8,000 available to Christian Aid in the United Kingdom to give help to the Ugandan Asians when they arrived. Nothing else was heard of public World Council reaction to the Ugandan situation. If racism is successful and eliminates the presence of the undesired race, then there is little left to pronounce about.

The Programme to Combat Racism has been criticized for being too polemical and too ideological. In reading its literature one might well be unaware that Christian teachings are being expounded. Solidarity with the oppressed is stressed, but no means of reconciliation seems to be left open as uncompromising measures are recommended and taken. A vocabulary which to one group sounds extreme may, from use, seem ordinary to another, so perhaps one should not deduce too much from the standard Marxist vocabulary used. The PCR assessment of its first five years, *A Small Beginning*, certainly appears to be ideologically oriented. For example, its praise of the East European churches for their support of the Programme seems excessive since they have not contributed a penny towards it, especially when compared with the charge that the 'Programme has not found much echo in the North American churches'.[122] This charge is made in spite of the internal examples of the anti-apartheid activities of the NCCCUSA, let alone its work in the American civil rights field. Funds have come from churches and church groups in the United States.

The Programme has tended to follow popular secular thinking somewhat uncritically, instead of formulating unique Christian solutions; for instance, it joined anti-apartheid groups contesting the building of the Cabora Bassa Dam in Mozambique and the Cunene Dam in Angola on the basis that such projects help 'to entrench racist and colonial régimes'.[123] No prophetic vision saw that the greater the capital improvement in colonial or neo-colonial areas, the greater the inheritance of the dispossessed when they come into their own. Such vision does require a certain amount of faith that they will, and the Cabora Bassa Dam is one of free Mozambique's greatest assets.

The efforts of the World Council of Churches in regard to racism in the world have taken place on three levels simultaneously. First of all Amsterdam (1948) and Evanston (1954)—and it must be remembered that each Assembly sets the tone for the period until the next Assembly—were concerned primarily with racism within the Christian community. Its political effects and its separate existence as an international problem were recognized, but to treat the issue as a Christian problem, it was felt, would help towards its solution in other spheres as well. At this time even the South African problem was regarded as soluble within the context of the Christian churches, a mistake that can partly be ascribed to the belief that, as the Dutch Reformed churches go, so goes South Africa; in the nature of things, it is more likely that, as South Africa goes, so go the Dutch Reformed churches.

As racism came to be recognized as a problem within the churches, so it was realized that one of the tasks of the World Council, through the churches, would be the formation of attitudes. This was achieved in various ways. The reports of the Assemblies and their consideration of racism reached parish level by means of the study sessions held before, during, and after each Assembly. Further, the statements directed to oppressed groups and oppressing groups were also publicized, thus further influencing opinion in the constituencies of the World Council. In specific cases the member churches were requested to act—by giving high priority to their anti-racist programmes and by making representations to their respective governments. In spite of the seemingly negative results in regard to South Africa, it cannot be said that there was not a great deal of self-examination among the English-speaking as well as Afrikaans-speaking churches. In the latter, minority voices did evolve to break the monolithic support for apartheid.

At the level of international organizations, where otherwise the CCIA was active as the arm of its parent bodies, the CCIA was strangely silent. This was explained as being due to a desire not to disrupt the inter-church talks which went on for some years. Although its officers kept UN delegates aware of the official World Council of Churches position on racism, the CCIA did not urge any particular resolutions on national delegates. On the other hand it did support the Convention on the Elimination of All Forms of Racial Discrimination at its various stages.

The World Council of Churches is an international, non-governmental organization; even so, it operates also at governmental levels through its members. It may wish to take action directly and address itself to the government concerned, or it may ask a member church to make representations to its government—or all member churches to approach their governments—on specific issues. Such action might relate to a national policy such as apartheid or it might be simply an attempt to gain support for an international matter such as the drafting and approval of a convention. The publicized activities at the international and national levels also influence the attitudes of World Council constituencies. In its fight against racial prejudice, it has used all these avenues.

Racism in Southern Africa acted as a catalyst for ecumenical activities against racism throughout the world. It has been claimed that ecumenical influence contributed to the arousal of the Christian conscience in South Africa against repressive racism. Such influence is more readily identifiable in a country such as South Africa, isolated not only geographically but linguistically and psychologically from the rest of the world. With a controlled press and the dominant opinion accepting injustice as a way of life, this one outside voice could penetrate the wall of isolation and silence and show that there was another viewpoint, a viewpoint which tried to see things in accordance with the idea that man is a creature of God, that all men are creatures of God, and therefore worthy of dignity. Making people aware that the 'generally accepted' mores are not *everywhere* generally accepted, is a contribution of the ecumenical movement in an era when individuals often abdicate their moral responsibility in favour of groups.

The importance of the problem of racism has been recognized for some time in present-day societies. Although the disciplines of psychology, sociology, anthropology, and political science have investigated the problem, relatively little is known of its causes and its cures. Perhaps, indeed, research into the problem has been too largely compartmentalized by each discipline. The non-white peoples of the world have long noted the connection between world poverty and racism, yet the economics of racism is too often neglected. The CCIA Executive Committee has called attention to this connection and urged its study, as well as research into the economic involvement in racist régimes of countries otherwise unconnected with racism—a welcome innovation of cross-national studies in contrast to the CCIA's previous work on individual racial situations, such as apartheid in South Africa. In addition, a small group of secular scholars has begun to study race as an independent variable in the making of political decisions. It is hoped that more scholarly attention can be given to the importance of racial perceptions in foreign policy formulation; for example, in political attitudes to foreign aid, in positions taken at UNCTAD conferences, or in potential conflicts in Africa or Asia itself.

A striking factor in the World Council's concern for racial justice and the elimination of racism has been the ever-increasing acceptance of violence as a means of change. Race was recognized as a problem at the Amsterdam meeting, but the urgency of the problem in a world of change was not. Six years later, at Evanston, the problem was seen more clearly and racism was condemned, but no clear plan of action was established—giving the lie to protestations of urgency. However, as the churches react to great popular moods, so they have awakened, with the non-white peoples themselves, to the immensity of the problem. Study, mediation, protestation on the part of the churches did not work; discussion, reasonableness, civil disobedience on the part of the African achieved nought; racial stratification in South Africa only became more solidified. The African in Southern Africa as a whole slowly and unwillingly turned to violence, at first alone; gradually the churches—more accurately many of their leaders—have come to accept that if they cannot actively advocate the use of violence, neither may they in every case condemn it. When violence is used to maintain injustice, violence has become acceptable to a large segment of white Christians and the overwhelming number of non-white Christians in the attainment of justice.

3. *Oikoumene and Economy*

MISSIONARIES in the nineteenth and twentieth centuries were often regarded by the native peoples as harbingers of imperialism, and some missionaries themselves felt this accusation was not without foundation. Indeed, as missionaries often supplied linguists and maps of local areas to government officials establishing their rule over uncharted Africa, they seemed one with the new rulers; nevertheless, missionaries in the field often attempted to correct, or at least ameliorate, injustices perpetrated by 'Christian' Europeans on non-Europeans, nearly always non-white. The missionary representatives gathered together in Edinburgh at the World Missionary Conference in 1910, publicly proclaimed a principle not enunciated officially as world policy until 1945, namely, that 'the interests of the inhabitants of these [colonial] territories are paramount'. (UN Charter, Article 73.)

The influence of the missionaries on their converts was recognized by the governments which ruled over the vast colonial empires. For example, the British government after the First World War required a pledge of all non-British missionaries working within the Empire that they would teach respect for the constituted government. The international political activities of the International Missionary Council at that time consisted primarily of trying to assure the freedom of missionaries to proselytize and freedom of conscience for their converts in colonies ruled by Roman Catholic governments, in League mandated territories, and in independent non-European states. Although the parts of the world in which the missionaries laboured were poverty-stricken by comparison with their home countries, no thought was given to urging the general economic development of these areas, for the very thought of comprehensive economic planning was alien to the times, except for a few obscure Socialists. The mission societies, however, often encouraged economic development by sponsoring agricultural experts or establishing model farms through which they hoped to treat the symptoms of under-development (a term they would not have recognized) and to raise their peoples from the slavery of grinding poverty.

The World Council of Churches had hardly been created in its provisional form when the Second World War tore countries asunder. When the firestorm subsided, the World Council's immediate post-war concern was reconstruction of European Christian institutions, that is, not only churches but also schools, seminaries, old people's homes, and orphanages; this policy paralleled that of the United States in reconstructing European economic, industrial, and political institutions in order to strengthen the whole body politic of that continent. There was no one agency organized for this particular task, since these now needy churches of Europe and their mission societies had once been the great channels for Christian charity across the oceans. The International Missionary Council had not been the means by which the mission societies had divided their largesse (they preferred to keep this power themselves), except in the case of 'orphaned' missions in both world wars; for this latter function funds had come primarily from the United States and neutral countries. Thus the IMC continued caring for the German missions, and for the younger independent churches of the Far East, while the American and British mission societies and those in countries not totally devastated by war maintained support for their dependent churches. The World Council undertook life-giving aid to European Christian institutions. The World Council is no more than the sum of its members, and its leadership (if not its members) at this time was primarily European-American; the reconstruction may be understood as the reconciliation of Europe. Reconstructed and reconciled, Europe could again become a source of Christian charity for the rest of the world.

The rest of the world, however, had passed beyond the stage of paternalism, even as recipients. India, Pakistan, and Burma received their independence; other peoples were becoming restless. New ideas about the responsibilities of these peoples for their own resources and development surged forward and took hold. These peoples did not believe any longer that they were solely responsible for their own poverty—because of improvidence, lack of intelligence or ability—but that it was primarily due to exploitation by the Europeans through superior technology and force. The World Council did not present its message in exactly this way, but it did preach the responsibility of the wealthy states to help the underdeveloped areas to achieve a minimal level of subsistence. The view that the wealthy, white, and Christian states (and now Japan) have a special responsibility towards the developing states is not favoured by many of those in power in the industrialized North. The view that the continuing inadequate economic growth rate is due to insufficient effort on the part of the developed states is the view of the World Council, of many economists, and of this author. To hold this opinion does not reject the knowledge that the developing states also have responsibilities for the transformation of their societies. However, the élites in states where no will to progress is often observed are supported by these same industrialized governments.

World Council action in the sphere of economic development flowed in three related streams: (1) carrying out its own programme of economic aid with funds from churches and governments; (2) preparing and urging governmental and intergovernmental aid for economic development and population control programmes; and (3) conducting a continuous study of the Christian responsibility in the developing areas of the world, with particular emphasis on the theological and ethical bases of rapid economic development which also affect the traditional social and political structures. Because the churches' own programme of economic aid was a natural consequence of Christian concern for the individual man, it was the earliest activity and is discussed first. From this immediate concern and the limited resources for implementing correctives, grew the programme for urging and planning governmental and international aid, including Dr Richard Fagley's nearly single-handed effort in promoting population control programmes, which are next discussed. In the ecumenical movement, since its beginning early in this century, action has always preceded its theological justification, or, as laymen might say, its rationalization: a discussion of this Christian rationale therefore ends this chapter. The study on Christian responsibility to areas of rapid social change, however, was more than a theological justification, it also helped to define need and plan aid, much as did the International Christian Social Institute of Life and Work with its disquisitions. In this sense, the three elements here separated for analysis were in fact overlapping and developing simultaneously.

Reconstruction and Inter-Church Aid

Although Christians claim certain unique insights into the nature of man, of the world, and of God, non-Christians in Western civilization often misinterpret these claims as meaning an omniscience in all spheres of life—which most Christian leaders themselves would deny. However, being made of the same clay as all men, some Christian leaders might accept any mantle of omnipotence proffered. Christians may be part of an international fellowship, but they are also members of families, clans, societies, nations, states. Their interests are identified not only in an ultimate Kingdom but in the here and now. It should not surprise anyone that in addition to Christian leaders looking at issues through the spectacles of the Christian ethic, the image they perceive will be tinted with the national ethos.

When the Second World War ended, the whole world was in

need, not only the countries that had been at war and those whose economies had been affected by lack of ability to buy and sell, but also those always living at a subsistence level, for whom the fighting in other parts of the world had meant nothing, if indeed it had even been understood. Thus one might have expected Christian leaders to devise plans for providing for the needs of all mankind. The biggest political problem for the Allies, at least the Western Allies, in 1945 even before the war in the Pacific was finished, was to restore order in the chaos of defeat and to provide minimum sustenance for those displaced—and misplaced—by human destructiveness. The secular response was the United Nations Relief and Rehabilitation Administration (UNRRA) and the International Refugee Organization (IRO).

The churches, too, were caught in this massive relief effort. In fact, one might say that their planning preceded that of the inter-governmental plans, for early in the war Dr Samuel McCrea Cavert journeyed to Geneva across still-Unoccupied France to discuss post-war aid; his memorandum on 'The Reconstruction of Christian Institutions in Europe' was submitted to churches in several countries. Throughout the war, the personification of the ecumenical movement, Dr Visser 't Hooft, laid plans for the day when help would be instantly needed. And even before the guns were finally silenced, representatives of the World Council and the American churches were in Europe making provision for relief supplies. Food and clothing were partially distributed through the Department of Reconstruction of the provisional World Council but to a much greater extent directly from the American churches to their sister churches in Europe.

This direct relief action was based both on the experience of the churches after the First World War and on the limited organization of the still small World Council. In 1919 American denominations gave extensive help to their European progenitors. In 1922 the European Central Office for Inter-Church Aid came into being due to the gigantic efforts of Dr Adolph Keller of Switzerland. Largely a one-man operation, this body provided a channel for the reconstruction of Christian institutions and churches without rich relatives beyond the seas and it was not meant to replace direct aid. It remained in existence under Dr Keller's venerable direction until its amalgamation in 1945 with the Department of Reconstruction.[1]

Besides immediate relief, the Allies were planning as early as 1943 for economic and reconstruction agencies. In July 1944 the Bretton Woods Conference drafted the Articles of Agreement establishing the International Bank for Reconstruction and Development; it came into existence in December 1945. But nature herself seemed to punish Europe for its holocaust; the winter of 1946 was severe, and the crops of 1946 and 1947 were poor. The resources of the Bank were too small and its scope not broad enough; in 1948 the United States launched the Marshall Plan (European Recovery Program) to put Europe back on its feet.

The churches did not wait for governments to reconstruct the Christian institutions of Europe. Their concern and efforts were not only for church buildings, but also for the re-establishment of organizations forbidden by the Nazis, for old people's homes, for orphanages, for the many charitable works which the term 'Innere Mission' defines; even the capacity of these organizations, had they retained their former vigour, would have been taxed by the new burdens placed upon them. Piecemeal assistance was not strengthening Christian witness in Europe; in the spring of 1947 the leaders of the American Church World Service asked the Director of the Department of Reconstruction to formulate a Four Year Plan for the spending of $10,000,000 a year for the rebuilding of European Christian institutions. Secretary of State George C. Marshall's famous speech to the Harvard graduating class was not given until 5 June 1947: he proposed a four-year American plan for European reconstruction. The rest of the world was ignored at this time by the World Council; though the ecumenical movement, in the form of the International Missionary Council, showed concern to the extent that the orphaned missions and their work throughout the world were helped. This, too, paralleled Caesar's world: the foreign assistance act of 1948 authorized $5.3 billion (US) for Europe (excluding Greece and Turkey, which were allotted $275 million), while China in that critical year was granted only $463 million. In the four-year period of the Marshall Plan, 86 per cent of all American aid was channelled to Europe; the Near East and South Asia accounted for 7 per cent, the Far East 5 per cent, and international organizations and other non-regional expenses 2 per cent. But as exciting and moving a story as the ecumenical reconstruction of European Christianity is one to be told elsewhere.[2] It is desired here only to point out the vigour with which the churches entered the field of service to their fellow Christians, and its European orientation, as a background to their later economic aid. Such an organized, ecumenical effort had not existed in the inter-war period. The World Alliance, for instance, refused a request for monetary aid from the Nansen Office of the League of Nations by replying that it was not a philanthropic organization. Only Dr Keller's European Central Office continued its lonely effort during that period without help from either the World Alliance or Life and Work.

The situation in Europe in 1948 had improved slightly over the immediate post-war conditions; in any event, with the Marshall Plan everyone had confidence that it would improve. It was noted at the Amsterdam Assembly that due to the improvement already seen in Europe there might be some revision in the reconstruction programmes. There were suggestions that the Middle East needed the ministrations of the World Council as urgently as Europe. Furthermore it was felt that 'the future work of the Department should more and more take into account the basic and continuing necessity of inter-church aid'. Christian charity, it would appear, was to be an ongoing policy not limited to crisis—or was it crisis that was to be unending? No definitive action was taken by the Assembly on the future areas and policies of operation of the Department of Reconstruction; this was left to the Central Committee.[3]

The change of name in 1949 from Department of Reconstruction and Inter-Church Aid to the Department of Inter-Church Aid and Service to Refugees (DICASR) was symbolic of two things: emphasis was changed from emergency help to a continuing concept of service and from an emphasis on Europe to a world-wide responsibility for this aid.[4] Since a concept of aid world-wide in scope required the co-operation of the International Missionary Council, the Joint Committee was given the task of studying the strategy of inter-church aid on an international scale. It was, however, the Central Committee which formulated the new mandate 'Emergency Inter-Church Aid Relief in Areas Outside Europe' in December 1952; and this new concept was later endorsed by the slower-moving IMC. This did not mean new resources for world distribution, at least not at first, but it provided for the co-ordination of all ecumenical relief measures through DICASR.[5] It evaluated appeals for projects from younger churches, consulted national and regional Christian councils in the areas concerned for local resources, and, if none were available, sought funding elsewhere. Not only did it consider European and American Christian bodies, for, if the project would be of interest to inter-governmental organizations, it co-operated with the CCIA in presenting an IGO with a formal request or gave full support to local leaders to do so.

The mission societies of the International Missionary Council may have been reluctant to co-operate fully in this new concept of ecclesiastical foreign aid as each could see its individual influence diminishing; much the same rationale lies behind the unwillingness of states to commit all bilateral aid to distribution by the United Nations. Much of the hesitation was overcome by maintaining individual aid for a specific project which had passed through the various evaluation processes of DICASR. One former World Council official saw this concentration of function in the World Council as a deliberate attempt to render obsolete the old paternalism of the mission societies. Here was an ecumenical agency in which both the giving and receiving churches were equally represented; the stigma of always being on the receiving end could be obscured. And DICASR did deal with the needs of Europe as well as those of Africa, Asia, and Latin America. During the inter-war years, the mission societies alone cared for what is now called the Third World, and Dr Keller's Central Office, mentioned above, aided only European churches and their welfare organizations, a factor which gave the ecumenical agencies an exclusively European, or at least white, appearance.

It is interesting to note that this change in World Council emphasis occurred about the same time as the United States entered a new phase in its economic aid programme in which it, too, emphasized the whole world. President Truman, in his Inaugural Address of January 1949, enunciated his famous Point Four to provide technical assistance to under-developed areas of the world. Put into force by the Act for International Development of 1950, it was regarded by many as 'a significant milestone in the evolution of American world policy'.[6]

By the time the Evanston Assembly met in 1954 DICASR had over a year of experience for it to evaluate. The Assembly declared that inter-church aid had become a permanent obligation of the World Council. (This should be compared with Harold E. Stassen's final report on the Foreign Operations Administration that foreign economic aid had 'become in fact an integral part of our total foreign policy . . .'.) In considering this factor, however, the Assembly continually stressed 'ongoing emergency situations', 'emergency inter-church aid', and 'emergency relief'.[7] This stress on 'emergency' aid is reminiscent of the Calvinist ethic that every individual should be able to stand on his own feet without assistance, save in very unusual and short-lived circumstances. It is also reminiscent of the capitalist ideological tenet that if an institution is not self-supporting, then somehow it is a faulty or unworthy institution.

There is evidence in the discussions of the Assembly and of the Central Committee that the term 'emergency' served the function for the World Council that 'defence' or 'mutual security' did for engaging the support of the United States Congress for a worthy programme which by another name would have smelt less sweet. If an emergency is 'an unforeseen combination of circumstances' then allied with 'ongoing' it becomes a contradiction in terms. In spite of semantic games, there was an indication that many within the World Council understood the awesome situation which faced the Christian communities throughout the world. The *Consultation on World Need and Strategy* at Les Rasses, Switzerland, called by DICASR in June 1955 declared that it was obvious that the needs of the Christian communities in the less developed countries would continue and that emergency aid and relief should be

151

reinterpreted to cover 'unmet needs which are beyond the strength of regular church or mission support'.[8] It proposed an enlarged role for DICASR as a clearing house for all projects (evaluated or not) and all resources available. Particular attention would be drawn to urgent needs and needs of special ecumenical significance.

The emphasis by the Evanston Assembly upon inter-church aid was continued by the Central Committee at its 1955 meeting where 'Inter-Church Aid and Assistance to Underdeveloped Areas' was one of two Main Themes of the meeting. Although inter-church aid was an annual topic in the discussion of the Central Committee —through the report of DICASR—its status as a Main Theme meant that it had the attention of the Central Committee meeting centred on that topic; special speeches are presented on Main Themes and discussion is extensive. This not only provides church leaders with additional information and understanding but it also plays a great role in the publicity disseminated after each meeting.

The speeches and the discussion limited the scope of the topic to what further aid the World Council and its member churches could supply to the under-developed areas; the obligations of the world generally were not considered. This meeting went significantly further than the Consultation at Les Rasses in prescribing the responsibilities of the churches. There the issue of emergency *versus* recurring needs of the younger churches was resolved, but here the Central Committee went beyond help intended only for its confessional adherents to benefits for the whole community in which Christians found themselves. It is coincidental that these recommendations were made during the same summer that Harold Stassen submitted to the President the final report of the Mutual Security Program of the Foreign Operations Administration and wrote that the American interest had evolved 'from preoccupation mainly with building of military defences to the aim of creating an economic base capable of both supporting necessary defence efforts and also of yielding a growing measure of economic progress and advance in human dignity and well-being'. The Central Committee urged that projects of benefit to the whole community as well as to the Christian one should be sponsored and supported. In addition, ecumenical action should lead the way with pilot projects of special importance and significance for a particular area, and relief work should be devoted to programmes of reconstruction for the total community, not only its Christian segment.

Although the goals and methods had been defined thus far, DICASR under the new leadership of Dr Leslie E. Cooke considered that a larger study of the role of the Church in the struggle for social justice should be undertaken. In spite of its efforts to ameliorate suffering, the results of social injustice, the Church was really peripheral to the decisions taken in governmental circles to root out the causes of the problem. It was with this in mind that DICASR co-operated closely with the Department of Church and Society in its study on 'The Christian Response to Areas of Rapid Social Change'. On the action side, it felt that the selection of key projects of considerable significance to the developing countries as a whole might bring the local churches to the centre of the decision-making scene.[9]

It acknowledged its lack of influence with governments, but it seemed to have no greater luck with member churches, for only about half of the projects evaluated and publicized received support. With the beginning of the American Surplus Commodities Program, the Division organized and co-ordinated an enlarged scheme of material aid distributed by Church World Service, Lutheran World Service, and the National Council of the Churches of Christ. Later in that decade, as the economies of Western European states began their phenomenal growth, this programme included German, Swiss, Dutch, Swedish and other *Hilfswerk* organizations. Some indication of the growth of aid for non-European lands is illustrated by the increase, from $185,000 in 1956 to over $1 million in 1960, in aid dispensed. In the period 1955–60, forty-four emergency appeals had resulted in $2.5 million in cash and $51 million of material aid from the churches; in addition, more than $195 million in US government commodities had been distributed by Church World Service alone.[10]

As the decade of the Fifties closed, new states in Asia and Africa gradually came into existence; it was obvious that many more would soon follow. The severing of political subordination was followed by the ending of ecclesiastical subordination and often of direct financial support. These circumstances and the completion of the first stage of the study on areas of rapid social change in 1959, led the Administrative Committee of DICASR to organize, in April 1960, a meeting of representatives from Specialized Agencies of the United Nations, of Christian bodies in Asia, Africa and Latin America, of missionary agencies and of national Inter-Church Aid Committees to develop an ecumenical strategy which came to be called 'The Christian Response to Areas of Acute Human Need'. Three main lines of action were defined: (1) the development of demonstration projects in selected areas; (2) the continued use of Material Aid; and (3) recruitment and training of Christian technicians to take part in development projects.[11] The Division desk for Areas of Acute Human Need, which was set up at this conference, stimulated churches and national christian councils to join national Freedom from Hunger Campaign Committees and to co-operate in projects calculated to raise food production. *The Times* reported that the Archbishop of Canterbury, Dr Fisher, felt 'uneasy' about the World Council development programme because it would be the beginning of continuing and recurring expenditures. The programme's supporters would not have denied its on-going aspect; indeed they would have pointed out its necessity.

The New Delhi Assembly, meeting in the first years of the United Nations Development Decade, approved the new route taken by the Division of Inter-Church Aid and granted it a new name in recognition of the permanent character of its world-wide activities: Division of Inter-Church Aid, Refugee and World Service (DICARWS). The Assembly particularly urged the churches to be generous in their response to the areas of acute human need. Affirming the Central Committee recommendations, the Assembly called upon the Division to intensify its efforts in undertaking specific comprehensive demonstration projects designed to aid the whole community.[12]

The younger churches attending the Thessalonica Conference on rapid social change in 1959 had suggested that the churches themselves engage more specifically in economic development by setting up a special fund for this purpose in addition to Inter-Church Aid activities. After much debate in the Central Committee in 1959 and 1960, a Committee on Specialized Assistance for Social Projects (SASP) was set up which reported to the Central Committee in 1962, when its programme was commended to the churches. SASP did not become the fund providing for economic development projects which the Thessalonica participants requested. Instead it became a technical assistance committee advising the World Council organs on the technical aspects of projects. Of the DICARWS projects, about 20 per cent were referred to SASP for expert analysis. All projects considered by SASP, however, were not DICARWS projects; in fact $75,000 of the SASP $200,000 budget was set aside for items on which the Committee might wish to take the initiative in order to pioneer an approach to economic development. Some $40,000 was provided for the thrice yearly meetings of the Committee of twenty experts. Because Committee members did not always have time to devote themselves to detailed work on an evaluation, $60,000 was provided for consultants' fees and costs.

SASP had over forty experts in the field, on such diverse items as leadership training in Latin America, reorganization of a farm school in Madagascar, publication of periodicals in French-speaking Africa, and colonization of the Amazon forest. It published Occasional Papers summarizing guidance given on similar projects which might be of help to other areas. The Committee on SASP, reporting on the Uppsala Assembly (1968), called attention to the unco-ordinated development aid of the World Council, the churches, and the mission societies. It recommended, and this was accepted by the Assembly, that a new Advisory Committee on

Technical Services (ACTS) should replace SASP.[13] This new committee is discussed below in conjunction with other development-
oriented organs created in 1969 and 1970.

With the amalgamation of the IMC into the World Council in
1961 and the increasing number of independent African and Asian
states—which multiplied those churches qualified to be members
of the World Council—interest in development aid within that body
waxed even more. The World Council through DICARWS undertook exceptionally large projects in several cases for the benefit
of non-Christian communities. It undertook to build a complete
village in Iran of 308 modern houses for Moslems who had lost all
in the earthquakes of September 1962. Increasing prosperity in
Europe broadened the base of donors of inter-church aid; more
than one-quarter of the $700,000 required for the Iranian projects
was provided by congregations in the Netherlands. In Algeria a
project for planting 22 million trees to arrest soil erosion was
undertaken; and, under DICARWS sponsorship, the Christian
Committee for Service in Algeria became responsible for providing
health and social services for 2 million people in that country for
an extended period beginning in 1962, when Algeria gained its
independence. These are but a few examples of economic development, sometimes coupled with emergency relief, engaged in by the
World Council of Churches.[14]

As with all large enterprises which have grown rapidly to tackle
a specific problem, certain difficulties of administration and co-
ordination arose; this was partly due to the large number of
agencies involved, many with only the slightest feeling of responsibility towards co-ordinated action. Recognizing the need for
co-ordination were the various World Council Departments and
Divisions, each acting through its own staff, and the member
churches using the World Council facilities. From a less universal
viewpoint the various churches in the requesting countries, operating through their national Christian councils or through the
regional council, if one existed, or through another ecumenical
body or through the mission agencies did not feel this need. In
addition, governmental and inter-governmental agencies co-operating with the World Council or with any one of the levels mentioned did not realize the necessity of world-wide co-ordination.
All this led in 1963 to a great self-evaluation regarding the aims
and functions of DICARWS (as well as an outside organizational
evaluation of the Division by a commercial firm). It was also in
1963 that President Kennedy appointed General Lucius Clay to
take a 'hard look' at the US government's foreign aid programme,
about which there had been dissatisfaction!

After decades of parsimony by the colonial powers in regard to
economic development and an equal period of frugality—due to

155

small resources and great demands—on the part of the churches, it was often a case of too much, too soon, too quickly. It was natural that inexperience should lead to waste. The donating churches demanded greater assurance that the projects they supported would be more responsibly formulated and executed. But the dissatisfaction was not one-sided; the receiving churches wanted a greater assurance that the resources which they felt they needed would be provided. These two demands resulted partially from an interest in larger and more technical development projects.

As a corrective DICARWS proposed that more information be disseminated on a regular basis about what the various churches were doing in the field of economic aid. Before beginning new projects, it recommended consultation among the receiving and donor churches as to the conditions and requirements of each. It proposed, however, that the co-ordinators of the information, requests, and offers be not the World Council but the regional ecumenical councils (e.g., the East Asia Christian Council or the All-Africa Conference of Churches) of the recipients. Ostensibly this was to give the new bodies experience and responsibility,[15] but it may also have been that the onus for inappropriate action would fall on the recipients themselves and not on the World Council officials who were primarily members of the donor churches. A similar plan was used by the United States for just this reason in the dispensing of Marshall Plan aid to Europe.

An *embarras de richesses* also contributed to the dissatisfaction: the churches had more resources at their disposal than ever before, both from their own congregations and from their governments. The problem of government aid to church bodies abroad was an old one and raised the spectre of past attitudes and past mistakes. It brought a shiver of fear that the World Council of Churches might become tainted as a harbinger of neo-colonialism. The acceptance by mission societies of government funds for social services, such as hospitals and schools, provided to dependent peoples had long been a subject of controversy in mission circles. The fear was always there that should they accept the money even for their innocent and beneficial work to native peoples, they would somehow become tools of the government which provided the funds. Many groups accepted, and indeed in the day of the national church, many were tools of the state. Unestablished bodies generally had disdained this status and refused the aid. There had been no satisfactory answer in the past; there was none now.

A request by the German churches for advice from DICARWS in responding to an offer of the German Federal government brought the question which had lain dormant since the Second World War again into full flower. The German government proposed to provide considerable sums for economic development to be administered by the German churches on projects of their own choosing. The World Council Executive Committee prepared an interim statement on the subject in February 1963. The Central Committee further considered the issue in August of the same year. Representatives of DICARWS advised that each such action should be considered on its own merits, rather than that the Committee should lay down strict rules to be followed. Regarding the German situation, it noted that the Evangelical Church in Germany (Evangelische Kirche in Deutschland, EKD) had established the Evangelical Central Agency for Development Aid (Evangelische Zentralstelle für Entwicklungshilfe) to receive government funds provided unconditionally. The Central Agency also wished to avoid the onus for refusing a project or the blame for an ill-conceived one and had provided that it would consider applications only when approved by the Lutheran World Federation or the World Council of Churches. It was this latter point that caused official World Council consideration of the issue. DICARWS proposed further that the church requesting aid should state whether it would be willing to use government funds; and that, if it were, it should be obliged to seek and receive the permission of its own government. DICARWS would then take the responsibility of requesting the funds from abroad. It should be a condition that the receiving church would in no way be answerable to the government which had granted the aid. In areas of the world where neo-colonialism was a real fear, this was a wise precaution. The types of projects for which it would use government aid would be the same as those it recommended for SASP.

Not all members of the Central Committee were happy with this report. Archbishop L. J. Beecher of Kenya felt that this might confirm the suspicion of a continuing colonialism with the churches as its vehicle, but he bowed to the argument that the receiving churches were protected. Dr Gerhard Brennecke of East Germany feared that a return to mission-society type dependence on government would bring some vague, ill-defined, disastrous results. Mission societies might give advice on aid use, he stated, but ought not to be a channel for the aid. From the recipient's point of view, Dr Moses of India stated that it was impossible for the Indian government to agree to mission agencies accepting aid from another government. Principal I. Russell Chandran of South India feared that the dispensing of government grants would cause others to think that Christianity was being propagated by foreign governments. Bishop Chandu Ray of Pakistan thought that the Indian argument was not valid for the rest of Asia. Such help—for example, from the United States and Denmark—had been given in the past without harm. The Central Committee 'took note' of the DICARWS advice but did not endorse it. DICARWS and the

Division of World Mission and Evangelism were requested to continue to deal with each situation on its merits as it arose.[16]

In 1960 the French African empire was for all practical purposes eliminated in one fell swoop. The dissolution of the British African empire, which had begun in 1957 with the granting of independence to Ghana, continued during the Sixties. It was, however, the independence suddenly given to a Belgian colony without advance preparation and to the trust territory of Ruanda-Urundi, as the two separate states of Rwanda and Burundi, that caused chaos in Central Africa. The Central Committee launched its Ecumenical Programme for Emergency Action in Africa (EPEAA) in 1964 as a project to care for refugees from the three former Belgian areas. It quickly developed into a programme to meet other emergency situations in Africa. To make WCC aid more effective and to act as an example to the world, whose short-term and often ill-advised (sometimes completely unadvised except for occasional World Bank studies) projects it frequently criticized, surveys of various parts of Africa were undertaken by experts, and a five-year programme with a budget of $10 million was drawn up. The programme itself was to be administered by the All Africa Conference of Churches.[17]

Of all the aid projects for the benefit of the younger churches and their communities, none contained help for any religious purpose. Aid to European churches after the Second World War fulfilled needs in worship as well as in fertilizer projects or other economic requirements. In the original agreement between DICARWS and the IMC (when inter-church aid was expanded to a world-wide basis), such 'non-emergency' aid as worship, supplies, and church buildings was excluded in order to avoid involvement in the financial programmes of the mission societies which were trying to wean the infant churches from the teat of subvention. The new independent churches of the new independent states, however, had needs beyond the capacity of the mission societies to fulfil in their religious as well as their secular programmes. The Central Committee authorized DICARWS to include all needs requested by member churches.[18]

It will be noted that the effort of the World Council in regard to its own actions for economic development was almost exclusively the responsibility of DICARWS. The CCIA had been concerned with the development policy of the industrialized states and of the United Nations. However, the World Conference on Church and Society and its discussion of economic development stirred the Executive Committee of the CCIA in 1966 to discuss economic aid at length, part of its discussion centring on direct World Council participation. Mr S. H. Amissah of the All Africa Conference of Churches appealed to the churches to help African states to achieve economic emancipation to match their political independence. Dr Rees of the CCIA staff urged direct participation in development assistance upon the World Council. A more conservative view was voiced by Professor Ulrich Scheuner of Germany, later Chairman of CCIA, when he questioned the Council's qualification to set up aid programmes and urged that the churches should confine themselves to alerting the conscience of nations. Dr Visser 't Hooft felt, however, that the World Council had a direct role to play in development assistance. In this he was supported by Dr Leslie Cooke, Associate General Secretary, who pointed out that the World Council had already played a large role in evolving aid programmes, for example, those concerned with agriculture. He also pointed out that, increasingly, Germany and Holland were channelling aid through their own churches. He felt that the World Council ought to have the same overall strategy of development for itself and its members which it urged upon the states of the world.[19]

The result of this discussion was 'A Memorandum on the World Council of Churches Approach to the Problems of Economic Development', destined for the WCC Executive Committee. It was 'generally received and approved' by the CCIA Executive, the adverb indicating that not all members agreed with its formulation and conclusions. The Memorandum urged upon the churches a realization of the extent to which they were already responsible for international economic development programmes within their own mission and service agencies. They must pursue, the memorandum continued, the advantage they had in this field by their closeness to people at the parish level. They could lead the way in economic development because they were freer to take risks than governments and international organizations bound by bureaucratic procedures (and, it might have added, by political considerations). The churches had to make clear to all who channelled aid through them, it declared, that their concern was with people and not with the political consequences for the donor states. Finally, the Memorandum criticized the churches for the same failures for which the CCIA had often chastised governments: the lack of co-ordinated development programmes. It recommended a central planning body within the World Council to co-ordinate not only its own Divisions and Departments but also the relevant activities of the donor churches. It urged that the Uppsala Assembly give full consideration to the issues of social economic justice.[20] Such a consideration was, in fact, a major task of Uppsala (see below) and a co-ordinating and planning body was recommended.

The World Council tried not only to meet emergencies, but also, in 1967, to prepare for the next one. The 'food gap', the difference between the food available and the food needed, appeared to be widening. The Executive Committee meeting in February 1967 urged that international co-operative action be undertaken to accelerate food production and even to build up reserves against threatening famine in Asia; and it suggested that the Central Committee should consider the issues further at its summer meeting. In a statement adopted at the meeting the Central Committee requested all nations to curtail military expenditures and use the saving to aid the hungry. Upon its own members it urged representation to their governments to aid in economic development and co-operation.[21] In a report on inter-church aid received by the Committee, the efforts of the churches and Christian agencies were acknowledged, but it was recognized that governments alone have the resources to develop the large-scale programmes which would assure success. DICARWS recorded with sorrow the death of its Director of eleven years, Dr Leslie E. Cooke. He had led the Division from the time it had begun to give non-emergency aid through an ever expanding role in economic development. Development of the concept of helping all men throughout the world was largely due to his thinking and efforts.

In keeping with its general emphasis on development, the Fourth Assembly directed that DICARWS give high priority to development in its total programmes. In addition to recurring and largely ignored requests that church aid be co-ordinated and that evaluation of projects be revised, the Assembly put forth a new idea in encouraging investment of church capital obtained from self-taxation of Christians. In spite of this novel idea, and its importance in inculcating a sense of responsibility in Christians of the industrialized North, these proposals were not framed in such a way as to impart a sense of urgency to the comfortable Christian citizens of Europe and North America.[22] The deliberations of the Economic Development section as a whole were viewed in a favourable light by the religion correspondent of the *Neue Zürcher Zeitung* who welcomed the humanistic rationality of the participants.[23] His prophetic feeling that the church community with this new interest and insight might well become a factor in the world community has not yet been completely fulfilled. But as governments retrench in their overseas aid commitments, the churches continue to expand theirs.

The Executive Committee of the Central Committee meeting in January 1969 announced that many churches had already pledged a regular percentage of their budget for economic development. Ten million dollars were expected the first year; an international consortium was being created to manage it.[24] The Central Committee meeting in August 1969 discussed fully the role of the churches and of the World Council of Churches in development. Dr Visser 't Hooft proposed that secular as well as religious channels be used for the dispensation of World Council aid for economic development. He was generally supported, but Dr Miguez-Bonino of Argentina noted that, although in many cases aid might be sent through secular channels without undesirable side-effects, in others that method would reinforce social and political structures which themselves hindered development. Dr Won Yong Kang of Korea urged that more people from developing countries be placed on the World Council's development planning bodies, an argument familiar also to those in secular organizations. He was happy to see that the World Council was acting as well as talking, but expressed the fear that aid might become another golden calf.[25]

The World Consultation on Ecumenical Assistance to Development Projects (Montreux Consultation held in January 1970, reported more fully in the second section of this chapter) proposed the creation of a Commission on the Churches' Participation in Development (CCPD) (a more precise formulation of the 1969 Central Committee's authorization for a 'committee on development') and an Ecumenical Development Fund. The Executive Committee established the CCPD in February 1970. The Montreux Consultation felt that this new Commission would give expression to the urgency of the situation which had thus far been missing from Christian and Northern secular discussion of the matter.

The tasks of the Commission on the Churches' Participation on Development are: (1) to co-ordinate all World Council efforts in the field of development; (2) to carry out a study of the theological bases of development and the churches' role in it; (3) to conduct education for development; (4) to provide a documentation service on development; and (5) to administer the Ecumenical Development Fund. In its short period of existence it has attacked these tasks with vigour. Being a part of Unit II on Justice and Service, the CCPD has had to maintain a close relationship with the other sub-units—CICARWS, CCIA, and the Programme to Combat Racism. CICARWS, it will be remembered, had heretofore carried out the churches' actual investment in development by acting as a clearing house for projects from developing countries and finding donors for them. As the CCPD now maintains the technical capacity of the World Council, it has a necessary relationship in the project system. The CCPD has pretty well assumed any residual role which had been left to the CCIA in the field of development; however, the CCIA still makes representations to intergovernmental organizations (with which it has consultative status) on behalf of the CCPD. The sub-units outside Unit II co-operated with CCPD at the programme level, for example, Church and Society on studies regarding simplified technology adaptable to field situations, and the Christian Medical Commission in the field of population control.

161

L

In order to test the hypothesis of direct participation by the churches and the World Council in development, the CCPD adopted the strategy of concentrating its work in four selected countries and regions: Ethiopia, Cameroun, Indonesia, and the Caribbean. In each instance there has been extensive discussion with local church leaders, and community and government leaders as well, on the priorities, areas for concentration, and the extent of local mobilization of resources. Processes were developed which allowed for participation by the peoples involved, as well as their leaders. Although concentrating in these areas, CCPD activities are not confined to them; needs are widespread. However, even in the short period in which this experiment has been under way, CCPD and local officials are pleased with the results.

The documentation service has grown apace. It provides a bibliographical service for World Council staff as well as for outside requests. It has published two catalogues and has indexed some 2,000 documents. Research will be shared with other interested groups, especially counterpart groups in developing countries, through dossiers prepared on specific topics such as rural development or new methods of education for development.

The best-known function of CCPD is its administration of the Ecumenical Development Fund. The setting-aside of a specific amount from church budgets, for development, was mentioned at the Uppsala Assembly; the Central Committee meeting in 1971 urged all churches to donate 2 per cent of their income to development. Since some of the World Council's projects had not always been regarded in the most favourable light in the donor countries, it was suggested that this 2 per cent could be spent by the churches directly on projects without the World Council handling it (as had sometimes been done), or through the Ecumenical Development Fund. This Fund was created to allow more local control than the project system did (it is true that projects were proposed by local church groups, but apart from that they had little discretion in their implementation). The Fund was to provide the opportunity to achieve social justice and self-reliance, for local groups would select priorities and plan. There are criteria to guide the disbursement of funds, but they are flexible. Even the primary one that they be church-related groups may be set aside in exceptional circumstances.[26]

Technical Service is now provided through the CCPD. The Uppsala Assembly had recommended the creation of the Advisory Committee to replace SASP in August 1969 when its first seven members were appointed. It had a Director and two executives but its backbone consisted of part-time consultants throughout the world who could be called on to evaluate projects: 276 specialists in 86 professional fields in 53 countries. In its first year it gave advice on 92 projects, counselling on improved use of church-owned agricultural land in Rwanda and Burundi and on integrating rural development projects in the Amazon Basin. Its independence was short lived, for in 1971 when the CCPD became operational it was integrated into that body, where its staff continues the work already begun.

Discussion of church investment in economic development began with the consideration of the ethics of investing in companies engaged in Southern Africa. It was suggested by the CCPD to the Central Committee at Addis Ababa in 1971 that a study should be made of this topic, and the Central Committee agreed that the CCPD should undertake an inquiry into the feasibility of such investment possibilities.[27] The result of this inquiry was presented to the Central Committee at its 1973 meeting. The Russian Orthodox delegates opposed the project as an extension of Western capitalism and colonialism, saying it would create an ideological confrontation of the churches.[28] Nevertheless the Central Committee accepted the report and set up the Special Committee on a Church Investment Corporation to provide a detailed proposal in time for the Executive Committee meeting in February 1974. This deadline was met by the Special Committee with draft articles of incorporation for a body to be called the Ecumenical Development Co-operative Society. The Executive Committee sent this draft to the churches for their comment and reaction. A report and revised articles were presented to the Central Committee in August 1974 and accepted. Newspapers headlined the creation of a 'Church World Bank'. By now the Russians had been won over to the plan, since the operation would be based on ethical as well as commercial considerations; also it would be run as a co-operative, a form of organization approved by Soviet communism. The Soviet churchmen indicated they might even become subscribers.[29]

The CCPD officials who presented the plan emphasized that it differed from existing financial institutions by fostering economic development 'based on the primacy of social justice and human self-reliance'.[30] The plan goes to great pains to illustrate that the production of a surplus from economic activity occurs in 'every kind of economic or political system, be it capitalist or socialist' [that is, communist]. It stated that the important point here was the need to control the distribution of profit; in fact there would be a controlled rate of return for the churches and any excess would be reinvested, the benefit accruing to those whom the Co-operative is meant to help.

The legal form for the investment corporation—that of a co-operative—was chosen in order to provide the most flexible organization, with final authority vested in a members' general meeting. Originally to be incorporated in Switzerland, the EDCS in August

1975 became a co-operative under Dutch Law (with headquarters in Amsterdam) in order to avail itself of more advantageous tax laws and the guarantee of work permits for its staff, which the Swiss government could not make. Membership is limited to member churches of the World Council, the Council itself, national councils of churches, and any church-related organization. A member may buy a share for as little as 500 Swiss francs; irrespective of the value of shares held, one vote per member was decided upon as a means of stressing the partnership between contributors and recipients and developing self-reliance.

Although criteria for investment were not written into the articles of incorporation, the report contained indications of what they are likely to be. From the point of view of the investor there arises the question of security and an adequate rate of return. Because the investors are Christian bodies, ethical consideration is important; unlikely areas of investment will be alcohol, tobacco, gambling, and armaments. For groups borrowing money, considerations will include the impact of a project on their communities, their readiness to develop self-reliance, and whether a project will provide more employment. It is hoped that the projects will help to correct gross imbalances in power and property in the developing countries. And regarding the project itself, it is desirable that in addition to helping those immediately concerned, it should act as a model for others.[31]

The Central Committee agreed that the World Council would become a founding member, subscribing 110,000 Swiss francs; it urged member churches and other Christian agencies to also become members. It agreed that the Society would be incorporated when a minimum of thirty members, of whom at least one half would be from the Third World, had pledged a minimum of 15 million Swiss francs.[32]

The organization of the aid programmes of the World Council has become more complex as the magnitude of the task of development has come to be understood. In the period of industrial prosperity in the Sixties, the resources of the churches grew and the aid programmes of all the churches, Protestant, Roman Catholic and Orthodox, became tremendous. Figures of all the Christian aid programmes have never been assembled, but some educated guesses are nevertheless impressive. As late as 1960 it was estimated that 90 per cent of all education south of the Sahara was conducted by Christian agencies. The Protestant churches are responsible for more than 1,200 hospitals and clinics in 85 countries, mostly in the developing world. Each year in Asia 150 doctors graduate from Protestant medical schools. In India there are 138 colleges related to the major Christian groups. The traditional areas of church activity—education, medicine and agriculture—are just those areas of great importance to economic development. In 1968 it was estimated that the total annual effort of Christendom, Roman Catholic, Protestant and Orthodox, was around $300 million.[33] The ensuing period of inflation and depression up to the mid-Seventies has reduced contributions to churches and the World Council; controversial programmes have been another limiting factor. Nevertheless the resources of the Christian churches, including those they are willing to dedicate to the use of others—especially self-taxation at 2 per cent—could stand as an example to the statesmen of 'Christian' nations.

CCIA Strategies for Development

The CCIA, as the official spokesman for the World Council of Churches before international organizations and governments, was the Christian agency which devoted most effort to offering suggestions and plans for world development to official bodies; except in very few instances, its concern was not, therefore, the direct participation of the World Council in the actual giving of aid; this it left to DICARWS. When asked to do so, it represented DICARWS before official world bodies as it does the CCPD at present. Inter-Church Aid had developed a full programme of relief and reconstruction before the CCIA thought of promoting world economic development; the later concern for the world was a natural outgrowth of the earlier distress over physical suffering.

Although certain themes run through CCIA development activity—for example, attempts to create favourable public opinion on behalf of development, using national Christian councils to urge action by the industrialized states, calling for an integrated, co-ordinated, balanced development programme, urging favourable trade policies and terms, and recommending a minimum national donation of 1 per cent of the GNP—it is proposed here to treat CCIA development work mainly in a chronological manner in order to illustrate the ever-increasing tempo of CCIA activities in this field. As with the World Council itself, or any new organization, all efforts at the beginning were restricted by lack of resources and personnel.[34] The attention of the young CCIA, like that of the secular world, had been hypnotically drawn to the Cold War contest. As the world was not cataclysmically destroyed by the two superpowers, attention turned to other matters; development of the full capacities of states and individuals to achieve self-fulfilment was one topic which commended itself to the Christian ethic.

The Amsterdam Assembly, held in 1948, came under the shadow of the World War and its immediate aftermath, and its delegates were too concerned with the political troubles of Europe and

America to consider the economic troubles of the majority of the world's peoples. The report of Section III on the disorder of society did note that 'the inhabitants of Asia and Africa, for instance, should have benefits of more machine production'; at the same time the Assembly breathed the hope that the new areas of industrialization might avoid the social evils experienced by the earlier industrialized peoples.[35] Section IV, on international disorder, protested against the exploitation of dependent peoples and proclaimed the interdependence of national economies: 'No nation has the moral right to determine its own economic policy without consideration for the economic needs of other nations and without recourse to international consultation'.[36]

This was the extent of the concern shown by the white man at that time for economic development; his world, his experience, after all, were different. The following year, from 3 to 11 December 1949 in Bangkok, the non-white Christian spoke on what he regarded as his most pressing problems; he explained how he proposed that the churches deal with them. Although the World Council and the IMC were sponsors of this Eastern Asia Christian Conference, its findings were not theirs but those of Christians living in the colonial and neo-colonial world. The great concern, of course, was the Communist government of China, but they had prophetic warnings for the Christians, churches, and peoples of the West concerning the 'majority of people both in the rural and urban areas [who] live in conditions of abject poverty and under oppressive systems that cramp their personality'. Although economic development had not yet evolved as a general international policy, the continuing emphasis on the duty of the churches to speak out for social and economic justice was a forerunner of the future concern in this area.[37]

In the autumn of 1948 the General Assembly requested ECOSOC and the Specialized Agencies to give full and urgent attention to the problem of the economic development of underdeveloped countries; it also budgeted $288,000 to provide limited technical assistance. President Truman's Point Four programme encouraged ECOSOC to prepare a proposal for an Expanded Programme of Technical Assistance (EPTA), which the General Assembly approved later that year. A Technical Assistance Board (TAB) was established, composed of representatives of the Specialized Agencies (ILO, FAO, UNESCO, WHO, ICAO, ITU, WMO and, later, IAEA, UPU, IMCO) that were taking part in the Expanded Programme of Technical Assistance.

Further impetus may have been given to ecumenical consideration of development by an increase in CCIA resources, which allowed more time to be devoted to following more aspects of international affairs. United Nations emphasis also increased and may have contributed to CCIA activity in the matter. Pledged amounts from UN member states for the technical assistance programme totalled more than $20 million. Point 6 of Trygve Lie's 'Twenty Year Programme for Achieving Peace through the United Nations' dealt with development: 'A sound and active programme of technical assistance for economic development and encouragement of large scale capital investment, using all appropriate private, governmental, and inter-governmental resources'. Welcoming this additional attention, the CCIA prepared memoranda on the United Nations programme, the American Point Four Programme, and the Colombo Plan of the Commonwealth for circulation to its constituency. In addition, more regularized contact with the Specialized Agencies—after they had granted consultative status to the CCIA—brought more opportunities to act in regard to economic development.

The Food and Agriculture Organization granted such status in November 1950. John H. Reisner, Secretary of Agricultural Missions, Inc. (USA) who was designated CCIA observer to FAO, described the technical assistance and economic development concerns of FAO to the CCIA Executive Committee at its 1951 meeting. The Committee approved a 'Statement on Technical Assistance' in which it noted that development was essential to international justice and peace. It contained general recommendations on development regarding the motivation of the donor and recipient states, the moral and technical qualifications of experts, and the need for training their indigenous replacements. The churches and Christians had the chief task, it noted, of helping to 'create and sustain the favourable climate necessary' for development programmes.[38]

The Economic and Social Council and the General Assembly discussed economic development extensively. CCIA officials gave informal support at the Sixth Session of the General Assembly for a resolution calling for expanded contributions for 1952 to the United Nations programme. In conversation with delegates, CCIA representatives expressed hope for well-conceived measures of land reform,[39] one of the topics discussed. The General Assembly debates, however, reached no conclusion—and that was to become a regular feature, since members of élite groups who would lose by reform measures were often the leaders of delegations from areas where the situation was acute.

The Enlarged Meeting of the Committee of the IMC, meeting at Willingen, Germany, in 1952, gave the subject of economic development more attention than the IMC had given it previously and more than it would subsequently. The report of Group IV on Technical and Welfare Services, adopted by the Enlarged Meeting, urged that it was the duty of Christians to encourage and assist governments in programmes for raising the standard of living of under-developed areas. Thus a previous admonition became a moral imperative. Urging upon governments and inter-governmental agencies points similar to those in the CCIA Statement of the previous year, it also called for the separation of technical aid from military aid. A worthy wish but highly unlikely of fulfilment, for the United States Mutual Security Act of 10 October 1951, barely ten months previously, had the very purpose of integrating the technical and military aid programmes. The missionary delegates further called upon the churches to take action promoting development, for they could draw upon their long experience among the peoples of the less developed areas in order to advise governments of local needs. Lest, however, the IMC appear unduly modern, a statement was issued warning the churches that, although technical assistance programmes would be welcomed, they should 'guard against undue diversion from the primary tasks of the church',[40] i.e. conversion.

The CCIA Executive Committee met after Willingen and reaffirmed its belief in the necessity of economic development; it pledged its support for such programmes and directed its officers to continue close co-operation with the United Nations technical assistance agencies.[41] At the same meeting a consideration of the population and food problem brought forth the Statement 'Christian Concerns in Regard to Food and Agriculture' which offered a programme of technical assistance for all agriculturally underdeveloped countries. As twin policies for national and international agriculture, it urged greater production of foodstuffs with equally vigorous measures for soil conservation. The Statement stressed the duty of the developed states and their special responsibility to help in the development of the less developed, for 'the obligation is the greater because of the frequently destructive impact of the more developed societies upon the social, economic, and religious systems of the less developed societies'.[42]

While the United Nations General Assembly continued to debate on the Cuban resolution of the previous year urging an integrated development scheme, the CCIA officers wrote to the chairman of the Technical Assistance Committee supporting the co-operative procedures being developed through the Technical Assistance Board with joint review of assistance projects by all agencies concerned and the appointment of a Resident Representative in each country to co-ordinate its projects. Although the CCIA had developed informal consultative relations with the UN technical assistance agencies, it and other NGOs interested in economic development considered it necessary to arrange a conference of NGOs to devise more adequate procedures of consultation with the Technical Assistance Administration. The use of these procedures, it was hoped, would result in better co-operation between inter-governmental and non-governmental representatives in the field.[43]

The Ecumenical Study Conference for East Asia, held at Lucknow from 27 to 30 December 1952, offered a report on 'The Responsible Society in East Asia in Light of the World Situation' as a general consensus but not 'as a statement unanimously accepted throughout'.[44] It put forward revolutionary proposals to meet the revolutionary needs of East Asia. While the General Assembly debated and adjourned the debate on land reform, these Asian Christian leaders discussed the feudal landholding relationships in existence in their area of the world. They urged the abolition of absentee landlordism, the ownership of farms of sufficient size to assure subsistence, freedom from moneylenders, land for the land-less, and use of unutilized land. They did not prescribe land reform as the panacea, rather they wisely urged a balanced programme of community development in the agricultural sector. While Western European delegates at the United Nations were urging private development capital as the answer to economic development, these Christian leaders were recognizing the need for centralized econo-mic planning and the nationalization of key industries. Was it a mere sop to the churches which paid the bills when they also recognized the place for private investment in this development? Industrial development could be achieved only with great amounts of technical assistance and economic aid from the developed countries, they added, but this aid should have no political strings. In Asian society the churches must be prepared to humanize the technical and social revolutions which would come with develop-ment.

In a Letter to Member Churches the Central Committee, meeting at Lucknow immediately following the Conference, gave special attention to development problems in Asia: 'Churches all over the world must ask how they can help the people of Asia in their efforts to obtain a standard of living which meets basic human needs, and in their search for a more just social and economic order'. It exhorted those in the more developed countries to urge their governments to strengthen programmes of technical assis-tance.[45] Metropolitan Juhanon of South India called the attention of the Central Committee to the Conference's insistence that the Church must deal constructively with poverty and injustice.[46] This warning to the churches of the West indicated that many Asians felt that the Church, in spite of four decades of ecumenical concern, was still not actively committed to the problems of the world.

The CCIA Executive Committee at its August 1953 meeting continued its consideration of technical assistance programmes. It adopted a resolution which urged better integration of the programmes of the United Nations and its Specialized Agencies in its Expanded Programme of Technical Assistance and closer co-operation between the latter and bilateral projects, in order to maximize the results of these efforts—matters of concern to many of the non-aligned recipients of aid and recommendations that many scholars had made concerning foreign aid programmes. Drawing upon years of missionary experience in introducing medical and agricultural technical improvements, the Committee stressed the importance of gaining the full co-operation and acceptance of all inhabitants at all levels in the developing societies. In addition, the resolution called for more effort on the part of the developed states to provide adequate financial support.[47] This point was the basis of CCIA contacts with members of the Second Committee of the General Assembly and of the Technical Assistance Committee of ECOSOC. The CCIA felt that it was these representations, reinforced by certain national commissions of the CCIA, that increased the amount pledged to EPTA to over $24 million, compared with the $22 million for the previous year.

The General Assembly continued consideration of proposals for a Special United Nations Fund for Economic Development (SUNFED) and for the foundation of an International Finance Corporation (IFC). The CCIA informed United Nations delegates that it supported the call for adequate financial backing for international economic and social development, but stated that it was not competent to comment on the technical aspects of the best way of achieving it. At the March 1954 meeting of the Technical Assistance Committee, CCIA officers made representations at an informal luncheon for the chairmen of the TAC and the TAB. At the meeting itself, the CCIA again stressed that it made no judgements on the technical issues discussed, other than to call attention to its previous resolution on the need for integration and co-operative procedures within the Expanded Programme.[48] To further its goal of a more integrated development programme, the CCIA brought before NGOs accredited to FAO a plan for closer co-operation between the national commissions of the CCIA and FAO field representatives. Through this means there would be some link between the FAO and the 120 technically trained agricultural missionaries and the hundreds of rural missionaries interested and knowledgeable in the problems with which the FAO dealt. Through the intervention of these NGOs, the FAO considered that this plan would be of mutual benefit.

With a great deal of international attention given to the economic problems of the world, it was not surprising that the Second World Council Assembly, meeting at Evanston, a suburb of Chicago, should also discuss the situation of the under-developed world at length. The report of Section III on social questions, 'The Responsible Society in a World Perspective', included a section on economic problems of the Third World. It noted the universal demand for rapid development and that the peoples of the under-developed world were tempted to use extreme political measures to attain it. The recommendations of the Lucknow Conference (noted above) were reproduced in full; perhaps the section chose this method of passing on recommendations that were too radical for delegates returning to their over-developed economies to identify themselves with at all closely. The report deplored the extent to which the Cold War militated against progress in the field of economic development and quoted Lucknow somewhat approvingly: 'When American foreign policy is determined primarily by the criterion of anti-communism, it generally strengthens conservative and reactionary political groups in the East Asian scene and tends to weaken the forces of healthy social reform'. Christians in general, it continued, must realize the sacrifices that peoples in the developed world would have to make to aid world development, and it called upon them to press their governments for self-denying action in helping these countries.[49]

Economic development was also considered by Section IV on international affairs in its report 'Christians in the Struggle for World Community'. It pointed out to those among the delegates, and to those who would read the reports, that aid was not a one-way street; though financial aid and technical assistance might flow from the developed to the less developed, the cultural contribution of older civilizations would flow in the opposite direction. The report emphasized the pittance of the effort in relation to the great need of the poor and the actual possibilities of the rich. It offered no specific programme, but it did note that a sustained effort over a period of time would be necessary.[50] In the shorter 'Appeal from the World Council of Churches', which the Evanston Assembly issued, economic development was found sufficiently important to warrant an entire paragraph. It recognized the discouraging slowness in raising standards of living in the under-developed world and urged greater sacrifices on the part of the richer nations. It appealed to the churches to hold before their members their responsibilities in this area and asked them to recruit Christian technicians in the service of international agencies.[51]

The United Nations continued its endless discussions of the matters meaning life and death to millions which had already been on its agenda for three years: land reform, co-ordinated development programmes, the Special United Nations Fund for Economic Development, and the International Finance Corporation. The CCIA in the efforts of Richard Fagley continued its representations on behalf of adequate financial support for the United Nations Expanded Programme for Technical Assistance; international aid grants, and a long-range evaluation of EPTA to assist it to fulfil still unmet needs. These efforts brought official recognition in a cablegram from Mr David Owen, Executive Chairman of the UN Technical Assistance Board, to the CCIA Executive Committee meeting in August 1954.

The importance and effectiveness of your work in promoting increased awareness and knowledge of international developments among the churches of the world has been notable. It is only in a society aroused to the great need in which more than half of mankind lives that effective means to meet this need can be mobilized. . . . Your immediate interest in this work of sharing skills and your active support of our efforts were a source of great encouragement in the often difficult and cautious first years of the Programme. . . . It is a source of great gratification to know that we can continue to look to the World Council of Churches for its help in mobilizing this support.[52]

The year after the Evanston Assembly, both the CCIA Executive Committee and the Central Committee devoted great attention to development. The Main Theme of the 1955 Central Committee meeting was 'The Implications of Christian Unity for Inter-Church Aid and for Assistance to Under-developed Countries'. Primarily it discussed direct aid by the World Council, though in the broader context it described the critical state of the peoples of the under-developed world.[53] The CCIA Executive was addressed by Professor de Vries, who indicated that a great amount of capital would be needed from the rich nations in order to achieve only a modest increase in the standard of living of the poorer. If these standards did not rise in a generation, he prophesied, the peoples of the under-developed world would lose interest in the democratic experiment and turn to authoritarian alternatives. Although United States bilateral programmes were beneficial, he continued, they were too closely related to American political requirements. The churches should help to guide some development capital to the social sector for the building of schools, hospitals, and other non-profit making but necessary social institutions.[54] The Committee did pass a resolution offering specific suggestions to both donor and recipient states.[55]

In 1955, after several years of preliminary discussions, the General Assembly approved plans for the International Finance Corporation (IFC), which came into being the following year with the required number of states becoming members. The under-developed states had wanted an institution that would grant low-interest loans or outright grants; they were given an affiliate of the World Bank, which was to make investments in private enterprises with government guarantees. In spite of the limited scope of the IFC, the CCIA welcomed it as one more source of development aid. The CCIA continued, however, to urge less stringent means of financing development, a development based on an overall strategy.

The CCIA continued its co-operation with the FAO, but no great projects were undertaken together. UNESCO also partook of the Expanded Programme and a working relationship was maintained by the CCIA with that organization. The UNESCO literacy programme was an area where the World Council was knowledgeable through the churches' and mission societies' activities with the vernacular in schools. The rapid social change study (see below), in which the CCIA co-operated, complemented a UNESCO study on 'Social Development in Areas of Rapid Technological Change and Industrialization'.

In 1956 the United Nations EPTA worked out a more co-ordinated and co-operative means of allocating funds to governments requesting assistance (which, in formulating their requests, would have the help of a TAB Resident Representative). This could hardly be construed as an international development programme, and it was just such a 'worldwide strategy of development' which the CCIA Executive Committee meeting in July 1956 urged upon the world. The statement went further in committing the World Council to supporting specific projects than it had previously done. Even so, the Committee expressed 'interest in the organization of sound international financial assistance' without committing themselves or the World Council to any of the various proposals. This was undoubtedly because of the controversial SUNFED, strongly opposed by the developed states led by the United States, who would be the principal contributor, and as fervently supported by the developing states. In fact, the assiduousness of the CCIA representatives in their activities with United Nations and governmental officials may have been vitiated by their vague stand on development in the early 1950s.

The mandate given to the CCIA officials by the Executive Committee statement was that 'A serious effort should be made to provide a mutually acceptable and effective international fund for grants-in-aid and long-term low-interest loans, establish basic structures for economic development, whether through the SUNFED proposal or a better alternative'. In a letter to the Economic Committee of the General Assembly, the Director and Executive Secretary of the CCIA urged positive action, whether SUNFED or the 'better alternative'.[56]

Partly due to CCIA arguments and partly due to representation by the American churches, the American delegation to the Twelfth General Assembly proposed a Special Projects Fund. This became the United Nations Special Fund, authorized in 1958 and officially established the following January. Although not the cornucopia envisaged by the Third World and the CCIA, the Special Fund became primarily a pre-investment fund, designed to provide pilot projects and economic surveys to encourage large development schemes financed by other means.

CCIA officers supported a Canadian-Norwegian proposal at the Eleventh General Assembly for an annual statistical survey of all aid programmes, both multilateral and bilateral, because it was 'a promising first step in the direction of a more responsible strategy for economic and social development'; they were disappointed, however, in that it led no further. The CCIA welcomed the founding of the Economic Commission for Africa in 1958, noting that it had made available to the United Nations Secretariat the experience of missionary leaders on African affairs in preparing for its establishment.

As colonial unrest grew and new states emerged politically independent but still economically dependent, development remained a major problem in international affairs. The Danish Church requested a statement on development for consideration by the Central Committee. CCIA officers drafted, and the CCIA Executive Committee approved, 'Christian Concern in Economic and Social Development', which, as amended, became the 'Nyborg Statement' of the World Council of Churches, a summary of what had been studied, discussed, and agreed upon in ecumenical organizations in regard to economic development. Noting the great disparity between the needs of the poor nations of the South and the abundant resources of the North, the statement called for increasing effort on the part of the industrialized nations; for the first time a specific amount was urged as the necessary minimum effort, an amount which the United Nations was to take up as its goal in economic aid: one per cent of the gross national product. Specific suggestions as to governmental policies were recommended, such as the necessity for balanced plans for development and the co-ordination of bilateral aid programmes. Probably because of the influence of delegates from Western Europe and North America, the 'important role' of private investment was stressed, and it was recommended that 'constructive' investment policies be followed by the receiving countries. This was urged in spite of the fact that the tremendous needs of these areas far exceed the available private capital (according to Dr Raúl Prebisch, world-renowned Argentine economist), the mistrust of neo-colonialism by the ex-colonial states, and the preference of private capital for lucrative rather than needed social overhead projects.[57] The statement also addressed itself to the tasks the churches themselves could carry out. These were primarily seen as the shaping of attitudes in the developed countries and in reviewing the technical contributions of the Christian institutions in the light of national development programmes.[58]

In addition to providing an educational function for the Christian constituency, such statements also provide the authority for representations by WCC officials to governments and international organizations. The clear call for increased support of aid programmes was stressed by CCIA officers in their contacts with governments, especially with governments of countries where the Christian churches were a powerful political force, and in contacts with national committees of the CCIA. International officials were also approached; Mr Paul Hoffman, Managing Director of the United Nations Special Fund, discussed with CCIA officials the needs of the Fund.

Non-governmental organizations do not press the inter-governmental ones to act more quickly, though where the latter want to act, the support of the former often gives added morale. For eight years the importance of stable primary commodity prices had been discussed in the General Assembly. The importance of this as a factor in international development was noted by the CCIA in 1956 and in the Nyborg Statement. Continual representations on the principle of stable prices, though not on the technical proposals to implement it, had been made by CCIA officers. In the Thirteenth General Assembly, a resolution urging that member states take notice of any harmful effects of their trade policies on the economies of developing countries was passed. Although no resolution so bold as the establishing of a co-ordinating body for development was proposed, one resolution of the Thirteenth Session did call for member states to plan 'their future courses of co-operative action' in the economic development of the less developed. The following year the General Assembly requested ECOSOC to report on means of stabilizing commodity markets.

The Secretary-General's report on speeding economic growth drew attention to the slowness of progress. In their contacts with governmental representatives CCIA officials stressed the need for a greater assistance effort if the struggle for development were to succeed. The first assembly of the East Asia Christian Conference (which met at Kuala Lumpur, Malaya, from 14 to 24 May 1959), also called attention to the great amount of capital urgently needed, in its report 'The Witness of the Churches Amidst Social Change in Asia'. The Commission of the assembly which prepared this report consisted of fifty members, many of them lay specialists in the fields of economics, politics, sociology, and other disciplines. Paying respect to the Nyborg Statement of the Central Committee, it nevertheless viewed Asian economic development from the viewpoint of those actively engaged in the travail and not of those merely academically interested. Seeming almost a riposte to the Nyborg praises for private investment and to United Nations debates where the role of private capital in development projects was annually extolled, a 'fundamental point' clearly stated that government planning of economic development was necessary and reliance on private investment was impractical.

Land reform, which appeared periodically on United Nations agendas, with no concrete results, loomed large in importance to these Asians, who regarded it as a pressing necessity if agriculture were to develop sufficiently. The indispensability of increased agricultural production was recognized, but so were the difficulties attendant thereon. In addition to simply increasing production, community development—with its concept of balanced growth and reform—was also urged; reform of the social fabric was acknowledged as necessary, but with gentle moulding and patching rather than a rendering asunder. The churches must become involved in the whole development process, these Asian Christians averred, infusing it with distinctive Christian insights and thereby forming it into new patterns.[59]

The CCIA Executive Committee meeting in August took note of the points raised by the Conference, but offered no suggestions for implementation. It also 'noted with appreciation the ECOSOC appraisal of UN programmes for the following five-year period'. It was 'gratified to note' that the Secretary-General emphasized in his latest report some concerns which had long been expressed in ecumenical statements, especially demographic pressures, stress on balanced approaches to economic development, and the need for a concerted effort for economic development through international channels.[60]

In September 1959 the governors of the World Bank decided to establish the International Development Association (IDA), as an affiliate of the Bank; it came into existence in 1960. It was to provide loans with low interest for fifty-year periods. The less developed countries were happy to see it, but still did not want it to take the place of a UN capital development fund. The United States, the principal financial supplier of all agencies, did not oppose the fund, but considered that there were not sufficient international resources at this time to begin still another one. The CCIA welcomed the establishment of the IDA as filling a great need; at the same time it urged the usefulness of a capital development fund.

The General Assembly passed a resolution on Concerted Action for Economic Development of Economically Less Developed Countries in December 1960. The resolution reiterated the duty of the UN to accelerate economic development; recognized the need for diversification and development of economic activity, including industrialization; urged increasing the provision of private and public capital; and called for recommendations to solve commodity trade problems. At the same meeting the Soviet Union proposed a

'Declaration on International Economic Co-operation', designed to extend the UN Charter provisions for economic co-operation into a solemn undertaking by states to abide by specific standards in their international economic dealings. The Western powers were opposed to such a Declaration, and action was averted by voting to have the ECOSOC consider it.

The CCIA Executive Committee meeting in August 1960 had a lengthy discussion on food, population, and development, covering the ground so often covered before. The Committee approved participation by the World Council through DICASR in the Freedom from Hunger campaign of the Food and Agriculture Organization. The continent of Africa, where the churches had long 'laboured in the vineyard of the Lord', was the subject of some discussion. The gaining of independence brought new problems to many African states. The former colonial governments, it was stated, had the duty to assist their former wards with the capital and technical assistance needed to develop complete independence. Giving aid through United Nations agencies was particularly recommended as a means to insure that these new states would be free of political domination through economic means.[61] Africa was also a subject of United Nations attention the following year. 'Africa, a United Nations Programme for Independence and Development' was a General Assembly agenda item proposed by the United States. Provision was made by the General Assembly for the creation of a programming institute within the Economic Commission for Africa to aid in an overall development plan. The ECA and UNESCO sponsored an African Conference on Development of Education to work out a long-range education plan for that continent.

If activity is equated with accomplishment, 1961 was a fruitful year for those in the United Nations concerned with economic development. The General Assembly requested the Secretary-General to create an Economic Projections and Programming Centre within the Secretariat to aid in economic development planning. The Committee for Industrial Development created the previous year met for the first time in March 1961. Although the United States, the United Kingdom and others opposed an Industrial Development Centre, a proposal for its study was passed and led to its eventual establishment. A great deal of discussion took place on the proposed United Nations capital development fund. Opposed by France, the United States, and the United Kingdom it refused to expire and the life of a committee studying it was prolonged.

In November of this same busy year the full Commission of the Churches on International Affairs met at Bangalore, India, prior to the New Delhi Assembly, and considered in detail once

177

more the elements of a strategy of development. Basically what emerged was a restatement of all the ideas previously expressed on development through the World Council as regards the responsibilities of governments, international organizations, and the churches.[62] Considering this report and others presented to it, the Assembly's Section on Service reiterated in more concise terms the major points made.[63]

In its 'Appeal to All Governments and Peoples', the Assembly expressed its concern for the many issues causing world tension. It devoted one paragraph to the need for development.

There is a great opportunity for constructive action in the struggle for world development. To share the benefits of civilization with the whole of humanity is a noble and attainable objective. To press the war against poverty, disease, exploitation, and ignorance calls for greater sacrifice and for a far greater commitment of scientific, educational, and material resources than hitherto. In this common task, let the peoples find a positive programme for peace, a moral equivalent for war.[64]

The churches were not the only bodies considering the goal of economic development that December. The General Assembly adopted on 19 December 1961 a resolution designating the 1960s as a United Nations Development Decade, as earlier proposed by President John F. Kennedy in a characteristically dramatic gesture. It was hoped that such a programme would catch the imagination of peoples and mobilize and sustain an effort to achieve a minimum annual growth rate of 5 per cent. The resolution required the Secretary-General to develop proposals for integrating the plans for economic development and the aid actually given by states, for eliminating illiteracy, and for promoting education and training. The concern was now widespread; the hopes of the Third World were high.

The CCIA Executive Committee meeting in Paris in August 1962 praised the General Assembly for its action on the Development Decade. It urged the national committees of the CCIA, the churches, and national Christian councils to make representations to their governments for increased help to, and to their peoples for their support of, the Development Decade and its goals. The Committee also commended the Secretary-General for his 'Proposals for Action';[65] Dr Fagley presented a memorandum in which he considered the proposals in relation to the eleven elements of development of the Bangalore Statement.[66] The Secretary-General had noted: (1) the lack of well-founded development plans; (2) a decline of primary commodity prices; (3) the absence of a sustained, assured, and widely distributed flow of capital; (4) the slow growth of agricultural output; and (5) the neglect of the social aspects of economic development. In each of these areas, Dr Fagley considered, the CCIA had definite possibilities to influence inter-

178

national policy. He noted that on several points, for instance, the need for research, price fluctuations of primary commodities, trade among developing countries, and increasing assistance, the Bangalore Statement had more definite suggestions than the Secretary-General.

When it appeared that the pledging conference would not reach the hopes of a large increase in aid for the first year of the Development Decade, Dr Fagley wrote to key figures on the national committees of the CCIA in the developed countries. It was noted the following year that the increases in pledges were primarily from states where the World Council constituency was significant, for example, Canada, Australia, Denmark, Finland, Norway, and the Philippines.[67]

Preparations were carried forward at the United Nations for the launching on 1 January 1963 of a World Food Programme, a three-year experiment of the UN and the FAO to distribute food surpluses to the hungry. Contributions would be in goods, services, or cash. The CCIA saw it as a worthy project but reiterated in informal representations the UN resolution itself that 'food aid is not a substitute for other types of assistance, in particular for capital goods'. In February 1963 the UN Conference on Science and Technology for the Benefit of Less Developed Areas was held. Point five of the Bangalore Statement had stressed the importance of scientific research in helping to relieve certain problems of the under-developed world. CCIA observers attended the conference and welcomed the founding of a UN Training and Research Institute which was proposed there and finally brought to fruition two years later.

The ecumenical meetings of 1963 saw attention still focused on the problems of the third world. The CCIA Executive Committee heard a brief report on the deteriorating economic conditions of the under-developed countries, a report similar to that which the General Assembly was to hear later that year. The Central Committee meeting had as one of its Main Themes 'The Church's Responsibility in the New Societies'. Although the Committee did not discuss specific points of economic development, it heard two addresses, one by an African, Pastor Jean Kotto, and one by a European, Dr Klaus von Bismarck, on the social problems resulting from the economic development of traditional societies.[68]

One cannot always find a cause and effect relationship between ecumenical statements and international action; yet it is at least indicative of the calibre of the CCIA staff that they anticipated so well UN trends and actions. In the Bangalore Statement of 1961 the importance of trade to economic development was stressed; in fact it was the subject of three of the eleven points. This was not some mystical prescience on the part of the CCIA officials, rather an indication that they had done their homework. The figures were there for all to see: in 1950 the trade of the less developed countries was one-third of the world volume, by 1960 this had declined to one-fifth. The terms of trade had declined about 9 per cent for the developing countries. For several years an annual General Assembly agenda item had been the fluctuations of primary commodity prices; in spite of General Assembly resolutions calling on the developed states to remember that their trade and economic policies affected the economies of the less developed, no one really paid much attention to the deleterious effects, except those adversely affected. Growing unrest on the part of the developing states, because they were in fact not 'developing', led to the acquiescence of the industrial countries to the calling of a United Nations Conference on Trade and Development (UNCTAD), which was finally convened in Geneva from March to June 1964. The purpose of the Conference was to find a new policy for trade to make it truly an instrument of development; the decline in terms of trade mentioned above, for example, meant that one-third of the aid given during the Fifties had to be used to make up for this loss of revenue.

Dr O. Frederick Nolde led the CCIA observers at UNCTAD, and he sent to each of the 119 delegations the statements of the CCIA and World Council on economic development. After the Conference he presented to the CCIA Executive Committee a report of its activities. In a statement, the Committee deplored the unfair terms of world trade and authorized the CCIA officers to seek the co-operation of national commissions and churches in harmonizing trade policies.[69] When the CCIA Executive Committee met in 1965 it had digested the full reports of UNCTAD, and it discussed at great length the trade relationships between the rich and the poor. Dr Leslie Cooke, speaking from his experience with Inter-Church Aid, considered it the duty of the richer to help the poorer nations, as in a national community the stronger sectors feel responsibility for the weaker. Since the Christian churches transcended national borders they could be mobilized, he felt, to bring this feeling of international community into being. Dr Patijn of the Netherlands pointed out the clash of philosophies between the developed and the developing worlds; he considered that it was the moral appraisal of these conflicting attitudes with which the churches had to concern themselves and not economic factors.

This is the crux of an important issue in the ecumenical movement: the contention that it is the duty of the churches to consider the moral aspects of a viewpoint on a technical issue without considering or knowing anything about the technicalities. Dr Nolde, in the covering letter to the delegates to the UNCTAD, wrote that 'the technical aspects of the Conference lie outside the competence of church agencies. But the great human issues of co-operation, justice and welfare underlying the technical problems are matters of very real concern.' [70] One hopes this was merely a case of false modesty. For if it is true that a technical matter is outside the competence of the CCIA, then it, the World Council of Churches, and all the Christian churches carefully hedge the efficacy of the condemnation of a particular action as immoral. Reticence to condemn or to guide because of doubt about capacity to understand an economic, financial, or trade policy might bring greater suffering upon those groups without voices which the World Council considered to be among its primary constituency.

Because the churches had no experts in economics during the heyday of laissez-faire capitalism, they could not criticize particular capitalist practices, or, if they did condemn, the 'experts' could, and did, say that the particular condemned practice was due to inexorable economic laws. In both cases the evils grew. Karl Marx and his followers, too, had moral pretensions, and they developed the technical capacity, that is they steeped themselves in economics and politics in order to fight the evils of industrialization. In so doing the Communist Party gained the allegiance of masses of the world's workers; Marx and his followers considered that the churches' excuse of lack of expertise was a weak excuse, that the clergy sat too comfortably on the lap of the industrial bourgeoisie. Socialists in England founded institutions such as the London School of Economics to give to the working class the technical expertise to enable them to fight at the bargaining table with the same economic jargon as their employers' officials. If the Church bows before the altar of expertise—and this is a sign of our secular times—it has nothing on which to base its moral judgement. It must seek out the experts on international trade (and on every other problem of concern to it) in order to give advice on the morality of a particular issue and of the alternative solutions to it. Indeed, the Commissioners of the CCIA were selected in part for their expertise in international affairs, though no attempt was made to ensure that there would be specialists in every phase of World Council interest. As indicated in the discussion of the organizational aspect of the CCIA, proper use was never made of the Commissioners nor of their specialized knowledge.

When the churches are told that their ignorance of economics invalidates their moral judgement it leaves their mouths agape; if they are told they are wrong about their economic solution to a specific problem it leaves their experts room to marshal data for a refutation, or, in Christian humility, for a reconsideration of the proffered solution and a look at its alternatives. There was some controversy within the World Council on this issue, too. Bishop Leaslie Newbigin told Dr Visser 't Hooft that he thought the CCIA should formulate the key issues confronting UNCTAD, for which the churches could press their governments to act.[71] Alan Booth, on the other hand, feared that the churches might go beyond their competence in their efforts to provide detailed solutions.[72]

After the discussion of the problems of international trade and development, the Executive Committee adopted the statement 'Trade and Development' in which it welcomed the establishment of UNCTAD as a permanent agency of the United Nations General Assembly. 'Without claiming competence on the more technical aspects', the Executive Committee urged specific reforms on the developed states' trade patterns to help the development of the Third World.[73] These suggestions were welcomed by Dr Raúl Prebisch speaking for UNCTAD.[74]

The UNCTAD Bureau (secretariat) was established in Geneva; the Conference itself was to meet every three years, and a United Nations Trade and Development Board (UNTDB) consisting of fifty-five members would meet between UNCTAD sessions. The question arose as to whether the CCIA should seek consultative status with UNCTAD. The UNTDB had talked of limiting such status to technical bodies, but since the Holy See was a member of UNCTAD, Dr Fagley felt that the CCIA should have consultative status.[75] The Bureau prepared a paper citing three criteria to be applied to a non-governmental organization seeking such status: it should (1) be concerned with trade, or (2) be able to provide information to UNCTAD, or (3) represent important elements of public opinion. In an interview with Raúl Prebisch, Director General of UNCTAD, Drs Nolde and Fagley and the Reverend Elfan Rees sought and were promised a good working relationship with UNCTAD. The CCIA officers stated they did not need consultative status in order to co-operate unless such status would be helpful to UNCTAD. It was noted, however, that as long as the Holy See was a member of UNCTAD, a refusal of status, if requested, would lead to political repercussions in Protestant countries.[76] It was later granted, but CCIA resources remained at a minimum, and it could not do justice to its duties to all the organizations with which it had consultative status.

It might be appropriate at this point to note the extent to which lack of proper financing is responsible for the WCC's use of amateur methods in international affairs; true, since World War II there has been increased professionalism, but, due to paucity of resources, it has been limited. A prime example of this is the degree to which the World Council and the CCIA have depended on non-professional representation at technical international conferences. At the second United Nations Conference on Trade and Development, held at New Delhi in 1968, the CCIA, lacking funds to pay the not inconsiderable air fare and expenses of its own officers or retain technical experts, selected individuals on the basis of proximity to the meeting. Dr Blake suggested that this did not provide adequate World Council representation. This became all the more noticeable as the Holy See had 'a pretty substantial presence' scheduled for that Conference.[77] Although the final delegation may have been of high quality, the question remains as to the effectiveness of *ad hoc* participation in a technical organization, a matter forcefully noted by CCIA officials at UNCTAD I. Although bureaucracy has a pejorative connotation in many circles, the modern complex organization of society, indeed of the business enterprises within it, would not be possible without a bureaucracy. The churches should not fear to create such an organization where it is called for in their best interests and in the interests of those they wish to serve. Admittedly the difficulty comes when the central organization must plead for funds, not having a regular Peter's pence (Wim Visser 't Hooft's gulden?) to rely upon.

In 1965 the EPTA and the Special Fund were reorganized into the United Nations Development Programme (UNDP), an effort to attain a more integrated strategy—though one must still look at the proliferation of agencies and committees all devoted to some aspect of economic development and wonder at the lack of an overall co-ordinating body. That same year the World Food Programme ended its three-year experiment and was established on a permanent basis. The following year saw a deterioration in the level of exports of the less developed countries; a report by the Secretary-General on the Development Decade saw 'no significant impact made on international actions by principles of the Development Decade'. In 1966 the World Conference on Church and Society, sponsored by the World Council of Churches, took place. Economic development played a significant part in its deliberations, but since it was a continuation of a study project of the World Council the result is considered below in the section on the rapid social change study (see below, pp. 212-13).

The CCIA Executive Committee met immediately after the Church and Society conference and discussed development in some detail—especially its human aspects, which it felt the Conference had largely ignored. The Committee approved the Statement 'Human Aspects of Development', which deserves to follow the Bangalore Statement in importance for its precise and comprehensive consideration of the largely neglected human aspects of the problem. Asserting that economics was not an amoral discipline but one with a duty to consider the effects of economic policies on human beings, the statement called for expenditures and planning for human beings in economic development by way of literacy campaigns, social reforms, food programmes, and the like.[78] In addition to issuing the statement, the CCIA Executive Committee judged it necessary to submit a memorandum on 'The World Council of Churches' Approach to the Problems of Economic Development' to the World Council Executive Committee, in which it summarized World Council activities to date and recommended that certain clarifications be undertaken. It emphasized the direct role of the churches through the World Council and the various Christian agencies in economic development, criticizing certain aspects of it (see above p. 159). Regarding public economic development, the churches, themselves a world community, must find a means of creating a world economic community in which the willing co-operation of the rich and the poor would overcome the ever-increasing chasm between them. The planners and developers must be made to realize, it continued, that their plans and developments are for the benefit of people and not the people for the benefit of their plans. It urged that the Uppsala Assembly give full consideration to the issues of social and economic justice. This latter wish was amply fulfilled at Uppsala.

The year 1967 saw an increasing population coupled with poor crops threaten famine. The World Council Executive Committee meeting in Windsor Castle in February of that year called the attention of the world to the diminishing food supplies, urging the creation of food reserves. The CCIA Executive Committee meeting the following August heard a report by Dr Fagley on the food problem, but it made no recommendations to the Central Committee which met immediately thereafter. Dr Fagley presented a summary of the sombre food situation and the ever-threatening famine that hung over the under-developed world. While he pointed out the many tasks which the Church through Christian agencies could carry out and a paper by Dr Heinrich Puffert of DICARWS gave examples of what the churches had done, it was recognized that the only true solution lay in large-scale programmes by governments. However, the churches, he stated, could help in this matter by shaping public opinion and influencing the decisions of governments.[79] The Committee adopted a statement on the food gap in which it spoke of its confidence that technology could solve the problem. It supported the World Food Programme and FAO's Freedom from Hunger Campaign, urging the continued co-operation of member churches. It called for family planning and a diversion of military expenditures as a solution of the food problem. It requested sacrifices by all peoples to assure the resources needed for the economic development of the poorer nations.[80]

In the spring of 1967 the public interest of the Roman Catholic Church in economic development was witnessed by the issuance of the encyclical *Populorum Progressio*. Under its authority the Pontifical Commission on Justice and Peace was established.

Dr Fagley, who was in Rome for consultations with officials of the FAO on the growing food crisis, made informal contact with members of the Commission during its first meeting in April. In June official exploratory talks considered the possibilities of joint or parallel action by the Pontifical Commission and the World Council in the field of development. Since the wheels of ecclesiastical bureaucracy built for eternity normally grind slowly it can only be described as a miracle that by 21 April 1968 a joint group, the Exploratory Committee on Society, Development and Peace (whose acronym SODEPAX conjures up a *spumante*) existed and had convened the Conference on World Co-operation for Development in Beirut.

The majority of the participants were laymen with competence in the field of economic development. Fifteen were observer-consultants from intergovernmental bodies. (Two were Moslem participants from the host country.) The co-chairmen were Dr Jan Tinbergen, Chairman of the United Nations Development Planning Committee and Dutch Protestant, and Dr B. T. G. Chidzero, United Nations Resident Representative in Kenya and prominent Catholic layman. Although the report of the conference went through several editings by both sides, it does not represent a unanimous view on any point. It provides, however, a general consensus on economic development by competent experts, who, at the same time, are dedicated Christians and who offer the report *to* the churches. The churches had requested advice on economic and technical aspects to help them make their own judgements on the doctrinal, moral, and ethical aspects of these issues.

The report of the conference is divided into four principal parts.[81] The first expresses the motivation behind Christian concern for economic development. The second describes the existing situation and need. The third offers a strategy for development to be followed by the states of the world. The fourth makes suggestions for the role the churches can play in this drama. One might describe the basic Christian motivation as a form of humanism, although the report carefully puts this concern in appropriate theological language. One point which gave man a greater responsibility today, theologically or humanely speaking, was that he actually possessed the power to remove the causes of the evil. Behind the immediate concern for economic development was the Christian concern for the full development of the individual personality; freeing man from the slavery of poverty would allow him to develop himself. Change must be recognized and welcomed into the world and not resisted. If violence was the only means to achieve the change required for economic justice, then it was permissible.

Economic conditions in the world were described and the inadequate international programmes noted. Particular obstacles to development were found within the developing countries, e.g., inadequate political structures which allowed special interests to prevail over the common good, blocking economic development. Often it was foreign interests within these countries which hindered appropriate reforms. But, in addition, the advanced countries had too easily become disillusioned with economic aid and its results. Development had not yet become a central concern for them; it could not compete with defence or space for public interest and public funds. The churches must develop a long-term education plan designed to produce new attitudes.

Although the strategy for development proposed was not detailed enough for the development plan of any one state, its breadth of coverage and understanding of technical difficulties indicate the competence of the drafters. Concern covered minimum growth rate, the importance of effecting an agricultural revolution, the provision for an adequate diet, the need for light industrial development suited to local conditions, and, surprisingly, the demographic factor in economic development. The need for education related to the scarcity of technicians and the lack of literacy as well as humanistic education. In this field there was an especially suitable role for the churches, for it was one in which they had long been active. The need for government planning in developing countries was recognized, as well as the need for regional economic groupings and institutions.

The role of the developed countries, in this strategy, was more precisely spelt out. The paucity of their effort was demonstrated by figures; the financial burden of aid which had to be repaid and the use by donor states of bilateral aid to achieve their national interests rather than the development of the recipients was deplored. The churches should support the reassessment of aid policy by the developing states. The particularly bad terms of trade offered to the developing states, and their need for some protection from fluctuating prices were emphasized. A paragraph which seemed rather out of place encouraged the use of private investment for international development. It urged the churches to support an international centre to which international investors and governments could voluntarily bring disputes for conciliation or arbitration. 'The churches should support this and other initiatives to extend the influence of law and contracts in international economic relations.'[82] Yet it is exactly the law of contracts of developed states that has denied—on the basis of law—economic justice to these states. It was these laws which took the control of a state's resources away from the people of a state or gave outrageously low returns for them, which were accepted due to ignorance or bribed officials.

The role of the churches, the report continued, is in education, in political action, and in creating more effective organization.

Education must be on an ecumenical basis, the collaboration of all Christian communions, and, where possible, inter-religious collaboration. To be successful, political action to commit governments to policies of development must be fully ecumenical, as well as be based upon local patterns of political action. The churches must create more effective structures for action. The Catholics have set up national Commissions for Justice and Peace; the national councils of churches in many cases already have national committees of the churches on international affairs. Close liaison between these confessional agencies should be established. The commissions should include lay experts or should arrange for outside consultation. To be an example, the churches themselves should be willing to devote more of their own resources to economic development. The vast number of Christian agencies in the field should also be co-ordinated by appropriate bodies created for this purpose.

While some nations laboured for the benefit of all mankind, other groups continued working for their own selfish interests. While terms of trade for the less developed continued to fall, the major trading nations seemed more interested in improving the conditions of trade among themselves in the 'Kennedy Round' of GATT talks which lasted into 1967. These same states inadequately prepared themselves for the negotiations of the Second UN Conference on Trade and Development held in February and March of 1968. Meeting at the mid-point of the Conference, the World Council of Churches Executive Committee issued from Geneva an admonishment to the developed states to act with a far-seeing selflessness—which they did not possess—and to the developing states to draw in their belts and look at closer horizons. Unrealistic Christian counsel was ignored, and the lack of results was unsatisfactory to all.

The CCIA met at Kungalv, Sweden, from 24 to 28 July 1968, prior to the Uppsala Assembly; its members commented in generally favourable terms upon the SODEPAX meeting in Beirut. Although papers analysing the economic development and world food situations were presented, no moves of great import were taken pending major action by the Assembly itself. In addition, a jurisdictional dispute regarding preparation of the topic of economic development for the Assembly had to a great extent been won by the Department on Church and Society.

The importance which the churches attach to this problem in world affairs is indicated by the extent to which it dominated the Assembly's thought at Uppsala. Contrast this with the two paragraphs given to it in the Amsterdam Report. Section III was devoted entirely to 'World Economic and Social Development'; Section IV, 'Towards Justice and Peace in International Affairs', reported, among other things, on development and world order; and Section VI, 'Towards New Styles of Living', touched directly if fleetingly on the unjust disparity between the rich and the poor nations. Further, the Assembly had invited the head of state of an under-developed country to speak on economic development. In his address, President Kenneth Kaunda of Zambia noted that the 'Decade of Impatience has become the Decade of Disappointment and Disillusionment. . . . The Church is called', he urged 'to be an instrument of peace and development; its involvement in economic and social problems is a moral issue.'[83] As a result of all this study and stimulation the Message of the Assembly also devoted some thoughts to this topic. But this emphasis should not be surprising now that the Church has publicly dedicated itself to this world and the care of those in it.

Dr J. M. Lochman, of the Evangelical Church of the Czech Brethren and Chairman of Section Three, in introducing the discussion of his report on 'World Economic and Social Development' before the Assembly declared, 'This is issue number one which the world provides for our agenda.'[84] Indeed, most students of international affairs today regard the economic development of the Third World as the most momentous problem of international relations in our time. In spite of the pressure of an agenda, the original draft report of Section III was considerably revised during discussion in plenary session, at which a report is normally accepted, and it was voted to send it back for redrafting and reconsideration at a hearing at which members of other sections might give their views on the subject. This action was taken to eliminate a bland 'balanced' statement and to sharpen the focus on the responsibility of those who control 'the riches and the economic and political structures of the world today', and to 'call in undeniably clear terms for a change of direction on the part of the western nations . . .'[85]

Dr Lochman described the necessity for a theology of development, and stated that this was not dealt with adequately in the report. The idea of a theology of anything often distresses many secular-minded people. It should be pointed out, however, that this is the justification for an action which any group attempts logically to set out for itself on the basis of its long-held values. Just as a conservative, liberal, or socialist party may each support social security, a public health service, or other social service for reasons which will appeal to its own constituency, so Christians, too, wish to find a rationale for their actions on the basis of their values and beliefs.

For greater detail in analysis and specific measures to promote development, the report of Section III recommended the report of the World Conference on Church and Society, as well as in a truly ecumenical fervour the encyclical *Populorum Progressio* and the report of the Sodepax Conference. Noting the disappointments and frustrations experienced in the Decade of Development, the Section found that the fault lay in the failure radically to change institutions and structures in the developing countries, in the developed countries, and in the international economy. The resources of the developing countries must not be monopolized by ruling élites. Revolutionary measures were needed, and while revolution need not be equated with violence, if violence were the only way then the churches could not condemn it. It further urged changes on governments in both the poor and the rich states. The churches could take political action, educational measures for their own constituencies, and could work with men of all religions and of none. The reports of Sections IV and VI as well as this one reiterated many of the recommendations made by other World Council organs at different times.[86]

It was in the Message itself that advice on development sounded strangely, and—many would say—characteristically, naïve and inappropriate. The fair participation of all in the resources of the earth was stressed: 'Therefore, with our fellow-men we accept our trusteeship over creation, guarding, developing and sharing its resources.' In a strange *non sequitur* it described the 'ever widening gap between the rich and the poor' as being 'fostered by armament expenditure'. The resources available to the industrialized states would undoubtedly allow both soaring armaments *and* aid budgets, if the industrialized world so desired. If it does not so desire, then a decrease in armament expenditure would have no meaning in relation to this gap, which could be fostered by indifference, greed, lust for power, but hardly by the cost of armaments. In any case, trade was also oddly coupled with arms: 'We shall work for disarmament and for trade agreements fair to all.' More useful and logical: 'We are ready to tax ourselves in furtherance of a system of world taxation.'[87] However, the good advice and trenchant analysis of the whole Assembly in the realm of economic development outweighs its few bad moments. Most important, the great amount of attention devoted to economic and social development is indicative of the dedication of the Church to the bettering of the conditions of those who otherwise have no advocate in the world.

Efforts since Uppsala have been mainly devoted to the aid dispensed by the churches themselves through the World Council. Perhaps because of the change in leadership of the CCIA, no fruitful or original suggestions came forth at the August 1969 meeting of its Executive Committee. Discussion consisted primarily of a recitation of the latest estimates of population figures and a summary of United Nations activities and plans. It did adopt a statement 'Towards the Second Development Decade', but no new ideas or recommendations were put forward in it.[88] The Central Committee meeting shortly thereafter busied itself with creating more internal organs to deal with development. It authorized an Ecumenical Consultation on Development to be held at Montreux, Switzerland, from 26 to 31 January 1970. The Consultation was attended by United Nations officials and governmental and former governmental advisers as well as non-official secular experts.[89] Its deliberations attracted widespread news coverage in German, Swiss, and British newspapers. A *Guardian* correspondent thought that the churches would make little impact on United Nations development programmes but that they might influence the existing development lobbies in Great Britain, Germany, Scandinavia, and Holland. The editor of the *Frankfurter Allgemeine Zeiting* understood the uniqueness of the churches' contributions because of their closeness to the people, but realized that the greatest development efforts would still have to come from the states themselves.[90]

Discussion at the 1970 meeting of the CCIA Executive Committee developed a more radical tone. Some churchmen at the meeting held that under-development was due to international exploitation by advanced countries using local oligarchies with a vested interest in the maintenance of under-development. An unspecified 'more radical' approach to development on the part of the churches, the states concerned, and the United Nations was urged. Still, the CCIA seemed to be floundering without a policy for development. Indeed, for a time the initiative was seized by SODEPAX. It produced in late 1970 observations on the Pearson Report on International Development (prepared for the Organization for Economic Co-operation and Development), on the FAO's role in development, and on the Report of the Committee for Development Planning of the United Nations; in addition it produced a critique of the resolution 'International Development Strategy' passed by the General Assembly in October 1970 at the beginning of the Second Development Decade.[91] SODEPAX also sponsored regional conferences on the problem of development in divers areas of the Third World.

The Second Development Decade was greeted with economic and monetary crises: an inflationary cycle began in 1970–1 which cut the value of many development programmes. In 1971 the most severe of several monetary crises led to the breakdown of the international monetary system devised at Bretton Woods in 1944. The dollar became inconvertible and was devalued: the value of the large American contribution to world economic development through bilateral arrangements and through donations to the United Nations Development Programme and to that of the churches was thereby reduced. In January 1971, at its Addis

Ababa meeting, the Central Committee issued a statement 'The Role of the Churches in Development'; it welcomed the launching of the Second Development Decade as a sign of hope but it also contained the warning that development depends on the political will to change political, social, and economic structures. It further declared that the church may not stand apart from this effort, for development from a Christian viewpoint is understood to be 'a liberating process enabling persons and communities to realize their full human potential, as purposed by God'. It is still not widely accepted in the developed world that the interrelated goals of development are social justice, self-reliance, and economic growth. There is a need for education to make those of the developing world aware of the need and their responsibility in fulfilling it as well as a need for education to create an indigenous leadership. The churches were encouraged to examine the structures of their national societies critically, ascertaining whether they helped or hindered development, and to motivate Christians to participate in development. They should also offer 'active support' for efforts to change structures that fail to guarantee the poor a fair share in the economic resources of their own country. Further they must make representations to mobilize national resources to benefit the world poor, and mobilize and redeploy the churches' own resources to that end. The statement ended with the following words:

Nothing short of universal, sustained and sacrificial action by all peoples will do. The Christian communities throughout the world need to play an active role in this universal venture. The vision that beckons the churches to move forward in the concern for development is the vision of the one human family, all of whose members have opportunity to live truly human lives and so as men to respond to the purposes of God.[92]

UNCTAD III met at Santiago, Chile, from 13 April to 21 May 1972. The developing states were particularly incensed at the inflation which they felt the developed countries had exported to them. Their commodity prices did not begin to rise until after mid-1972, and they were feeling the pinch of producing more in order to buy less. The World Council was represented at this conference by Dr Marion Gallis, a German economist working with the CCPD. It was a meeting which, according to the *Economist,* achieved little except ill will.[93] Even Mr Manuel Perez-Guerrero, Secretary-General of UNCTAD, stated that the conference 'had not spurred development efforts as it should have because of the attitude of major industrial and trading states'.

In the report year 1972–3, the United Nations Development Programme achieved part of the goal enunciated by the CCIA in 1953, two decades earlier. It began a country-oriented approach with five-year estimates of the funds available for development.

Planning would be for the development of a country as a whole, and where planning was needed for two or more states together, inter-country plans would be made. The Central Committee meeting in 1973, busily occupied with planning the Ecumenical Development Co-operative Society, did not consider intergovernmental development efforts.

Upon a proposal by President Houari Boumédienne of Algeria, a Special Session of the General Assembly was called from 9 April to 2 May 1974 on the problems of 'raw materials and development'. The two main resolutions emanating from this meeting were a Declaration on the Establishment of a New International Economic Order and a Programme of Action on the Establishment of a New International Economic Order. The changing of existing political and economic structures is a topic dear to the heart of the World Council; in fact, one could say that since the beginning of the Programme to Combat Racism there has been in many of the reports a persistent call for alteration of these structures, internally within states and within the international order itself. The Declaration called for this new economic order 'based on equity, sovereign equality, interdependence, common interest and co-operation among all States, . . . which shall correct inequalities and redress existing injustices . . .' [94] The Programme of Action provided greater detail on how to achieve the new economic order.

The CCIA Executive Committee meeting from 29 July to 2 August 1974, following the Special Assembly, gave a prominent place on its agenda to the Assembly resolutions, especially that on change of the international economic order. Relevant background documents by CCIA Commissioners and staff were circulated. All viewpoints supported the need for change of the existing system. Mr Hulugalle, Chief of the Tropical Product Section, UNCTAD, spoke to the Committee also asserting the necessity for change. He saw the churches' role as being to increase the awareness of the affluent world to the needs of the poor and to work for change in the policies of the rich states. [95] The results of this discussion were summarized for the Central Committee in a document entitled 'The Economic Threat to Peace'. This document held that the present conjunction of crises in the world—food shortage, possible exhaustion of resources, pollution, political tensions between poor and rich—were the result of disobedient (selfish) human stewardship of the earth. In secular terms, the document continued, it meant that 'through indifference, greed, envy, fear, love of power, and short-sighted stupidity' an unjust economic order has arisen. It contrasted the millions of underfed who were denied human dignity with resources 'lavished on the extravagant and lethal accumulation of weapons of destruction'. It cited the demand for change of the Sixth Special Session of the UN General Assembly, quoting at length from the Declaration and the Programme of Action. Though generally endorsing both, the Committee members did not accept the latter uncritically, for it could not fully endorse the 'steadily accelerating economic growth' called for by the General Assembly. The Committee's understanding of development was 'progress towards a just and humanly satisfying social system, appropriate to the needs and aspirations of each developing country, and not crudely as growth only in Gross National Product'. It condemned the over-consumption of resources especially in the waste so evident in the developed world. It cited with approval some of the principles of the Declaration which would bring about the 'establishment of a new, just alternative system'. Finally, it appealed to the member churches 'and to all people of goodwill' to urge their governments to support initiatives that would change international economic structures.[96]

At the 1974 Central Committee meeting the CCIA document, with a CCPD report dramatically setting forth disparities between food production and consumption, was considered. The CCPD document devoted a section to the role of the churches in which it emphasized their dedication to change of the international economic structure. It indicated roles at three levels: the international, the local, and the Christian parish level. At the international level, the churches would have to react to emergencies such as famine while working for fundamental changes in the system. At the local level they must help the poor to become aware of their situation and of the means to correct it. 'Social justice, self-reliance and people's participation are emerging as true pillars of development and must therefore be basic to the work of the churches in fostering social change.'[97] Among their own constituents the churches must undertake an educational task to make acceptable the retrenchment in living standards which may become necessary. 'Church people must come to see that the dominant world-wide economic system is as great a threat to human justice and survival as are . . . population explosion and hunger, real as these are.' The Central Committee accepted the two papers and agreed to give the widest publicity to their contents so that Christians might seek ways of effecting the political will for change.[98]

The Central Committee in 1974 also called upon its member churches to bring the contents of the CCIA and CCPD documents to the attention of their governments preparing for the United Nations World Food Conference, to be held in Rome; the staff of Unit II on Justice and Service was asked to prepare critical reviews of government proposals for the conference. The WCC co-operated with more than 100 non-governmental organizations at the Rome Conference, held from 5 to 16 November 1974, which had the responsibility of resolving the world food problem! The con-

193

N

ference called for four major initiatives: the creation of a World Food Council to co-ordinate the activities of all international agencies in the agricultural field; the creation of an international fund for agricultural development; the creation of nationally held cereal reserves as 'world food security'; commitment by the richer states to provide a three-year guarantee of food-aid commodities.

On the withdrawal of extensive Vatican support from SODE-PAX in mid-1972, most of the development work of the ecumenical movement fell on the newly created CCPD, with the CCIA acting as intermediary in relations with intergovernmental organizations. The greater part of international development work and strategy is conducted by the United Nations through the UNDP and the Specialized Agencies. In spite of the importance the churches attach to development, the New York office of the CCIA will continue to be manned by one officer. After Dr Fagley's retirement at the end of 1975 the post remained vacant throughout 1976, awaiting an appropriate Third-World candidate.

The World Council's CCIA officers acted as a voice for the poor of the world before they had their own political voices. The CCIA urged a comprehensive world-wide development plan long before the colonial empires disintegrated and the new developing states were able to urge the same thing, though it must be admitted that neither the World Council nor the developing states nor the more far-seeing economists of the developed world have been able to achieve this goal because of the self-interest which piecemeal bilateral or multilateral grants serve.

The World Council urged the general goal of economic and social justice in the world, with the responsibility of the richer, and therefore the stronger, to bring this about, again to no avail. Since 1970, its demands have become more radical, not only in the matter of economic development but also in its Programme to Combat Racism, as it has begun to call for a change in international power structures—a shift of power from the rich to the poor, from the strong to the weak. Its richer constituency does not yet realize the import of this change . . . or refuses for the moment to understand the implication for its own comfort and well-being.

Responsible Parenthood

No discussion of World Council activities in the realm of development of the Third World would be complete without recording the unique role played by the CCIA and one of its officers in particular, Dr Richard F. Fagley, in the field of population control. The function was unique because a greater semblance of Protestant-Orthodox consensus on the issue of family planning was achieved than ever before; and this was due primarily to the efforts of this one man, continually prodding—sometimes goading—ecclesiastics into taking a stand.

As Dr Fagley pointed out in his book,[99] there was no mention of the population problem in the *Aims* of the CCIA nor in the founding documents of the World Council. Few realized in 1945 that overpopulation had already become the major problem of the century; indeed, man had just finished great slaughtering of his own kind and was most worried about a depleted population. But by 1952 some prophetic voices were beginning to be heard in the world and in the ecumenical movement. At the CCIA Enlarged Executive Committee meeting held that year, the issue was first raised in a discussion on the 'Statement of Christian Concerns in Regard to Food and Agriculture'. A delegate from the United States broached the subject and he was quickly seconded by Dr E. C. Bhatty of India, who indicated that this was a problem of great concern to the developing world. A final point was added to the Statement: 'Educational measures should be undertaken to raise the quality of family life and reduce the pressure of population.'[100] In addition the Executive proposed that 'an agency of the ecumenical movement should consider problems of family limitation or planned parenthood with reference to questions of governmental policy'. This represented the first definite step, and therefore a bold one, for an ecumenical agency to take, because of the divergent views among the various confessions, especially the Orthodox, on this point.

While Protestants and Orthodox of the developed world could afford to be reserved on the subject, the peoples of Asia and Africa could not, for their population growth constantly outstripped any economic gains they were able to achieve. In December 1952 the Lucknow Ecumenical Study Conference for East Asia discussed economic development and stated, regarding population, 'Many underdeveloped countries, especially in Asia, are very densely populated in relation to their resources. Redistribution of population nationally and internationally, family planning and birth control are burning questions. The profound ethical, political and social issues which they raise need to be courageously examined and guidance should be given by the churches.' [101]

Another representative of the developing world spoke out at the Evanston Assembly for all to hear: Mrs Karefa-Smart of Ghana (then the Gold Coast) accused the churches of inactivity before the needs of Africa, while 'the pressure of an increasing population upon an increasingly unproductive soil' was felt.[102] The problem of overpopulation had not yet become so familiar to all that the Assembly wanted to take action, though Section III on 'The Responsible Society' did note the Lucknow stand on it. In

195

1955, despite Dr Fagley's urging that attention be devoted to the world population problem in relation to economic development, the CCIA Executive Committee included this obtuse paragraph in its resolution on International Assistance Programmes: 'In the interest of more effective assistance, consideration should be given to greater concentration of effort on the more crucial projects, and particularly in those densely populated countries where a rapid acceleration of economic and social development is imperative.' [103] This ambivalence is ameliorated only by Dr Fagley's assurance that CCIA representatives had been less cautious in their conversations with United Nations delegates and officials and other churchmen.[104]

The following year, Dr Fagley's articles, memoranda, and personal contacts began to bear fruit. At the Arnoldshain Conference, which he attended, churchmen of varying nationalities (though all from industrialized, white countries), and, more important, varying denominations, passed a strongly worded resolution: 'In view of the rapidly increasing pressure of population on the means of subsistence and in view of the need for a clearer ecumenical position on the problem of population, we recommend that serious consideration be given to the population problem, *including family planning by the appropriate agency of the World Council of Churches'*.[105] Meeting a week later, the CCIA Executive Committee quoted the Arnoldshain resolution approvingly, and, further emphasizing the urgency of the problem, urged the Central Committee to set up procedures for the study of the theological and ethical issues of family planning. The Central Committee meeting shortly thereafter 'received' a resolution introduced by Sir Kenneth Grubb on the CCIA view of the urgency of the population problem and requesting Central Committee support in studying it,[106] but took no further action. However, the First Assembly of the East Asia Christian Conference convened in Kuala Lumpur in May 1959, on the continent where the population was indeed exploding, recognized the seriousness of the problem while acknowledging that some of the churches did not wish to discuss it. It preferred limitation of births by contraception rather than abortion and affirmed that the decision to limit the size of the family belonged to the husband and wife alone.[107] Two months later the Thessalonica Conference, where for the first time at an ecumenical meeting the number of participants from the Third World equalled those from the developed, also took cognizance of the problem.[108]

The most important ecumenical meeting that year for future policy was, however, a small study group called together at Mansfield College, Oxford, by Dr Norman Goodall in his capacity as secretary of the Joint Committee. The convening of the study group was in no small measure due to Dr Fagley's persistent efforts. Although representative of several disciplines, confessions, and even of the younger churches, it was only an exploratory group intending to lay the groundwork for future, and perhaps more official, consultations. No little consternation was caused when the *New York Times* identified this small group as 'a world-wide Protestant conference . . . to develop a common attitude toward birth control . . . ', and this under the headline 'Protestants Act on Birth Control—World Parley is Convoked to Define Attitude'.[109] The concept of 'responsible parenthood' as the more positive formulation of family planning or birth control was conceived by this group.[110]

The present book has so far focused entirely on *ecumenical* actions and thought on this issue. Social scientists and economists concerned with economic development were also, of course, becoming more familiar with it as a world-wide problem. More and more studies on it began to appear.[111] The United Nations and most Western governments remained coolly detached from this pressing international issue, due primarily to Roman Catholic pressure or feared Roman Catholic pressure in individual countries and to the governments of Roman Catholic countries at the United Nations. The United Nations *Special Report on World Population Trends*, issued on 29 June 1958, told, for the first time in that organization, of the danger of continued population growth. The alternative to a decline in births, it boldly stated, was a rise in mortality.

The CCIA Executive Committee, meeting in August 1959, welcomed the Mansfield College Report and urged that 'appropriate ecumenical agencies might give careful consideration to the suggestions'. In authorizing CCIA support for the FAO Freedom from Hunger Campaign, the Executive instructed Dr Egbert de Vries, Director of the Institute for International Development at The Hague, and Mr John Metzler who would represent it at the FAO Conference 'to be on guard against any tendency to describe the campaign for food as a "solution" for the population problem'.[112] However, in his speech launching the campaign on 1 July 1960, Dr B. R. Sen, Director-General of the FAO, supported the Roman Catholic position and stressed that the problem was not one of overpopulation but of underproduction. Dr Sen evidenced a similar sensitivity to the Roman Catholic attitude at the Tenth Conference of the FAO in October 1959 to which Dr Arnold Toynbee delivered the Frank McDougal Memorial Lecture on 'Population and Food Supply'. In the course of his speech, Dr Toynbee mentioned that eventually birth control might become an international necessity. Dr Sen felt constrained to issue a statement that the assumption at this time would have to be that the food supply must be increased. Dr Fagley noted the difficult position of Dr Sen *vis-à-vis* the Roman Catholic organizations and governments; he felt their power was exaggerated by the fact that no non-Catholic Christian body—for example the CCIA, the World Council of Churches, or the International Missionary Council—had taken an official position on the population problem or on family planning. In such circumstances it appeared to Dr Sen, as it would to most national politicians, that those who cared passionately about an issue should be heeded, since those who had no opinion, or had many divided and not strongly held opinions, would not care. Fagley urged de Vries to give encouragement to Dr Sen on this matter.[113]

On looking in from the outside, it is understandable why Dr Sen and other international officials in other agencies paid attention to the Roman Catholic position on birth control and sometimes on other matters. Pressure may be put on intergovernmental organizations by the governments of Roman Catholic countries heeding the strictures of the church; it may also be applied by full-time Vatican observers (of which there is one at the FAO). An interesting variation on the theme of a Roman Catholic presence in IGOs occurs at the ILO where, since its inception, a Jesuit priest has been employed on the staff in the section dealing with non-governmental organizations. Contrasted with this profuse and professional representation is the rather small though very professional CCIA staff, dependent upon a more diffuse presence in the form of part-time, interested individuals to represent the world Protestant-Orthodox interests. Furthermore the Vatican emphasizes not only its role of central Defender of the Faith but also its rights and duties as an international person (state). This must be compared to the decentralized concept of Protestantism and the autocephalous practice of Orthodoxy in which the grandeur of the international Christian fellowship is not always apparent, even to its workers, much less to outsiders.

Dr de Vries reported to the CCIA Executive Committee meeting in August 1960 on his work with the FAO and co-operation in the Freedom From Hunger Campaign; he noted that in international quarters there was a reluctance to take the population explosion seriously. During the discussion of his presentation it became clear that the members of the Committee recognized the importance of the problem; they urged the special responsibility of the churches to bring the question before the world's authorities because of the exceptional religious pressure to which they were already subjected, and they called for a clear Christian stand on this issue.[114]

Dr Fagley's persistence and the publication early in 1960 of his book *The Population Explosion and Christian Responsibility*, written from a Protestant viewpoint, and increasing secular concern about the issue brought about a consideration of these matters by the Central Committee which met the following week. A substantial part of its business was devoted to an examination of responsible parenthood. The Right Reverend Stephen F. Bayne, Jr, Anglican Executive Officer, presented an address on 'Population and Family Problems' and Dr de Vries spoke on 'Population Growth and Christian Responsibility'. In the discussion which followed, it became clear why there had not been a clear ecumenical word on this issue. The Orthodox representatives Archimandrite Emilianos Timiadis and Professor Florovsky pointed out that it was against their doctrine to approve artificial means of birth control. Principal Chandran of India, however, vehemently supported the study of population control, pointing out its great importance to states like India; at the same time he acknowledged the need to maintain dignity and moral standards in any programme of family planning offered to peoples in developing countries. Following an exchange of ideas on the Christian basis, or lack thereof, for family planning, a rather weak statement was adopted by the Central Committee to be transmitted to the churches along with the addresses of the meeting and a request for a theological examination of the problem. Hope for more positive action rested in the Central Committee's directions to the World Council Executive Committee to keep this concern before the churches.[115]

The next opportunity to speak publicly on the issue arose in conjunction with the New Delhi Assembly in November and December 1961. The Commission of the CCIA, which met in Bangalore in November, approved 'Elements of a Strategy of Development' (later known as the Bangalore Statement) in which it called for co-operation in national family planning programmes; however, in order not to offend and alienate people it felt the churches should not attempt to initiate such programmes.[116] The New Delhi Assembly, in spite of meeting in an area where the population problem had become acute, exhibited great timidity in bringing this major issue before its constituents and the world. In addition to calling for a survey of the views expressed by the various member churches, the report of the Assembly's Committee on the CCIA dealt in one paragraph with the need for population control, urging developed countries to grant technical assistance when requested to do so by the developing countries. In spite of the rather diffident handling of the subject by the Committee, Archimandrite Emilianos Timiadis, representing the Ecumenical Patriarchate of Constantinople, made known his apprehension about the paragraph.[117] One might ask, however, whether the churches can afford to criticize states for putting politics before development if they themselves put doctrine before development.

In spite of the World Council's quiescence, CCIA cognizance of the problem had led to action where possible. In 1961, but prior to the Bangalore meeting, Mrs Ulla Lindstrom, Swedish Minister of State and Representative to the United Nations, asked Dr Fagley's advice on a Swedish-Danish draft resolution on technical assistance for family planning. Fagley tried to discourage her acting at this time, but as she persisted he suggested certain tactics she might follow. However, in the Second Committee of the General Assembly there was no time to discuss the draft, but it was put on the agenda for the next year, when the Second Committee held its first debate on population growth in relation to economic development. On Dr Fagley's advice Mrs Lindstrom had toned down her resolution, and, also on his suggestion, had found members from the under-developed areas to co-sponsor it. Although the Second Committee approved the point that the United Nations could give technical assistance for national population programmes, the relevant paragraph was rejected in the General Assembly, where the voting was 34–34 with 32 abstentions. The amended resolution was passed 69–0 with 27 abstentions, primarily of the Soviet and Roman Catholic blocs. In spite of the weakened form of the resolution, Fagley was elated, feeling that the 'emerging Protestant consensus' helped to give delegates courage where it had been previously lacking.[118]

The year 1963 saw Dr Fagley more active as this emerging consensus became apparent to others. The British, Japanese, and United Arab Republic delegations discussed with Fagley an 'ad hoc approach to co-operation on fertility regulation'. He felt that Roman Catholic delegations had overplayed their hand with intransigent, dogmatic attitudes, ignoring and thereby underestimating the attitudes towards population control which the new countries were displaying. Indeed, the widening of United Nations membership to include countries throughout Asia and Africa had created an organization interested in new problems and new solutions. Fagley sent an aide-mémoire to those governments potentially favourably disposed to population control, proposing that ad hoc multilateral co-operation along the lines of the Colombo Plan be developed to institute it. (The Colombo Plan, originally begun as a means to bring technical assistance and limited economic aid from developed to developing members of the Commonwealth, broadened its base to take in recipients throughout south and south-east Asia and donors from the United States and Western Europe. With a small Secretariat in Colombo, it acts as a clearing house, matching requests for technical experts with offers from developed states.) Fagley offered the advice of the CCIA to those wishing to set up such a plan, but pointed out that the CCIA would lack the technical staff to assist in the actual running of it. Apparently delegations receiving the *aide-mémoire* were enthusiastic, and several turned to him for moral support before essaying a more adventurous role.[119]

Although Dr Fagley reported to each CCIA Executive Committee meeting from 1962 through 1965, no new statements were issued. Activities continued, however, among the churches and the intergovernmental organizations. Under the sponsorship of the United Nations Economic Commission for Asia and the Far East, an Asian Population Conference was held in New Delhi in December 1963 at which the CCIA was represented by an Asian observer. Dr Fagley considered that his plan for *ad hoc* co-operation, put forward at the previous United Nations General Assembly session, was recommended by this conference.[120] He himself attended a consultation on 'The Churches in Asia and Responsible Parenthood', sponsored by the East Asia Christian Conference which met in Bangkok in February 1964. The results of this conference, urging positive programmes of family planning, were circulated to churches and governments in Asia.

The 1964 meeting of the United Nations Economic and Social Council saw the adoption of a resolution calling, among other things, for United Nations technical assistance to be available for family planning programmes to those states requesting it, although the General Assembly did not discuss this or any population resolution since it was awaiting the outcome of the United Nations Second World Population Conference scheduled for Belgrade in 1965. Addressing that Conference, Monsieur Philip de Seynes, Under-Secretary for Economic and Social Affairs, warned delegates that the United Nations remained neutral regarding limitation of population, but that it would aid those states which had decided to embark upon such a policy. Although this Conference was one of governmental experts, Dr Fagley attended on the invitation of the Secretary-General and read a paper on 'Doctrines and Attitudes of Major Religions in Regard to Fertility'; in discussion he also put forward arguments against the simplistic solution offered by some Roman Catholic delegates. Dr Fagley privately complained that the CCIA's status as a non-governmental organization restricted it to one observer with no voice or vote (Fagley, as just explained, was not attending as its representative and Mr Sjollema of the World Council Geneva staff attended as the observer) while the Holy See, treated as a government, was able to have three expert participants and an observer.[121] This again illustrates the advantage of operating as a state in intergovernmental organizations as opposed to trying to make one's voice heard through the lesser status of NGO.

The General Assembly session of 1965 conducted a rather inconclusive debate on population growth and economic development.

A draft submitted by the Scandinavian states in conjunction with some Third World states was opposed by Ireland, and the Brazilian proposal that further consideration of the draft be postponed until the following year was carried. The significance of this debate lay not in decisions reached but rather in the evolution from negative abstention to positive support by the USSR, the Netherlands, and the Philippines of attempts to deal with overpopulation.

The 1966 World Conference on Church and Society made no mention of the population explosion in its 'Message', but the need for family planning was treated extensively in the various section reports. These reports were received by the Conference and their conclusions adopted for transmission to the World Council and its member churches for their study, consideration, and appropriate action. In all cases the stress was on the positive aspect of population control: responsible parenthood. This was described as encompassing concern for mothers used as breeding animals and concern for the provision of training which a child in modern society requires. It recognized the divergence of ecclesiastical tradition but urged that traditional answers were not enough; in fact the churches had failed to consider both the recognized needs of the world and the aspects of new methods of preventing conception. All sections discussing this problem reiterated the responsibility of the churches to lead the way and to participate actively in national and community programmes where established.[122] This rather revolutionary conference did not take the revolutionary action that might have been expected of it and which the problem called for; in this matter perhaps its delegates had spent their energy in a demonstration in the streets of Geneva.

At the General Assembly session that autumn, Dr Fagley actively participated in the Assembly's clarification of its position on overpopulation. He worked for a positive resolution commanding a large majority. In order to increase support, he suggested to the sponsors of the draft that reference to the right of parents to determine the size of their families should be included; they were amenable and additional support was garnered. The operative clauses of the resolution asked the Secretary-General to implement training, research, information, and advisory services regarding the overpopulation problem.[123]

Against the background of a report on the food gap by Dr Fagley, the World Council Executive Committee recorded the following minute at its meeting in February 1967 regarding family planning and nutrition: 'Deep and growing concern must be aroused by the narrowing margins of subsistence for vast numbers of human beings in the poorer societies as indigenous food production tends to lag behind population growth and world food reserves diminish. Even though many developing countries are undertaking programmes to promote family planning, essential to any human solution, no early reduction of population pressures is to be anticipated . . .' [124]

The Central Committee, meeting in August, took a definite stand while sitting in a stronghold of Orthodoxy. 'We recognize that even the most promising combination of measures for increased food production will only postpone catastrophe unless there is a vast increase in responsible family life and planning.' [125]

While the Committee kept speaking, Dr Fagley kept acting and making use of their pronouncements. He attended part of the Assembly of the FAO in November 1967 where he supported a report of the Advisory Committee on the Application of Science and Technology on 'Feeding the Expanding World Population', in which recommendations for international action to avert the impending protein crisis were made. He then attended the United Nations Population Commission followed by the Second Committee of the General Assembly, endorsing the policy objectives recommended by the experts.

The Roman Catholic–World Council SODEPAX conference on economic development, held in Beirut in April 1968, showed a surprisingly positive attitude towards limiting population growth. While using such euphemisms as 'population problems and policies', 'rights and claims of the family', 'population pressures', 'new pattern of family life', 'responsible parenthood', the issue was always that of family planning. The conference recognized that governments had the right and duty to make all their citizens aware of the problems of overpopulation; on the other hand it was the duty of the churches to emphasize the right of the parents to decide on the number of children they wished to have, albeit taking into account the 'claims of the social situation'. The methods of fertility regulation should not conflict with the religious teachings of the parents. Nevertheless the findings of this conference recognized that 'rapid increase of population of the low-income societies would lead to vast social, economic and political problems' and that programmes of population regulation should be integrated into the development programmes.[126] In spite of the fact that this was a report *to* the churches and not *by* the churches, it was hailed as a fitting beginning to Roman Catholic–Protestant co-operation in this doctrinally delicate field.

The population explosion with its worldwide implications would seem to be an area in which inter-governmental organizations could best formulate an international plan for control of further population growth. Such an international problem with specific religious undertones would seem just the type of problem in which the World Council of Churches and its foreign office, the CCIA, should be interested and active. Yet in April 1965 Sir Kenneth

Grubb raised the question with his population expert, Dr Fagley, to what extent family planning was a proper subject for policy-making by international agencies or governments. He also queried the role of the World Council in formulating population policy, inasmuch as the Overseas Development Institute in London was hesitating to encourage governments to follow any one policy. Sir Kenneth felt that real damage might be done by 'ecumenical enthusiasts' actively proposing new policies.[127] However, this apparent lack of confidence by the Chairman of the CCIA did not reduce Richard Fagley's momentum, for his own fervent belief in the gravity of the issue and his reputation as an expert drew officials to him. He advised the delegates of India and Sweden, who were proposing a resolution in the United Nations, to get Philippine co-sponsorship to dispel 'the idea of a monolithic Catholic opposition'.[128] Like all good lobbyists (in the neutral sense of the term, representatives of the interests of groups to their legislators), he also received advice: when India, the United Arab Republic, Pakistan, and Yugoslavia suggested that he and the CCIA should lie low in order not to engender religious controversy during a debate on the population problem he agreed to do so.

The Uppsala Assembly made no mention in its 'Message' of the population problem despite the fact that the emphasis of Uppsala was development. Note of the problem, however, appeared in the reports of several sections. The Section on World Economic and Social Development called attention to the 'world's unprecedented population explosion' and noted that many churches agreed on the necessity to promote family planning and birth control, but it also noted that 'some churches may have moral objections to certain methods of population control'. Two other Section reports made brief mention of this problem.[129] It was therefore the more disappointing to the Protestant churches and to General Secretary Eugene Blake that the spokesman for the Roman Catholic Church, soon after the Uppsala Assembly, issued the encyclical *Humanae Vitae*, reaffirming his opposition to any 'artificial' means of birth control. However, although posing certain difficulties for a Christian consensus, it has so far had no noticeable impact on international aid for national programmes: in fact a SODEPAX consultation on development held in Montreal in April 1969 again spoke of support for the consensus on the population problem achieved at the Beirut Conference mentioned above.

The 'Statement on Development' of the CCIA Executive Committee adopted at its 1969 meeting called for co-operation 'to help developing countries to implement their population policies', as well as 'international assistance on national family planning programmes' to be placed within the framework of family health and welfare schemes.[130] This mention of the population explosion, as in other World Council statements, stressed the right of the individual couple to decide on the size of their family, and as did the 'Declaration on Social Progress and Development' adopted by 119 to 0 with 2 abstentions at the December 1969 meeting of the General Assembly. A population expert, albeit one who uses rather emotive language, Dr Paul R. Ehrlich, has stated that just such formulation by family planners is an evasion of the problem, which is not to give families the number of children they want, but to give society the number of children it needs.[131] It is unlikely for some time, however, that one could get from the churches a statement of such harshness.

Church and Society sponsored the Exploratory Conference on Technology and the Future of Man and Society, held in Geneva from 28 June to 4 July 1970. As a result of the findings of the conference, Church and Society undertook to produce a broad study on this topic in which demographic issues figured prominently. The Central Committee commented, *inter alia,* that Church and Society should consider this study in the light of the distinctive problems of the Third World and that, particularly, the relationship between population increase and industrial and agricultural production should be examined. The Central Committee urged its member churches 'to develop local and regional meetings to awaken public opinion to this population increase. . . .'[132] The resulting study was the basis of the 1972 Central Committee request that a 'substantial' report on 'the quality of life in relation to methods of population control' be submitted to it in August 1973 for circulation to the churches preparatory to the United Nations World Population Conference in June 1974.[133]

The report 'Population Policy, Social Justice and the Quality of Life' was prepared by Church and Society in co-operation with the CCIA, Christian Medical Commission, CCPD, and the Office of Family Ministries; it caused some controversy between Orthodox representatives and others, even though it did note that 'The Eastern Orthodox tradition favours abstinence as a means of family limitation'. It recognized the danger of concentrations of power in the modern state, but appreciated the need for government population policies to provide for a higher quality of life, especially the right of the child to health and education. In calling for population planning it cited the need for social justice, both within a country and on the international level; the imbalance between population and resources—the population crisis—was aggravated by developed states having a much higher *per capita* use of resources. It warned the developing nations, where the crisis is most visible, not to commit themselves to economic goals based on the over-use of resources, as in the developed world, but rather to search for a different economic system.

The shift from earlier pronouncements on population control is interesting. Whereas they concentrated mainly on the quality of life and on the right of the family and the child to a higher standard of living, there has now crept in the call for institutional change, a characteristic introduced by the Programme to Combat Racism in its attempt to give power to the powerless. With a change in institutions, measures to achieve social justice and respect for human rights would include raising the standard of living and creating higher aspirations, so that a better life for one child was preferable to a miserable life for several; reducing infant mortality through child-care programmes; improving educational opportunities and providing for security in old age so that parents were not totally dependent on the number of children for their well-being.

The report cited the UN Conference on Human Rights at Teheran which recognized as fundamental the right of parents to determine the size of families. 'We add that these rights need to be exercised in the light of the parents' obligation to the larger society.' It commended this specifically to the World Population Conference of the following year.

Such ecumenical reports are always the result of many compromises among the various value systems represented. In this case, while one sector called for institutional changes and whole-heartedly recognized the rights of governmental intervention, another section put limitations on these rights, evincing almost a *laissez faire* attitude with the requirements that a 'government must (i) demonstrate that continued unrestricted liberty poses a direct threat to human welfare; that the common good is threatened; (ii) demonstrate that the proposed restrictions on freedom promise in the long run to maximize options of choice; (iii) see that the restrictions on free choice fall upon all equally; (iv) choose the programme that entails least intervention.' It went on to list incentive measures which were morally acceptable, and coercive ones, such as forced sterilization or abortion, which were not. The Central Committee, in spite of potential problems with Orthodoxy, commended this report to the churches both for study and as a basis for the ecumenical contribution to the United Nations World Population Conference.[134]

This conference, which took place in Bucharest from 19 to 30 August 1974, was the international high point of World Population Year. The Secretariat's draft Plan of Action was supported mainly by the capitalist, developed countries and opposed by the Vatican, several Latin American countries, and the communist states. In addition Third World delegates in rhetorical speeches implied or stated that population control was some plot on the part of the developed world. A revised Plan of Action, adopted on 30 August —and supported by an overwhelming majority of Third World states, in spite of their earlier fears—provided for a reduction in national birth rates by 1985 and offered family planning advice and services to those who wanted them. The Vatican representative dissociated the Vatican from the resolution. Other resolutions urged that: (1) a solution to the population problem implied the elimination of the gap between developed and developing states; (2) those countries consuming an excessive share of resources (the developed states) should reduce their consumption; (3) the equality of men and women should be part of the development effort; and (4) population programmes should ensure respect for human rights and the preservation of the dignity of the family.

An impressive team of World Council observers headed by Dr Fagley attended the conference. The others were Dr Paul Abrecht of Church and Society, Dr Nita Barrow of the Christian Medical Commission, and the Reverend Leslie Clements of the Office of Family Ministries. (These three bodies have now taken the ball from the CCIA on matters of population control.) Some 150 clergymen and laymen attended the conference as representatives of accredited non-governmental organizations. One judgement was that their viewpoints were so conflicting that little Christian impact was made. Prior to the conference, a World Council delegation had travelled to Rome to try to arrive at a unified Christian position . . . or at least to work out a *modus vivendi* for collaboration at the conference. In the end it was wasted effort because of sharp Vatican opposition to the World Population Plan of Action. From the viewpoint of World Council officials, the conference was unproductive not only because of its appeal to national interest and sovereignty but also because of the visibly deep division which separated the World Council and Roman Catholic stands.[135]

The Christian Medical Commission has developed family planning as an integral component in several community health projects which provide low-cost medical care where there was none before. The intention is to make family planning services more acceptable by enhancing confidence in local health workers. Five such programmes, two in northern India and one each in Bangladesh, Korea, and Botswana, have indicated to the CMC the correctness of its thesis. In fact, such has been the success of the provision for health care and family planning that the WHO has developed a relationship with the Christian Medical Commission held by no other NGO. Now all new CMC projects will be reviewed by the WHO and its expertise will be made available to the Christian body. The CMC expects that this will increase its potential for innovations in the health care field in co-operation with governments.[136]

In spite of the necessary weakness in the formulation of compromise statements, the work of the World Council of Churches

207

in dealing with this world issue could well serve as a model for its tactics in other issues. The prime mover was a World Council (more specifically, a CCIA) official, with sufficient interest in the problem to become an expert on it—not a dilettante among the clergy, but one whose views were sought by international and national organizations. Thus the churches gained respect for their competence on this issue. Much of the activity was carried on in personal contacts before the churches had issued a statement on it. The advice sought, and offered, was not solely of a biological nature; it also contained something of tactics in regard to the United Nations. One can see that not only a technical expert but also a diplomatic/parliamentary expert is needed by the churches. Although the issue was one in which there is a religious interest, it was Roman Catholic activity against population control which motivated, indeed compelled World Council reaction. It was of recognized religious interest because it touched ecclesiastical dogma; and it would appear that the lesson here is for the churches to point out to the world the doctrinal reason for their interest, possibly fervent interest, in an issue. Hence the importance of the study function of the World Council, which is recounted and discussed in the following section.

Church, Society, and Theology

It has been characteristic of the Ecumenical Movement since its inception that it has acted first and tried to find a theological justification afterwards. Life and Work eschewed theology completely; Archbishop Soederblom wanted to accomplish things, not to discuss the biblical text which may or may not have authorized the action. But Life and Work soon added a Theological Commission to its organization, for it had to defend itself in theological language against attacks by the ecclesiastical establishment. In the case of ecumenical action on the economic development of the Third World action also came first, then a justifying study was proposed. It should be made clear, however, in commendation of the Department on Church and Society, that in carrying out the mandate of the Evanston Assembly with the long study on 'The Common Christian Responsibility toward Areas of Rapid Social Change', the Department was not seeking theological justification alone. Rather the whole phenomenon of change from agrarian to industrial societies had been too little studied and was too poorly understood by secular as well as religious authorities; so it was proposed to find out what this process was, how it came about, the problems which it brought into being compared to those of famine and poverty which it ameliorated, as well as the theological rationale behind Christian concern with the procedure. This study

—conducted by active Christian clergy and sociologists, economists, political scientists, and other lay experts—was not strongly influenced by dogmatic theologians. And while the study and its consequences were useful for those Christians active in international affairs, the need for subjective justification, or rationalization, provided by theological terminology was still felt by clergy, especially theologians. The consideration of a theology of development, begun by SODEPAX in 1969, can be considered a successor to this pioneer study.

Dr de Vries described 'rapid social change' not only as rapid development but as an overspringing of stages of development: people were flying in airplanes who had never ridden horses or used cars. Since it was industrialization from the Western world that was a cause of this social turmoil, the churches of the West and the industrial states had a special responsibility to help these societies to help themselves. The Central Committee accepted the proposal for a study and suggested that it be carried further by a conference the following year in which lay consultants would participate with members from all participating World Council departments.

A Working Committee met in July 1956 at Herrenalb, West Germany, to guide the study further and it produced 'The Common Christian Responsibility toward Areas of Rapid Social Change: 2nd Statement'. This statement indicated which areas the continuing study would follow and further defined the issues. Basically it consisted of five main subjects: (1) the theological foundations of Christian concern for these issues; (2) the impact of the West on such phenomena as nationalism, racial tensions, problems of international trade and investment; (3) social change in rural communities; (4) industrialization and urbanization; and (5) responsible citizenship, e.g., development of political institutions and political participation.[137]

To ensure participation by the churches of the underdeveloped states, a Japanese, Mr Daisuke Kitagawa, an Indian, Mr M. M. Thomas, and an African, Dr John Karefa-Smart, were persuaded to accept positions with the study. Research projects and study conferences were planned at the national and regional levels with a final international conference to draw the results of the research, conferences, and reports together. To aid in this ambitious programme, John D. Rockefeller gave $100,000, and the Phelps-Stokes Fund gave an additional $25,000, designated for work in Africa.

To ensure wide participation of member churches and to act as an educating influence as well as a research factor, national conferences were held at which the research programmes were discussed. The national programmes were integrated at regional

209

o

conferences in Asia, the Middle East, Africa, and Europe. (Because of the unsettled conditions in the Middle East generally and the Anglo-French-Israeli invasion of Egypt in 1956, in particular, the results from that area were peripheral.) The study culminated in the International Ecumenical Study Conference held at Thessalonica, Greece, from 25 July to 2 August 1959, at which there were 140 participants, mainly laymen, representing 34 countries, but with over half from the Third World, and, for the first time in any ecumenical conference, a large number of Africans. The Conference considered Christian responsibility in political action as well as in economic and community development. The large number of participants from the under-developed countries ensured that the discussion would reflect their views rather than those from the over-developed West.

The Conference did not wish to urge consumption as the way to salvation; nevertheless, it recognized that a higher standard of living freed man from the slavery of ignorance and want. The unequal division of wealth in the world cannot be overcome all at once; action is required at many different levels from individuals, voluntary groups, governments, and international agencies. But individual responsibility cannot be shirked by leaving it to group responsibility at any level. Moreover, charity is not enough; to eliminate the root causes of poverty is the essential job.

Churchmen *qua* churchmen cannot prescribe technical programmes. But the Thessalonica Conference consisted mainly of laymen, many with experience in international economic development. The prescriptions of the Conference, therefore, have their own technical validity. Nevertheless, their Christian origin meant that they were based on values other than the strictly economic or technological. The recommendations generally accorded with those of independent studies of economic development. The report urged upon its readers the difficulty of accumulating capital in a subsistence economy and the need for more capital from the developed areas.[138] The need for public capital was urged—capital that would, unconcerned with profit, build the necessary infrastructure.[139] Recognizing that it was supremely important for the agricultural revolution to precede the industrial, a whole section was devoted to rural development.[140] Realizing the inevitability of urbanization, the Conference urged that international economic development be planned and carried out in such a way as to avoid the sufferings undergone by Europeans during their industrial infancy.[141] The Conference commended its findings to the Central Committee for approval and action.

The Central Committee, pleased with the report rendered to it at its meeting immediately following the Conference, accepted the report and recommended it to the churches for their consideration. In addition to the report from the whole conference, the participants from Asia, Africa, and Latin America requested the World Council to make this study, which they had found valuable, an ongoing one with centralized direction. The participants from each continent had specific suggestions; generally, however, they wished help for widespread dissemination of the materials produced by the study and help in establishing church and society committees and in strengthening those that already existed.[142] The Central Committee authorized the continuation of the study, to include carrying on existing activities, pursuing new research projects and collating the results.[143] These same participants urged that the World Council itself engage directly in economic development by establishing a fund under international control for social projects. The Central Committee requested a joint recommendation from DICASR, the Division of Studies, the Division of Ecumenical Action, and the CCIA. This resulted in the creation of the Specialized Assistance for Social Projects (SASP) whose results are recounted above.

The World Council of Churches, its officials, and the Third Assembly felt that this report, which had cost about $250,000 was well worth the effort and cost. At the inception of the study it had not been clear what role the Church had in areas of rapid social change. This study helped the World Council understand better its function in economic development. It indicated the weakness in the structure of the various churches and Christian councils which were not organized to carry out effective study on social problems. Its results also helped DICASR to evaluate the projects for which aid was requested. The theological issues had not been resolved, none had agreed exactly how many angels danced on the pin of development, yet the study had illumined the issues at stake. The young churches had been aided in formulating their problems, the old churches in analysing their responsibilities.

A plenary session of the New Delhi Assembly was devoted to the study. The Assembly received the report of the Committee on the Department on Church and Society and authorized a continuation of the rapid social change study as 'Moral issues in the change from traditional to dynamic societies'.[144] The Assembly also authorized a study of 'the social, political and moral problems of modern industrial societies' and on 'racial and ethnic tensions in a changing world community'. The Working Committee of the Department considered that these studies could best be combined and carried out by means of a world conference. This proposal was accepted by the Central Committee in 1962. In order to encourage as much participation as possible from the 'new' nations, regional conferences were held, and scholars from the various regions of the world contributed articles to the four volumes of preparatory material for the forthcoming conference, for which the 1965 Central Committee meeting approved the final plans. It was decided that the participants would not be delegations of member churches but representative groups of competent laymen and theologians; had they been official delegates, it was felt, too much emphasis on ecclesiastical representation would result, the Western churches would predominate, and the conference 'would not have the freedom to obtain the pioneering and creative thinking on the Church's responsibility in society . . .'.[145] One might accept this as an indictment of the arthritic minds of some ecclesiastical leaders!

The technological progress which speeds up the development of society, of its economic capabilities, of its destructive capabilities has not been matched by the churches in the development of an ethic to regulate the problems caused by industrialization and the amassing of capital. The pioneering thinking predicted for the World Conference on Church and Society did come about, especially as eminent economists from both the developed and underdeveloped countries exchanged views on international economic development, as did other experts on their subjects. Here, for the first time, the ethical problems of world economic relations were systematically explored; the responsibilities both of those with economic power and those receiving aid were formulated.

The report of Section I, 'Economic Development in a World Perspective', stressed the need for 'human' criteria to be considered as well as economic factors in judging economic change. It declared that 'the biggest issue in the world today' was economic development; in this judgement the conference agrees with many international political scientists, economists, and sociologists. The countries undergoing economic development, the report continued, have to face the complete restructuring of their political, social, and economic systems. The physical resources required for development must, to a large extent, come from abroad; the human resources of the developing states must be trained to the areas of need. The report recognized the need for an agricultural revolution to occur first in order to provide food and labour for industralization; to minimize human suffering, the industrializing sector must grow at the same rate as labour is released from the agricultural sector. International organizations were suggested as the vehicle for long-term commitments, so that the required continuity of planning would be possible. (To corroborate the accuracy of the analysis and prescriptions, readers may consult other studies on economic development; for example, John Pincus's *Trade, Aid and Development: the Rich and Poor Nations* provides an analysis by a Westerner that is sympathetic to the less-developed states.[146]) The astute insight into the issues of importance to developing countries indicates the stature of the specialists who drafted it.

Nor were the responsibilities of the developing states ignored. Reform of political, economic, and social structures was prescribed as well as the need for internal planning and the honest application of aid. The churches themselves, and the World Council acting for them, were given advice on their duties in this sphere. The Conference did not eschew the possibility of the churches' offering technical advice but saw also their particular ability to provide 'an ethic of altruism and justice' that would make the technical measures intelligible within a Christian context. The churches' diffusion of this ethic would result in an enlargement of their educational functions: in theological education they would give attention to the ethics of economic problems and in economic education an understanding of human problems; positive attitudes on the part of statesmen and peoples in support of development aid would result.[147]

Although the report of Section I, like those of the other three Sections, was received by the Conference and commended to the churches, there was not unanimous agreement on every point. The speeches in the plenary session devoted to this report indicated the dichotomous views within the churches themselves. Professor Roy Blough of the School of Business Administration at Columbia University stated that American businessmen would doubt the wisdom of giving aid to states which had not learnt to control their population growth, ignoring the enormous resources that need to be put into any family planning campaign, resources which those countries do not have. He stated, moreover, that businessmen would ask whether such countries were making the best use of their resources, again disregarding the fact that states of the Third World were often unable to afford the comprehensive economic survey that would tell them fully what resources they had and evaluate their use. Furthermore, he continued, American businessmen could not understand why these countries were hostile to foreign private enterprise, for American businessmen did not regard themselves as neo-colonialists or imperialists. Professor Gilbert Blardone of France noted that inequalities in powers of negotiation and decision-making enabled developed countries to influence the economies of the under-developed states. These adverse influences, as noted in the Section report, might help Professor Blough's businessmen to realize why some people regard them as neo-colonialists.[148]

The Uppsala Assembly recognized the Conference report as 'a significant source for Christian social thinking' and commended it to the churches. It also approved four studies proposed by the Department on Church and Society, three of which could be regarded as continuations of the original study on rapid social change: (1) the structural changes necessary for effective world development; (2) the functions of law and the realization of social justice in time of change; and (3) the significance of the human being in world-wide technological change.[149] These will be part of the Humanum Study—the Study of Man—which the Uppsala Assembly authorized. The exact content of the study, really several studies from various World Council departments, was left to the study adviser Canon David Jenkins and an *ad hoc* consultative committee.

In response to the oft-expressed need for a theology of development the Committee on Society, Development and Peace (SODE-PAX) convened in November 1969 at Cartigny, Switzerland, twenty-eight Roman Catholic, Orthodox, Anglican and other Protestant theologians from the developing and the developed countries. It was not meant to produce *the* theology of development, and indeed did not, but those who participated from many theological traditions considered the results were encouraging and that SODEPAX should pursue this theme further.[150]

It was reported in April 1972 that conservatives in the Vatican were displeased with the comparatively radical attitude of SODE-PAX both to development and to dictatorial régimes and racism. The budget, depending on agreement between the WCC and the Pontifical Commission on Justice and Peace (PCJP), was drastically cut and the Roman Catholic staff dispersed, leaving a small Secretariat in Geneva headed by an elderly Belgian missionary from Japan.[151] The Joint Working Group of the WCC and PCJP decided that SODEPAX would no longer draw up its own programme and that it should be, more simply, a link between the PCJP and the WCC's Commission on the Churches' Participation in Development. Both sides reduced their contribution to the staff of SODE-PAX and theoretically enlarged the staff of the two responsible bodies.[152] The Central Committee agreed to this change in order to maintain the semblance of continued collaboration, biding its time, perhaps, for more liberal days.

Since these changes in 1972, the activities of SODEPAX—compared with those of its first three years—seem very small. It has sponsored the Asian Inter-religious Forum for Social Action as a long-term project of the Asian Christian Conference and Asian [Roman Catholic] Bishops Conference, headed by Dr Kinhide Mushakoji of Sophia University, Tokyo. A Church Alert Service to keep the problems of development before the churches, with a quarterly bulletin and a peace education programme for Northern Ireland, are two other reduced spheres of its activities.[153]

It is important for the churches and for the World Council of Churches, that Christian experts interpret to the churches the technical aspects of the complex problems which face all mankind. The studies discussed here all deal with the development of the 'new' societies, new in the sense that they are being quickly changed by the 'technical and social revolutions of our time', as the Conference on Church and Society called them. The realism with which these topics were considered, the suggestions which were offered, brooked no Utopia. The World Council personnel are worthy followers of the tradition established by the International Social Christian Institute of Life and Work: a concise scientific analysis coupled with Christian value judgements. The reports on the changing societies were more than statements prepared by an amateur group of do-gooders; they demonstrated knowledge of the problems to be met, combined with Christian insight into the value of man. Some might call it humanistic and support it for that reason, but these Christians who revealed a depth of feeling for those who suffered under present unjust social and economic conditions and who were ready to help them across the pains of change said it was 'because the love of Christ constraineth us'.

The World Council of Churches works through its own structure and through that of its member churches, mission societies, regional and national Christian councils, and church agencies; the choice of agent depends on the situation and the desired result. From the foregoing review of the actions and thought of the World Council regarding the economic and social advancement of under-developed areas it can be seen that there have been four major areas of action. The first is the education of its own con-stituencies—its ecclesiastical and lay leaders, and then the mass of its own followers—in favour of development. The second lies in initiating and carrying out its own projects of development, as the early missionaries initiated and carried out social services which the colonial governments could not or would not institute, namely education and health services. The third area was concerned with achieving recognition of the danger of overpopulation and over-coming a Roman Catholic taboo in the heterogeneous United Nations against even its discussion. The fourth area of action, attempting to influence decision-makers at the national and inter-national levels, is that which receives most attention when international ecclesiastical action is under observation.

The educational function of the theologian is as important as that of the Christian pastor and layman, even in the seemingly worldly field of economics. For the latter two groups, this function may be considered in a sense as propagandizing in that the pre-sentation of facts is combined with persuasion to accept the concept of development as a Christian responsibility. The educational function of the theologian is carried out while he develops the theological rationale for the churches' concern with this problem.

The summary of ecumenical activities in international affairs given in the first chapter of this book indicates how recent is Protestant-Orthodox responsibility for such areas of concern. Although action in these areas was taken pragmatically by concerned clergymen, every innovation (for example, the concern with the concept of economic development in 1950) had to be followed by the theological basis for such action; this Christian concern in social and economic matters is still not accepted by all,[154] hence the need, constantly felt by ecumenical Christians, of self-justification in these areas expressed in theological terms.

Once a theological rationale is developed (one must really say while it is being developed, since there is never a final, definitive dogma), it is transmitted to the parish level in simpler terms. Through the 'theology of development' the Christian populace is taught the positive value of a secular idea as well as its theological significance and justification. Both activities are so closely related that one cannot always distinguish one from the other. The study of the 'Christian Responsibility to Areas of Rapid Social Change' was both an exercise in the development of a theological position and a dissemination of ideas favourable to economic and social development. This was accomplished through national, regional, and international study groups and reports of their progress in both scholarly journals and the popular religious press. In Great Britain, Germany, France, and Switzerland élite newspapers such as *The Times*, *The Guardian*, the *Frankfurter Allgemeine Zeitung*, *Le Monde*, and the *Neue Zürcher Zeitung*, carry regular news of ecumenical occurrences and press releases. The élites of these countries are regularly 'educated' to ecumenical thinking.

Although it could have limited itself to preaching, the World Council began practising what it preached when its post-war relief activity was transformed into inter-church aid. With the help of the Rapid Social Change study, the World Council itself was committed to participating directly in economic development projects, as well as acting as intermediary for its member churches in other projects as it had done theretofore. Indeed, the wide variety of Christian agencies participating in development activities called forth many requests for an integrated World Council programme, as similar unco-ordinated activities at the intergovernmental level did there. The restructuring called for by the Uppsala Assembly, and carried out since that meeting, resulted in the Commission on the Churches' Participation in Development.

One area in which a CCIA representative gained a reputation as an expert was that of population control. Dr Richard Fagley understood the danger of this phenomenon before there were many 'population experts'. He became an authority on the subject and first fought the bar against even mentioning the problem in the

United Nations and the Specialized Agencies. Later he actively worked with the FAO in proposing actions to be taken by that body.

Until the World Council's own programme of development was initiated under CCPD the most visible ecumenical effort in the field of development was directed towards influencing decision-makers. This pressure is exerted at the national and at the international levels. National decisions in the developed states may concern the amount of aid that will be pledged, whether a policy of development aid should be vigorously pursued, and whether recipient governments are likely to act honestly and efficiently. In the pluralistic societies of Western Europe and North America, the national Christian organizations made up of members of the World Council can exert the influence of any large group in those societies. In the socialist countries of Eastern Europe, influence on the decision-making process will be more indirect; but in the case of churchmen like the late Professor Joseph Hromadka in Czechoslovakia, it may be no less real. In some developing countries, Christians may be in such a minority and of such a class that they have no influence at all; in other developing states, especially African ones where the leaders were educated primarily at mission schools, this influence may be significant. That the President of an African state should accept the invitation and make the journey to a World Council Assembly indicates the esteem in which that body is held in his country.

The decisions of intergovernmental bodies are no less impregnable for being decisions of a culturally heterogeneous group. The organizations and agencies administering the development programme of the United Nations—the FAO, UNESCO, the Secretariat, and the ECOSOC—are looking for support from every possible source. They would be interested in the opinions of the World Council regarding development, especially as influence at the national level becomes visible in the amount of aid pledged. As students of pressure groups at the national level know, the more groups that join their resources behind a particular project, the greater its chance of being adopted by the governmental power structure. So at the international level, the CCIA and the CCPD actively co-operate on behalf of the World Council, with other NGOs to try to effect certain decisions of intergovernmental organizations.[155]

The effectiveness of the World Council in the field of economic development may be compared to that of the weak developing states themselves. One scholar in considering 'the politics of the powerless' has pointed out that a major element in effecting changes of attitude has been argument. 'The function of argument is to convince rather than to compel.'[156] She concludes that the

217

most important effect of the activities of these states has been to familiarize the world with the need for development. This has also been an important result of the World Council's efforts; it has used the weapon of argument with governments, intergovernmental organizations, and with its own constituents.

In order to remain effective, however, the World Council of Churches must not be afraid of engaging experts in the fields in which it wishes to give advice. Although its resources may not be as great as those of most governments, it should be prepared to use them in experimental development projects, as it most certainly has done through the CCPD and its strategy of concentration of direct investment. It can thus demonstrate the validity of its own experts' claims. Able to offer technical advice (even if, for political reasons, it does not always wish to prescribe a programme) and experimenting to show its good faith, it can hardly fail to carry its constituency with it; and since this is the strongest in the developed North, it can with more efficacy help those in the South so long exploited by Christian states.

4. Disarmament Bedevilled

THE Christian Church has been interested in the problem of arms and armaments and the killing of man in the name of the state since the earliest Christians refused to serve in the Roman legions. When Christianity became the state religion under Constantine the apparent blessing of the Church was given to the maintenance of order by the Empire by whatever means were required. Warfare, of course, was primarily a face-to-face affair. The invention of, *inter alia,* the crossbow changed that and the Second Lateran Council in 1139 forbade its use as 'deadly and odious to God'.[1] The Church at this time also appeared to be interested in suppressing war altogether, but the well-established doctrine of the just war prevented it from progressing further than outlawing 'private wars', or feuds, among the medieval Christian princes, an act accomplished by the Third Lateran Council in 1179. To most in the world, Christian and non-Christian alike, it would seem that the Church has indeed failed to prevent its adherents not only from slaughtering each other but from devising more and more horrible ways to do so in greater and greater quantities. This is not to imply that Christian doctrine has been held by the majority of Christians to be pacifist; it has not been. But attempts have sporadically been made to stop particular wars and to prohibit the use of specific weapons.

The first inter-church action of this century, an action that was to lead to the founding of the ecumenical movement in our time, was a public petition to the leaders of the world calling for a cessation of the arms race.[2] This petition, signed by Protestant, Catholic, and Jewish ecclesiastical leaders was presented to the Second Hague Peace Conference in 1907; it further urged upon political leaders the need for persistent efforts to maintain international peace. In the various organizations which followed upon this action and led up to the founding of the World Council of Churches,[3] arms control and the elimination of war and the conditions which give rise to it have been persistent themes of ecumenical activity in world affairs.

The World Alliance for International Friendship through the Churches regularly discussed disarmament and armaments problems at its meetings after the First World War; it also supported the French quest for security and the German obsession for equality without encountering the necessity to tie all these points together.

219

After the Locarno treaties had been concluded and the problem of security apparently solved, there was little excuse left for the Allied Powers not to carry out their obligation under the Covenant and disarm. The World Alliance loudly proclaimed this factor in 1928 when a scandal over a secret Anglo-French agreement to disagree, so that the Disarmament Conference would not be called, was discovered. In 1929 when it became certain that a Disarmament Conference would in fact convene, the World Alliance initiated a petitioning campaign among the churches in support of it.

The League Disarmament Conference which began its long life in February 1932 provided an example of ecumenical co-operation. The World Alliance, the Universal Christian Council on Life and Work, the YMCA, YWCA, and the International Missionary Council's Department of Social and Industrial Research joined with some international denominational groups such as the Quakers and formed the Christian Disarmament Committee in Geneva, the site of the Disarmament Conference. Thus the meetings of the politicians and the technical experts were carefully followed during their two-and-a-half-year duration. Although the ecumenical movement had been active in international affairs for nearly a quarter of a century by this time, the lack of a Christian theology concerning the type of action which it should take—for example, whether it should make general statements or present technical plans—hindered effective lobbying by the Christian Disarmament Committee.

The world and the churches faced a multiplicity of social and economic crises which diverted their energy and attention away from disarmament. The Oxford Conference of 1937 could find strength only to condemn uncontrolled rearmament. It is obvious from the historical record that the efforts of the churches did not achieve the desired results: a world without war. However, only the foolhardy would deny that the churches' efforts were entirely in vain or that the three decades of reiterating a standard of behaviour in international affairs—which the greater part of Protestantism had not done since Luther's death—had no future influence on men's minds.

Raining on the Just and on the Unjust

The atomic age dawned for the Christian as well as for the non-Christian; as the rain falls 'on the just and on the unjust', so too radioactive fallout would fall on the baptized and the unbaptized. The leaders of the churches and in the ecumenical movement, as the leaders in all walks of society, realized the awesomeness of this new dawning, even if no one, the scientists included, comprehended its full extent. The Christian journals of the post-Hiroshima period were filled with mistrust of this new source of power.

Thus ecumenical concern for the control of destructiveness centred, first, on atomic power and its taming; secondly, on the strict control of nuclear weapons and other weapons of mass destruction (generally unspecified but understood to include chemical and biological agents); thirdly on the control of conventional weapons, in the context of proposals for an unspecified general and complete disarmament. After the hydrogen bomb became a reality there was a concentration on the issue of nuclear testing. When this goal was partially achieved there was concern for the prevention of the spread of nuclear weapons to non-nuclear powers. An often-voiced concern throughout this period when states remained in deadlock was that each side should take the first step to begin negotiations again. One theme becomes clear through all the moves of the World Council on the disarmament question: the concern for man. Indeed many might say that it was a purely humanistic campaign on the part of the churches—to which the answer would be that their rationale was not based on man for his own sake, but on man as the crowning achievement of creation.

The Provisional Committee of the WCC, meeting in February 1946, devoted the greater part of its time to making plans for the alleviation of suffering caused by the war just ended; the critical world political situation gave it occasion in its Message to denounce war as a result of man's selfishness and to express hope in the efficacy of the United Nations. 'But the time is short. Man's triumph in the release of atomic energy threatens his destruction. Unless men's whole outlook is changed, our civilization will perish.' [4] At this stage of its organization, the Provisional Committee was not prepared to offer prescriptions for its admonitions.

At its First Session the General Assembly of the United Nations also took up the armaments issue and on 24 January 1946 the United Nations Atomic Energy Commission (UNAEC) was created; the task of this body was to eliminate from national arsenals atomic weapons and other weapons of mass destruction and to provide effective safeguards for complying states; it was also to ensure that atomic energy was developed for peaceful uses only. At the first meeting of the Commission, in June 1946, the United States presented the 'Baruch Plan' which would have established strict control over all phases of the development and use of atomic energy, at that time an American monopoly. The Soviet Union's counter-proposal was simply the outlawing of atomic weapons and the destruction of existing stockpiles. This was not acceptable to the United States without the strict controls it envisaged in its proposal.

In December of that year the General Assembly called upon the

Security Council to formulate 'practical measures' for disarmament; it responded with the creation early in 1947 of the Commission on Conventional Armaments (CCA), comprised of the member-states on the Security Council. It met first on 24 March 1947 to consider proposals for its plan of action. The Soviet Union tried to combine disarmament of conventional weapons with the question of nuclear armaments. The United States, on the other hand, wanted to keep the two issues separate, ostensibly so that deadlock over conventional disarmament would not block action on a plan of control for atomic energy. In fact, if there had been a *bona fide* desire by both sides to reach agreement it could have been reached; rather there was a tacit agreement to disagree. The Working Committee of the CCA based its discussion on the control of conventional arms only, in spite of the continued objections of the Soviet Union. Its report to the Security Council was the subject of a Soviet veto.

In the midst of these negotiations the First Assembly of the World Council of Churches met at Amsterdam from 22 August to 4 September 1948. Section IV of the Assembly, 'The Church and the International Disorder', had to consider all the problems that then beset world affairs. It recognized both the fearfulness of atomic power and the destructiveness of conventional weapons. 'Moreover, the immense use of air forces and the discovery of atomic and other weapons render widespread and indiscriminate destruction inherent in the whole conduct of modern war in a sense never experienced in past conflicts.'[5] In addition to this condemnation of war, the report prescribed that the churches 'should also support every effort to deal on a universal basis with the many specific questions of international concern which face mankind today, such as the use of atomic power and the multilateral reduction of armaments'. However, other than the vague injunction to strengthen the United Nations, no means were suggested in detail and no programme of action was offered either for the CCIA or for the states of the world to follow. A delegate of the Church of South India, Mr George Vadanayagam Job, moved that the report should recommend the destruction of all atomic weapons then in existence, but this suggestion failed for lack of a seconder.

Whether the churches offered programmes or not, the world continued, as did the discussions in the UNAEC and in the CCA. The General Assembly itself considered the armaments question in September 1948; the Soviet Union proposed that all permanent members of the Security Council reduce their armed forces by one-third during one year. The Assembly failed to support this proposal and only recommended that the CCA continue its work. Within the UNAEC the main differences between the USSR and the Western position concerned the timing of the outlawing of weapons and the inspection procedures that were to ensure compliance. The Soviet Union also opposed the proposal that an international control agency should own all dangerous facilities and nuclear fuel, thus adopting a position surely inconsistent with the Marxist theory of non-private ownership of the means of production. The Western powers also wanted to eliminate the right of veto in the Security Council when the imposition of penalties for violation of the rules was being voted upon. However, the USSR, facing a bloc with a built-in majority, could not accept the position of permanent inferiority that would have followed.

The Soviet Union used the negotiations to stall for time while mastering the secret of atomic power, an objective that was achieved in September 1949 with the explosion of an atomic bomb. Negotiations on the international control of atomic power came to an end in January 1950 when the Soviet Union walked out of the CCA in protest against the presence of the representative of Nationalist China. It reconvened in April 1950, without the USSR. Soviet success with atomic power and her failure to continue negotiations convinced President Harry S. Truman that it was necessary to order the United States Atomic Energy Commission to pursue the development of a hydrogen bomb.

The failure of the UNAEC and President Truman's announcement prompted the World Council of Churches Executive Committee to make a public statement in February 1950 against the development of the hydrogen bomb. 'The hydrogen bomb is the latest and most terrible step in the crescendo of warfare which has changed war from a fight between man and nations to a mass murder of human life. . . . All this is a perversion; . . . it is sin against God.' As a response to the walkout of the Soviet Union from UNAEC and the Security Council, the statement continued, 'The governments have an inescapable responsibility at this hour. . . . But sharp political conflicts continue and the atomic danger develops uncontrolled. We urge the governments to enter into negotiations once again. . . .' [6] It further urged that each government should take the initiative to resume negotiations and not wait for the 'guilty party' (always the other side) to do so. Governments should be willing to 'take reasonable risks' to secure agreement on arms control.

But the Cold War mentality on both sides prevented one part of the world from heeding this advice. The Cold War became a hot one as North Korean forces invaded South Korea in the early morning hours of 25 June 1950. On 9 July the WCC Central Committee gathered in Toronto for its annual meeting; its proximity in time to the recent invasion provided an unprecedented opportunity for the whole Central Committee to speak out on a major international incident. The CCIA had drafted a 'Statement on the

Korean Situation and World Order' which, after modification, was adopted by the Central Committee. One paragraph referred specifically to the control of atomic weapons. 'Such methods of modern warfare as the use of atomic and bacteriological weapons and obliteration bombing involve force and destruction of life on so terrible a scale as to imperil the very basis on which law and civilization can exist. It is therefore imperative that they should be banned by international agreement and we welcome every sincere proposal to this end.' [7] It went on to urge both immediate and continuous inspection after such weapons and methods had been outlawed. Thus the World Council, which had never considered atomic and conventional weapons as separate problems, embraced both the American and Soviet proposals which had been before the deadlocked Atomic Energy Commission. The London *Daily Worker* quoted approvingly the Central Committee condemnation of atomic and bacteriological weapons, without, however, stating that in the same resolution it had also censured the North Korean invasion.[8]

In March 1950 the Stockholm Appeal, a worldwide petition issued by the Congress of Partisans for Peace, a communist-front organization, had also demanded the outlawing of atomic weapons and stated that the first country which used such weapons would be committing a crime against humanity. There was a great deal of pressure for the World Council to join in this appeal. However, its patent communist source and the fact that it followed the Soviet proposals for less stringent inspection led the CCIA to advise its constituencies and the World Council itself not to associate themselves with it. The following year, at the CCIA Executive Committee meeting, the statement 'Christians Stand For Peace' was adopted; it summarized CCIA and World Council views and statements on peace in order to counter still further the pressure and propaganda that was coming from the World Peace Council (ex-Partisans for Peace) regarding the Stockholm Appeal. It was a general statement containing the affirmation, 'We condemn equally the proposal of a preventive war, or the use for aggressive purposes of atomic weapons'. In January 1951 Monsieur Joliot-Curie, a leading figure in the WPC, made another attempt to gain the support of the WCC, which replied in a letter by Baron van Asbeck, K. G. Grubb, and O. F. Nolde in which they stressed the interest of the churches in effective international control of weapons of mass destruction but declined to co-operate with the World Peace Council.[9]

On 24 October 1950, the fifth anniversary of the United Nations, President Truman proposed to the General Assembly that it should now consider consolidating the work of the United Nations Atomic Energy Commission and the Commission on Conventional Armaments. This step did go some way towards meeting the Soviet position and followed the injunctions of the World Council of the previous February and August, but it is more likely that secular rather than religious events influenced him. It has been suggested that this proposal was made to gain favour with members of the United Nations who feared the rearming of the United States in its preparations to help in Korea. The Stockholm Appeal, which had had a great success on a world scale, had put the United States on the defensive where propaganda was concerned. In any case, the ending of the American monopoly of atomic power, even though the Soviet Union had not yet a delivery system, brought about concern for types of control other than those envisaged by the Baruch Plan.

At the request of the Presidents of the World Council, the officers of the CCIA, in February 1951, prepared a communication in which they expressed 'strong agreement with the progressive reduction and eventual abolition of all national armaments, including atomic weapons and all weapons of mass destruction, and of all national armies, subject always to certain conditions which we put forward provisionally for consideration . . .'. The communication further stressed the possibility of gradual reduction of forces and weapons under the protection of a United Nations combined force. The World Council Executive Committee (also meeting in February 1951, at Bièvres in France), addressed a letter to the churches in which it considered the increasing armaments of the world. It saw the West arming for fear of Communist aggression; it understood the East to be arming for fear of a preventive war by the West. But whatever the circumstances, it urged, Christians must not let armaments 'dominate the whole life of national and international society'.[10]

As a result of President Truman's speech of 24 October 1950 the General Assembly created a Committee of Twelve which recommended to the 1951 (Sixth) session the creation of a Disarmament Commission. In addition, the three Western powers proposed that limits of national armed forces and weapons be devised and that, if these limits were agreed upon, systems of control and continuous inspection be instituted for both conventional and atomic weapons. Such a general programme of disarmament could not, however (they asserted), be put into effect while the United Nations was fighting in Korea. The Soviet Union's counter-proposals were basically as already stated under different circumstances: immediate prohibition of atomic weapons, with unspecified international control subject to veto in the Security Council, and immediate reduction of conventional forces by one-third for each of the Big Five.

Deadlock was quickly reached but there were hopes that it might be broken by means of a Sub-Committee. Dr O. F. Nolde addressed a letter to the members of the Sub-Committee (the President of the General Assembly, the representatives of the United States, United Kingdom, France, and the Soviet Union) in which he stressed that 'the reduction of armaments is not an arithmetical proposition but a political and, above all, a moral problem'.[11] This was in laudable contrast to the attitude of the Christian international organizations at the 1932 Geneva Disarmament Conference, when some representatives of Christian bodies hesitated to make any recommendation for fear of treading upon the 'technical' aspects of disarmament. Subsequent agreements on arms control proposals more than a decade later, when, for political reasons, the United States and the USSR reached a compromise, are proof of Dr Nolde's assertion. The CCIA states that the views in the letter to the Sub-Committee were extensively discussed at informal meetings with delegates. In two addresses, 'Rearmament and Reconciliation' and 'Disarmament', Dr Nolde also tried to publicize and interpret the views advanced on behalf of the churches.

During the first meeting of the Sub-Committee the three Western powers presented a plan calling for a ceiling on the armed forces of the five great powers. Predictably, these proposals were denounced by the Soviet delegate, Mr Malik, who stated that they did not go as far as his proposals. The latter included prohibition of bacteriological warfare and other weapons of mass destruction. The Western proposals provided only arbitrary ceilings, Mr Malik claimed, and he counter-offered with the Soviet formula of an immediate one-third overall reduction in armaments and armed forces of the major powers. To a deadlocked Sub-Committee, Dr Nolde's letter claimed to reflect

the deep concern for peace and justice which moves many millions of people in our churches and missions throughout the world. . . . If present positions are maintained, agreement on first steps toward reduction can in all probability not be found solely in the area of armaments, but will have to take into account concomitant factors. For example, if there is to be provision for verified assurance that atomic weapons will not be used, there must also be provision for verified assurance that powerful nations will permit peoples in all countries freely to choose their own forms of government, to determine their own policies, and to bring about necessary changes by peaceful means and with the preservation of freedom. Similar considerations of equity will apply to all other arms and armed forces . . . [12]

On the recommendation of the Committee of Twelve, the General Assembly created the United Nations Disarmament Commission (UNDC) on 11 January 1952, composed of the members of the Security Council and Canada. Its mandate was to negotiate a system of disarmament with safeguards acceptable to all. Reflecting President Truman's proposals of late 1950, atomic armaments were included within its scope, a concession designed to please the Soviet Union. Meeting for the first time on 4 February 1952, the Disarmament Commission adopted a compromise French proposal for its plan of work (after a deadlock between Soviet and American plans seemed certain). This permitted the Commission to begin work, but in May the Western powers again proposed their same numerical limitations; again the Soviet Union countered with their demand for prohibition of atomic weapons and a one-third reduction in armaments and armed forces.

Under such Cold War conditions as these, the CCIA Executive Committee, meeting in July 1952, passed a resolution welcoming the establishment of the Disarmament Commission and recognizing the 'urgent importance' of progressive reduction of arms. Its advice to the Commission called for: (1) an assessment by an international inspection team under the United Nations of the armaments situation in the various states; (2) continuous inspection and control with adequate safeguards; and (3) a schedule to fix stages of reduction of arms.[13] It noted that an international police force would aid such a reduction; a first step in this direction would be forces earmarked for use by the United Nations. It was a vain hope both by the nations of the world and the churches of the world to expect two powers whose forces or surrogate forces faced each other in Korea to agree on a reduction of armaments.

The existence of the American hydrogen bomb, tested at Eniwetok Atoll on 31 October 1952, was not announced until 8 January 1953. The United States, once again, had a lead in destructive capability. Josef Stalin died in March. The consequent power-shuffle in the Kremlin may have led to the Korean Armistice Agreement signed on 27 July 1953. Stalin's posthumous gift to the world was exploded on 12 August 1953, bringing the Soviet potential nuclear capability on to a par with the American. Reflecting these conditions, the Disarmament Commission, which met only once during 1953, adopted its report unanimously, expressing 'the hope that recent international events would create a more propitious atmosphere for the reconsideration of the disarmament question'.

Atoms for Peace . . . and War

In April 1954 the Disarmament Commission, acting on the General Assembly Resolution of 28 November 1953, established a Sub-Committee 'of the powers principally concerned', i.e., Canada, France, the United Kingdom, the United States, and the USSR. President Dwight Eisenhower, in an address before the General Assembly on 8 December 1953, endorsed the idea of a sub-committee in which private conversations could take place. He further offered his 'Atoms for Peace' proposal in which the nuclear powers would contribute fissionable materials to an international atomic energy agency. This plan, Eisenhower felt, would give the two nuclear super-powers the opportunity to co-operate without actually having to set inspection procedures and controls. The CCIA took no formal action pending the 1954 Evanston Assembly, but was generally favourably disposed towards President Eisenhower's proposal. It, too, felt that in addition to any intrinsic worth, the proposal did provide the means by which the two super-powers could become accustomed to co-operating.

The Evanston Assembly in 1954 did not discuss the problem of disarmament to the same extent as other international issues, for example racism. Nevertheless a significant portion of the report 'Christians in the Struggle for World Community' was devoted to the evils of arms and the virtue of their regulation. 'Without forsaking their conviction that all weapons of war are evil, the churches should press for restraints on their use. Christians in all lands must plead with their governments to be patient and persistent in their search for means to limit weapons and advance disarmament.' [14] It urged the elimination and prohibition of atomic, hydrogen, and all weapons of mass destruction, as well as the reduction of all types of armaments. It recognized that an impasse had been reached on the issue of the control of nuclear weapons and that the first constructive step to help restore confidence would be the renunciation of their use or threat of use. It also called for safeguards in the testing of the hydrogen bomb.

The same section also proposed 'An Appeal from the World Council of Churches' [15] which was adopted by the full Assembly and addressed to the world. It again urged the prohibition of all weapons of mass destruction, with provision for international inspection and control along with the reduction of all other armaments. The peace, it was felt, was gravely endangered by the armaments race. This appeal was distributed to more than five hundred delegates at the Ninth Session of the General Assembly.

As a matter of policy, the CCIA had concentrated on finding agreement on a starting point for disarmament. On 19 April 1954 it distributed an informal memorandum which illustrated how it was already possible, under the United Nations Charter, for members to outlaw any threat or use of force, including atomic, hydrogen or other weapons of mass destruction, against the territorial integrity of any state and at the same time to recognize the inherent right of self-defence if an armed attack should occur. Its stated policies had even penetrated the Iron Curtain, as evidenced by East German Deputy Premier Nuschke's action in writing to Bishop Bell, Chairman of the WCC Central Committee, requesting the World Council to join in demanding a ban on all nuclear weapons. *Die Neue Zeit,* the East German Democratic Party newspaper, devoted almost the whole of its front page to Bishop Bell's reply, which promised that the World Council would do its utmost to further the gigantic effort that states must make to attain international agreement. The newspaper described the letter as approval of the Communist demand for banning all weapons of mass destruction, though in fact Bishop Bell did not mention a ban.[16] Such prominence given to World Council thought on the problem of disarmament, even if purely for purposes of propaganda, indicates that even in atheistic countries ecumenical approval is sought.

A proposal similar to that of the CCIA was made jointly by France and the United Kingdom at the meeting on 11 June 1954 of the Sub-Committee of the UNDC. The Soviet Union rejected it at the time. However, the Soviet proposal at the Ninth Session of the General Assembly was based on the Franco-British proposals. The final proposal before the General Assembly was sponsored by France, the United Kingdom, Canada, and both the United States and the USSR. It concluded that a further attempt should be made to achieve an international disarmament treaty to regulate, limit, and provide for the reduction of armed forces and conventional armaments (as desired by the Western Powers) and to include the total prohibition of use and manufacture of nuclear weapons and other weapons of mass destruction (as proposed by the Soviet Union since 1945). The resolution also made provision for international control and inspection in sufficiently all-inclusive but general terms as to please both the Soviets and the Americans.

The Sub-Committee of the UNDC reconvened in the spring of 1955 with the same cordiality among the great powers that was exhibited prior to adjournment. On 10 May the Soviet Union put forward a plan that accepted gradual implementation of disarmament, as proposed by France and the United Kingdom, the United States presented the chief obstacle to agreement, maintaining that technical difficulties stood in the way of exercising control over nuclear weapons. This was not regarded as too serious a problem, for the leaders of the four major powers had agreed to a summit meeting in Geneva that July. At this meeting President Eisenhower made his famous 'open skies' proposal whereby states would allow inspection by overflight, a plan advantageous primarily to the West which found intelligence activities in the Soviet closed society more difficult than did the Russians in Western societies. For Philip Noel-Baker, the Soviet proposals represented the 'Moment of Hope', for John Strachey rather the 'moment of despair'. American academics tended to view the Soviet proposal negatively through cold-war lenses.[17]

Sir Kenneth Grubb and Dr Nolde, on behalf of the CCIA, communicated in very general terms with the heads of government during their Geneva summit meeting, sending each of them a copy of the WCC Presidents' 'Call to Prayer'—a request that all should pray for the good guidance of the statesmen and the success of their deliberations. Replies were received only from the American and British governments. Meeting immediately after the summit meeting and heartened by the 'Spirit of Geneva' and apparent Soviet acceptance of disarmament proposals, the CCIA Executive Committee issued a 'Statement on Disarmament and Peaceful Change',[18] adopted in August by the Central Committee.

This statement was a more detailed and thoughtful analysis than the World Council had heretofore issued on disarmament. It brought to the attention of the seven hundred national and international officials to whom it was sent the knowledge that the message came not from a naïve Christian group but from one well up on its international reading. To many supporters of disarmament the very act of disarmament is the magical motion that will bring peace and euphoria. However, as many modern studies of disarmament have shown,[19] the building-up of arms is a symptom more than a cause of lack of confidence and friendliness, and also perhaps of a lack in the international system itself. In its introduction the statement tied the problem of disarmament ('the process whereby all armaments will be progressively reduced under adequate international inspection and control') to that of discovering a means that would enable existing unjust situations to be rectified. Furthermore, it urged participation in the United Nations programme for the peaceful use of atomic energy.

The old concern was stated in new words: the elimination and prohibition of nuclear and other weapons of mass destruction coupled with a reduction of conventional arms. The statement saw the problem as twofold: (1) agreeing on a system of inspection and control acceptable politically and technically; and (2) arriving at the psychological starting point from which armaments reduction could begin. To provide for technical inspection possibilities without political propaganda, it proposed that scientists should be appointed by the United Nations to work on this matter. To find a point from which the start could be made, it advised that small ways of co-operation, where compliance could be tested on a day-to-day basis, should be created. The ensuing relaxation of tension would lead to still greater co-operation.

The World Council was itself aware that what it suggested was beyond the realm of possibility at the time; its main desire was to stimulate discussions among the governments to develop methods of peaceful change and peaceful settlement. As its own suggestion for beginning these discussions, it recommended that procedures be followed where the veto did not apply. If a situation arose which endangered international peace and security, a cease-fire should be recommended and a Peace Observation Commission should be sent to the area to supervise it. An impartial agency would then identify the causes of the conflict and would submit its findings to the governments concerned, also, if necessary, to relevant organs of the United Nations. This latter recommendation almost takes one back to the days of the League, when it was believed that rationality was all that was needed. If only states could be prevented from rushing into war, they would calm down and think things over. When their error was shown them, they would recant. There is no evidence that the desired discussions were, in fact, stimulated.

The UNDC Sub-Committee reconvened in August at United Nations Headquarters. The United States presented a plan based on President Eisenhower's 'Open Skies' proposal; the Soviet Union's was based on Chairman Bulganin's proposal for ground control posts. These were discussed until the Tenth Session of the General Assembly met that autumn, when all proposals were transmitted to it. The General Assembly again urged continued efforts by the UNDC and that special consideration should be given to the Eisenhower and Bulganin proposals, as well as 'all such measures of adequately safeguarded disarmament as are now feasible', the latter a rebuke for American insistence on excessive inspection guarantees, referred to by some as 'inspection without disarmament'.

Deputy Premier Mikoyan, speaking at the Twentieth Party Congress, informed that body and the world that the Soviet Union had the capacity '. . . to deliver atomic and hydrogen bombs by aircraft or rockets to any spot in the world'.[20] The United States countered this claim with the deed of the first successful air-dropped hydrogen bomb on 21 May 1956. The UNDC Sub-Committee met in spite of the apparent attempts to assert superiority by both sides. The Soviet delegation submitted a proposal for partial disarmament; the US position was that an immediate beginning could be made on one proposal, but that a more comprehensive attempt must await the solution of important political issues. The churches were still seeking the optimum results for their action in international affairs, a posture no different from that of many powerful states. Lay and ecclesiastical leaders from Eastern and Western Europe and the United States met at Arnoldshain, West Germany, to confer on 'The Responsible Society in National and International Affairs'.[21] Among its topics was disarmament. No resolution was passed, and the report indicated both consensus and dissension on various points. It was well understood by these men that disarmament was the 'by product of a relatively stable international order' and not that it created such an order. The way in which the churches could help to achieve order and disarmament was by urging governments and peoples to recognize the urgency of the situation and their responsibility to co-operate in all attempts to achieve a just international order. Where nationalism or ideology reared its head, the churches were to denounce it. In order to create the confidence necessary for achieving the just international order, Christians were also to encourage the use of nuclear power for peaceful means and support the establishment of the proposed International Atomic Energy Agency.

The continuing attempts of both the United States and the USSR to develop bigger and better bombs and to this end to continue atomspheric testing were viewed by the churches not only as gratuitously inflicting the ill effects of fall-out on the by-stander in world affairs who happened to be in the way of prevailing winds but also as a basically inflammatory act. The Arnoldshain conference supported efforts to ban the testing of nuclear weapons. The CCIA Executive Committee meeting, held shortly after Arnoldshain in late July 1956, discussed at length the necessity for cessation of tests. A statement was adopted on the issue for the guidance of CCIA officers, supporting the discontinuance of nuclear tests by international agreement as soon as possible. This was qualified by several 'observations' attempting to show the ecclesiastical grasp of *Realpolitik*.[22] One concerned the wisdom of unilaterally abandoning the tests; another observed the inter-connection of the tests and of the overall armaments effort. It also urged the necessity of informing public opinion on the effects of radiation. The Central Committee meeting one month later in Hungary issued a summary statement: 'We call upon the churches to appeal to their governments for the discontinuance, or limitation and control of these tests . . .'

The crises over Suez and Hungary distracted the attention of the world from disarmament, but 1957 brought renewed efforts in the UNDC Sub-Committee where it appeared that both the American and the Soviet delegates were willing to negotiate seriously. The discussions, however, ended in acrimonious accusations prior to the General Assembly meeting that autumn. This Twelfth Session of the General Assembly was to be the last to see the item 'Regulation, limitation and balanced reduction of all armed forces and all armaments' on its agenda. The Soviet Union refused to participate in further meetings of the Disarmament Commission or its Sub-Committee, even though the latter was to be increased by fourteen states to make it more representative of the world. What the Soviet Union wanted was a permanent disarmament commission of all members of the United Nations. This proposal was, however, defeated.

That same year of 1957 saw a greater level of activity in nuclear testing and consequently greater activity on the part of the churches. Primarily because of the anti-test statements of Pope John XXIII, Albert Schweitzer, a group of German scientists, and Prime Minister Macmillian of Great Britain, the initiative for a CCIA Executive Committee statement was requested by Dr Visser 't Hooft. A long and thorough 'Atomic Tests and Disarmament Statement' was adopted.[23] In a moving introduction, it noted the fear upon the peoples of the earth—a fear of nuclear weapons, a fear of the consequences of their use, and a fear of the unknown consequences attendant upon radiation, both for this generation and those yet unborn. The Statement recognized the extent to which all aspects of a strategy for this end were interrelated, especially: (1) the cessation of nuclear testing by international agreement; (2) the cessation of production of nuclear weapons, with strict controls; (3) the development of measures to reduce both nuclear and conventional armaments, again with appropriate safeguards; (4) the acceleration of international cooperation in developing atomic power for peaceful purposes; and (5) the establishment of effective measures for peaceful settlement and peaceful change. The Statement ended on a less than optimistic note about the progress possible. It did urge Christians in states preparing for nuclear tests to urge unilateral abstention from testing for a trial period in order to establish the confidence necessary for international agreement on the subject.

The Central Committee at its meeting in July and August in New Haven, Connecticut, thoroughly discussed the Statement, on which opinion was sharply divided. In its own lengthy resolution on the subject, the Central Committee commended the CCIA statement to the churches for their consideration and addressed itself to the moral issue of two states taking decisions affecting many peoples who had no part at all in the decision. This universal responsibility was urged upon the super powers as a consideration in decision-making on testing in addition to the usual considerations of national defence. Member churches were urged to submit both this resolution and the CCIA Statement to their governments.[24] The CCIA itself made full use of the texts. It sent copies to all delegates at the Twelfth Session of the General Assembly, as well as to the Secretary-General and members of the Secretariat. The Statement was informally discussed with the Secretary-General when the latter was host to the Archbishop of Canterbury after the New Haven meeting. CCIA representatives had many informal consultations on the Statement with delegates so requesting it.[25]

The actions of the member churches were of three kinds. In some cases there was no action beyond publication of the texts in church newspapers and discussions in church circles. As is to be expected, this occurred in countries where the Protestant-Orthodox churches were weak, such as Austria, or where Christianity was weak, as in Japan. Then there were areas where unofficial comment was made to governments; this occurred in New Zealand and Norway (where a Commissioner of the CCIA was also a member of Parliament and leader of the Christian Folk's Party). In still other countries, the national councils of churches transmitted the statement officially to government officials with their comments. This took place in Australia, Denmark, France, the two Germanies, the United Kingdom, and the United States.

Interestingly enough, General de Gaulle replied to the French Reformed Church, certainly a minority church, stating that the matter would receive his full attention. Later activities of the French government regarding nuclear testing indicate this was indeed the case—but to schedule further tests. It appeared as no surprise that Chancellor Adenauer received leaders of the churches in the German Federal Republic; however, Prime Minister Grotewohl in East Berlin not only acknowledged the statement and criticized it in part, but also suggested that it be read from the pulpits. Government permission was also granted for the printing of the statement.[26] Thus Christian educative efforts were aided, even if for non-Christian reasons, by those who normally denounced them.

American church leaders submitted the documents in person to the Secretary of State, John Foster Dulles, on 13 September 1957. The United States had already made an unannounced decision to conduct a series of tests in the summer of 1958, and the Secretary could only express agreement with the churchmen's objectives, without committing himself. When the resumption of tests was publicly announced Dr Nolde wrote to the Secretary requesting that the United States offer to forgo the tests if Soviet co-operation in the disarmament area were evidenced. It was not ecclesiastical leaders alone who were disturbed by the seemingly obsessive compulsion of the nuclear powers to increase their destructive power in 'overkill' at the cost of unknown damage to future generations, for on 13 January 1958 Dr Linus Pauling, the American nuclear physicist, presented a petition to the Secretary-General of the United Nations, signed by some 9,000 scientists from forty-three countries, urging an immediate cessation of nuclear testing.

Both religious and secular activity in the United States failed to influence the course of events. On 26 March 1958 President Eisenhower announced that American scientists had succeeded in reducing fall-out and invited qualified experts under United Nations auspices to observe the explosions. On 31 March 1958 the Supreme Soviet adopted a decree ending nuclear testing; Premier Khrushchev in a personal letter requested President Eisenhower to suspend testing. This declaration of conditional cessation of tests and the way in which the United States could use it productively were 'forcefully brought to the attention of the Secretary of State' by Dr Nolde and Dr Barnes, Executive Secretary of the NCCCUSA. They urged Mr Dulles to consider suspending the tests as an act of conciliation, but he adamantly refused. Although the World Council has often been accused of following the capitalist 'line', this is one indication among many that it was, and is, an independent body which critically examines action by all sides. In spite of the planned continuation of the tests, a Conference of Experts on Detection of Nuclear Tests met in Geneva from 1 July to 21 August to consider the technical feasibility of detection.

The CCIA Executive Committee in August praised the ability of the Conference of Experts to reach agreement. It then adopted another statement on disarmament and nuclear tests, basically reiterating and reaffirming its statement of the previous year. It emphasized the necessity for inspection and controls but still advocated a suspension of tests, at least for a trial period, to encourage the growth of trust and confidence between the super powers. The report to the Central Committee was presented by the German physicist Dr C. F. von Weizsäcker, who stated that he could not in any way take part in the making or use of atomic weapons. He had not always held that position, he affirmed, but he did so now. The Central Committee received and approved the CCIA Executive Committee statement and adopted a shorter one, again calling for cessation of tests.[27]

The Soviet Union, the United Kingdom, and the United States agreed to begin negotiations with the Conference on the Discontinuance of Nuclear Tests, meeting at Geneva on 31 October 1958. President de Gaulle of France was not represented; as he had informed Premier Khrushchev, France would not agree to any cessation of nuclear tests unless it were accompanied by disarmament measures. Both the Americans and the British, whose tests had been scheduled for October, agreed that all nuclear tests should be suspended for the duration of the Conference. The Soviet Union, which had been observing a unilateral moratorium based upon no testing by others, carried out a short series of tests during the first days of the Conference in order to 'catch up' with the West. It suspended tests by 3 November and negotiations continued. By early 1959 the United States appeared to be the recalcitrant one, with demands for ironclad detection techniques. In fact, the World Council Executive Committee in a statement adopted that February indicated that 'any agreement, however carefully framed, involves a measure of calculated risk for all parties', and urged perseverance—and realism—in attempting to achieve fraud-tight inspection.[28] The statement was commended to member churches who were urged 'to do everything possible to build an informed public opinion . . . and to make such representations to their governments as they deem proper'. Sir Kenneth Grubb, Dr Nolde and Dr Elfan Rees personally submitted the World Council Executive Committee statement to the heads of the delegations: the Rt Hon. David Ormsby-Gore of the United Kingdom, Ambassador Semyon K. Tsarapkin of the USSR, and Ambassador James J. Wadsworth of the United States. Although all delegations allowed ample time for discussion of the issues involved, there was no noticeable change in the attitudes of any of the great powers.

The test-ban negotiations of 1959 finally reached some agreement on a control organization and its relationship to the United Nations. The Western leaders' proposal to ban atmospheric tests, 'the partial test ban', was not acceptable to the Soviet Union or to France, which continued preparations for its first atomic test in the Sahara. In the summer of 1959 the Thessalonica Conference on Rapid Social Change, sponsored by Church and Society, representing many delegates from Africa and Asia, requested the World Council to oppose the French tests. In a statement adopted at its August meeting, the Central Committee urged that 'so long as international control is under discussion, powers which have not made tests as yet should not launch them anywhere for military purposes'.[29] Stated with the obliquity of a papal declaration, it had no deterrent effect on the plans of General de Gaulle to make France once again a power of the first order. The statement also had words of advice and exhortation for those negotiating at Geneva: a treaty to cease all types of nuclear tests should be concluded (the Soviet position) and all tests for peaceful purposes should be under international control (the Western position). The Central Committee also urged the complete cessation of nuclear weapons testing, and, furthermore, that testing not be unilaterally resumed, so that people of other nations—who had not given their consent—would not have to bear the consequences of the decisions of others.

The General Assembly was more forthright than the Central Committee, and in a November resolution it urged France to refrain from atomic tests. France had stated, however, that she would halt her tests only for equal treatment with the other nuclear powers and as part of a general nuclear disarmament programme applicable to all. One minor though encouraging agreement reached between France, the USSR, the United Kingdom, the United States, and eight other states was the Treaty on the Antarctic, signed in Washington on 1 December 1959. It provided primarily for scientific co-operation in the Antarctic, but Article V also prohibited 'any nuclear explosion in Antarctica and the disposal of radio-active waste material'. More important were the provisions for observers and inspections. In such a case, without the doctrine of sovereignty looming over their shoulders, states can sometimes be reasonable.

In December 1959 President Eisenhower, speaking for the Western Powers, stated that they no longer looked upon themselves as bound by the unilateral undertaking of test-suspension, but that they would not resume tests without first announcing their intention to do so. In January 1960 Premier Khrushchev stated that the USSR would not resume testing unless the Western powers did so first. In February the Western powers put forth a new proposal to ban all testing in the atmosphere, outer space, under water, and underground above a seismic magnitude of 4.75. The World Council Executive Committee, meeting in Buenos Aires in February, expressed its appreciation of the progress made thus far in the negotiations, and urged a treaty covering those forms of nuclear tests which could then be detected; for smaller underground tests, it considered that a voluntary moratorium would preclude disagreement over inspection procedures.[30] In another statement, noting the announced intention of France to continue its tests in the Sahara, the Executive Committee asserted that states which had not yet conducted nuclear tests for military purposes should not begin to do so.

Although the Soviet Union replied to the Western proposal with a similar one in March, little further progress was made pending the summit meeting of President Eisenhower, Prime Minister Macmillan, President de Gaulle, and Premier Khrushchev in May. Nevertheless, CCIA representatives, according to their annual report, conducted extensive lobbying for a treaty based on the two proposals. On 16 May 1960 Dr Nolde addressed an open letter [31] to the heads of government at the Summit Conference in Paris, in which he expressed the opinion that they ought to be able to resolve the few remaining differences standing in the way of an agreement. Further, he called attention to the need for measures to halt the manufacture of nuclear weapons. Alas, the abortive conference did not give the leaders a chance to sit down and negotiate.

In March 1960 the Ten Nation Disarmament Committee convened. It had been created by the Foreign Ministers of France, the Soviet Union, the United Kingdom, and the United States to be independent of, but linked to, the United Nations in order to continue the disarmament negotiations interrupted two years previously. Made up of five East European delegations and five Western ones, the Committee soon became bogged down in discussing its relationship to the United Nations. No decision of substance had been reached before the five East European states withdrew, after the U-2 incident and the breakdown of the summit meeting in Paris. Strangely enough, the Conference on the Discontinuance of Nuclear

Tests reconvened on 27 May, and some proposals were put forward. Although no progress was made in the negotiations, the Conference remained in session for the greater part of that year.

This lack of progress in reaching agreement on the cessation of nuclear tests and the failure to begin any form of disarmament naturally disturbed the CCIA Executive Committee, which devoted extensive discussions to these problems at its meeting at St Andrews, Scotland, in the summer of 1960. No statement was issued, but a minute was adopted for the guidance of CCIA officers on several aspects of the international situation.[32] Among the issues mentioned was the need to reduce and regulate armaments, and, at the least, to resume serious negotiations. It was felt that a good beginning would be an agreement on the cessation of nuclear testing, where accord seemed so close. The Executive considered that success in that area might produce the mutual confidence necessary to make other disarmament proposals work.

The World Council Executive Committee in February 1961 welcomed the return of the great powers to the nuclear negotiating table. It repeated its stand that success there would aid deadlocked disarmament negotiations. 'We express the hope that disarmament negotiations will be reopened at the earliest possible moment, giving appropriate place to the responsibility of the United Nations in this area.'

The Conference on the Discontinuance of Nuclear Weapons Tests resumed its work in March 1961. Not surprisingly, the Soviet Union pointed out that, although it had discontinued tests, France —an ally of Great Britain and the United States—had not done so and that the Western Powers therefore had an advantage. After President Kennedy's meeting with Premier Khrushchev, the Soviet Union proposed that a test ban treaty be concluded on the basis of the USSR's proposals or at least that it be considered within the context of general and complete disarmament. This again produced dead-lock. On 30 August the Soviet Union announced that it was compelled by the aggressiveness of the NATO bloc to resume experimental nuclear explosions. The President of the United States declared that his country would be obliged to take whatever steps its national interests required. On 3 September both the United Kingdom and the United States proposed an end to all atmospheric tests without international control. This act of generosity was too late. After months of quibbling over ways in which the Soviet Union could cheat, the United States was faced with a simple, direct end to the moratorium much less devious than imagined.

Upon the announcement by the Soviet Union, the Officers of the World Council urged that there should be no testing without international consent or control. In October, when the USSR declared its intention to explode a 50-megaton bomb, Dr Nolde suggested that the General Assembly should issue 'a solemn appeal' against such action.[33] A resolution embodying the appeal was approved by the General Assembly on 27 October but the test was still carried out—in Novaya Zemlya on 30 October. Dr Nolde declared that the action invited escalation in the nuclear arms race.

Meanwhile the United States announced that it would conduct underground tests. Since World Council opinion was divided on this issue Dr Nolde decided not to protest. In speaking with Ambassador Arthur Dean, he took the informal position that the United States should not resume atmospheric tests until after the General Assembly debate that autumn. He was then told that the United States was indeed contemplating the resumption of such tests.[34] The Conference reconvened on 28 November with a new Soviet proposal rejected by the Western powers. It adjourned on 29 January 1962 *sine die*.

Yet international schizophrenia was surely at its height in 1961: in March, when the Soviet Union and the Western powers were haggling over plans for the cessation of tests, the US special representative in charge of disarmament, Ambassador John J. McCloy, began talks with Ambassador Zorin concerning future disarmament negotiations. It was agreed to meet informally in Moscow in July. Perhaps imbued with an overwrought sense of the churches' importance, Dr Nolde consulted World Council leaders on the question of whether he should go to Moscow at that time. They agreed to his going, provided that political circumstances were favourable and that Metropolitan Nikodim also agreed. In the end, after a talk with McCloy in Washington, Nolde decided not to go.

The CCIA met in plenary session in Bangalore, India, in November 1961 just before the Assembly. Such meetings are policy-planning sessions devoted to a study of policy recommendations to be made to the Assembly. Disarmament and East-West tensions received a great deal of attention. The greatest contribution of churches, it was felt, was to create a public opinion concerned about disarmament.

The New Delhi Assembly was itself apprehensive of the international situation, especially the Cold War and the threats of hot war that were borne into the air with every nuclear test. The recent books from the 'think-tanks' did not pass the churchmen by, for example, Herman Kahn's *On Thermonuclear War*, and Henry A. Kissinger's *Nuclear Weapons and Foreign Policy* and *The Necessity for Choice* in which speculation upon 'megadeaths' and how a nation might survive in nuclear war seemed to make but a cipher of human beings. The report of the Section on Service commented on this thought: 'The habit of thinking of persons as potential victims or potential destroyers in nuclear war will surely reduce sensitivity to their worth. Such sensitivity is blunted by callous use of abstract speculation concerning the millions who will die or survive in nuclear war. . . .' [35]

The same Section, in its paragraphs on disarmament, condemned the resumption of nuclear tests and the use of weapons which kill indiscriminately. 'In this situation the churches must never cease warning governments of the dangers.' The churches must fight the growing conviction that weapons of mass destruction will inevitably be used. Christians must not only urge their governments to eliminate nuclear weapons; governments must also be warned that, pending such elimination, they must never get into a position where they would contemplate their first use. 'Christians must also maintain that the use of nuclear weapons, or other forms of major violence, against centres of population is in no circumstances reconcilable with the demands of the Christian Gospel.' Total disarmament must be the goal, but it was realized that it was a long-term goal. It would be reached by many small steps. 'Experts must debate techniques, but the churches should constantly stimulate governments to make real advances.' [36]

The report of the Committee on the Commission of the Churches on International Affairs also tackled the issues of disarmament and nuclear testing. (Each Assembly Committee on a particular organ or department of the World Council is the overseer, on behalf of each Assembly, for the review and future policy of that body until the next Assembly.) This report was approved in substance by the Assembly and commended to the churches for study and appropriate action. The Committee noted that the goal of general and complete disarmament would necessarily be reached in stages. It cited the three disarmament proposals of the United Kingdom, of the United States, and of the USSR then before the Sixteenth Session of the UN General Assembly. It proposed that the CCIA should analyse each proposal and indicate which points were common to all and where the stumbling blocks lay. It proposed that a consultation should be held at the Ecumenical Institute between Christians from various countries and government specialists, who might explain in a confidential meeting the policies of their governments, especially those of the United States and the Soviet Union. The Committee endorsed the CCIA's condemnation of the nuclear tests by France and the resumption of those by the Soviet Union.

The Committee's proposed 'Appeal to all Governments and Peoples' [37] on the international situation was opposed in plenary session by the Methodist Professor C. A. Coulson of the United Kingdom, who wished to substitute a much shorter and more platitudinous statement. The Assembly adopted the original

'Appeal', slightly abridged, which emphasized that a halt in the arms race was imperative. General and complete disarmament was the goal; nevertheless, there must be a first step, and the cessation of nuclear tests could be that step. Indeed, referring to the objections of both sides, the 'Appeal' concluded that to break through mutual distrust might require the acceptance of an inspection system less than foolproof or one which might exceed its stated duties.

The Executive Committee of the World Council met in Geneva after the Eighteen Nation Disarmament Committee (which had been created by the General Assembly in December 1961) convened for the first time on 14 March 1962. On 21 March the ENDC established a Sub-Committee comprised of the Soviet Union, the United Kingdom, and the United States (France refused to participate in the work of the ENDC) to continue consideration of the cessation of nuclear testing. The WCC Executive Committee passed a resolution on disarmament in which it urged the participants 'not to continue or resume the testing of nuclear weapons and, as a warrant of their good faith, to agree on a system of information and verification which will assure all parties that treaty commitments are being honoured'. This statement was sent to the heads of the delegations to the ENDC. The exhortations were for nought, as the United States resumed testing in the atmosphere on 25 April. The officers of the World Council of Churches publicly condemned this—as they had done the Soviet resumption. The Director and Chairman of the CCIA issued a joint statement beginning with the categorical, 'The testing of nuclear weapons without international consent or control must cease'.[38] It proposed that an effort be made to devise a graduated system of information and verification, and that the use of non-aligned scientist inspectors might be acceptable to all. It announced that the governments concerned should be willing to conclude a treaty without air-tight assurances. If the nuclear powers refused such reasonable proposals and continued to test, a special session of the General Assembly should be convened to appeal to them, it recommended. Finally, if this action had no effect, the General Assembly should propose a summit meeting. In April the non-aligned members of the ENDC submitted a memorandum in which it was proposed that the monitoring systems then in use, supplemented by non-aligned experts, should be considered as affording adequate inspection. The nuclear powers agreed to use the memorandum as a basis for negotiations.

In fulfilment of the New Delhi mandate for a consultation with individuals from all sides of the disarmament question, the Consultation on Peace and Disarmament was convoked in Geneva, from 20 to 22 June 1962, during a recess of the ENDC. The first day was devoted to hearing the representatives from the ENDC:

Sir Michael Wright of the United Kingdom, Mr Alexander Akalovsky of the United States, and Ambassador Semyon Tsarapkin of the USSR. Baron von Platen of Sweden interpreted the position of the eight non-aligned members of the ENDC. The World Council participants included leading churchmen from Eastern Europe, including Archbishop Nikodim of the Soviet Union and Dr J. L. Hromadka of Czechoslovakia. In its final statement, the Consultation welcomed the Eight Non-Aligned Powers' Memorandum and felt that it offered the first step necessary to achieve an agreement. It recognized that public opinion had become considerably less interested in disarmament and that the churches in several states had not spoken out for it as they might have done.[39] Here it should be recognized that, simply as a public relations exercise, the great-power delegations could each have sent any representative, a junior secretary, merely to placate groups interested in disarmament. In fact, the heads of delegations appeared before World Council leaders, even the Soviet Ambassador who might have considered a church group unworthy of Marxist attention. The admission of the Russian Orthodox Church as a member of the World Council at New Delhi seemed to put the World Council in a different light and may account for this Soviet co-operation. It could be deduced that any body which can call upon such high co-operation would at least be heard out in the councils of the great.

Meeting at the beginning of August in a deserted Paris, the CCIA Executive Committee gave considerable thought and discussion to disarmament. A statement was issued which reiterated the positions taken so often before on cessation of testing and effective disarmament. A new emphasis was introduced in which the opinion-shaping role of the churches was stressed and the directions it should take were prescribed. The Central Committee, meeting shortly thereafter, generally approved the statement and urged that it be given the widest publicity.[40] Copies were sent to the heads of delegations of the ENDC and to the delegates at the Seventeenth Session of the United Nations General Assembly.

An example of the workings of the CCIA is the amount of correspondence sent to leading public officials. When the United States resumed testing, letters of protest were sent by Dr Nolde to Secretary of State Dean Rusk, and to Ambassadors Arthur Dean, Jacob Beam, and Adlai Stevenson. At a meeting of the United States Conference for the World Council of Churches on 26 April 1962, Dr Nolde gave an address calling for the cessation of atmospheric testing. In letters to the UN Secretary-General U Thant, to Sir Patrick Dean of the British delegation, and to American Ambassador Jacob Beam he drew attention to the urgency of this matter. Personal and informal relations were used concurrently with open letters for publication. These relations were reciprocal: often an official would be just as keen to advance his views as the churchman, either in order to justify himself or to act as a sounding board for possible policy changes. In the broader context of all World Council individual contacts, the importance of personal relationships will be elaborated in the final chapter.

In August the United States and the United Kingdom submitted alternative draft treaties (while the United States continued testing), one for a comprehensive treaty banning all types of tests, the other banning only tests in the atmosphere, outer space, and under water. At last what so many had suggested as a means to break the dead-lock was being proposed. Throughout the Cuban missile crisis the meetings continued, and further proposals and counter-proposals were made. The ENDC went into recession in December, seemingly no closer to agreement. The first months of 1963 witnessed a general relaxation after the tense days on the brink of nuclear war the previous September. The Eighteen Nation Disarmament Committee reconvened on 21 February 1963, with apparent agreement on three principles: (1) the use of nationally manned and con-trolled seismic stations; (2) the installation of unmanned seismic stations on territories of the nuclear powers; and (3) an annual quota of on-site inspections. The exact number of inspections and unmanned stations was still a matter of negotiation. Once political situations in the world developed to bring about Soviet-American co-operation, the results could be astoundingly quick. On 10 June talks between the three nuclear powers were announced to begin on 15 July in Moscow. The Soviet Union dropped its demand that a moratorium on underground testing must accompany any partial test ban treaty. By 25 July agreement had been reached on a treaty banning nuclear tests in the atmosphere, in outer space, and under water; the treaty itself was signed on 5 August.

Statesmen are not used to receiving praise from the churches. The Central Committee, however, at its late August meeting at Rochester, New York, addressed letters of gratitude to the three statesmen who had made the Nuclear Test Ban Treaty possible. It is true that the letters ended with the admonition that much remained yet to be done and that they were accompanied by the statement 'The Test Ban Treaty and the Next Steps: from Co-exist-ence to Co-operation'.[41] This statement, drafted by the CCIA Executive Committee and adopted by the Central Committee, also praised the new treaty, noting, however, that it did not slow down the arms race nor prevent the spread of nuclear weapons to states which did not yet have them. (This foreshadowed the need for a non-proliferation treaty, at this time still a future consideration for the nuclear powers.) The goodwill thus far shown, it suggested, should be used to begin negotiations for general and complete disarmament. It was hoped that a way would be found whereby France and China could associate themselves with the treaty; the latter, it was feared, would feel more isolated than before and attempts at new means of contact were advocated. Although the WCC opposed the proliferation of nuclear weapons, it realized the danger of the concentration of such great power in so few hands and recommended that responsibility for nuclear weapons be shared within the alliances of the nuclear powers to mitigate the corrupting influence of power. Furthermore, underground weapons-testing should be halted and outer space should be protected from military competition. The latter case is another example of prophetic vision in that the disarmament of outer space became a matter of general concern, and a treaty on this subject was concluded in 1966.

This statement was sent to the governments of the nuclear powers, to all commissioners of the CCIA, all National Commissions on International Affairs, to 1,000 delegates at the Eighteenth Session of the UN General Assembly, to the Secretary-General and key members of his Secretariat, and to officials of numerous governments. Many churches made use of it in consultations with their governments and in forming opinion within their denominations. When the Eighteen Nation Disarmament Committee resumed deliberations in January 1964, it was sent to the delegates and served as a point of reference in consultations with the heads of delegations representing the nuclear powers.[42] Although it would be naïve to give the World Council of Churches credit for the test ban treaty, one must see that its constant preoccupation with this goal led it to publicize the desirability of such a treaty to its constituencies. This provided a source of information other than the Cold War news which was the daily diet of the populations of both West and East. Here was an institution in Western society which political leaders were accustomed to hearing, if not to heeding. The publicity and opinion disseminated by the World Council made the treaty more acceptable to those of its Western constituents who were imbued with extreme anti-communist feeling by existing social forces. The use which the press in the communist countries made of World Council pronouncements against nuclear weapons and tests has been noted above and it will be examined more closely in chapter 5 below.

Problems and Opportunities

Meeting in Odessa at the invitation of the Russian Orthodox Church, the World Council Executive Committee issued a statement on 'Problems and Opportunities Today', welcoming the relaxation of tension between the major powers and hoping that the 'opportunity would be seized to advance from competition in armaments to co-operation in disarmament'. It reviewed the political world of the mid-sixties: 'Local conflicts multiply and this confronts powerful nations with the temptation to seek ideological or territorial gains—whether by military aid, economic exploitation, or acts of subversion'. Nevertheless, the Executive Committee urged that recent proposals by both sides in regard to disarmament were close enough to make agreement a possibility. It called upon states to take unilateral measures—for example, the reduction of military budgets and of standing forces—and to exercise restraint in the face of political provocation in order to instil confidence and enable further multilateral agreements to be reached. This text, too, was communicated to the delegates at the Eighteen Nation Disarmament Committee and was discussed individually with some delegations. Subsequent to this statement, the CCIA has pointed out, unilateral announcements were made by the three nuclear powers of a decrease in the production of fissionable material for military purposes.

While the Eighteen Nation Committee discussed the various proposals before it, CCIA officials prepared for a Second Consultation on Peace and Disarmament. These preparations again indicate the extent to which CCIA officials were known to government officials, if not the extent to which they might have been privy to information. Dr Nolde had spoken to Secretary of State Dean Rusk concerning the Second Consultation and had been assured informally of State Department co-operation. Dr Elfan Rees in Geneva had discussed it with Peter Thomas of the United Kingdom delegation to the ENDC and had been assured of 'favourable consideration' by Her Majesty's Government. In New York Dr Nolde discussed the Executive Committee meeting at Odessa with the Soviet Representative to the United Nations, Ambassador Fedorenko, explained CCIA interests to him, and told him about the contacts with American and British officials, as well as that with Ambassador Tsarapkin regarding the Second Consultation. Much to Dr Nolde's embarrassment, Ambassador Fedorenko indicated that he would be willing to fly to Geneva to address it. Elated with the indication of the high regard in which the CCIA was held even by Soviet representatives, Nolde was nevertheless embarrassed about the rather unimportant consultation which was to take place.

When the Consultation convened in Geneva, from 16 to 18 June 1964, the United States was represented by the Honourable William C. Foster and Ambassador Clare Timberlake, the United Kingdom by Ambassador Sir Paul Mason, the Soviet Union by Ambassador L. I. Mendelevich, and the non-aligned states on the ENDC by Ambassador L. C. N. Obi of Nigeria. Again each speaker interpreted his government's viewpoint. The Consultation's final statement welcomed the Nuclear Test Ban Treaty and the relaxation of East–West tension and attempted to draw the lines of agreement and disagreement between the powers. It seemed that the negotiating powers agreed that a reduction of arms must not disturb the nuclear balance—upon which they felt that security rested—and that general and complete disarmament would not be achieved in a short time. They were separated, however, by many points of disagreement: on the stages of disarmament, on verification, on how best to prevent the proliferation of nuclear weapons, and, perhaps most significantly, on the political problems of Germany and Southeast Asia, seemingly far removed from the disarmament negotiations. The Consultation differed on how best to maintain peace and security while disarmament proceeded by stages; in fact the participants admitted that the role of the churches in this phase of international politics was not clearly understood. The only clear duty of the churches was to help mould an intelligent public opinion.[43]

Little further progress had been made by the time the Central Committee met in January 1965 at Enugu, Eastern Nigeria. That meeting was more forthright than the Consultation had been, and less modest in offering advice; the armaments race continued; more ought to be done to stop it. It stated, too, that France and China had to be brought into the negotiations in order to achieve maximum results. The primary purpose of disarmament talks was to limit destructive power, and that could be done by limiting nuclear warheads and delivery power as well as by the establishment of nuclear-free zones, as the Organization for African Unity had recently proposed for Africa.[44] To this, as to so many other proposals of Christian leadership, there were no public responses by governments or the United Nations.

The United Nations Disarmament Commission, meeting for the first time since 1959, was convened in New York on 21 April 1965 in response to a request by the Soviet Union. The general debate emphasized that possible proliferation of nuclear weapons was now the major problem in the field of disarmament. The thirty-five African and Asian states on the Commission and Yugoslavia took the initiative and called for a world disarmament conference which all states, clearly including the People's Republic of China, would attend. The United States did not support this move, but neither did she oppose it. The CCIA Executive Committee meeting in July acknowledged the convocation of the United Nations Disarmament Commission and welcomed the suggestion to call a world conference on disarmament in which China could participate. The lack of any progress in the field since the Nuclear Test Ban Treaty was noted with disappointment.[45]

The Eighteen Nation Disarmament Committee reconvened on 27 January 1966. The WCC Central Committee met shortly afterwards (also in Geneva) and adopted a 'Statement on Disarmament', in which it addressed itself to its member churches but also sought 'to encourage governments to press forward in this task upon which the fate of mankind may hang'.[46] As it had done so often before, the Central Committee urged that underground tests also be included in the test ban. The potential proliferation of nuclear weapons was still a matter of concern to the Central Committee; realistically it understood that the non-nuclear powers, in forgoing the possession of nuclear weapons, had a claim to protection from nuclear attack and to the benefits of nuclear power for peaceful uses. These objectives lay within the power of the Eighteen Nation Disarmament Committee to achieve, it asserted. The Central Committee also welcomed the proposal for a world disarmament conference.

The lay and church leaders participating in the World Conference on Church and Society in Geneva, from 12 to 26 July 1966, were often political leaders and technical advisers in their home countries. Section III of the Conference dealt with the issue of nuclear weapons and warfare in its report 'Living Together in Peace in a Pluralistic World Society'.[47] Although recognizing the historical division in Christian thought concerning the acceptability of war in self-defence, the Section categorically declared that 'nuclear war is against God's will and the greatest of evils'. In considering the relations between the United States and the Soviet Union, the Section estimated that they were now ready to accommodate each other because of the terror of nuclear weapons, world economic interdependence, and the exchanges which had removed the false images each nation had of the other. The Section was divided as to the best way to achieve disarmament: one group held that the immediate establishment of nuclear-free zones and general and complete disarmament was a prelude to still closer co-operation; the second, more realistically, believed that more modest steps would have to precede the desired goals. The churches could help to reduce the mutual mistrust of these giants by challenging the tendency to make ideologies absolute and by acting as a community that transcended nations.

In attempting to limit their dependence on the two super-powers, states have developed their own nuclear capabilities, as exemplified earlier by France and China, and more recently by India. The problem of proliferation, as the Section noted, could be solved only by guaranteeing small powers against nuclear blackmail, the creation of nuclear-free zones, and the control of fissionable material. As it was at the moment, the power of the two nuclear giants over the non-nuclear states was in no way checked. Although the Section recognized the limited usefulness of world public opinion through the United Nations as a control on the superpowers, it appeared to be the only possibility at that time. The Section affirmed that 'it is the first duty of governments and their officials to prevent nuclear war'. It further requested 'control and inspection of armaments by international agencies to ensure an equilibrium of power and regulate the different phases of disarmament'. In keeping with the widespread representation from the Third World at this Conference, most comments on disarmament linked the potential saving in resources with additional aid to under-developed areas.

The stands of the various meetings, consultations, and conferences of the World Council organs provided further opportunity for CCIA officials to communicate with delegates to the United Nations. The CCIA explained the World Council's position on disarmament both to the delegates to the Twenty-first Session of the General Assembly in September 1966 and to those attending the ENDC when it reconvened early in 1967 in Geneva. CCIA officials reported numerous personal consultations, as well as correspondence, with various delegations. One of the major areas of concern in the disarmament negotiations was the non-proliferation of nuclear weapons, a care of the Central Committee since the previous year. CCIA officials reported that correspondence and consultations on this point with non-nuclear powers indicated that such powers had two aims: in addition to their desire for a clearcut commitment by the nuclear powers to halt the nuclear arms race they also wanted assurances that there would be no interference with their own development of nuclear energy for peaceful purposes. These views were transmitted by the CCIA to the participants in the ENDC at their late May meeting in Geneva.[48]

In response to the negotiations for a non-proliferation treaty, the WCC Executive Committee, meeting in mid-February 1967, adopted a minute welcoming this subject as an item on the agenda at the UNDC meetings and pointing out that it was a cause which the CCIA and the World Council had consistently supported. It wished to involve in the treaty, however, every nation which possessed nuclear weapons, not just the three powers at Geneva. It also praised the Treaty on the Principles of the Activity of States in the Exploration and Use of Outer Space, including the Moon and Other Celestial Bodies (the Outer Space Treaty, for short), which had been endorsed by the Twenty-first Session of the General Assembly two months previously. This treaty prohibited the placing in orbit of objects with nuclear weapons or other weapons of mass destruction or their installation on celestial bodies. This prevented the 'military exploitation of outer space', the Executive Committee pointed out, and was in conformity 'with the long-standing concern of the World Council of Churches . . .

that military rivalries are too dangerous to project into outer space'.[49] Although sixty states had signed it by the following month, it could not come into force until ratified by the United States and the Soviet Union.

The busy month of February 1967 also saw fourteen Latin American states sign a treaty banning nuclear weapons from Central and South America and the Caribbean area. The fulfilment of this objective depended less upon the will of the Latin American countries themselves than upon the assent of the nuclear powers, principally the United States and the United Kingdom, which had bases in the area; their agreement was obtained in the following months. China and France remained aloof from this treaty until a state visit by President Luis Echeverria of Mexico to both countries in March and April 1973 elicited their promise of adherence, which they carried out in 1974. The Soviet Union has not become a party to the treaty, alleging that it contains loopholes. The ENDC reconvened on 21 February to continue its negotiations on a non-proliferation treaty; France continued her boycott of the Committee.

The CCIA Executive Committee meeting in August discussed the disarmament situation as it had developed. Emphasis shifted slightly to ways of ameliorating war: states were advised to adhere strictly to the Geneva Conventions of 1949 and to outlaw such new devastating weapons as napalm bombs. The CCIA Executive's statement 'Limitations in Modern Warfare' did not mention the non-proliferation negotiations then going on.[50] It urged governments to take positive and urgent action on the declaration of the International Conference of the Red Cross at Vienna in 1965, which asserted that recognition of the principle of maintaining a distinction between the civilian population and combatants and recognition that the general principles of the law of war apply to the use of nuclear and other weapons of mass destruction was imperative. The Executive Committee also requested governments which had not yet done so to become parties to the 1949 Geneva Conventions and those which had already subscribed to them to honour their commitment. Then followed the rather astounding claim: 'Furthermore, all governments should be aware that they are bound by such laws of warfare as have grown into general rules of customary international law (e.g., the prohibition of chemical and biological warfare).' This was followed by the more modest wish: 'In addition . . . the laws of warfare should be expanded to include more recently developed weapons which produce new horrors of human suffering, such as napalm bombs.' Although this statement was independent of one on Vietnam which did not, in fact, mention the horrors of war, it was undoubtedly the escalation of more and more cruel means of warfare in that country that brought the need for this statement before the CCIA Executive. The Central Committee which met the following week gave only tepid endorsement to it.

On 24 August, however, the United States and the Soviet Union submitted to the ENDC identical drafts of a non-proliferation treaty. This good omen was strengthened by the coming into force of the Outer Space Treaty upon deposit of the American ratification on 10 October. Meanwhile in the ENDC the two superpowers were united against the criticism of the non-nuclear states. Adjourning on an optimistic note for the Christmas holidays, it reconvened on 18 January 1968 and identical drafts—further developed—were again presented by the superpowers. *In absentia* France denounced the proposals as detrimental to all except their originators. By 14 March pressure from the two nuclear giants forced reluctant approval by the ENDC of the final draft; this was forwarded to the United Nations General Assembly to be considered in special session. On 12 June the General Assembly commended it to its membership for ratification.

The fourth Assembly of the WCC convened at Uppsala on 4 July 1968, with the good news of the fulfilment of a task the World Council had so long advocated. However, the report of Section IV 'Towards Justice and Peace in International Affairs' [51] took cognisance of the newly completed treaty, recognizing this as only one small step on a long journey to safety and security for mankind. It began the plenary discussion of its report with a rather pessimistic documentary film, *An Armed World*. Although CCIA staff members judged this film to be equally condemnatory of armaments policy in East and West, it was attacked by a group of delegates and Youth Participants (the latter seeming to attack any and every issue at Uppsala) as a Cold War manifestation.

The report, adopted by the Assembly, condemned war and noted that 'Of all forms of war, nuclear war presents the gravest affront to the conscience of man'. It was the duty of the churches to urge that 'the first duty of governments [was] to prevent such a war: to halt the present arms race, agree never to initiate the use of nuclear weapons, stop experiments concerned with, and the production of, weapons of mass human destruction by chemical and biological means'. It particularly urged that China and France be among the signatories of the Non-Proliferation Treaty. Further steps still to be taken, it asserted, included the cessation of underground tests and the prevention of anti-ballistic missile systems being established in the United States and the Soviet Union, since they amounted to an escalation of nuclear capability.

The report also noted the problems caused by the concentration of nuclear weapons in a few hands: the difficulty of guaranteeing the security of non-nuclear states and the tendency to freeze the *status quo* at the expense of needed change. In return for the small states accepting 'nuclear abstinence', the nuclear powers should be willing to undertake phased disarmament. Not only ought the great powers to disarm; they should not furnish weapons to others to fight their wars by proxy. Criticisms of this part of the report again came from two Youth Participants, Mr Suhail Aranki of the Arab Episcopal Church, and Mr Theodore Buss of the Swiss Reformed Church, both of whom wanted a clear statement that participation by Christians in the manufacture of nuclear or bacteriological weapons or the threat to use them was incompatible with Christian obedience. This was put as a motion on behalf of the Youth Participants by Dr Harold A. Bosley, a delegate from the Methodist Church in the United States. It died for want of a seconder, leaving many dissatisfied Youth Participants. But as they aged, their day would come.

On 16 July, before the Assembly adjourned, the ENDC reconvened with further American and Soviet proposals for disarmament. These new proposals were presented without much discussion; the Committee went into recession on 28 August to await the results of a United Nations Conference of Non-Nuclear-Weapons States. This conference sat for nearly a month and adjourned on 28 September but without reaching agreement on a plan to protect non-nuclear states against nuclear blackmail. They were concerned particularly with this problem because it seemed that the safeguards under the Nuclear Non-Proliferation Treaty were inadequate, for action to enforce them required Security Council authorization. The Treaty itself did not fare well in the American presidential campaign, as Republican candidate Richard M. Nixon made the ratification a political issue. Apparently this was a ploy to appeal to the ultra-conservative vote—after taking office, he asked for and received Senate approval of ratification. The Soviet and American ratifications were exchanged in November 1969, and the treaty came into force on 5 March 1970.

On 18 March 1969 the ENDC reconvened after a seven-month recess. Both the United States and the Soviet Union submitted proposals for the prohibition of nuclear weapons and other weapons of mass destruction on the sea-bed and the ocean floor. On 21 August the membership of the Eighteen Nation Disarmament Committee was enlarged to twenty-six and its name changed to the Conference of the Committee on Disarmament (CCD). On 30 October the United States and the Soviet Union again submitted revised identical proposals for a sea-bed free of nuclear weapons, which they insisted on recommending to the Twenty-fourth Session of the General Assembly, being held at the time. Several of the smaller states criticized the proposals rather for the lack of time to study them than for their content. The superpowers were adamant that the treaty proposals be sent to the General Assembly, with or without CCD endorsement—which in the end was reluctantly granted. The medium powers at the Twenty-fourth Session, however, did not take kindly to this attempt by the superpowers to push their desires down unwilling throats. Canada, Brazil, Iran, and Mexico sponsored a resolution to send the treaty back to the CCD for further study. This was successfully passed. The following year (1970) the General Assembly commended the reconsidered Sea-Bed Treaty; on 11 February 1971 it was signed in London, Moscow and Washington, but not until 18 May 1972 were enough ratifications received from non-nuclear states for it to enter into force.

In 1969 the same General Assembly unanimously passed a resolution declaring the 1970s the Disarmament Decade. If the Development Decade were to be taken as an augury, disarmament would be delayed! In fact, however, 17 November saw preliminary bilateral negotiations between the United States and the Soviet Union in Helsinki at the Strategic Arms Limitations Talks (SALT). An astounded world watched the eager co-operation between the erstwhile enemies with ever-increasing pessimism as the talks dragged on for three years.

The CCIA kept the pronounced views of the churches before the delegates at the United Nations; it sent a summary of World Council pronouncements on disarmament to more than 1,000 delegates of the 1968 Session of the General Assembly. In 1969 it judged that there was at that time no reason to make a statement in regard to the Geneva deliberations nor in regard to the planned European Security conference. It was then preparing—by mandate of the World Council Executive Committee, as an aspect of its representation function—the Third Consultation on Disarmament, which it convened in June 1970 in Geneva; [52] this was attended by CCIA Commissioners, representatives of national committees of the churches on international affairs, and guest participants from the YMCA, YWCA, World Federation of United Nations Associations, the International Quaker Centre and others. At separate times various outside officials joined the discussions of the Consultation to give the views of those they represented: Mr W. Epstein, Deputy Special Representative of the Secretary-General to the United Nations Conference of the Committee on Disarmament, Mrs A. Myrdal, the Swedish Minister for Disarmament, Ambassador Husain, Representative of India to the Conference, Ambassador A. A. Roschchin, Head of the Soviet delegation to the Conference, and Ambassador Leonard, Head of the American delegation.

In spite of the importance of the participants, the report of the Consultation appears to be fairly light-weight material. However, as a communication aimed at the churches for use in publicizing disarmament information at local levels, it is probably quite adequate. Among its contents it noted support for the United Nations Resolution declaring as contrary to international law the use of chemical agents. It also spoke approvingly of the SALT talks, urging the two powers to halt the arms race. And like many United Nations resolutions, it closely tied in disarmament with the possibility of accelerated development.

The SALT talks continued in 1971 but the sole agreement between the United States and the Soviet Union was on what to talk about. The CCD in Geneva made some progress when the USSR reversed its position of linking together the questions of chemical and bacteriological warfare and agreed to discuss proposals to ban bacteriological warfare on its own merits. Agreement on these proposals was reached by 10 April 1972 when the Convention on the Prohibition of Development, Production and Stockpiling of Bacteriological (Biological) and Toxic Weapons and Their Destruction was opened for signature in London, Moscow, and Washington. Although it did not require the destruction of existing weapons, it was intended to stop further research on development and production of more bacteriological weapons. During President Nixon's visit to the Soviet Union that year he and party Secretary Leonid Brezhnev signed two products of the bilateral SALT talks. The first was the Treaty on the Limitation of Anti-Ballistic Missile Systems which became effective immediately after ratification on 3 October 1972. The other, An Interim Agreement on Certain Measures with respect to the Limitation of Strategic Offensive Armaments, which limited the number of ballistic missile launchers on submarines, came into force on signature.

The CCIA Executive Committee meeting in August 1972 gave its attention to several background papers on disarmament and the European security conference-to-be, but virtually ignored the progress made at the conference table. Ambassador George Ignatieff, head of the Canadian delegation to the CCD, gave an address on disarmament and the Committee decided to make this topic a major agenda item the following year. It also adopted the 'Statement on European Security and Co-operation' which was later submitted to, and adopted by, the Central Committee. The Statement looked at the European conference in its world-wide context, viewing it as part of the general détente illustrated by West Germany's *Ostpolitik* and the progress made in the SALT talks. It saw the proposed 'mutually balanced force reduction' as a positive factor in terminating the military confrontation in Europe. Interestingly enough, it retained its non-European spectacles to see clearly that a Europe without East-West tensions would be a stronger Europe: that 'there could follow in a new guise new attempts at still further increasing European domination in other areas of the world'. The new strength, it urged, should be used for attaining social justice through trade and aid with the developing states.[53]

Following the General Assembly call at its 1972 session for a World Disarmament Conference, the CCIA joined with fourteen other non-governmental organizations in addressing letters to Secretary Brezhnev and President Nixon on the eve of the former's visit to Washington in June 1973. These letters asked for a complete ban on nuclear testing, and support for the World Disarmament Conference requested by the General Assembly. At the same time the CCIA and sixteen other NGOs wrote to President Pompidou of France, urging the cancellation of the projected nuclear tests at Mururoa in the South Pacific. In both cases the ink seemed wasted, for no immediate results were attained. In the long run, however, Christian opinion, and that of the constituencies represented by the other NGOs—communicated to the political leaders, and, through newspaper reports, to a far wider public—played one part in reinforcing the creation and preservation of norms in international affairs.

The CCIA Executive Committee met in Visegrad, Hungary, from 14 to 19 June 1973 and adopted a memorandum on disarmament. It began by noting the continuing growth in the number of weapons held and of military budgets, though it did allot a legitimate place to enough arms for self-defence. It feared that, in developed societies, there were broad sectors which benefited economically so much from arms production that they would struggle against a reduction. It urged the rechannelling of resources from the arms industries to the development of the Third World. (This tying together, probably unrealistically, of economic development and the resources that could be released by disarmament has also been the subject of General Assembly resolutions and United Nations reports.[54])

It laid a special responsibility on the churches to develop a public opinion to accept disarmament. It judged a comprehensive nuclear test ban treaty to be the next step in the SALT talks (see below for the accuracy of this prophecy) and stated that all nuclear powers, including China and France, should be invited to participate. It also supported ratification of the Nuclear Non-Proliferation Treaty by those states on the threshold of developing nuclear weapons, though it did not name them. Although welcoming the 1972 Convention on Bacteriological Weapons it did not take the opportunity to urge its ratification, whereas it did make a 'most urgent plea . . . to ban the production, possession or use of chemical weapons'. Until that aim had been realized it urged observation of the Geneva Protocol of 1925. (Other forces were at work besides the churches, and the American Senate finally gave its advice and consent to US ratification; President Gerald Ford signed the instrument of ratification of the Geneva Protocol on 22 January 1975; at the same time the Convention on Bacteriological Warfare was ratified by him.)

The document urged the World Council and its member churches to support the move to strengthen the humanitarian rules of warfare, to be discussed at the 1974 Red Cross Conference, as well as prohibition of the production and use of anti-personnel weapons, the elimination of starvation as a weapon of war, and the use of environmental warfare, 'indiscriminate weapons', and torture. It ended on an appeal to all member churches and Christians to work harder than theretofore for disarmament. They must fight apathy and hopelessness; Christians should support the willingness of their states to take 'reasonable risks' for disarmament.

One section dealt with 'Disarmament and Change'. It was strange to read—in the middle of this document calling for the destruction or regulation of arms—a plea for the right of the oppressed to use arms. This paradox would be solved, it predicted, if change produced international social justice.[55]

Visegrad also witnessed the passing of a resolution on great power rivalry in the Indian Ocean. On 15 December 1970 it was announced in London and Washington that the construction of an Anglo-American naval communications facility on the British island of Diego Garcia was beginning. It appeared to many south Asian states that the area of arms utilization was spreading rather than diminishing. In December 1971 the United Nations General Assembly passed a resolution declaring the Indian Ocean a zone of peace and calling on the major powers to withdraw their military bases and nuclear weapons from the area. The Assembly repeated the resolution the following year, feeling that if one resolution made no impact on the countries involved, two might; however, the United States and the United Kingdom continued their work on Diego Garcia and the Soviet Union maintained its naval presence, albeit intermittent, in the Indian Ocean. The CCIA Executive Committee made a statement deploring the fact that freedom of the seas was 'being used by powerful maritime nations as a façade behind which almost unrestrained military activity in support of the strategic interests of nations not bordering on the Ocean is taking place'. It judged that this constituted a threat to the peace and called upon its member churches to support the United Nations resolution by urging the major powers to demilitarize the Indian Ocean.[56]

At the Conference on Mutual Reduction of Forces and Armaments and Associated Measures in Central Europe, convened in

Vienna on 30 October 1973 as the military counterpart to the Conference on European Security and Co-operation, the Warsaw Pact and Nato negotiators made no progress; however, during President Nixon's last visit to the Soviet Union, the United States and the Soviet Union reached a minor accommodation. One of President Nixon's final attempts to regain domestic stature and popularity required some type of agreement on his visit, and he left with two arms control measures. The first was a Protocol to the Anti-Ballistic Missile Treaty which reduced from two to one the number of sites allowed to each side. In fact neither side had constructed the second one and at that time neither wished to spend the money. The effective date of the second agreement indicated its use for domestic political effect, based as it was on future promises. The Treaty on the Limitation of Underground Nuclear Weapon Tests provided for the complete cessation by 31 March 1976 of all tests of weapons above the equivalent of 150 kilotons of TNT and placed a limit on the number of tests of weapons smaller than that.

The CCIA Executive Committee, meeting from 29 July to 2 August 1974, apparently ignored that year's gains and engaged in a somewhat sterile debate on disarmament. Documents circulated on the topic included a description of the failure of the Red Cross Conference on Humanitarian Law in Armed Conflicts in February and March and its adjournment until the spring of 1975. The CCIA offered the churches no strategy for guiding governments in this traditional area of concern of the Church. This is indeed unfortunate, for if general and comprehensive disarmament seems as distant as ever, the activities of the many non-governmental organizations as well as the efforts of medium and small powers, appear to have goaded the super-powers to a few halting steps along the path of disarmament.

This chronological compendium of the development of World Council thought and action in regard to disarmament reveals successive and distinct stages of concern. Immediately after the Second World War church leaders were horrified at the seemingly limitless power of atomic weapons, which grew to incomprehensible proportions as fission gave way to fusion. During the period when the organization of the World Council was being established this overwhelming knowledge led at first to vague concepts of disarmament with no distinct programmes of suggestions. As the terror grew with the development of the H-bomb, efforts were primarily directed to convincing states not to use it, or at least not to use it first. A further concern grew out of the continuous testing to perfect still more deadly weapons; many scientists pointed out how harmful such tests were; the World Council pointed out that nations which did not possess the bomb, and which had no desire to possess it, were equally at risk with the others. A continuous campaign for the cessation of nuclear tests was conducted until finally the tests which polluted the atmosphere and the food of the world were stopped, at least by the two powers who tested the most, the Soviet Union and the United States. Hardly had the Nuclear Test Ban Treaty been signed when the World Council understood that a further danger, both directly in destructive force and indirectly in pollutants, existed in the spread of nuclear weapons to other states. The campaign for a non-proliferation treaty was begun even before the earlier treaty came into force.

Concurrent with these dangers, the first trip of man into space also drew attention to the possibility of man's destructive capabilities being extended beyond the earth, both in the contamination of space and in aiming great destructive potential towards the earth from orbiting arsenals. The space states also recognized the danger and in the Outer Space Treaty provided for the limitation of nuclear power and weapons in the conquest of space. These concerns developed one from the other, among the states as well as within the World Council of Churches and other non-governmental organizations. Throughout all these aspects runs a slender thread of hope for general disarmament. It is mentioned from time to time in the statements of the World Council, more as a distant ideal than as a practicable possibility. The resolutions of the United Nations General Assembly have also reflected this human yearning, but the progress achieved has been the result of tackling each problem separately and not of attempting the immediate fulfilment of Utopia.

The two primary means of action by the World Council of Churches were statements and consultations. Statements were issued by the CCIA, either from its Executive Committee or individual officers; by the World Council of Churches—from its Central Committee, Executive Committee, or its Presidents; by the Assemblies of the World Council, the only body in which all members are represented; and by *ad hoc* conferences. Pronouncements, of course, bind no member of the World Council; they are compromises created by delegates to represent a consensus—but always an unofficial consensus—of ecumenical Christian thought on the subject. As William Temple noted in the early days, World Council statements would have only that authority inherent in the wisdom of their content. Nevertheless, Christians recognized in them the best understanding of disarmament issues (in this case) based on Christian values.

These statements did not contain detailed plans; indeed such plans would have been of little use, because disarmament agreement is based primarily on political considerations, technical decisions are secondary. Although not detailed in this sense, the pronouncements were specific in seeking a particular goal, cessation of nuclear tests, for example, rather than just some vague disarmament. These statements (whether of the CCIA or of any other World Council organ) when publicized by the CCIA helped to fulfil some of the *Aims* defined for the CCIA at its founding in 1946. The first *Aim,* though this may not indicate its priority, refers to the education of Christians to their responsibilities in world affairs. There is a whole array of statements addressed to the churches collectively, or to Christians as individuals, designed to help mould and build Christian opinion on the particular issue of disarmament.

Another *Aim* is the study of selected problems of world order and publication of the findings to member churches. CCIA statements are the result of a great deal of study by the officers in charge of subject areas. And these studies are the basis on which Central Committee or its Executive makes a separate pronouncement or adopts that prepared by the CCIA. Dr Fagley, for example, has read, digested, kept up to date on, and summarized the technical information on the dangers of radioactive fall-out, one of the continuous studies used to arrive at a World Council position on disarmament. This meant that the campaign for cessation of testing was based on hard considerations and not on wishy-washy do-goodism. Still another *Aim* follows from these studies and that is to suggest ways in which Christians may act effectively upon a particular international problem. In the statements, either national churches or individual Christians were often called upon to petition their governments for particular ends—for example, the ratification of the Nuclear Non-Proliferation Treaty—or to publicize the results of a CCIA study in order to build up a Christian consensus.

Sometimes the statements were addressed to the governments of the world and their citizens, whether Christian or not. In such instances the World Council separately and through the CCIA was acting as the Christian conscience of the world in accordance with the seventh *Aim* which states that the CCIA will 'discover and declare Christian principles with direct relevance to the inter-relations of nations, and . . . formulate the bearing of these principles upon immediate issues'. For example, when a new source of power was discovered in 1945 and again in 1950, the proper attitude for Christians to the use of this new power had to be examined and then declared. One might also consider that, in addressing the governments of the world, the World Council is acting as an international pressure group in a pluralistic society. The World Council represents on the international level a social institution which exists at the national level in Christian countries—and also, with severe limitations, even in some communist states—

the church. In addition, the role which the World Council plays in the international sphere is likely to affect the attitudes of government and other officials who act at the international level.

The statements examined in this chapter were often vehicles through which formal communications could be opened or maintained by official correspondence. They were sent regularly to delegates at the United Nations, to the various disarmament bodies, and to the foreign ministers of the great powers as well as their heads of government. Although the heads of government might remain remote, foreign ministers did not, at least in the United States where the ecclesiastical hierarchy seemed to have the entrée to John Foster Dulles and Christian Herter, and in the United Kingdom where the Archbishop of Canterbury, due to his high social/ecclesiastical/political position, could communicate directly with the foreign secretary. More usual were the informal consultations, to which the correspondence led, with members of the various delegations.

Consultations provided another means of achieving the aims of the CCIA (and thus of the World Council of Churches). The formal presentation of the ecumenical statements to international and national officials led to both formal and informal consultations. Since the first kind were often widely reported by the news media, they also had the incidental effect of reinforcing creation of a Christian opinion. Furthermore, this public contact added to the prestige of the World Council of Churches in its activities in international affairs. Formal consultations also took place when officials visited the World Council. This they did at the Consultations on Peace and Disarmament recounted above, and at the World Conference on Church and Society. It may be that national and international decision-makers pay an iota of extra attention to the results of a consultation in which national and international officials have played at least a small role.

The informal consultations may be more important for actually achieving a particular goal. Such consultations were held between CCIA officials and delegates to the United Nations and the various disarmament bodies. They were the result of, or led to, personal relations between the officials and the delegates concerned. Information might be garnered and information given. Always the CCIA officer acted as a kind of World Council presence, ever reminding the international officials of abiding Christian interest in their activities.

In evaluating the activity of the churches in the field of disarmament one has to keep in mind the goals which they expected to achieve. The idealists working for the churches in international affairs were realists enough to recognize that there could be no sudden conversion of the great powers to complete disarmament.

Yet that has always been kept as an ultimate goal, the World Council constantly reminding its constituents of its desirability and helping to form a Christian opinion on disarmament. The creation and shaping of this opinion has been a continuing activity. The acceptability of any degree of disarmament may indicate considerable achievement in this field.

Specific goals were proposed: international control of atomic energy, cessation of nuclear tests in the atmosphere and later underground, peaceful use of outer space, prevention of the spread of nuclear arms. By their constant reiteration in ecumenical statements they became acceptable goals to many Christians who made their views heard in pluralistic societies where it was possible to do so. The international control of atomic energy has not yet been achieved; underground tests continue. On the other hand, nuclear tests in the atmosphere by the two superpowers have ceased, nuclear weapons have been kept out of outer space, and a non-proliferation treaty has been accepted by all nuclear powers except France and China, the two with the least capability of supplying others. To give the World Council of Churches credit because its opinions on some aspects of disarmament have been implemented in international relations may be to exaggerate its importance. There were many other groups in these societies who sought similar goals for ethical, ideological, or financial reasons.

However, although international political phenomena such as the Sino-Soviet rift may have given the final impetus to Soviet-American *rapprochement,* leading to the conclusion of the limited arms control agreements between those two powers, one must also consider the groundwork of the ecumenical movement (and other groups) in making the idea of disarmament acceptable to the various élites and their followers in Western democratic countries. The continual process of education through World Council pronouncements, reports, and recommendations helped to change the perception of the élites in the West concerning the trustworthiness of the Soviet Union in disarmament negotiations, as well as the perception of what 'national security' actually required.

One might perhaps accept the opinion of Dr Fagley in his assessment of twenty years of CCIA activity in regard to disarmament. 'Disarmament is obviously an area where the criterion of Christian witness is patient obedience rather than worldly success. A good cause can be made for the time and effort devoted to the Geneva negotiations in the hope that a slight nudge in the right direction at the right moment might tip the balance in favour of a step forward. . . . Since so little real headway is being made in an area so fateful for contemporary civilization, the search for new approaches must be unflagging.' [57]

5. *The Christian Constituency*

THOSE Christians who have given their mites or their fortunes in support of the World Council of Churches and its ideals may justly inquire how well the stewards of their money have exercised their responsibility. Have the resources allotted to international work been justified? Have the talents of its officers applied to international goals produced positive results? In the words of W. A. Visser 't Hooft himself, 'Has it been worthwhile?' [1]

In order to answer this succinct, simple and probing question, the World Council and its activities as recounted in the foregoing chapters will be analysed as an international political interest group. On the international level the World Council has acted in the same way as interest groups at the national level act when they wish to influence public policy—to hinder a proposed policy, to alter an existing one, or to introduce a new policy.

An evaluation of the effectiveness of this *international* political interest group—the World Council of Churches—requires that it be examined at different levels as it attempts to achieve its goals. At the international level it interacts with the international bureaucracy, the civil servants of the world; at what I call the international-national level it negotiates with national delegates to intergovernmental organizations and meetings. At the national level it makes its requests and desires known to governments, primarily through its member churches but also directly. At the transnational level it deals with other NGOs, multinational corporations, and Christian bodies; also, through pronouncements and messages, it addresses individual Christians and all men of goodwill.

Any international non-governmental organization poses a greater problem of evaluation than does a national political interest group,[2] because of the more heterogeneous nature of international society and its greater size. In an assessment of WCC effectiveness, the World Council must also be examined as representative of a still major social institution, organized religion. This role as a social institution is particularly visible in the attention paid to it by the world press; apparently what the World Council does and says is considered to be of interest to large bodies of people. In the absence of financial power, and, in many countries, voter power, it must be the social role which accounts for this interest and for the status of its leaders and their interaction with other élites; this

261

interaction has been and remains a major aspect of World Council activity. This role as a social institution helps to explain, in the context of a communications model, the attention which has been paid to it, if not to the proven efficacy of its actions.

Lobbying in the Corridors

At one time the lobbyist and pressure group were seen as undesirable products of representative democracy,[3] and the United States Congress was considered the example *par excellence* of their illicit work. More recent studies have shown them to be an integral and desirable part of the pluralistic industrial societies in which we live.[4] Although political interest groups are praised by many as making representative democracy truly representative, they still have their critics, who claim that they have certain built-in qualities which render them altogether too powerful (and this might explain why statesmen and civil servants bother to continue communications with them).[5] These qualities include possession of money and credit, the existence of some type of bureaucratic organization, some control over jobs, some control over a supply of expert knowledge, control over a supply of votes through a large membership, and prestige inherent in the group through the status of its members. All these qualities do not apply to all political interest groups, but all such groups possess one or more of them. These capabilities should not be assumed to imply solely a power model of politics, rather they represent potentialities of sustained communication in the policy and decision-making process. The amount of attention which the target pays to the group depends on its perception of these endowments.[6] The extent to which the target will be susceptible to group blandishments will also depend on its evaluation of the group's aims in relation to the national (or international) interest.

At the international level several independent élites, sharing power (a plural élite model), appear to be more characteristic than a single élite dominating the decision-making centres of important issue areas (a power élite model).[7] The religious élite, sometimes joined by technical élites such as groups of economists, physicians, physicists and so on, communicates with intergovernmental élites. It is obvious that the intergovernmental élite will be the instrument by which policy is changed or continued, but one élite may wish to engage the support of other élites in its communications proceedings. This is facilitated by the fact that there is an overlapping of élite membership: just as an individual has divided loyalties so he identifies in varying degrees with several social groups.

In all these interactions there is a reciprocal flow of influence, favours, and information.[8] The national pressure group may be able to deliver votes, campaign funds, or volunteer labour, or simply prestigious approval of the action undertaken (e.g., nuclear physicists approving a government's nuclear power policy). So it is also with the international political interest group. The international civil servants may wish to have information on a specialism of the NGO and may request its help and that of its national members in gaining the support of national governments for an international programme. The institutionalization of contact with NGOs in the United Nations Charter (Article 71) evinced this flow of communications and has aided its further development.

The World Council of Churches can be considered an actor at the international level, just as political interest groups are at the national level.[9] The activities of the World Council, where it has hoped to influence international behaviour, have been pursued on the levels noted above. Numerous examples at the international level have been cited throughout this study; other topics it has not covered, such as World Council Refugee work, required co-ordination with the United Nations High Commissioner for Refugees and the United Nations Relief and Works Agency for Palestinian Refugees. This international level may be particularly susceptible to the blandishments of an NGO, for in the international civil servant you have a person whose whole livelihood is inextricably intertwined with his organization. Its continued existence—and his livelihood—will depend to a great extent on the fulfilment of its purpose in the world, i.e., to further international co-operation within the particular limits set by its constitution. In addition, he may have a truly international idealism that allows him to visualize issues from an international point of view. Thus, for example, economic development is not perceived primarily as an instrumentality to extend the national influence of a donor state, but rather as a means of developing the economies of the underdeveloped states of the world.

At the international-national level, the World Council has attempted to change or initiate policies by exerting pressure on national delegations to the General Assembly or to international conferences such as UNCTAD. Reference was made in the third chapter of this study to the close co-operation between the Swedish delegation and Dr Fagley when the politically sensitive issue of family planning was first put before the United Nations General Assembly. The national delegate is sent to represent first and foremost the interests of his government in deliberations with other states. The very fact that he is sent, however, indicates that the organization is accepted by the policy-making authorities of his state. It may be that in certain instances national delegates are sent in order to throw a spanner into the consultations, but normally they are there to make the organization work—true, to work for the

263

interests of their respective states but nevertheless, in many cases, to succeed in solving the international issue under deliberation. The *raison d'être* of a national delegate is bound up with the smooth running of his IGO so that he may present his national viewpoint. Like the international civil servant, he has a vocational interest in the promotion of this particular multilateral diplomatic process, but he must also represent his government. The ambivalence of this position was exemplified in the rivalry which developed between the American Secretary of State, Dean Rusk, and his Ambassador to the United Nations, Adlai Stevenson; one might ascribe this conflict to personality differences, but their understanding of the role of the Secretary of State and of a delegate appears to have been a contributory factor.[10] The World Council has recognized this dual interest by communicating not only with governments but also with the individual delegates themselves (and, in this latter case, not merely on specific issues but regularly at each United Nations General Assembly session).

At the national level the World Council has communicated directly with governments which have taken, or were about to take, a decision with international ramifications which it judged inimical to its own interest morally or materially. This study has given examples of direct communication to the government of South Africa, letters to heads of states, and advice to both donor and recipient governments on the problems and issues of specific economic development projects. In addition to aiming at the target of its interests directly, the World Council has also tried to persuade sympathetic governments to act as a source of additional communication or pressure upon the target state. Examples from this study include petitioning the British government on two separate occasions to influence South Africa and the Central African Federation on racial issues.

The WCC's communications with governments are most often handled, not directly by the Council, but through its national members. Members of the World Council are always national churches, since this global institution reflects in its ecclesiastical membership the political divisions of the world. For example, the Lutheran Church as such is not a member but the two ecclesiastical organizations the Lutheran Church in America and the American Lutheran Church are separate members, as is the Lutheran Church of Sweden, and so on. The Lutheran World Federation, which encompasses them all, is not a member. Nor are national councils of churches members, but according to the Constitution they may have a special status (Article VI : 2 of the Constitution and Article X of the Rules). It is through a national council, a national established church, or a national majority church that the World Council most often communicates with national governments on problems best dealt with at that level. In addition to the national councils just mentioned, regional councils of churches also enjoy special status with the World Council; the three so far in existence are the Conference of European Churches, the Christian Conference of Asia (formerly the East Asia Christian Conference), and the All Africa Conference of Churches. World Council co-operation with this last body in approaching the government of the Sudan resulted in the solution of internal guerrilla problems in that country (discussed in chapter 2 above).

At the transnational level the World Council addresses its religious adherents directly, and, in some cases, 'all men of goodwill'. Many of its pronouncements are directed at a wide constituency and the Message of each Assembly is always broadly addressed. The transnational community of those who heed the messages and pronouncements of goodwill can be considered analogous to the 'justice constituency' of Julius Stone, an international community of people sharing goals and norms which express the justice sought by them and embodied in their institutions.[11] It is with compassion and regard for the human person that the World Council has fought for justice and equality for the non-white, the poor, and those who suffer from war. Those who listen to its counsels, even when they do not obey them, are certainly more widespread than simply its member churches, as the reporting and approval even by Communist newspapers discussed below illustrates. Both the World Council membership and the Communist parties would no doubt be horrified to find themselves classed together in such a way; nevertheless, both are appealing to many of the same goals and norms. All who share the concern of the World Council for social justice and who still recognize the WCC as a significant social institution (some, even, as a divine one) could be counted as part of the 'Christian social justice constituency'.

The WCC has also directed itself, at the transnational level, to multinational corporations and banks, attempting to change their policy towards Southern Africa. Its communications with these organizations are often handled through member churches or national or regional Christian councils. Apart from enlisting Christian help, it has also co-operated with organizations such as the Anti-Apartheid Movement in several countries.

Uppermost Rooms and Chief Seats

'But it is in the nature of the case that the success of the CCIA cannot be estimated,'[12] Dr Visser 't Hooft concluded in answering his own question, 'Has it been worthwhile?' And yet those who

265

furnish the sustenance want an estimate of the role of the World Council in international affairs; perhaps even those who are subjected to its admonitions would like to have an impression of its efficacy. One may look for circumstantial evidence in the general influence of NGOs. One aspect of their success may be explained by the plural élite model already mentioned. By taking cognizance of those whom the World Council addresses, and, more importantly, those who seek its views or its endorsement, and even those who refute its stands, one may deduce that some reciprocal influence and communication does take place. The reporting of its activities by the press, Western and communist, is also testimony to a recognized role in society and thereby in the decision-making process.

The membership of national political interest groups is overlapping: in the case of a Christian businessman who was a member of the United Nations Association it would be difficult on most issues to define a single, predominant interest simply on the basis of his identification with these groups. With the present emphasis in both the Protestant and Roman Catholic churches on the role of the laity, it will become more and more usual for the business, educational, and social élites to overlap with the Christian; the role of leadership in matters of interest to the church will be reserved for the cloth even less than in the past.

Such an overlapping of the roles of a decision-maker among the ecumenical and political-economic élites has already occurred to some extent. The wealthy corporation lawyer, John Foster Dulles, was a leading layman in the Presbyterian church; he was also active in the founding of the CCIA and the World Council. On becoming Secretary of State under President Eisenhower he resigned his World Council posts; but a man cannot so easily give up his interests, feelings, previous friendships, and psychological framework. When called upon by his former associates, Secretary Dulles interceded with the Attorney General of the United States on behalf of churchmen from communist countries, so that they might be admitted to capitalist America to attend the Evanston Assembly.[13] Another example similar among the ecumenical decision-makers is Dr Jan Tinbergen, Dutch head of the United Nations Committee for Development Planning, who was elected a CCIA Commissioner in 1968. The Reverend T. Paul Verghese (now Metropolitan Paul Gregorius), as priest of the Indian Orthodox Church and former private secretary to Emperor Haile Selassie, chief adviser to the Haile Selassie Welfare Foundation, and Executive Secretary to the Ethiopian governmental committee for the distribution of relief aid was named an Associate General Secretary of the World Council in 1962.[14] However, these few examples do not indicate the extent to which Christians of the political, social, and economic élites who do not hold World

Council office also feel themselves part of its constituency, nor do they indicate the extent to which they hold national lay and ecclesiastical office. But they do direct attention to the fact that the World Council leaders are not an isolated élite immune from interaction with others.

This study has furnished the reader with examples of many conspicuous and manifest interactions between the ecumenical élite and other élites. At times these have consisted of ceremonial receptions of ecumenical leaders or the attendance at World Council Assemblies of heads of state and government. At other times they have been formal visits to national figureheads followed by serious talks with political leaders; politicians have addressed messages, sometimes important, to the Assemblies and Central Committee meetings. The political élite has sometimes sought out World Council leaders to ask their opinions; at other times secular technocrats have attended ecumenical consultations as advisers and for the exchange of information. At intervals the ecclesiastical leaders have denounced national actions (though never abusing the government or individual statesmen); and from time to time they themselves have been publicly reviled. Both the praise and the obloquy heaped upon the World Council have enhanced its stature, and its ability to communicate values has thereby grown.

There are some members of the political élite whose primary function is ceremonial; ceremonial reception by those who are not decision-makers should not be regarded as a useless gesture. Life and Work had been honoured by royalty at the Stockholm Conference in 1925, and Princess Juliana, soon to be crowned queen, and Prince Bernhard attended a plenary session of the Amsterdam Assembly. The following year the members of the Central Committee, meeting in England, were received by King George VI and Queen Elizabeth at St Catherine's Lodge, a Christian foundation for multi-disciplinary academic studies, in Windsor Great Park.[15] Even the officially atheistic government of the Hungarian People's Republic gave a reception attended by the Chairman of the Presidium Istvan Dobi [16] for the Central Committee meeting held at Galyatető, shortly before the uprising in 1956. The King and Queen of Denmark attended a special service commemorating the tenth anniversary of the World Council, and the Danish government gave a reception in its honour.[17] The Vice-President of India, Dr Radhakrishna, held a reception on behalf of the President, who was ill, for the New Delhi Assembly delegates. King Gustav VI Adolf of Sweden attended the opening ceremonies of the Uppsala Assembly in the great cathedral of that town.[18] The fact that even a nominal leader's time was allotted to World Council meetings and officials bespeaks the symbolic function of the ecumenical movement in international society.

Political leaders or their representatives have addressed World Council meetings. This is in addition to those individual politicians whose personal interest has caused them to undertake extensive responsibilities at the meetings, such as John Foster Dulles at Amsterdam or Senator George McGovern at Uppsala and many others in between. Prime Minister Jawaharlal Nehru spoke to the Central Committee meeting at Lucknow in 1953. His previously benevolent attitude towards Western religions had changed by the time of the New Delhi Assembly, and he refused to address it until the great interest shown by India's press resulted in his acceptance of the Assembly's invitation.[19] The Evanston Assembly saw many political and diplomatic luminaries. Dr Charles Malik, Representative of Lebanon to the United Nations and prominent Maronite Christian in his own land, spoke critically to the Assembly on the work of the churches in world politics.[20] He was followed the next day by President Eisenhower who challenged the World Council: 'We see religion as a practical force in human affairs. . . . We shall listen if you speak to us as the prophets spoke in the days of old.'[21] The Secretary-General of the United Nations, Dag Hammarskjöld, journeyed from New York to Evanston to address the assembled Christians.[22] In addition to Premier Nehru, Sir Francis Akanu Ibiam, Governor of Eastern Nigeria, attended the New Delhi Assembly (though because he was delayed on official business his speech to the assembled delegates was read by his wife).[23] He was at the Uppsala Assembly as a retiring President of the World Council. President Kenneth Kaunda of Zambia spoke at Uppsala, but took no part in the deliberations of committees.

When the Central Committee met in Paris in 1962 the French Foreign Minister, M. Couve de Murville, personally welcomed the Committee to France.[24] The following year in Rochester, New York, members of the Central Committee were shocked to hear President Kennedy's personal representative to them, Mr Averell Harriman, make a political speech critical of the Soviet Union in the presence of the newly admitted Russian Orthodox clergy. It was fortunate that the Orthodox guests were more magnanimous than their American hosts and did not take offence.[25] At the Central Committee meeting at Heraklion in 1967 the attentions of the new revolutionary Greek government were gingerly received, and the Committee was relieved to learn that the Prime Minister would not attend. King Constantine, at that time still in favour with the junta, spoke on the topic of church unity. At a consultation on economic development in the same area, Archbishop Makarios, President of Cyprus, addressed participants. As already mentioned, the President of Zambia, Kenneth Kaunda, participated in the deliberations of the Uppsala Assembly as well as Dr Akanu Ibiam.[26]

As more conferences were devoted solely to non-ecclesiastical topics, high-ranking leaders from political and economic élites became still more numerous. At the 1966 World Conference on Church and Society, the eminent included Dr Julius G. Kiano, Minister of Labour in Kenya, M. Jean Rey from the European Economic Community, and Mr Raúl Prebisch, Secretary-General of UNCTAD, among many others. The Montreux Consultation on Ecumenical Assistance to Development Projects, in January 1970, was the scene of mutual exchanges of information between ecumenical leaders and members of the political and economic *élites* of several countries: the former finance Minister of Liberia and sometime adviser to President Tubman, Dr Charles Sherman; a former economic adviser to President Lyndon Johnson, Dr Edward Hamilton; Dr Erhard Eppler, Minister for Economic Co-operation in the West German government, and Dr Robert Gardiner, Secretary of the UN Economic Commission for Africa. Thus not only did the ceremonial élite allot time to the World Council, and not only did the political élite address its gatherings informationally and ceremonially, but the highly trained technocratic élite also devoted time to them.

Participation in public meetings is not the only, nor perhaps the primary, way in which communication is undertaken. Individual members of the political élite have asked World Council officials to take collective action, sometimes concrete assistance and at other times spiritual guidance. President Kekkonen of Finland asked an Anglican Bishop visiting his country whether the European churches had no word for the world on the problems of co-existence, *his* problem as well as the world's. The Christian conscience was being asked to speak out.[27] With a rather more concrete proposal, Ambassador Myron Taylor, President Truman's personal representative to the Vatican, visited WCC headquarters in Geneva before the Amsterdam Assembly and offered his services to make Amsterdam 'serve the interests of peace'. The offer was politely declined,[28] but this incident shows that even the president of the United States wished to have the co-operation of this infant organization without power in the accepted political sense.

Although the Russian Orthodox Church denounced the World Council of Churches, at the time of its founding, as a tool of the capitalists, communist governments, too, have found cordial relations with it useful. As early as 1950, in the tensest years of the Cold War, President Wilhelm Pieck of the German Democratic Republic received the representative of the World Council, Propst D. Högsbro, in the presence of the Deputy Prime Minister, Herr Otto Nuschke. This meeting, reported by newspapers in both East and West, included a friendly discussion of possible co-operation between the World Council and the government of the Republic.[29]

Meeting at Galyatető in 1956, the Central Committee inquired of the Hungarian government about the imprisoned Lutheran Bishop Lajos Ordass, after which his 'rehabilitation' was announced.[30] In 1969, two years after taking office, General Secretary Eugene C. Blake was received by President Gustav Heinemann of the German Federal Republic and later had talks with Chancellor Kurt Kiesinger and Foreign Minister Willy Brandt concerning aid for ecumenical development projects; longer discussions were arranged with the Minister for Economic Co-operation. At the time a leading German newspaper expressed the opinion that, in view of the common interests of Bonn and Geneva in regard to peace and economic development, relations ought to have been opened earlier.[31] Such conversations with government leaders and their technocrats indicate at least an informational exchange (input) involving decisions to be made or already made (feedback).

The hostility of some statesmen towards World Council actions or opinions bears witness to their desire to discredit the WCC. A claim made by Pastor Jean Kotto of Cameroun, at the 1966 meeting of the Central Committee, that the government of the Sudan had perpetrated massacres of the Southern Sudanese in a 'war' caused by racial and religious tensions, drew the following reply from Mr Muhammed Mahgoub, Prime Minister of the Sudan: 'This is yet another red herring; professional religionists prey on man's distress everywhere'.[32] Dr Verwoerd was reported 'extremely worried' about the decisions of the Cottesloe Conference in 1960, especially because of the support given to its findings by the churches of South Africa. The single World Council decision which has brought the most reactionary criticism was that giving financial aid to victims of racial discrimination; as reported in chapter 2 above, this brought forth immediate, vehement, and vituperative reaction from Prime Minister Vorster of South Africa. If, in fact, ecclesiastical statements consist of just so much hot air, why do busy political leaders spend time answering them? Why have other leaders in their private capacity (but widely reported) communicated with the World Council, as did Princess Wilhelmina of the Netherlands in 1951, urging the Executive Committee to help relieve the suffering of refugees and displaced persons,[33] and as did her daughter, Queen Juliana, when she gave money from her privy purse for the World Council's fund for aiding the victims of racial discrimination? The answer can only be that its voice does carry weight and that its actions are efficacious.

The relationship between élites is most often one of mutual benefit. At times the politicians or the administrators need the advice, the opinion, or favour of those who represent segments of their societies. It is not a case of trying to force an élite to take an action to which it is unalterably opposed but a case of giving information on the way in which particular policies will affect the constituents of the World Council (or the political interest group in question). One former CCIA officer has remarked that when one of his colleagues lunched with the director-general of a Specialized Agency, or had coffee in the United Nations delegates' lounge, it was difficult to know who had influenced whom. Sometimes civil servants even volunteer information of particular interest to the World Council, as when 'reliable sources' in the American State Department warned a CCIA official that Swedish students were planning demonstrations against American participants at the Uppsala Assembly. The correspondence files give many more examples of a much less sensational nature but still illustrative of a regular relationship in which information is exchanged as a matter of course.

The interaction of elites and their reciprocal usefulness were recognized in the United Nations Charter, Article 71, which provides that the Economic and Social Council 'may make suitable arrangements for consultation with non-governmental organizations which are concerned with matters within its competence'. Similar arrangements are provided for in the constitutions of the Specialized Agencies. This resulted from the League experience with private international associations (including the Universal Christian Council on Life and Work). Special facilities such as the provision of documentary information, attendance at briefing sessions and special conferences, and other perquisites are extended to the NGOs. They are grouped into two major categories; Category I NGOs have broad interests and have the right to comment, orally or in writing, on matters before ECOSOC. Category II consists of NGOs with more specialized interests, which may comment in writing only; the CCIA is in this category.[34] However, once formal liaison is established, informal contacts can and do continue with delegates and officials in their day-to-day decision-making, as the voluminous correspondence of the CCIA concerning matters before the United Nations organs attests.

The status of the World Council of Churches (through the CCIA) is to be contrasted with that of the Holy See which is recognized in international law and everyday relations as a state. The Vatican is thus able to maintain a permanent observer at the United Nations of equal status to that of representatives of other non-member states—for example, Switzerland, Korea, Vietnam, and, before its entry into that body, the Federal Republic of Germany. When the United Nations has dealings with these observers, it is interacting with ambassadors of states; when contact is made with a representative of the Holy See, he is accorded the respect, courtesy, and attention due to such an official. The World Council's representatives, on the other hand, approach most officials (all except those appointed to deal with NGOs in the ECOSOC) as suppliants rather than by right.

The facilities which the Specialized Agencies provide for the NGOs are similar. The CCIA has formal consultative status with the FAO, UNESCO, UNICEF, and the United Nations High Commissioner for Refugees. It is on the Special List of Non-Governmental Organizations maintained by the ILO, but it has only informal contacts with the World Bank (IBRD). The Christian Medical Commission of the World Council of Churches applied for, and was granted, a consultative relationship with the World Health Organization in 1970. This use of several World Council organs instead of one well-known spokesman on international affairs—as the CCIA had been—may portend a still weaker role for the CCIA. Unless there is close co-ordination, announced by the WCC as desirable (but not inevitable), the voice of the World Council itself might lose force.

In its relations with the Specialized Agencies, the Holy See may have observer status for the asking, where it is not already a member, as is the case with the International Telecommunications Union, the Universal Postal Union, the International Atomic Energy Agency, and the Office of the United Nations High Commissioner for Refugees. The Vatican is also a contributing government to the United Nations Development Programme. Even the according of NGO status to the World Council does not give it the voice in the world's problems that the Vatican has by reason of its 200 sovereign acres. A further drawback is that the CCIA has not a big enough staff to maintain a permanent NGO representative at the various agencies where its interests lie; this has been noted throughout the study. Although not a member of the FAO, the Holy See has the right to maintain a full-time observer at that organization. Full-time observers and full-time staff provide the continuity and possibility of immediate reaction that are necessary for effective and decisive action in world politics. With its part-time specialists and its small staff, the wonder is that the World Council should succeed in being noticed at all in its international political ventures.

The reciprocal influence between interest group and target is illustrated in the case of the World Council not only by these formal arrangements but also by the informal contacts which evolve; the latter indicate an inclination on the part of states to communicate and, therefore, a greater susceptibility to influence. A leading United Nations official gave Dr Fagley an advance copy of the proposals to be presented to the Sixteenth General Assembly concerning the Development Decade for his critical comments. This willing use of NGOs emphasizes the need for mutual exchanges, as well as confidence in the technical ability of CCIA officials.

At the Tenth Conference of the FAO in 1959 an official requested Dr Egbert de Vries, the CCIA representative, to speak early in a debate, so that there would be positive endorsement of the Freedom From Hunger Campaign.[35] Seeking the same goal, he readily agreed to do so. Representatives of interest groups may let themselves be tactically used by international officials, when their interests coincide, and hope for reciprocity another day.

The Fourth Estate

The great fourth estate of democracies, the press, is probably more discriminating in its judgement than many politicians. It has limited space and reports what is important or of particular interest to its readers. The newspapers have regularly published news of the World Council, of meetings of its Central Committee and of its Assemblies, as well as its press releases on specific international issues. They have reported the moves of its General Secretary and often of its Central Committee chairman. The movements of Dr Potter have been the subject of news reports whether at national church conferences, ecumenical meetings, or on his visits to political and religious leaders; Dr Blake's open letter to U Thant about violations of human rights was published in *Le Monde*, this World Council viewpoint being apparently of concern even in a predominantly Roman Catholic country.[36] His predecessor Dr W. A. Visser 't Hooft, who for many *was* the World Council, appeared continually in the pages of the world press; his leadership was recognized by the German Publishers and Booksellers Association in their award to him and Cardinal Bea of their 1966 Peace Prize.[37] This acknowledgement of two individuals was also indicative of the importance of the social institution which they represented in German society and in international society.

The attention of the press has not been limited to simple reporting; its editors have also entered the lists in praise and criticism of the World Council. The founding of the World Council was occasion for welcoming the arrival of a Christian's 'spokesman' in the affairs of the world.[38] The editor of the *Manchester Guardian* (as it was then), in an editorial on coexistence and the forceful turning-back of communism, spoke in terms of the moral and the immoral, quoting from the preparatory volumes for the Evanston Assembly.[39] The voice of the Christian conscience was important enough for secular power to consider, to quote, and to discuss. In 1958 the same newspaper praised the churches for their service to refugees and their help in the areas of rapid social change.[40] The following year, this same secular paper did not find it out of place to publish an editorial in favour of the integration of the World Council with the International Missionary Council, a

273

S

step that had been taken in order to strengthen the international Christian movement.[41] The editor of *The Times* saw fit to devote two editorials of his important newspaper to Christian unity and the social position of the churches at the time of the New Delhi Assembly.[42] The *Frankfurter Allgemeine Zeitung* and the *Neue Zürcher Zeitung* have also had frequent editorials on the position of this international ecclesiastical institution; more surprisingly, *Le Monde* has regular features on ecumenical news. Issues of importance to particular countries or regions have received attention from the newspapers most concerned—a recognition of the importance of ecumenical opinion or actions to their areas. The South African papers nearly always had a comment on World Council pronouncements concerning racism. The more emotional the issue, the more publicity in reports, articles, and editorials. The financial aid given to groups to alleviate the suffering caused by racial discrimination and to stop the discrimination itself occasioned unprecedented editorial comment on World Council action, as noted in chapter 2 above.

The press in the communist states is more the second arm of government than the fourth estate of society. One might suppose that it would ignore Christian activities of any kind, because to recognize them publicly, even negatively, would endow them with a certain stature. Yet the communist press of East Germany, as well as of Great Britain and France, has given prominence to the World Council by invective, criticism, and selective praise of statements and actions which upheld communist positions. It is not surprising that the fewest comments and the most negative appeared in the coldest days of the Cold War. The *Tägliche Rundschau*, organ of the Soviet Military Government of Berlin, and *Neue Zeit*, newspaper of the Christian Democratic Union of the Russian Sector, both wrote of the 'Marshallization' of the Amsterdam Assembly. Since the Marshall Plan had been condemned by the Soviet Union as a tool of the American imperialists, these comments certainly carried hostile overtones.[43] *L'Humanité* published a reply in 1951 from the Reformed and Evangelical Churches of Hungary to the World Council Executive Committee's Statement on Nuclear Tests, criticizing it for ignoring other more pressing international issues.[44] As late as 1957 *Neue Zeit* wrote a polemical article against the meeting of the ecumenical Committee on Christian Responsibility for European Co-operation, whose function was to encourage European unity. If its existence, action, and opinions had not been considered to some degree influential, there would have been little point in attacking it. In addition to criticism of the World Council itself, individuals particularly obnoxious to the communist régime of East Germany were vilified even when the World Council was not; such an individual was Bishop Otto Dibelius of Berlin. *Neues Deutschland* wrote with admiration of a World Council sub-committee's refusing a 'provocative proposal . . . of the chief of the German NATO-church . . . .' [45]

If hostile mention implied that the World Council was sufficiently important to warrant criticism the practice of citing selected World Council pronouncements, in order to point out how they agreed with communist policy, unwittingly added to its stature among communists. In 1950 the *Daily Worker* (London) quoted a Central Committee condemnation of atomic and bacteriological weapons as well as reporting its recommendations to governments regarding conciliation in the Korean affair, without stating that the World Council had condemned the invasion that had just taken place. [46] In 1954 one issue of *Neue Zeit* was devoted almost entirely to a letter from Bishop G. K. A. Bell to Deputy Premier Nuschke of the German Democratic Republic. In this letter, a reply to Nuschke's request that the World Council subscribe to the demand for a ban on all nuclear weapons, Bishop Bell stated that a 'gigantic effort to secure international agreement' on this subject was necessary and that the World Council would do its utmost to further this effort. *Neue Zeit* described this as approval of the communist demands. [47] Later that year *Neues Deutschland* gave prominent coverage to the Evanston Assembly, and in an article this communist party paper claimed that the Assembly Message was a defeat for Secretary of State Dulles and President Eisenhower in their own land: 'The resolutions of the world conference show that the peace policy of the German Democratic Republic lies not only in the interests of the whole German people, but also finds itself in agreement with the whole of Protestant Christianity and many other churches as well.' [48]

The highly selective quotations used in the communist press showed a preference for World Council calls for peace and the ending of nuclear tests. [49] In passing, they sometimes mentioned the other items discussed, but more often that was not the case. When an international item was of special interest to a particular state, as Algeria was to France, the World Council stand on that issue would be announced or denounced according to the party line. All in all, it would seem that the communist press—naturally atheistic—both reacted to the status of the ecumenical movement in international society and contributed to its enhancement.

World Council Capabilities

The qualities of a political interest group mentioned at the beginning of this chapter can, *mutatis mutandis,* be applied to NGOs in general and to the World Council of Churches in particular;

those qualities, it will be remembered, ensure that the group is able to sustain communication and influence over a period of time. The possession of money and credit applies to all NGOs; the amount they actually possess indicates the possible extent of their efforts to influence international policy. The World Council's expenditure (see Table II) exceeds that of many small states. The existence of a bureaucratic structure is also common to NGOs and also depends on their finances. The World Council staff in international affairs in the first twenty years of its existence earned the respect of many international and national civil servants because of its expert knowledge, not only in the field of faith and morals, but also on some of the technical questions it had to face, such as the population explosion. Its present leaders are still earning this respect.

TABLE II

Expenditure of the WCC 1949–1975

(US $ million)

Year	Amount	Year	Amount	Year	Amount
1949	1.425	1958	3.916	1967	5.336
1950	1.358	1959	4.249	1968	6.067
1951	1.140	1960	4.605	1969	6.087
1952	2.006	1961	5.422	1970	7.307
1953	2.840	1962	5.971(a)	1971	7.054
1954	3.241	1963	6.332	1972	6.665
1955	3.279	1964	5.584	1973	10.189
1956	3.559	1965	5.427	1974	13.444
1957	3.647	1966	5.345	1975	16.471

(a) Absorption of the International Missionary Council increased expenditure.

Note: Since the WCC issues no single budget showing all income and all expenditure, these figures are based on the Council's annual *Financial Statement*. They show expenditure only, and include internal payments by one Department to another. Amounts paid to the Ecumenical Centre in Geneva and amounts transferred to Reserve are excluded. Nevertheless, the figures do give a rough idea of the financial power of the WCC.

The prestige of eminent national leaders has been reflected onto the World Council, leaders such as the Archbishop of Canterbury and the Ecumenical Patriarchs among its many divines. And it has the prestige of being the only Protestant-Orthodox world voice; the International Christian Council of Churches is a Protestant body only. Social institutions change slowly and even in this secular century the societal place of the church seems to be high even among those who complain of its present irrelevancy.

The World Council neither controls many jobs as patronage nor, directly, any large number of votes, though some of its national members may do so. However, every group cannot expect to have all the possible qualities enabling maximum influence and communication. The World Council appears to be well endowed and may even not make full use in international affairs of the endowments it possesses.

The targets of World Council communication, national leaders or international bureaucrats, will perceive any given topic in terms of the national or international interest respectively. For example, Dr Sen, Director-General of the FAO, reasoned that it was *not* in the international interest of his organization to consider problems of family planning, because to do so would antagonize Roman Catholic members. This negative reaction came in spite of the fact that the opinion of WCC officials on this topic could be considered by international secular officials to be as authoritative on this matter of faith and morals as that of the Vatican.

National interest groups are most effective when several groups unite to seek a common goal, each able to communicate with a variety of persons in the decision-making process. As an international interest group the World Council has co-operated with non-Christian groups both on procedural matters (e.g. concerning IGOs) and on such substantive matters as refugees, migration, and human rights (e.g. with the International Red Cross in the Nigerian-Biafran war).[50] It co-operates actively with the NGO Committee on Disarmament in Geneva and with individual anti-apartheid movements in several European countries. Nevertheless it maintains its claim to its unique role as the Christian conscience of the world.

The continuing capabilities of the World Council are illustrated by its long-term commitment to research and education in world affairs. It has carried out its educational function more often through national and regional Christian bodies (by providing them with a documentation service on issues before the United Nations and background research papers on political problems) than by direct contact with individual Christians. Nevertheless it has addressed itself to individuals by supplying information material on the needs of refugees and of developing countries. Its pronouncements, too, are publicized to all its constituents. They reach the religious constituency through the church press and the Ecumenical Press Service; through the secular press they reach those who do not necessarily consider themselves Christians but who may feel part of its 'justice constituency'.

Research has been carried out by several World Council bodies. With one exception the CCIA has never conducted the broadly based studies which the Cambridge founders envisaged. (Its one attempt to do so concerned elaboration of an international ethos and collapsed for lack of funds.) It has, however, thoroughly researched the problems with which its officials have been engaged. The Department on Church and Society has carried the brunt of the in-depth studies of a more theoretical kind. The usefulness of its work on rapid social change has been noted at length in this present book. Study is still considered important, but the Structure Committee, proposing changes in World Council organization noted that, 'The new structure must surmount the old separation between study and action. . . . It [study] must be integrated with the work which is primarily "action" or service oriented'.[51] Research and education on world affairs since its inception is one visible proof to international officials of the sustained capabilities of the World Council, and, what is more important, its sustained interest in international affairs and social justice.

Manifold Complexity

A further opinion of Dr Visser 't Hooft on the evaluation of the CCIA, and hence World Council, effort in international affairs: 'For international decisions are the result of a complicated process and it is practically impossible to estimate correctly just how much or how little each group participating in the general discussion has contributed'.[52] Reference to any political scientist's model of foreign policy decision-making will confirm the veracity of such a statement. Amidst the enormous complexity of the process, the World Council should be set alongside the various private interest groups and governmental bodies that supply information to the decision-making process.

Figure 7 indicates only part of this complexity. It represents a hypothetical case of the World Council communicating to several levels at once. World Council information and judgement (output) concerning a particular issue, e.g., family planning, goes to its international constituency (input), to the government of State A, to the United Nations delegations of States A and B, and to the United Nations Secretariat. Within the decision-making process of each of these, this information is processed along with that of other interest groups and public bodies. Each delegation in turn communicates its decision (output) to the General Assembly Main Committee debating the issue (input). All new viewpoints are digested there, and a resolution is prepared for the General Assembly (output). This resolution also is information which goes back to the suppliers of the original input (feedback). This reactivates all those who had an interest in the original proceedings. (For the sake of simplicity, feedback in Fig. 7 is shown only to the World Council.) A re-evaluation produces a modified ecumenical opinion (output²) which is communicated as previously. Other private interest groups and public bodies also put in new informa-

Fig. 7. A Communications Model of the WCC in International Decision-making

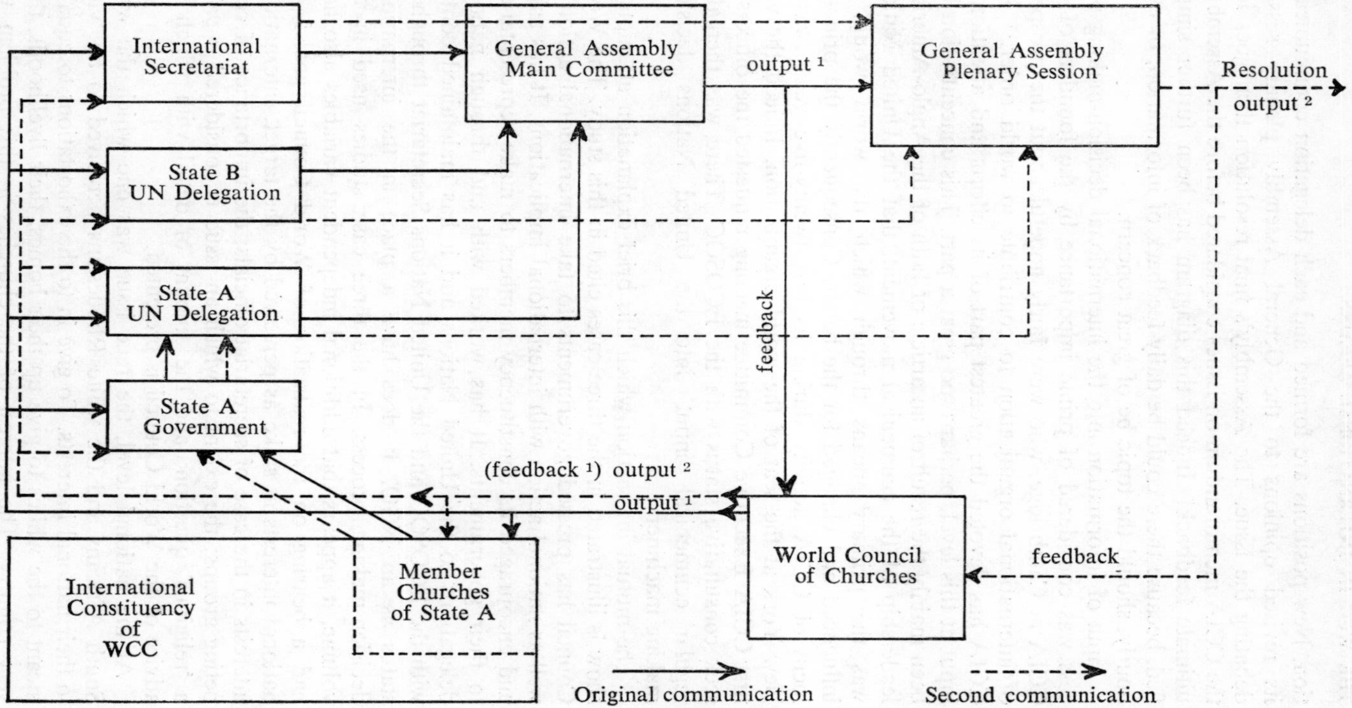

General Assembly Plenary Session

World Council of Churches

General Assembly Main Committee

International Secretariat

State B UN Delegation

State A UN Delegation

State A Government

Member Churches of State A

International Constituency of WCC

Resolution output [2]

feedback

Second communication

Original communication

output [1]

feedback

(feedback [1]) output [2]

output [1]

tion. New positions are formed and each delegation communicates its revised opinions to the General Assembly plenary session debating the issue. The Assembly's final resolution then goes into the CCIA memorandum on issues considered before the Assembly: ultimate feedback! Indeed this diagram has been further simplified, because there could be daily feedback of information, or even hourly, should the topic be of great concern.

Input of information into the international decision-making process was considered of prime importance by the founders of the CCIA at Cambridge, who were fairly hopeful about the prospects of international organization to contribute to world order.[53] The CCIA has devoted the greatest part of its efforts and attention to input at this level, perhaps too great a part. This concentration has been mainly the result of an article of faith of the Anglo-American leadership of the ecumenical movement, that the United Nations was the primary means through which the world would be influenced and changed for the better. Consequently the principal locus of CCIA activity during its first twenty-five years was in New York at the seat of the world organization. Indeed the very first CCIA Executive Committee meeting requested the officers to seek consultative status with the ECOSOC. There was thereafter regular ecumenical 'input' into the United Nations decision-making machinery.

The mutual interaction which this brief explanation attempts to show is illustrated in the three cases cited in this study. The World Council has pressed governments to take international action as well as national action with international implications. It has asked and encouraged its constituency members to make representations to their governments. It has worked with and through national delegations to the United Nations and it has maintained contact with the ECOSOC and the United Nations Secretariat through its status as an NGO. It does have a place in the international decision-making process. In the three case studies used in this volume, it appears that additional independent variables also have had a bearing on the realization of World Council goals: the national interests at stake as perceived by the target, international interests in the case of secretariat officials; the importance of competing groups; the extent to which an issue is considered *a priori* a 'religious' question; and the amount of detail with which the advice of the World Council is presented.

At the national level, the race issue was one which the white South Africans and the white Rhodesians perceived to be 'vital' to their national interests. To give in to the exhortations to equality meant to the whites to give up their homes, their livelihoods, their very country. The interest of the churches in this problem was recognized by most as legitimate; one notable insufficiency was that they could offer no plan for solving the social, economic, and political issues of apartheid—certainly not surprising, as neither sociologists nor politicians have been able to offer a workable solution. At the international level, the United Nations officials and delegates from most states of the world regarded racial equality as in the international interest. Of course other international pressure groups were also proponents of racial equality. The work of the World Council in formulating human rights has been prodigious, though reciprocal communication is evident in its earlier empathy with the South African churches and its attempt to avoid a break between itself and them and the United Nations and South Africa. The international standard espoused was a Christian standard; the international action by the World Council and by the United Nations has not yet produced results.

Economic development seems hardly a legitimate concern of religious bodies (from the perception of secular-minded *élites* used to the Pauline doctrine of subjection to the powers that be); yet this became a religious issue through the backdoor of Christian charity for those in distress. Inter-church aid developed into the ecumenical concern for the growth of production in the Third World. Generally there has been no vital interest opposed to aid, though donor national interests have been better served by bilateral than by multilateral aid. In this case, proposals by the churches have gone into great detail, because the churches themselves are actively involved in spending their own money for development. Again reciprocal influence is seen when Christian bodies, co-ordinated by the World Council, act as distributors for surplus commodities of the West. International officials have supported many of the goals of the World Council, especially an overall plan of development; the World Council has helped the international organizations in the Freedom From Hunger Campaign, gaining publicity for other humanitarian actions of the intergovernmental bodies.

The disarmament negotiations deal with an area, that of war and peace, in which the religious interest has long been acknowledged; at the same time it is an area in which decisions are regarded as vital to a state's existence. Although the CCIA has preferred to recommend negotiations and first steps rather than provide technical plans for disarmament, CCIA officials have had to use a great deal of technical information (for example, on fall-out) as the basis of their value judgements. International civil servants have been generally so helpless in their relations with the major powers in the disarmament negotiations that primary communication by the World Council has had to be with the national delegations. A surprisingly large percentage of the goals enunciated in the field of disarmament have been achieved.

281

The popular appeal of the World Council's interests is indicated by the widespread reporting of its pronouncements, studies, and meetings in the world's newspapers. They represent a growing Christian consensus on international social justice. Far more important than a Christian consensus is the fact that the Council's immediate preoccupation with helping only the baptized has given way to concern for the whole community in which Christians live, even as a minority. It is only on this basis that economic aid can be given by the churches; and only on this basis that the World Council can plead for the racial equality of all people. Its strength lies in its not speaking for powerful groups in society, as was the Church's custom in the past, but for the poverty-stricken, the sufferers from discrimination, and those weary of war and injustice, whether they are Christian or not. This evolution was prophesied in the very first message of the newly formed World Council of Churches at Amsterdam: 'We have to make of the Church in every place a voice for those who have no voice, and a home where every man will be at home'.[54]

Epilogue: Nairobi 1975

THE preparations for each Assembly begin when the previous one has ended: inevitably Uppsala 1968 led to Nairobi 1975.[1] Each succeeding Assembly is thus a continuation of the previous one, but each is also unique and has its own character. The intervening septennium allows each to develop in accordance with the mood of the time. Uppsala was a restless Assembly in a revolutionary period: 1968 saw the student-led revolt in France and student unrest in Germany, and riots occurred at the US Democratic National Convention in Chicago that same summer. Uppsala suffered—or benefited—from this unrest. A counter-assembly of youth and activists kept Assembly leaders on their toes. This revolutionary pressure led to the creation of a priority programme to combat racism and to the recognition of the urgent need for economic development.

Nairobi was an Assembly of the seventies. Several commentators noted the absence of divisiveness, characteristic of a decade that can ill afford the luxury of revolt.[2] This is not to say that there were not tense moments over the Programme to Combat Racism or the condemnation of religious persecution in the Soviet Union. In fact, however, the major tension occurred at the opening ceremonies when the Reverend Jack Glass of Glasgow seized the microphone and shouted, 'This is an assembly of the anti-Christ', before being escorted from the hall by ushers.[3]

In spite of its large non-official attendance, the Nairobi Assembly was smaller than Uppsala. Seven hundred and forty-seven delegates —from a total of some 2,300 participants—represented 286 churches throughout the world (including 15 newly admitted ones). Uppsala boasted 2,700 participants, with 704 delegates—as a venue it was more accessible to the richer countries of Christendom, and the starker economic realities of the seventies were still to come. The delegates at Nairobi were considered more representative than at Uppsala; the number representing each church is set by the constitution, but 20 per cent of the delegates were women compared with only 9 per cent at Uppsala; 10 per cent were under thirty years of age compared with 4 per cent at Uppsala; and 40 per cent consisted of lay people compared with 25 per cent in 1968. Eighty per cent of the delegates were attending their first Assembly;[4] this could account for the complaint that staff and observers, rather than delegates, seemed to be directing the events.

While it is desirable that as many individuals as possible gain experience in ecumenical meetings, the extent of the usefulness of so many novices at major ecumenical deliberations must be questioned for future assemblies.

By its nature, such a large meeting is unlikely to produce anything worthwhile without a great deal of preparation. This preparation is inevitably carried out by the paid staff. And so it was at Nairobi; it should have astounded no one, but apparently did.[5] An attempt was made to ensure more participation by holding not only the usual Section meetings (on specific topics) but also 'hearings' on World Council programmes and committees on matters of special concern. These all reported to overburdened plenary sessions, where restrictions on speakers by denomination and geographical region did not allow the dynamic input desired by the majority. One ecumenical delegate has suggested that, in future, a more decentralized programme culminating in a shorter plenary session would be a useful reform.[6] However, such a change might not be welcomed by delegates and their churches, since it would limit participation in the most popular debates.

Fresh innovative programmes were not the norm for the Nairobi Assembly, although women's rights—already introduced at Uppsala —became an established field of interest and a major topic of debate. In fact two women were elected to the six-member presidium of the World Council: Justice Annie Baeta Jiagge of the Court of Appeal of Ghana and Dr Cynthia Wedel, psychologist and former president of the NCCCUSA. Their four male colleagues are Archbishop Alof Sundby, Primate of the Lutheran Church of Sweden, the Reverend J. Miguez-Bonino, Argentine Methodist theologian, former General Tahibonar Simatupang, President of the Indonesian Council of Churches, and Metropolitan Nikodim, Archbishop of Leningrad. World Council presidium candidates are traditionally presented as a group, with the proper mix of church affiliation and worldwide distribution; however, because of anti-Soviet feeling on the part of some American and French delegates, an attempt was made to enter a candidate to oppose Metropolitan Nikodim.[7] Rulings from the chair prevented this unprecedented action. All six presidents hold office until the next Assembly.

The more conservative *Zeitgeist* of the seventies combined with financial problems to make innovation difficult; consolidation was the keynote of Nairobi. Even to maintain existing programmes requires great effort in the face of worldwide inflation and the relative depreciation of the dollar and the pound (the currencies of the major contributors until the West German churches stepped in with the saving D-Mark); furthermore, the relative appreciation of the Swiss franc has greatly added to headquarters costs. Stringent financial cutbacks and the use of reserve funds will help, but the WCC still risks a deficit in 1976. Part of the savings will be attained by not filling several vacant positions. The retirement of Dr Richard Fagley at the end of 1975 threatened closure of the CCIA office at the United Nations. Not only was it proposed to leave this position unfilled, but all CCIA activities were to be centralized in Geneva (a culmination of Dr Blake's centralization policy discussed in chapter 1 above). The Assembly protested against such an attitude to the United Nations and its work and requested the General Secretary to maintain this CCIA post. At the time of writing, Dr Fagley has been persuaded to remain as a part-time consultant and the office remains temporarily open. The International Affairs Department of the NCCCUSA is considering how it can co-operate in maintaining the office as an outpost of Christianity in world affairs.

The Racial Issue

The Programme to Combat Racism continued to be attacked by those who felt it was being applied in an unchristian manner. The attack failed, possibly because, for the first time, there was a 38 per cent plurality of delegates from Third World countries, in addition to 109 East Europeans. While it was primarily delegates from capitalist countries who attacked the PCR, the attack was supported only by a relatively small group of those delegates. The Bishop of Truro, the Right Reverend Graham Leonard, brought before the Assembly once again the red herring of Christians not being able to support violence to attain social justice. In a committee meeting the Bishop led a walkout with eleven others from Western Europe and North America to protest against 'undue emphasis' on violence to combat racism. They returned with a seven-point proposal which was incorporated into the committee report.[8] Dr Potter, in a BBC interview, observed that those who criticized the PCR 'have been the most racist in history, especially Britain. Wherever the British have gone in the world they have established a racist system.'[9] Dr Donald Coggan, Archbishop of Canterbury, agreed that the British, as well as other nations, 'had much to repent of over past racist attitudes', but the British had done much in the last thirty years to atone for past sins.[10]

The West German church delegates also came in for their share of criticism by Africans—the result of an abrupt refusal by Bishop Class, Chairman of the Council of the Evangelische Kirche in Deutschland, to consider protesting to his government against nuclear collaboration between certain West German firms and South Africa. (Prior to the Assembly, Bishop Gatu, Chairman of the AACC, had written to request him to take such action.) Bishop Class's schoolmasterly tone, as well as his refusal, caused repercussions among Christians in Germany also.[11]

The Assembly concerned itself with this problem of multinational companies financing and constructing nuclear power plants in South Africa. It named firms in the United States, the Netherlands, Switzerland, West Germany, and France and called upon the member churches in those states to 'make public the political and military implications' of continued collaboration with South Africa and to urge their governments and companies to revise their policies by weighing the strengthening of apartheid against the paltry economic advantages to be received.

The report of Section V, 'Structures of Injustice and Struggles for Liberation', dealt not only with racism but also with all violations of human rights, including women's rights and religious freedom. A survey of racism throughout the world revealed what the report called 'a litany of shame of the whole human family'. It specifically deplored racism within the churches, some of which are still organized along racial lines and others are not without feelings of superiority that are unconsciously racial. It condemned institutional racism, whether in a form enforced by law or as illustrated in the trade patterns of the North Atlantic states. The internationally racist structures which serve and are served by multinational corporations can best be met by the churches at the ecumenical and international levels, it stated.[12]

Section V's recommendations to the churches on racism included continuing support for the PCR, especially the financial commitment. It urged that, wherever possible, representatives of minority or racially oppressed groups should join the churches' decision-making bodies. Theological study on racism and on the causes of violence should continue. South Africa was singled out for special attention by the churches. Member churches were urged to become active in campaigns within their states to stop the arms traffic with that country, to work for the withdrawal of investments from it, and to discourage white migration there. These recommendations break no new ground and should not offend the most ardent West European champion against violence in World Council programmes. This writer believes that nothing less than acceptance of the international *status quo* would, in fact, satisfy these critics.

Some religious leaders in Western Europe and North America have regarded the anti-racism bias of the World Council as being somehow undesirable.[13] This negative attitude has sometimes been attributed, ungenerously, to the benefits which those societies derive from the existing international structures of racial and economic subordination; more generously, others have considered such an attitude to be simply a manifestation of unconscious racism due to the normal socialization processes of those societies. One consistent complaint by the religious leadership in question has been the singling out of Western (i.e. capitalist) societies as racist while communist societies have escaped criticism for their equally reprehensible suppression of human rights, especially in the form of religious persecution, a matter of natural interest to an organization of churches. It is this writer's opinion that these two questions are politically related within ecumenical circles.

An appeal by two Russian Orthodox priests in a letter to the Nairobi Assembly for help against religious persecution in their country paved the way for action by the Assembly after some bitter debate. Metropolitan Filaret, Vicar of Moscow, stated that an Assembly resolution concerning this issue might create new problems for the Russian Church. In the compromise reached, the Assembly issued a public statement calling on all signatory states to the Helsinki Agreement on Security and Co-operation in Europe to observe and carry out their commitments under it, especially regarding the protection of human rights. In the statement the following simple, innocuous sentence pleased neither the Soviet churchmen nor the Western hardliners: 'The Assembly has devoted a substantial period to the discussion of the alleged denials of religious liberty the USSR'. The editor of the *Frankfurter Allgemeine Zeitung* stressed the word 'alleged' in the title of his article; the correspondent of *The Times* interpreted the statement as a 'Sidestep by churches on Soviet curbs'.[14] Only the correspondent of *Le Monde* showed understanding for the restraint of the reprimand.[15] The Russian Church's only link with the outside world is the World Council, and a majority of the Assembly delegates felt that this one opportunity for Christian fellowship ought not to be endangered. Public debate did occur; the World Council did respond publicly as it has done many times privately. Its restrained wording, like that of a papal encyclical or a diplomatic note, is none the less efficacious for its restraint.

A period of consolidation for all the World Council programmes makes no exception for the Programme to Combat Racism. It continues without hope for an expanded role in the immediate future. Criticism of its grants to victims of racism, which included some guerrilla groups, has not led to an abandonment of those grants but has increased emphasis on the non-violent aspects of its programme, such as withdrawal of investments from firms doing business in South Africa, boycotts of banks lending money to South Africa, halting the arms trade with South Africa, and attempting to halt white migration to that country.

Economic Development

The World Council has continued its innovative thinking on development matters, discussed at length in chapter 3 above. It no longer considers development as economic development but

287

as human development. According to WCC thought, this expansion of the term includes the concepts of social justice for all and self-reliance on the part of the recipient states as well as the more usual idea of economic growth. Although the churches have their own development programmes, they realize that the primary responsibility will continue to be that of secular agencies, i.e. governments and intergovernmental organizations, primarily because the resources needed are so great as to be available from public sources only. Nevertheless, the Assembly sees a specific role for Christians and the churches in defining and articulating just social, political, and economic goals.

These just goals include ethical regard on the part of recipient states for the way in which the money is used, and, on the part of the donor states, undertakings to give a fixed percentage of their wealth; this concept of ethical values in development has been extended to a consideration of the life-style of the industrialized states, not only what the donor gives, but how he husbands what he has. The conservation of energy, the ethics of the type of energy chosen—whether nuclear or solar or other—and the extent to which the wealthy consume a disproportionate share of the earth's resources are all ethical factors which should become part of the decision-making process in 'Christian' societies. Ecological thought has become ethical thought.

Recommendations to the churches on development included renewal of a request that 2 per cent of church budgets be assigned to development aid, consideration of the population problem as an integral part of development, and the education of Christians and the churches about development. The churches were asked to consider the possibility of action to influence the development policy of their respective governments (action already undertaken by some of them), to participate directly in the development programmes of churches or Christian councils in the developing countries, and to work in partnership with secular bodies, including governments and United Nations agencies.

The report recognized the ecological aspects of development in recommendations on the 'quality of life'. Warnings were issued regarding the pollution resulting from technology and urban concentration. The wealthy were urged to modify their consumption patterns as well as to provide a minimum for the poor. Indeed, a plenary speech was devoted to this problem. Professor Charles Birch, Head of the School of Biological Sciences at the University of Sydney, spoke on 'Creation, Technology and Human Survival'. He noted that of the three commands in the book of Genesis—be fruitful and multiply, have dominion over every living creature, and replenish the earth—man had willingly carried out the first two but had grievously failed to replenish the earth. He also created *the* aphorism of the Assembly: 'The rich must live more simply that the poor may simply live'.[16]

In development, as in other World Council programmes, the keyword was consolidation, to keep the programmes already approved alive. The main exception was not a programme that would cost money but rather in the emphasis of the programme; the earth should not only be developed but be developed wisely, with due respect for the earth and for future generations. In continuing development projects through CCPD as well as the newly founded Ecumenical Development Co-operative Society, as described in chapter 3 above, the World Council proceeds with its strategy of experimental development.

Disarmament

The traditional Christian concern with destruction and war was voiced in an Assembly statement which contained an analysis, from the ecumenical point of view, of the world armaments situation. It went beyond simple platitudes but avoided technical details, which were left to later consultations, and it showed perspicacity in recognizing that the build-up of tactical nuclear weapons reduces 'the potential importance of a threshold between conventional and nuclear warfare'. Military bases on foreign soil were pronounced to be as great a threat as armaments themselves; the military build-up in the Indian Ocean was cited as an example of bases having created tensions in an area relatively free from them previously. World military expenditure was criticized in general, and it was particularly deplored that Third World countries expended on arms three times the amount they received in official foreign aid.

In this statement, entitled 'The World Armaments Situation', the Assembly showed discernment when it noted the internal (as distinct from external) forces encouraging the arms race: the military-industrial-bureaucratic complex whose *raison d'être* can be seen as the creation of new and better arms. The statement's analysis represents a step forward in an area which has been mainly a source of emotional rhetoric. As in the cases of racism and development, where the WCC conducted scientific studies of their underlying causes, it is now beginning to treat the arms control problem with similar detachment.

In its 'Appeal to the Churches' the Assembly asked the churches to study this statement and also called for the Central Committee to organize a consultation on disarmament. This would differ from those described in chapter 4 in that it would propose a strategy to be followed by the churches at their national levels and by the WCC at the international level to prevent increased military

T

expenditure. The Assembly also recommended that nostrum of the ecumenical movement since the Universal Christian Council called for a League of Nations Disarmament Conference in the 1930s, a United Nations World Disarmament Conference. As a placebo given by a doctor often produces a positive result in his patient, so this remedy proposed by the ecumenical movement might produce positive results were it tried.

Disarmament has been a perennial concern of the WCC, as of its predecessors. The subject is, however, one to which states are extremely sensitive; they consider it a matter within their 'vital' interests. It is an area in which the churches can themselves take no practical action as they have done in other areas, such as undertaking development projects or giving aid to liberation groups. It is unlikely that the churches can do more than keep the ethical value of disarmament and arms control before their constituencies and before statesmen. Here the WCC continues in patient obedience, searching for new approaches.[17]

The Nairobi Assembly, like previous Assemblies, created its own spirit and put forth its own programme with its own emphases. It marked, however, neither a beginning nor an end. Its results have not called for change in the basic analysis presented in the body of this book. The WCC remains a non-governmental organization, an institution in international society. The churches which are its members remain social institutions in their own lands, even in avowedly atheistic states. The importance to the Soviet Union of criticism of religious persecution is an illustration of this. One head of government, Prime Minister Michael Manley of Jamaica, travelled half-way round the world to deliver a speech to the Assembly; the delegates were received by Mzee Jomo Kenyatta, President of Kenya. Observers from both intergovernmental and non-governmental organizations participated in the Assembly. All these factors uphold this author's concept of a World Council of Churches in international society partaking in international decision-making by publicizing its views and ideas, by input into the decision-making process. Its input is acceptable, whether or not its specific recommendations are used, because of its role in international society, which derives partly from the institutional position of its member churches to their own societies.

Even the critics of the Assembly voiced the same criticisms as in previous years. One was that the Assembly enunciated general goals without specifying the means to achieve them.[18] As noted throughout this work, this has been a point of contention ever since 1948. It is based on a misunderstanding of the function of an Assembly, which is to set the policy and programmes for the next septennium: the Central Committee and the WCC staff and experts will propose (through a myriad consultations, workshops, and meetings with each other and with Third World Christians and Christian experts as well as the experts and statesmen of the industrialized world) concrete ways to carry out the Assembly's policies. When the more detailed reports are issued, the critics then normally point out that the churches should not attempt to provide specific solutions but rather should limit themselves to offering general ethical guide-lines. As in any organization, the WCC has bodies which set policy and other bodies which prepare the means to implement it.

There was also the perennial complaint that the WCC does not criticize communist countries, specifically the USSR, sufficiently— or at all. Some compliments from the more conservative critics were meant also as implied complaints of past WCC activity. There was praise for a return to piety and theology and a retreat from political activism, which they detected at Nairobi. This was seen as a counterwave to the 'crusader's spirit' of the PCR in its first seven years, and was thought to indicate a return to the centrality of faith and tradition in the ecumenical movement.[19] In fact, it is the financial situation of the World Council which makes it appear more modest in its political, social, and economic endeavours. It is, as the more sympathetic writers noted, a period of consolidation of the daring programmes of the sixties. If there were the desired 'return' to the centrality of the ecumenical movement's origins, those who desire it would find the centrality one of Christian activism in the Universal Christian Council for Life and Work, while they would find theological discussion and the quest for unity in a much weaker, less well-organized World Conference on Faith and Order.

If the World Council of Churches were to turn inward and discuss the primarily theological problems of Christian unity, it would silence its Western critics. It would, however, not be true to those of its constituency who look to it to help them achieve human dignity which the 'Christian' states of Europe in their period of colonialism did not allow them. If it retreats from the world, it can no longer serve as a voice for the voiceless nor lend the helping hand of the Good Samaritan.

Appendices

APPENDIX I

A. *Meetings of the World Council of Churches in Process of Formation*

Organ	*Date*	*Place*
Provisional Committee	13 May 1938	Utrecht, Netherlands
	28-30 Jan. 1939	St Germain France
Administrative Committee	21-22 July 1939	Zeist, Netherlands
	7-8 Jan. 1940	Zilven, Netherlands
IMC-WCC Joint Committee	14-15 Feb. 1946	Geneva
Provisional Committee	20-23 Feb. 1946	Geneva

B. *Assemblies of the WCC and Meetings of the Central Committee*

Organ	*Date*	*Place*	*Main Theme*
First Assembly	22 Aug.-4 Sept. 1948	Amsterdam	Man's disorder and God's design.
1st Central Committee	6-7 Sept. 1948	Woudschoten, Netherlands	None.
2nd CC	9-15 July 1949	Chichester, England	1. What should the Churches expect from the WCC? 2. Contemporary issues of religious liberty. 3. Christian action in international affairs.
3rd CC	9-15 July 1950	Toronto	1. Dominant religious liberty. 2. The ecclesiological significance of the WCC. 3. Nature and theme of the 2nd assembly.

Organ	Date	Place	Main Theme
4th CC	4-11 Aug. 1951	Rolle, Switzerland	1. The calling of the church to mission and unity. 2. The role of the WCC in times of tension.
5th CC	31 Dec. 1952-8 Jan. 1953	Lucknow	1. The two primary goals of the ecumenical movement: mission and unity. 2. The relevance of Christian hope to our time. 3. The Asian situation as a concern of Christians everywhere.
6th CC	12-14 Aug. 1954	Chicago, Illinois	None.
Second Assembly	15-31 Aug. 1954	Evanston, Illinois	Christ, the hope of the world.
7th CC	27, 31 Aug., 1-2 Sept. 1954	Evanston, Illinois	None.
8th CC	2-8 Aug. 1955	Davos, Switzerland	1. Implications of Christian unity for inter-church aid and/or assistance to under-developed countries. 2. The meanings of unity, and the unity which the WCC seeks to promote.
9th CC	28 July-5 Aug. 1956	Galyatető, Hungary	1. Christian witness, proselytism, and religious liberty in the setting of the WCC. 2. The churches and the building of a responsible society.
10th CC	30 July-7 Aug. 1957	New Haven, Conn.	The calling of the Church to witness and to serve.
11th CC	21-9 Aug. 1958	Nyborg Strand, Denmark	Special reports. No theme.

Organ	Date	Place	Main Theme
12th CC	19-27 Aug. 1959	Rhodes, Greece	The significance of the Eastern and Western traditions within Christendom.
13th CC	16-24 Aug. 1960	St Andrews, Scotland	1. The role of the WCC in regard to unity. 2. Responsible parenthood and the population problem.
14th CC	17 Nov. 1961	New Delhi	None.
Third Assembly	19 Nov.- 5 Dec. 1961	New Delhi	Jesus Christ, the Light of the World.
15th CC	6-7 Dec. 1961	New Delhi	
16th CC	7-16 Aug. 1962	Paris	The finality of Jesus Christ in the age of universal history.
17th CC	26 Aug.- 2 Sept. 1963	Rochester, New York	1. The Churches' responsibilities in the new societies. 2. The meaning of WCC membership.
18th CC	12-21 Jan. 1965	Enugu, Nigeria	The call to conversion and service, and its meaning for the Churches' participation in God's work.
19th CC	8-17 Feb. 1966	Geneva	The ecumenical way.
20th CC	15-26 Aug. 1967	Heraklion, Crete	The concern of the WCC for evangelism.
21st CC	2-3 July 1968	Göteborgs Nation, Uppsala, Sweden	None.
Fourth Assembly	4-20 July 1968	Uppsala	'Behold, I make all things new.'
22nd CC	18, 20 July 1968	Uppsala	None.
23rd CC	12-22 Aug. 1969	Canterbury, England	None.
24th CC	10-21 Jan. 1971	Addis Ababa	The WCC and dialogue with men of other faiths.
25th CC	13-23 Aug. 1972	Utrecht, Netherlands	Committed to fellowship.
26th CC	22-9 Aug. 1973	Geneva	None.

APPENDICES

Organ	Date	Place	Main Theme
27th CC	11-18 Aug. 1974	West Berlin	None.
28th CC	7 Dec. 1975	Nairobi, Kenya	None.
Fifth Assembly	23 Nov.- 10 Dec. 1975	Nairobi, Kenya	Jesus Christ frees and unites.
29th CC	11 Dec. 1975	Nairobi, Kenya	None.
30th CC	10-18 Aug. 1976	Geneva	None.

APPENDIX II

World Council Grants to Organizations Combating Racism: 1970, 1971, 1973, 1974, 1975 and 1976

US $

	1970	1971	1973	1974	1975	1976
AFRICA						
Angola						
National Union for the Total Independence of Angola (União Nacional Para a Independencia Total de Angola, UNITA)	10,000	7,500	6,000	14,000	—	—
People's Movement for the Liberation of Angola (Movimento Popular de Libertação de Angola, MPLA)	20,000	25,000	10,000	23,000	—	—
Revolutionary Government of Angola in Exile (Governo Revolucionario de Angola no Exil, GRAE)	20,000	7,500	10,000	23,000	—	—
Guinea-Bissau						
African Independence Party of Guinea and Cape Verde Islands (Partido Africano da Independencia da Guiné e Cabo Verde, PAIGC)	20,000	25,000	25,000	100,000	—	—
Mozambique						
Mozambique Institute of Frelimo (Frente de Libertação de Moçambique)	15,000	20,000	25,000	60,000	—	—
Rhodesia						
African National Council (Zimbabwe)	—	—	—	—	83,500	—
Zimbabwe African National Union (ZANU)	10,000	5,000	—	15,000	—	*85,000
Zimbabwe African People's Union (ZAPU)	10,000	5,000	—	15,000	—	—

* "Will be distributed on the authority of the WCC officers as soon as the situation in Zimbabwe is clarified." (WCC Press Release CC/16, 18 August 1976.)

	1970	1971	1973	1974	1975	1976
South Africa						
African National Congress (South Africa)	—	—	—	—	45,000	50,000
Lutuli Memorial Foundation of African National Congress	10,000	5,000	2,500	15,000	—	—
Pan Africanist Congress of Azania	—	—	2,500	15,000	45,000	50,000
South African Congress of Trade Unions	—	—	—	—	—	5,000
South West Africa (Namibia)						
South West African People's Organization (SWAPO)	5,000	25,000	20,000	30,000	83,500	85,000
Tanzania						
Sixth Pan African Congress	—	—	—	12,000	—	—
Zambia						
Africa 2000 Project	15,000	5,000	—	—	—	—
Total Africa	**135,000**	**130,000**	**101,000**	**322,000**	**257,000**	**275,000**

ASIA AND AUSTRALASIA

	1970	1971	1973	1974	1975	1976
Australia						
Federal Council for the Advancement of Aborigines and Torres Strait Islanders	10,000	—	14,000	—	—	10,000
National Tribal Council	15,000	—	—	—	—	—
Aboriginal and Islanders Development Fund	—	—	—	—	10,000	—
Southern Africa Liberation Centre	—	—	—	—	—	5,000
Japan						
Anti-Apartheid Movement of Osaka, Japan	—	—	—	—	—	5,000
International Committee to Combat the Immigration Bill in Japan	2,000	—	—	—	—	—

	1970	1971	1973	1974	1975	1976
Japan Anti-Apartheid Committee, Youth Section ...	—	—	—	—	7,500	—
Legal Defence Committee in Japan (Korean Minority) ...	—	5,000	—	10,000	—	—
National Committee Combating Discrimination against Ethnic People	—	—	—	—	20,000	—
New Hebrides						
New Hebrides National Party ...	—	—	—	—	—	10,000
New Zealand						
National Anti-Apartheid Co-ordinating Committee ...	—	—	—	4,000	—	7,500
Total Asia and Australasia ...	27,000	5,000	14,000	14,000	37,500	37,500

SOUTH AMERICA AND THE CARIBBEAN

	1970	1971	1973	1974	1975	1976
XLII Congreso Internacional de Americanistas ...	—	—	—	—	—	13,000
Bolivia						
Bolivian Project in Aid of Indian Liberation (Proyecto de Acción Liberadora de Indígena en Bolivia) ...	—	12,500	—	—	—	—
Centro de Coordinación y Promoción Campesina ...	—	—	—	—	20,000	—
Colombia						
Asociación Nacional de Usuarios Campesinos ...	—	—	—	—	15,000	10,000
Colombian Foundation for the Defence of Natural Resources and Black Workers (Fundación Colombiana para la Defensa de los Recursos Naturales y de los Trabajadores Negros)	—	—	10,000	—	—	—
Committee for the Defence of the Indian in Colombia (Coordinación de Movimientos Indígenas en Colombia) ...	15,000	5,000	—	—	—	—

	1970	1971	1973	1974	1975	1976
Indigenous Rural Alliance in Struggle for the Land (Alianza Campesina Indígena en Lucha por la Tierra) ...	—	—	—	15,000	—	—
Native Regional Council of the Cauca (Consejo Regional Indígena del Cauca, CRIC) ...	—	—	10,000	10,000	5,000	15,000
Ecuador						
Imbabura Indian Peasant Organization ...	—	—	—	—	20,000	—
Paraguay						
Indigenist Association of Paraguay (Asociación Indigenista del Paraguay) ...	—	2,500	—	—	—	—
Caribbean						
Christian Action for Development in the Eastern Caribbean ...	—	5,000	—	—	—	—
Total South America and Caribbean ...	15,000	25,000	20,000	25,000	60,000	38,000

NORTH AMERICA

Canada

	1970	1971	1973	1974	1975	1976
Committee for Original Peoples Entitlement (COPE) ...	—	—	—	—	—	10,000
Indian Brotherhood of the Northwest Territories (IB.NWT) ...	—	—	7,500	—	—	—
Inuit (Eskimo) Tapirisat of Canada ...	—	2,500	—	—	—	—
National Indian Brotherhood (on behalf of Cree—Inuit Council of James Bay) ...	—	—	7,500	5,000	—	—
Toronto Committee for the Liberation of Southern Africa ...	—	—	—	—	6,000	6,000
United States of America						
Akwesasne Notes ...	—	—	—	—	5,000	—

300

	1970	1971	1973	1974	1975	1976
All African News Service (AANS); for 1975, see Southern Africa Committee, below	—	—	3,000	—	—	5,000
American Indian Movement (AIM)	—	—	6,000	15,000	15,000	15,000
Americans for Indian Opportunity (Oklahoma Indians)	—	⁝	—	5,000	—	—
Center for National Security Studies: Africa Project	—	—	—	—	7,500	—
Coalition of Concerned Black Americans (earlier, Legal Protection of Civil Rights of Minorities in the USA)	—	7,500	6,000	—	—	—
Delta Ministry, Mississippi	—	—	6,000	—	15,000	15,000
El Paso Education Research Project	—	—	5,000	5,000	—	—
Free Southern Theatre	—	—	—	5,000	5,000	—
Haitian Refugee Concerns	—	—	—	—	—	10,000
Institute for the Development of Indian Law in Washington DC	—	2,500	—	—	—	—
Malcolm X Liberation University	—	7,500	6,000	—	—	—
National Association for the Advancement of Colored People—Legal Defense Fund	—	—	—	—	—	10,000
Puerto Rican Minority	—	—	6,000	—	—	—
Puerto Rico Solidarity Committee	—	—	—	—	—	15,000
Southern Africa Committee (in 1975, grant shared with AANS)	—	—	—	4,000	5,000	—
Southern Election Fund Inc.	—	7,500	—	—	15,000	15,000
United Farm Workers Organizing Committee AFL-CIO	—	2,500	—	15,000	15,000	—
Washington Office on Africa	—	—	—	—	—	5,000
Total North America	—	30,000	47,000	49,000	73,500	106,000

EUROPE

	1970	1971	1973	1974	1975	1976
Belgium						
Belgian Anti-Apartheid Committee (Comité de Soutien à la Lutte Contre le Colonialisme et l'Apartheid) (1976 total shared with Aktiekomitee Zuidelijk Afrika and Boycot Outspan Aktie)	—	2,500	2,000	—	6,000	7,500
France						
Association des Marocains en France	—	—	—	—	5,000	10,000
Collectif des Organisations Africaines en France	—	—	—	—	5,000	10,000
Comité des Travailleurs Algériens en France	—	—	—	—	5,000	10,000
French Anti-Apartheid Committee (Comité Français Contre l'Apartheid)	—	2,500	—	—	—	—
Germany						
Informationsstelle Südiches Afrika and Anti-Apartheid Bewegung	—	—	—	—	—	6,000
Italy						
Liberazione e Sviluppo	—	—	—	—	—	5,000
Netherlands						
Angola Committee and Dr Eduardo Mondlane Foundation, for their Foundation for Information about Racism and Colonialism (in 1975, grant shared with Anti-Apartheid Movement and Boycot Outspan Aktie)	5,000	—	2,000	4,000	—	—
Anti-Apartheid Movement	—	—	—	4,000	10,000	—
Boycot Outspan Aktie	—	—	—	—	—	5,000

302

	1970	1971	1973	1974	1975	1976
Switzerland						
Anti-Apartheid Movement	—	—	2,000	4,000	5,000	5,000
United Kingdom						
The Africa Bureau	2,500	—	—	—	—	—
The Anti-Apartheid Movement	5,000	—	2,000	4,000	10,000	10,000
Committee for Freedom in Mozambique, Angola and Guinea	—	—	—	4,000	—	—
Europe-Africa Research Project—Black Press International, later Europe-Third World Research Centre	—	—	—	5,000	—	—
'Free University for Black Studies'	—	2,500	—	—	—	—
Institute of Race Relations, UK	—	2,500	7,500	—	5,000	5,000
International Defence and Aid Fund	3,000	—	—	—	—	30,000
Race Today Collective Association	—	—	—	—	—	—
Towards Racial Justice	—	—	—	10,000	—	—
West Indian Standing Conference	7,500	—	—	—	—	—
Migrants in Western Europe						
Community of Agape, Italy, Migrant Seminar (Comunità d'Agape—Centro Ecumenico)	—	—	2,500	—	—	—
Migrant Workers Co-ordinating Committee (Paris)	—	—	—	5,000	—	—
Total Europe	23,000	10,000	18,000	40,000	51,000	103,500
GRAND TOTAL	200,000	200,000	200,000	450,000	479,000	560,000

SOURCES: WCC press releases: 3 Sept. 1970; Nb/16-71, 9 Sept. 1971; Nb-4/73, 22 Jan. 1973; Nb 4/74, 20 Feb. 1974; Nb 7/75, 16 Apr. 1975.

303

Notes

INTRODUCTION

Source materials not available in published form were consulted at the WCC archives in Geneva and at the former CCIA office in London.

[1] Michael Haas, 'A Functional Approach to International Organization', *The Journal of Politics,* vol. 27 (1965), p. 500.

[2] Jean Meynaud, *Groupes de Pression* (1961), p. 390.

[3] Ibid. Also Edward Miles, 'Organizations and Integration in International Systems', *International Studies Quarterly,* 12: 2 (June 1968), p. 199, note 8; and Michael Banks, 'Systems Analysis and the Study of Regions', ibid., 13: 4 (Dec. 1969), pp. 335-60.

[4] The monthly publication *International Associations* provides articles on this topic. The UIA also publishes the *Yearbook of International Organizations* and many other worthwhile studies.

[5] See Chadwick F. Alger, 'Research on Research', a paper presented to the American Political Science Association Annual Meeting, Sept. 1969, cited in Anthony J. N. Judge, 'Visualization of the Organizational Network —the UAI as an International Data Bank', *Union of International Associations 1910–1970, Past, Present, Future* (1970), p. 90.

[6] Robert O. Keohane and Joseph S. Nye, Jr, eds, *Transnational Relations and World Politics* (1972).

[7] It would be incorrect to state that this was so of all societies throughout the world. On the other hand confining it to countries of traditional Judeo-Christian heritage understates its importance. The influence of Christian thought on leaders of Africa is seen by noting those who have attended the World Council Assemblies: these include President Kenneth Kaunda of Zambia, Sir Akanu Ibiam of Nigeria, Robert Gardiner of Ghana and others. The active participation of General T. Simaltupang of Indonesia in the Central Committee indicates that Asia, too, may be included.

CHAPTER 1: AN INTERNATIONAL WITNESS

[1] Bryan Wilson, *Religion in Secular Society, a Sociological Comment* (1966), *passim* but esp. Pt III.

[2] The first meeting was held in Manchester on 15 Apr. 1907, where the original proposal was made. On 27 Apr. 1907 invitations were sent out calling a London meeting (held in Exeter Hall, Strand, 6 May 1907), signed by the bishops of Hereford and Ripon and others. *Report on the Memorial of the Churches for Peace Presented to the Conference at The Hague, 25th June, 1907* [1907].

[3] Carnegie Endowment for International Peace, Division of International Law, *The Proceedings of the Hague Peace Conferences, the Conference of 1907,* vol. 1: *Plenary Meetings of the Conference* (1920), pp. 60-1.

[4] The two books giving accounts of the visits are *Peace and the Churches* [1908] and F. Siegmund-Schultze, ed., *Friendly Relations Between Great Britain and Germany* (1910).

[5] 'Minutes of the Conference on the Situation in Korea at the Aldine Club, New York, October 11, 1912' (typescript), provides some informa-

tion. The richest source is the correspondence files of the IMC, now located at the World Council Library in Geneva.

6 World Alliance for Promoting International Friendship Through the Churches, *The Churches and International Friendship, Report of the Conference held at Constance, August 1914* (London 1914).

7 The publication of the British group of the World Alliance entitled *Goodwill* relates most of these efforts.

8 For a fuller description, see Darril Hudson, *The Ecumenical Movement in World Affairs* (1969).

9 Nathan Söderblom, *Christian Fellowship* (1923), p. 203.

10 George K. A. Bell, ed., *The Stockholm Conference, 1925* (1926).

11 Walter Moberly and others, *The Churches Survey Their Task* (1937), Appendix B.

12 W. A. Visser 't Hooft, *The Ten Formative Years, 1938–1948* (1948).

13 WCC, 'Conference on International Affairs, Cambridge, August 4th to 7th, 1946', Paper 1 (typescript).

14 *New York Times*, 6 and 7 Aug. 1946.

15 Ibid., 5 Aug. 1946.

16 As n. 13 above, Minutes (typescript), p. 7.

17 Ibid., p. 8.

18 Several instances are cited in Hudson, *passim*. For example, the CMSGBI was responsible for the establishment of the Blanesborough Committee which recommended repayment to German missionaries of their property confiscated during the First World War.

19 Hudson, p. 24.

20 As n. 13 above, Paper III (typescript), p. 11; my italic.

21 WCC, Second Assembly, *International Affairs—Christians in the Struggle for World Community* (1954).

22 WCC, Central Committee, *Minutes 1969*, p. 65.

23 'The Present and Future of the Ecumenical Movement', *Christian Century*, 30 Aug. 1972, p. 847. This article reported an interview with Dr Potter.

24 Ibid., p. 849.

25 N. Goodall, ed., *The Uppsala Report 1968* (1968), p. 495.

26 Indeed it is difficult to stamp out useless concepts which agree with ideology; Chairman Dahlén writing in 1973 stressed the importance of the future effort to build up the role of Commissioners and national and regional committees. CCIA, *The Churches in International Affairs: Reports 1970–1973* (Geneva, 1974), p. 14.

27 The latest changes in the Constitution and Rules were approved at the Central Committee meeting in 1972. These were ratified by the Nairobi Assembly. They may be found in David M. Paton, ed., *Breaking Barriers: Nairobi 1975* (1976), pp. 317-40. The previous ones are in Goodall, ed., *The Uppsala Report 1968*, pp. 466ff; see Article V regarding the Assembly.

28 Rule IX.1. Cf. the previous Rules X.1 and X.2.

29 See previous Rule X.3 and X.4, as well as the present ones.

30 Rule IX.4.

31 Rule IX.5; cf. previous Rule X.5.

32 Rule IX.2.

33 WCC, Central Committee, *Report of the Structure Committee to the Central Committee, Addis Ababa, January 1971* (1970), pp. 26ff.

CHAPTER 2: WHITE DEVILS

1 *The Times*, 'The Churches in South Africa', 4 Sept. 1970.

U

2 Conference on Church, Community and State, *The Churches Survey Their Task: the Report of the Conference at Oxford, July 1937* (London, Allen & Unwin, 1937), p. 234.

3 'Statement from the Provisional Committee of the WCC in Process of Formation (1939)', in WCC, *Ecumenical Statements on Race Relations* (1965), p. 13. See also Ruth Rouse and Stephen C. Neill, eds, *A History of the Ecumenical Movement 1517–1948,* 2nd edn. (1967), p. 707.

4 See almost any articles on taxonomies of races, e.g., Stanley M. Garn and Carleton S. Coon, 'On the Number of Races of Mankind', *American Anthropologist,* 57: 5 (1955), pp. 996-1001, and J. Beaujeu-Garnier, *Geography of Population* (1966), pp. 17-28.

5 *Statement on Race and Racial Prejudice,* UNESCO, 26 Sept. 1967.

6 This report appears in W. A. Visser 't Hooft, ed., *The First Assembly of the World Council of Churches: the Official Report* (1949), pp. 51-6.

7 Section III appears ibid., pp. 74-82.

8 Section IV appears ibid., pp. 88-100.

9 This debate is recorded in Central Committee, *Minutes 1949,* pp. 17-19.

10 Three leading newspapers reported the debate on racism. The *Manchester Guardian* and *The Times* both on 23 July 1949, and the *New York Times* on 13 and 16 July 1949.

11 W. A. Visser 't Hooft, 'A Visit to the South African Churches in April and May 1952', *Ecumenical Review,* 5:2 (Jan. 1953), p. 175.

12 *Keesings Contemporary Archives* for 1950.

13 *New York Times,* 5 and 15 July 1950. The specific recommendations of the resolution were as follows. First, it was agreed that the statements on race by the World Council would be gathered together and widely circulated. Secondly, the General Secretary was to ask churches involved in racial problems what help the World Council could give towards their solution at the local level. Thirdly, it authorized the sending of a multi-racial delegation to South Africa, under joint World Council-IMC auspices for 'conference and fellowship', if invited. Any invitation which did not include multi-racial delegates would have to be referred back to the Central Committee for consideration. Central Committee, *Minutes 1950,* p. 28.

14 See CCIA, Executive Committee, Minutes (mimeograph) for 1952 and 1953.

15 The specific recommendations: (1) Regular meetings between members of the World Council inside and outside South Africa should be undertaken. (2) The churches of South Africa ought to provide a Christian Press Service to offset the sensation-seeking secular press. The most important Afrikaans documents should be translated into world languages, thus alleviating somewhat the isolation felt by these churches. (3) South African theologians should be invited to share in the preparation of the biblical foundation of the forthcoming World Council Assembly Message on race. (4) Opportunities should be sought to increase contacts between South African churches and the rest of the world. W. A. Visser 't Hooft, *Christianity, Race and South African People. Report: an Ecumenical Visit* (1952).

16 'Theologian Hits World Council's African Report', *New York Herald Tribune,* 12 Jan. 1953. This article also contained the information that Professor Matthews's home institution, the University College of Fort Hare, had been warned by the government of South Africa that if Dr Matthews appeared before the United Nations Ad Hoc Political Committee, the College would suffer financially. Professor Matthews did not appear.

17 WCC, Central Committee, *Minutes 1953–54,* p. 20.

18 Norman Goodall, 'The Challenge of the Pretoria Conference', *Ecumenical Review,* 6:4 (July 1954), pp. 398-407.

[19] WCC, *Response to Evanston,* Geneva 1955, p. 42.

[20] W. A. Visser 't Hooft, *The Evanston Report* (1955), p. 45.

[21] Ibid., p. 158.

[22] The second resolution recognized that the absence of political participation, due to lack of the franchise, exacerbated the racial problem and urged Christians to take measures to diminish this source of tension. This would apply presumably to parts of the world other than South Africa. The third resolution urged the inclusion of anti-Semitism in further work and study on prejudice. Ibid., p. 159.

[23] Ibid., p. 3.

[24] Donald C. Dearborn of the Evangelical and Reformed Church in America, in *The Messenger,* Nov. 1954, p. 8.

[25] Rena Karefa-Smart, 'Africa asks Questions of the West', *Ecumenical Review,* 10 : 1 (Oct. 1957), pp. 43-55.

[26] WCC, Department on Church and Society, *Dilemmas and Opportunities: Christian Action in Rapid Social Change, Report of an International Ecumenical Study Conference, Thessalonica, Greece, July 25–August 2, 1959* (1959), pp. 26-9. Hereafter cited as *Dilemmas and Opportunities.*

[27] The *Guardian* headed its article 'Danger of Split in WCC', 12 Apr. 1960. See also the *Johannesburg Star* of 12, 14, and 16 Apr. 1960.

[28] This Minute was reproduced in the Central Committee, *Minutes 1960,* pp. 146-7.

[29] The results of this consultation are recorded in WCC, *Mission in South Africa, April-December 1960* (1961).

[30] As reported in the *Sunday Times,* 18 Dec. 1960.

[31] 15 Dec. 1960. See also its editorials of 7 and 28 Dec. 1960.

[32] This was reported in the *Guardian,* 29 Dec. 1960. Other dissenting voices within the Dutch churches also existed. The book *Vertraagde Aksie* (Delayed Action), written by eleven leading theologians and ministers of three of the Dutch Reformed churches, was published on 11 Nov. shortly before the Consultation. On 29 Nov. 1960, the book was condemned by the Commission of the Assembly of the Dutch Reformed churches. A month later, a group of white and non-white Dutch Reformed clergymen maintained that it was morally indefensible to deny political and other rights to Africans permanently settled in white areas. Although this kept alive the light of Christian justice and humanity, it had no effect on the government nor on the leadership of the Dutch Reformed churches in actual policy changes.

[33] Visser 't Hooft, ed., *The New Delhi Report,* pp. 182-8, 322-5.

[34] *The Times,* 29 Aug. 1963.

[35] A full report of the Consultation is to be found in WCC, Department on Church and Society, *Christians and Race Relations in Southern Africa* (1964).

[36] CCIA, Executive Committee, Minutes 1964, Annex 6.

[37] All Africa Conference of Churches, *Consultation Digest: a Summary of Reports and Addresses . . . Inter-Church Aid Consultation, Enugu, Eastern Nigeria, 4–9 January 1965* (1965), pp. 104-6.

[38] 'Clerics Hear Islam is Spreading Swiftly in Africa', *New York Times,* 14 Jan. 1965.

[39] WCC, Central Committee, *Minutes 1965,* p. 43.

[40] CCIA, Executive Committee, Minutes 1965, Annex 6.

[41] World Conference on Church and Society, *The Official Report* (1967), pp. 135-7.

[42] Ibid., pp. 175-6.

[43] *Le Monde,* 20 Feb. 1968.

[44] James Baldwin, 'White Racism or World Community', *Ecumenical*

Review, 20:4 (Oct. 1968), pp. 371-6.

⁴⁵ Lord Caradon, ibid., pp. 377-84.

⁴⁶ Goodall, ed., *The Uppsala Report 1968* pp. 49-50.

⁴⁷ Ibid., pp. 65-6.

⁴⁸ Ibid., p. 83.

⁴⁹ Ibid., p. 90.

⁵⁰ Ibid., p. 192.

⁵¹ Ibid., p. 5.

⁵² 'World Council Seeks Catholic Church Membership', *New York Times,* 19 July 1968.

⁵³ *The Morning Star* (London), 20 July 1968, is a British communist newspaper.

⁵⁴ *The Ecumenical Review,* 21:2 (Apr. 1969), p. 161.

⁵⁵ WCC, Central Committee, 'Report on the World Council of Churches Sponsored Consultation on Racism Held in Notting Hill, London, May 19–24, 1969 to the Central Committee Meeting in August 1969' (mimeograph), 33 pp. plus Appendices. The more picturesque aspects of the Consultation appeared in 'Racism and Revolt', *Christianity Today,* 13:19, pp. 33-4, and 'Preparation for Separation and Reparation: the Churches' Response to Racism?', *The Christian Century,* 25 June 1969, pp. 862-5.

⁵⁶ The specific points were (1) The WCC and its members should apply economic sanctions against corporations which practice racism, and (2) should influence governments to apply similar sanctions. (3) It should support and encourage the principle of 'reparations' to exploited peoples and countries, an exploitation in which the churches had joined. (4) An agency within the World Council should be established with adequate resources to deal with the eradication of racism. (5) The World Council and the CCIA should act as co-ordinator for the application of strategies in the struggle by the churches against racism in Southern Africa. (6) Should all else fail, the churches should support revolutionary movements aimed at the elimination of the power bases which make racism possible. See the Report and articles cited in n. 55 above.

⁵⁷ Central Committee, *Minutes 1969,* pp. 35-40 and Appendix XX.

⁵⁸ 'Churches and Guerrillas', the *Guardian,* 19 Aug. 1969.

⁵⁹ 27 Aug. 1969.

⁶⁰ 'World Council to Admit African Church', *New York Times,* 24 Aug. 1969.

⁶¹ *The Times,* 12 Jan. 1971.

⁶² *Daily Telegraph,* 7 Sept. 1970.

⁶³ Edward R. Fiske, 'Church in South Africa Defies Edict', *New York Times,* 27 Sept. 1970.

⁶⁴ World Conference on Church and Society, *Official Report* (1967), p. 206.

⁶⁵ Ibid., p. 116.

⁶⁶ *Study Encounter,* 7:3 (1971), SE 09. The outline of the study agreed upon by the Working Committee appears in 'Violence, Nonviolence and the Struggle for Social Justice', ibid.

⁶⁷ WCC, Central Committee, *Minutes 1971,* p. 55.

⁶⁸ The *Guardian,* 7 Sept. 1970.

⁶⁹ WCC, Department of Communication, Press Release of 23 Sept. 1970 (mimeograph).

⁷⁰ The *Guardian,* 28 Oct. 1970.

⁷¹ *New York Times,* 5 Sept. 1970.

⁷² WCC, Department of Communication, Press Release of 24 July 1970 (mimeograph).

⁷³ The *Frankfurter Allgemeine Zeitung,* 15 Oct. 1970, reports a con-

frontation between General Secretary Eugene C. Blake and West German church leaders.

[74] *New York Times*, 11 Jan. 1971.

[75] *The Times*, 12 Jan. 1971.

[76] *Frankfurter Allgemeine Zeitung*, 18 Jan. 1971.

[77] *The Times*, 17 and 26 Feb. 1971.

[78] *The Times*, 26 Feb. and 4 Mar. 1971.

[79] See Appendix II for breakdown of all grants.

[80] The CCPD made a contribution of $50,000 to the Mozambique Institute of Frelimo for its economic development programme.

[81] This and the following evaluation of the grants was taken from WCC Central Committee Meeting, Utrecht, 13-23 Aug. 1972, Document 40(d), 'Extension of the Special Fund to Combat Racism' (mimeograph, 13 pp.).

[82] 'Violence, Nonviolence and the Struggle for Social Justice', *The Ecumenical Review*, 25:4 (1973).

[83] Richard Shaull, 'Revolutionary Challenge to Church and Theology', *Princeton Seminary Bulletin*, vol. 60, Oct. 1966, pp. 25-32. Jürgen Moltmann, 'Racism and the Right to Resist', *Study Encounter*, 8:1 (1972), SE 21. Other sources of the debate are Edwin H. Rian, ed., *Christianity and World Revolution* (1963); Peter L. Berger and Richard John Neuhaus, *Movement and Revolution* (1970); John C. Bennett, ed., *Christian Ethics in a Changing World* (1966).

[84] Peter Schmid, 'The Clergyman and the Guerrilla: a Conversation with Dr Philip Potter', *Encounter*, vol. 39, Dec. 1972, pp. 58-61.

[85] *Frankfurter Allgemeine Zeitung*, 18 Aug. 1972.

[86] *The Times*, 14 Aug. 1972.

[87] For background and reasons for this policy, see WCC, Programme to Combat Racism, *Time to Withdraw: Investments in Southern Africa* (1973).

[88] Merle Lipton, 'South Africa: Authoritarian Reform?', *The World Today*, 30:6 (June 1974), pp. 247-58.

[89] WCC, Central Committee, *Minutes 1972*, pp. 71-2.

[90] In Aug. 1972 the Central Committee of the WCC, meeting at Utrecht from 13 to 23 Aug. 1972, adopted the following resolution:

'The World Council of Churches, in accordance with its own commitment to combat racism, considering that the effect of foreign investments in Southern Africa is to strengthen the white minority régimes in their oppression of the majority of the people of this region, and implementing the policy as commended by the Uppsala Assembly (1968) that investments in "institutions that perpetuate racism" should be terminated:

(i) *instructs* its Finance Committee and its Director of Finance to sell forthwith existing holdings and to make no investments after this date in corporations which, according to information available to the Finance Committee and the Director of Finance, are directly involved in investment in or trade with any of the following countries: South Africa, Namibia, Zimbabwe, Angola, Mozambique and Guiné-Bissao; and to deposit none of its funds in banks which maintain direct banking operations in those countries;

(ii) *urges* all member churches, Christian agencies and individual Christians outside Southern Africa to use all their influence, including stockholder action and disinvestment, to press corporations to withdraw investments from and cease trading with these countries.' WCC, Central Committee, *Minutes 1972*, pp. 28-30.

In Dec. 1972 a first list of Dutch, Swiss, UK, and USA corporations directly involved in investment in or trade with Southern Africa and Guinea-Bissau was published as a guide to the implementation of the above resolution. A second list was published in Aug. 1973. It included the corporations already listed and added many others from the following countries: Australia, Belgium, Canada, France, New Zealand, Sweden, and West Germany. See WCC, PCR, *Second List of Corporations Directly Involved in Investment in or Trade with South Africa, Namibia, Zimbabwe, Angola, Mozambique and Guiné-Bissao* (1973).

91 *New York Times,* 23 Jan. 1973.

92 WCC, Central Committee, Geneva, 27-29 Aug. 1973, *Withdrawal of Investments from Southern Africa* (Document 2a, mimeograph, 19 pp.).

93 *Frankfurter Allgemeine Zeitung,* 27 Aug. 1973.

94 *Guardian,* 12 Mar. 1973.

95 'HMG Hints', *The Economist,* 31 Mar. 1973, p. 66.

96 *The Times,* 14 May 1974.

97 *Daily Telegraph,* 23 May 1974.

98 *Guardian,* 15 Mar. 1974; *Daily Telegraph,* 19 Mar. 1974.

99 *Frankfurter Allgemeine Zeitung,* 12 Aug. 1974.

100 This information and that following was originally published in NCCCUSA, Corporate Information Center, *The Frankfurt Documents: Secret Bank Loans to the South African Government* (New York, 1973) and is cited in Counter Information Services (CIS), *Business as Usual: International Banking in South Africa* (1974), *passim.*

101 WCC, Central Committee, *Minutes 1974,* pp. 37-8.

102 CCIA, 'From Uppsala to Jakarta: Report of the CCIA of the WCC' (Geneva, 1974, mimeograph, 13 pp.), p. 10. This is probably a draft of the CCIA section of the normal pre-Assembly report, later called *From Uppsala to Nairobi* (1975).

103 *The Times,* 18 and 22 Feb. 1966.

104 *Johannesburg Star,* 'What the Africans Think', 11 Sept. 1971.

105 CCIA, *Annual Report 1957–58,* p. 16.

106 At the 1959 meeting a rather innocuous resolution was passed requesting CCIA officers to keep the situation under review; it also requested World Council and IMC officers to address a letter to the churches and Christian councils of the Federation, expressing appreciation of their efforts at easing tension between the races and their continuing concern for the rights of all peoples in the Federation. CCIA, Executive Committee, Minutes 1959, p. 13.

107 CCIA, *Annual Report 1965–66,* pp. 18-20, 45-7.

108 WCC, Central Committee, *Minutes 1966,* p. 67.

109 CCIA, *Annual Report 1967–68,* p. 43.

110 The Five Principles were:

'(1) The principle and intention of unimpeded progress to majority rule, already enshrined in the 1961 Constitution, would have to be maintained and guaranteed;

(2) There would also have to be guarantees against retrogressive amendment of the Constitution;

(3) There would have to be immediate improvement in the political status of the African population;

(4) There would have to be progress towards ending racial discrimination;

(5) The British Government would need to be satisfied that any basis proposed for independence was acceptable to the people of Rhodesia as a whole.' Cmnd 4835, *Rhodesia: Proposals for a Settlement* (Nov. 1971), p. 3.

111 On 1 Jan. 1972 a clause of the American Defence Procurement Act came into force forbidding the President to prevent the importation of any strategic material from a non-communist country if the same material was

being imported from a communist country. Since chrome was the main commodity fitting these qualifications, the Act was seen as applying primarily to Rhodesia. The UN General Assembly called on the United States to maintain the Rhodesian chrome embargo. In February a Security Council resolution called for continued sanctions against Rhodesia and stated that importation of Rhodesian chrome would undermine these sanctions. Further UN resolutions condemned the United States, but importation of chrome continued. Mr William N. Lawrence of the US Office of Emergency Preparedness told a House of Representatives sub-committee that an American surplus of chrome meant there was no national security basis for the imports. USA House of Representatives, Committee on Foreign Affairs, Sub-committee on Africa and Sub-committee on International Organizations and Movements, *Hearings*, 93rd Congress, 1st sess., 21, 22 Feb.; 15 Mar. 1973, p. 66.

[112] Mr Kodwo E. Ankrah, Africa Secretary of DICARWS in 'Sudan: the Church and Peace', *Africa*, no. 9 (May 1972), pp. 58-63.

[113] WCC, Department of Communication, *Press Release Nb–4/72*, 'WCC Discloses Contribution to Peace Agreement for Sudan' (mimeograph, 2 pp.).

[114] For texts of the agreements, see the final issue of the organ of the SSLM published in London, *Grass Curtain*, May 1972.

[115] WCC, Central Committee, *Minutes 1963*, p. 141.

[116] *Guardian*, 22 May 1973.

[117] For a biased report of the first five years of the PCR see Elisabeth Adler, *A Small Beginning: an Assessment of the First Five Years of the Programme to Combat Racism* (1974).

[118] WCC, Central Committee, *Minutes 1972*, p. 32.

[119] See WCC, PCR, *FRELIMO—Frente de Libertação de Moçambique* (1970); WCC, PCR, *PAIGC—Partido Africano de Independencia da Guinee e Cabo Verde (Guinea-Bissau)* (1970); WCC, PCR, *Portugal and the EEC* (1973).

[120] See WCC, PCR, *Cunene Dam Scheme and the Struggle for the Liberation of Southern Africa* (1971); WCC, PCR, *Cabora Bassa and the Struggle for Southern Africa* (1971).

[121] WCC, Central Committee, *Minutes 1972*, p. 31.

[122] For instance, see charges in Adler, pp. 54-5, and compare with isolated descriptions of American churches' positive role, e.g. pp. 24, 55, and 102 *re* contributions.

[123] Ibid., p. 38.

CHAPTER 3: OIKOUMENE AND ECONOMY

[1] For more detailed treatment of this period, see Visser 't Hooft, *The Ten Formative Years 1938-1948*, pp. 32-4; and WCC, *The World Council of Churches, Its Process of Formation: Minutes and Reports of the Meeting of the Provisional Committee of the World Council of Churches held at Geneva from February 21st to 23rd, 1946, the Constitutional Documents of the . . . and an Introduction by W. A. Visser 't Hooft* (1946).

[2] For a small part of this story see Paul Bock, 'Ecumenical Reconstruction in Europe' (unpublished MST thesis, Yale Divinity School, 1957).

[3] W. A. Visser 't Hooft, ed. *The First Assembly of the World Council of Churches: the Official Report* (1949), pp. 167-8.

[4] WCC, Central Committee, *Minutes 1949*, pp. 25, 119-21.

[5] WCC, Central Committee, *Minutes 1952/53*, pp. 53-4.

[6] Richard P. Stebbins, *The United States in World Affairs, 1950* (1951), provides much insight into American aid policy at this time.

7 Visser 't Hooft, ed., *The Evanston Report*, pp. 233-6.

8 WCC, Central Committee, *Minutes 1955*, pp. 94-7.

9 WCC, Central Committee, *Minutes 1957*, pp. 112-13.

10 From 1961 the average was twelve emergencies a year, with response to these needs varying unpredictably from $1 to $3 million a year in cash. To this must be added the value of great quantities of material aid. Visser 't Hooft, ed., *The New Delhi Report*, pp. 120-2. An interesting comparison with American aid under the Mutual Security Act shows shifting emphasis, too. The following figures include military as well as economic aid, a ploy by the administration to facilitate passage of appropriations bills.

	1953-7 % of total	1958-61 % of total
Europe	25	6
Near East and S. Asia	22	34
Far East	42	34
Latin America	3	8
Africa	1	9
Other	7	9

11 WCC, Central Committee, *Minutes 1960*, pp. 130-1, and *New Delhi to Uppsala, 1961-1968* (1968), p. 126. See 'Church's Aid for Developing Areas', *The Times*, 18 Aug. 1960.

12 Visser 't Hooft, ed., *New Delhi Report*, pp. 242-6.

13 Goodall, ed., *The Uppsala Report 1968*, pp. 51-4, 192-6. See also Richard Dickinson, *Line and Plummet: The Churches and Development* (1968).

14 Central Committee, *Minutes 1963*, pp. 64, 69. In addition to direct action, DICARWS is also authorized to make agreements with national, confessional, or service agencies of churches to carry out specific projects for economic development or emergency relief. For example, the Lutheran World Federation Commission on World Service was requested to conduct operations connected with the refugee problem in Tanganyika in 1963.

15 Ibid., pp. 76-81.

16 Ibid., pp. 22-4.

17 Ibid., 1965, pp. 128-32.

18 Ibid., 1966, pp. 108-23. In 1967 DICARWS set up a Secretariat for Material Aid to co-ordinate supplies of foodstuffs and goods to help in emergencies and to support projects. In addition, a Secretary for Development Education was appointed to develop ways in which the churches might inform their members on areas of need. WCC, Central Committee, *New Delhi to Uppsala, 1961-1968*, pp. 129-30.

19 CCIA, Executive Committee, Minutes 1966, pp. 6-7.

20 Ibid., Annexure 8.

21 WCC, Central Committee, *Minutes 1967*. The Statement appears on pp. 46-7. Another discussion of development appears on pp. 179-85.

22 Goodall, ed., *The Uppsala Report 1968*, pp. 254-66.

23 Hans ten Doornkaat, 'Einheit der Kirchen in der einen Welt', *Neue Zürcher Zeitung*, 2 July 1968.

24 'Kirchliche Entwicklungshilfe', *Neue Zürcher Zeitung*, 1 Feb. 1969.

25 WCC, Central Committee, *Minutes 1969*, pp. 50-5.

26 For examples of the Fund's disbursements, see WCC, CCPD (meeting at Albano, 24-30 June 1973), 'How the CCPD has used the Ecumenical Development Fund' (Document no. 18, Geneva, 1973).

27 WCC, Central Committee, *Minutes 1971*, p. 63.

28 *Guardian*, 27 Aug. 1973.

29 Ibid., 16 Aug. 1974.

[30] WCC, *Draft Proposal for an Ecumenical Development Co-operative Society* (Geneva, 1974), p. 8.

[31] Ibid., pp. 36-7.

[32] WCC, Central Committee, *Minutes 1974*, pp. 35-6.

[33] Dickinson, p. 46. Indeed Robert Gardiner estimated all non-governmental non-profit organizations' aid at one billion dollars at the Ecumenical Consultation on Development in Jan. 1970: *Fetters of Injustice*, p. 95.

[34] CCIA, *Annual Report 1949/50*, p. 25.

[35] Visser 't Hooft, *The First Assembly . . . Report*, p. 75.

[36] Ibid., p. 91.

[37] WCC, *Statements of the World Council of Churches on Social Questions*, 2nd edn. (Geneva, WCC, 1956), pp. 25-9.

[38] CCIA, Executive Committee, Minutes, 1952, Annex VII.

[39] CCIA, *Annual Report 1951/52*, p. 38.

[40] Enlarged Meeting of the Committee of the IMC, *Minutes*, Willingen, Germany, 1952.

[41] CCIA, Executive Committee, Minutes 1953, p. 22 and Annex XI.

[42] Ibid., pp. 14-15 and Annex V.

[43] Letter of 20 Mar. 1953, CCIA to M. Philippe de Seynes. CCIA, *Annual Report 1952/53*, p. 40.

[44] WCC, *Statements of the World Council of Churches on Social Questions* (2nd edn., 1956), pp. 31-8, excerpted from original report *Christ —the Hope of Asia* (1953).

[45] WCC, Central Committee, *Minutes 1952/53*, pp. 96ff.

[46] Ibid., p. 37.

[47] CCIA, Executive Committee, Minutes 1953, p. 22 and Annex XIV.

[48] CCIA, *Annual Report 1953/54*, pp. 41-2.

[49] Visser 't Hooft, ed., *The Evanston Report*, pp. 112-26.

[50] Ibid., pp. 137-8.

[51] Ibid., pp. 146-9.

[52] CCIA, *Annual Report 1954/55*, pp. 46-7.

[53] WCC, Central Committee, *Minutes 1955*, pp. 18-21.

[54] CCIA, Executive Committee, Minutes 1955, pp. 18-21.

[55] Among these suggestions were: (1) An overall survey of the needs of the under-developed world should be made; (2) all agencies in the field should consult to decide on the priorities of their activities in a given area; (3) assistance programmes should be evaluated on the basis of unmet needs of the areas; (4) preparatory plans should be instituted so that when the resources became available, through disarmament, for example, they could. quickly be put into operation. Ibid., Annex 10.

[56] CCIA, *Annual Report 1957/58*, p. 45.

[57] For a discussion of private capital in economic development, see John Pincus, *Trade, Aid and Development: the Rich and Poor Nations* (1967), p. 31.

[58] Other points of the Nyborg Statement included urging that the effects of national trade and monetary prices on development programmes be carefully considered, and that commodity prices be stabilized. In regard to the role of the churches, they were urged to encourage qualified Christians to enter employment in development programmes; the churches' especial responsibility for those uprooted in the social change that was bound to come with development was recognized. WCC, Central Committee, *Minutes 1958*, pp. 124-5.

[59] *The Witness of the Churches Amidst Social Change in Asia* (Geneva, WCC, 1959), pp. 10-19.

[60] CCIA, Executive Committee, Minutes 1959, p. 14.

[61] Ibid., 1960, pp. 9-10.

⁶² The main points were as follows: (1) Both the developed and the developing should realize the need for increasing the tempo of development. (2) Balanced development should be sought, a condition calling for considerable planning. (3) Emphasis should be on simple improvements which benefited the masses and not on dramatic manifestations of aid. (4) The need for training technicians was obvious, but the need for efficient administrators ought not to be forgotten. (5) Research on urgent problems of under-developed states, such as the conversion of sea water, should be undertaken by developed states. (6) The importance of trade as a primary source of funds for development was stressed. The developed states were encouraged to maintain trade policies which did not discriminate against the under-developed states. (7) Prices of primary products should be stabilized. (8) The possibility of encouraging regional trade agreements among the developing should be explored. (9) The devotion of at least 1 per cent of gross national product for aid was reiterated. (This goal had not been supported by the General Assembly, but a resolution of 19 Dec. 1961 hoped that the flow of aid would reach 1 per cent.) (10) Lip service was again given to private investment, but it was noted that private capital preferred the more developed areas. A background paper, supplied to the commission, cited the inadequacy of private capital as a factor in development. (11) The United Nations was again suggested as the co-ordinator of all aid programmes, bilateral and multilateral.

⁶³ Visser 't Hooft, ed., *New Delhi Report,* pp. 106-7.

⁶⁴ Ibid., p. 281.

⁶⁵ Doc. E/3613.

⁶⁶ CCIA, Executive Committee, Minutes 1962, Annex VIII.

⁶⁷ Correspondence R. Fagley to A. Booth, 4 Oct. 1962 and R. Fagley to K. Grubb, 18 Oct. 1963.

⁶⁸ For the full text of these two speeches, see the *Ecumenical Review,* Oct. 1963.

⁶⁹ CCIA, Executive Committee, Minutes 1964, p. 11.

⁷⁰ Letter dated 27 May 1964.

⁷¹ Letter 6 Apr. 1964.

⁷² A. Booth to Sir K. Grubb, 14 Apr. 1964.

⁷³ The specific points urged were: (1) A commitment by all developed states to expand trade to at least the point which is required to maintain the desired economic growth of the new states; (2) trade barriers against developing countries should be eliminated; (3) positive efforts, such as trade preferences, to aid products from developing states should be made; (4) intergovernmental commodity agreements to prevent wide fluctuations of prices must be concluded; (5) a substantial portion of aid should be used to increase the trading capabilities of these states, e.g., improve processing, design of products; (6) aid should also be used to overcome obstacles to trade among the under-developed states by providing transportation, credit, or storage facilities. CCIA, Executive Committee, Minutes 1965, Annex 4.

⁷⁴ Letter to Nolde of 9 Aug. 1965.

⁷⁵ Letter R. Fagley to the Revd. E. Rees, 27 May 1965.

⁷⁶ Letter R. Fagley to Sir K. Grubb, 15 Nov. 1965.

⁷⁷ Evaluation by A. Booth in letter to E. Rees, 27 Dec. 1967.

⁷⁸ The principal points were: (1) Economics is not an amoral discipline and should be concerned with human beings. (2) The CCIA's Bangalore Statement was quoted in urging simple improvements for masses rather than dramatic innovations of little immediate economic effect. (3) Continuing war against hunger was urged. (4) While recognizing the necessity to concentrate on training skills directly related to development, the need for broad campaigns to end illiteracy was also recommended. (5) Social

reforms to overcome prejudices against disadvantaged social or ethnic groups must be pursued in order fully to utilize the human resources for development and to promote justice for all. (6) Realistic assessment of priorities led the statement to plead for special programmes of aid to peasants, not only to increase food production but to enrich their lives. (7) At the same time, however, industrialization should be undertaken, not an industrialization abstractly conceived but one related to the actual conditions of each country. (8) Trade within the under-developed areas of the world should be encouraged in order to conserve hard foreign exchange needed for basic imports not available within those areas. (9) There must be mutual respect between donor and recipient states, but especially ought the donors to respect the 'sovereign equality' of those they are able to influence against their wills. (10) The affluent must accept development as being in their long-term interest; if half-hearted development continues, the final cost may be greater in coping with famine, chaos, and war. (11) The oft-mentioned minimum of effort, 1 per cent of gross national product, was reiterated. (12) The use of multilateral agencies for the disbursement of economic aid was urged. (CCIA, Executive Committee, Minutes 1966, Annex 7.)

79 Central Committee, *Minutes 1967,* p. 184.

80 Ibid., pp. 46-7.

81 This summary was taken from Committee on Society, Development and Peace, *World Development: the Challenge to the Churches. The Conference on World Co-operation for Development, Beirut, Lebanon, April 21–27, 1968* (Geneva, 1968).

82 Ibid., p. 40.

83 Goodall, ed., *The Uppsala Report 1968,* p. 168.

84 Ibid., p. 39.

85 Ibid., p. 44.

86 The reports of these three sections should be read by all interested in the thinking of the churches on development. The following is a summary of their major points concerning development. Section III urged that a means within the international economic structure be found to prevent poor terms of trade, burdensome debt repayment, and excessive return to private investment. The developed nations must accept a new international division of labour, give aid that leads to self-sustained growth, and donate at least 1 per cent of their GNP to this cause.

The Section recognized the need to create political instruments for development; wisely it understood that in the present organization of the world, they had to be based on the nation-state. It saw the need to create a national identity within states that were still divided by tribal or caste loyalties and thereby to mobilize the masses of people. The developed states must cease seeking to exploit and dominate the poorer nations. National policies must be oriented towards world development, transcending the narrow political interests of the developed state. At the international level, a supra-national structure was called for to deal with regional and world economic planning, an international taxation system, and an increase in multilateral aid programmes. In creating a positive public opinion for these measures, the Christian community would be an effective force.

The report proclaimed that development was not for development's sake but for the sake of humans. Agricultural policies must be geared to feeding the world. Training for the new technical jobs should be undertaken; jobs should be brought to the people as well as forcing migration to jobs. The particular task of the churches was co-operation one with another, Protestant, Catholic, Orthodox, as well as with non-church organizations, other religions, and men of no religion, in order to meet the challenge of development. The churches could educate their members to understand the need for development and to be more politically effective. In carrying out the political task, the churches should influence political parties and governments of industrialized countries to increase their aid to 1 per cent of GNP by 1971, to stabilize prices of primary products, and to offer markets to developing countries' manufactures. The World Council in its restructuring process should organize a new expanded development service. In addition to offering tasks for the individual Christian in economic development, the report stressed the new theological urgency in coming to grips with the interaction of technology and social justice. Theologians must get together with technicians, administrators, and industrialists who would 'give knowledge and receive vision'. (Goodall, ed., *The Uppsala Report 1968*, pp. 45-55.)

Section IV considered the gap between the rich and the poor nations and the relationship between economic justice and world order. Noting a cause and effect between the areas of poverty and injustice and violence, the Section urged vigorous international action to reduce the disparity of growth between the industrialized and unindustrialized states. Especially were the developed states counselled to change their economic structures so that their economic prosperity would no longer be at the expense of the developing states. To achieve economic justice, the Section recommended old standbys: an overall strategy of development correlated by the UN, increased aid, expanded trade with fair terms of trade, and programmes of family planning. The churches, themselves, it continued, must strive to reform the consciences of the peoples of the world in favour of international justice. To act, they should utilize political parties, trade unions, and other groups which influence opinion. They must stress the need for sacrifice to achieve international economic and social justice; they should also support an international development tax to help this become a reality. (Ibid., pp. 67-9.)

In Section VI a discussion of styles of living brought again to the attention of the delegates the inequality in standards within states and between nations, and the ways in which this inequality resulted in hate, racism, and violence. It asked that Christians should use the power they had to take action; on the international level this would be support for development and participation in nation-building. (Ibid., pp. 89-92.)

[87] Ibid., pp. 5-6.

[88] The statement noted the limited gains of the First Development Decade and emphasized 'a few considerations deemed important for a valid international strategy of development': (1) '. . . the sharing of resources will be seen as a matter of justice and not generosity'. (2) 'Truly effective regional agencies need to be developed' to overcome social obstacles to development such as unjust land tenure, exploitation by foreign concerns, and widening inequalities in income. (3) Development distorted for the political or economic domination by others, e.g. tied aid, must be opposed. One per cent of the GNP of developed states administered by multilateral means would correct this problem. (4) Trade barriers must be lowered so that trade became a more dynamic factor in development. (5) Research into local economic problems should be encouraged; it must not be assumed that industrial societies' experience is always appropriate. (6) Educational expansion including technical training, vocational training, and adult education must be encouraged. CCIA, Executive Committee, Minutes 1969, Annexure 9.

[89] The complete report of the consultation is found in Pamela H. Gruber, ed., *Fetters of Injustice: Report of an Ecumenical Consultation on Ecu-*

menical Assistance to Development Projects, 26–31 January, 1970, Montreux, Switzerland (1970).

90 Hella Pick, 'Churches Discuss Role in Third World', the *Guardian,* 29 Jan. 1970; see also her article on the Sodepax report, 'Call for new look at world poverty', ibid., 20 Oct. 1970. The *Frankfurter Allgemeine Zeitung* followed the Consultation closely in articles on 27, 28, 29, 30, 31 Jan. and 2 Feb. 1970. The opinion of the editor of the *FAZ*, referred to in this paragraph, is taken from a report on the previous year's Central Committee meeting: Karl-Alfred Odin, 'Die Christen—ein Drittel der Menschheit', *FAZ*, 27 Aug. 1969.

91 Committee on Society, Development and Peace, *Partnership or Privilege? An Ecumenical Reaction to the Second Development Decade* (1970); also *A Supplement* with the same title (1970).

92 WCC, Central Committee, *Minutes 1971*, p. 64. Due to a misprint the statement did not appear in the *Minutes* until 1972, pp. 272-4.

93 *Economist*, 20 May 1972, p. 116.

94 Resolution 3201 (S-VI).

95 CCIA, Executive Committee, Minutes 1974, pp. 5-6.

96 Mimeographed document circulated to the CCIA 29th Executive Committee meeting (1974), entitled 'The Economic Threat to Peace (Crisis and a New International Economic Order)', 5 pp. This was reproduced in full in *Ecumenical Review*, 27:1 (1975).

97 'Threats to Survival', later published in *Study Encounter*, 10:4 (1974), SE/67, p. 10.

98 WCC, Central Committee, *Minutes 1974*, pp. 22-3, 38. For another presentation by a WCC official on the need for change of international structures, see Charles Elliott, 'Do the Poor Subsidize the Rich?', *Study Encounter*, 9:4 (1973), SE/51.

99 Richard Fagley, *The Population Explosion and Christian Responsibility* (1960).

100 CCIA, Enlarged Executive Committee, Minutes 1952, pp. 14-15 and Annex V.

101 Visser 't Hooft, ed., *The Evanston Report*, p. 125.

102 Ibid., p. 59.

103 CCIA, Executive Committee, Minutes 1955, p. 19 and Annex 10.

104 Fagley, p. 214.

105 WCC, Division of Studies, *The Responsible Society in National and International Affairs: the Arnoldshain Report 1956* (1956), p. 13; my italic.

106 WCC, Central Committee, *Minutes 1956*, p. 36.

107 'Report on the Witness of the Churches Amidst Social Change in Asia', *Ecumenical Review*, vol. XI:4 (July 1959), pp. 453ff.

108 WCC, Department on Church and Society, *Dilemmas and Opportunities*, pp. 88-9.

109 *New York Times*, 28 Feb. 1959 and Memo from R. Fagley to N. Goodall, 5 Mar. 1959.

110 'A Report on Responsible Parenthood and the Population Problem', *Ecumenical Review*, vol. XII:1 (Oct. 1959), pp. 85-92.

111 e.g. Robert C. Cook, *Human Fertility: the Modern Dilemma* (1951); Roy Francis, ed., *The Population Ahead* (1958); Paul K. Hatt, ed., *World Population and Future Resources* (1952); Frederick Osborn, *Population: an International Dilemma* (1958).

112 CCIA, Executive Committee, Minutes 1959, pp. 14-15.

113 Letter R. Fagley to E. de Vries, 5 Nov. 1959.

114 CCIA, Executive Committee, Minutes 1960, p. 5.

115 WCC, Central Committee, *Minutes 1960*, pp. 12-13, 85-6.

116 CCIA, Third Commission, Minutes 1961, Annex L.

117 Visser 't Hooft, ed., *The New Delhi Report,* pp. 276 and 279.

118 Memoranda R. Fagley to K. Grubb, 13 Oct. 1961, 12 and 19 Dec. 1962.

119 Memoranda R. Fagley to K. Grubb, 8 and 15 Feb. 1963 and aide-mémoire, 8 Feb. 1963.

120 CCIA, *Annual Report 1963/64,* p. 57.

121 Memorandum R. Fagley to W. A. Visser 't Hooft, 27 Aug. 1965.

122 World Conference on Church and Society, *Official Report* (Geneva, 1967), pp. 72-3, 167-70, 178.

123 CCIA, *Annual Report 1966/67,* p. 55. Memorandum R. Fagley to K. Grubb, 9 Dec. 1966 and 19 Dec. 1966. Dr Fagley felt the resolution had been unnecessarily weakened in Committee.

124 WCC, Central Committee, *Minutes 1967,* p. 46. See also CCIA, *Annual Report 1967/68,* p. 53.

125 WCC, Central Committee, *Minutes 1967,* p. 46.

126 Committee on Society, Development and Peace, *World Development: Challenge to the Churches, The Conference on World Co-operation for Development, Beirut, Lebanon, April 21–27, 1968* (Geneva, 1968).

127 Memoranda K. Grubb to R. Fagley, 7 Apr. 1965, 12 and 20 Oct. 1966.

128 Memoranda R. Fagley to K. Grubb, 16 and 30 Nov. 1966.

129 Goodall, ed., *The Uppsala Report 1968,* p. 50; this work contains the reports *Towards Justice and Peace in International Affairs* (p. 68) and *Towards New Styles of Living* (p. 92), which made note of it.

130 CCIA, Executive Committee, Minutes 1969, Annex 9.

131 Paul R. Ehrlich, *The Population Bomb* (rev. edn., 1971), p. 79.

132 WCC, Central Committee, *Minutes 1971,* pp. 74-6 and 293-7.

133 Ibid., 1972, p. 43.

134 Ibid., 1973, p. 71. The report is found in full in *Study Encounter,* 9:4 (1973), SE/49.

135 Ecumenical Press Service No. 26, 19 Sept. 1974.

136 'Report of the Population-Related Activities of the Christian Medical Commission 1972-1974' (typescript, 2 pp. Geneva, Jan. 1975); see also, WCC, CMC, 'Comprehensive Rural Health Project: Jamkhed, India' (mimeograph, 18 pp., Geneva 1972).

137 WCC, Central Committee, *Minutes 1956,* pp. 18-21.

138 cf. Robert L. Heilbroner, 'The Engineering of Development', in Lewis P. Fickett, Jr, ed., *Problems of the Developing Nations* (1966), pp. 53ff., and Raymond F. Mikesell, *The Economics of Foreign Aid* (1968), chs. 3-4, 8.

139 cf. Stephen Enke, 'Agricultural Innovations and Community Development', in Fickett, ed. (see previous note), pp. 21ff.

140 cf. ibid.

141 WCC, Dept. on Church and Society, *Dilemmas and Opportunities,* pp. 22-9.

142 WCC, Central Committee, *Minutes 1959,* pp. 184-6.

143 Two further volumes appeared as a result of this study: Paul Abrecht, *The Churches and Rapid Social Change,* and Egbert de Vries, *Man in Rapid Social Change* (both 1961).

144 Visser 't Hooft, ed., *The New Delhi Report,* p. 176.

145 WCC, Central Committee, *Minutes 1966,* p. 82.

146 For the view of an economist from an underdeveloped country see Jagdish Bhagwati, *The Economics of Underdeveloped Countries* (1966).

147 The report made specific suggestions on several topics. In detail it prescribed a role for the churches: to encourage attitudes on the part of statesmen which favour the recommendations made by the churches and

on the part of the people to support their statesmen. It continued with other prescriptions: (1) the Church must develop and maintain its competence in technical areas; (2) Christians in positions of importance should be guided by a Christian ethic in their decisions and not relinquish their moral responsibility; (3) the WCC in co-operation with the Roman Catholic Church must develop international institutions to plan and promote economic and social justice through an international system of taxation; (4) the churches must continue their research in technical areas. World Conference on Church and Society, *Official Report,* pp. 51-119.

[148] Ibid., pp. 30-1.

[149] Goodall, ed., *The Uppsala Report 1968,* p. 239.

[150] Committee on Society, Development and Peace, *In Search of a Theology of Development: Papers from a Consultation on Theology and Development held by Sodepax in Cartigny, Switzerland, November 1969* (1970). It is a companion volume to Fr Gerhard Bauer, ed., *Towards a Theology of Development: an Annotated Bibliography* (1970).

[151] *The Observer,* 2 Apr. 1972, and 'Rome's Ecumenical Retrenchment', *Christian Century,* 5 July 1972, p. 835.

[152] 'Report on the Joint Working Group between the Roman Catholic Church and the World Council of Churches', WCC, Central Committee, *Minutes 1972,* pp. 215-19.

[153] WCC, Central Committee, *Minutes 1973,* p. 78. See also summary of SODEPAX activities by its General Secretary, Joseph J. Spae, 'SODEPAX: an Ecumenical and Experimental Approach to World Needs', *Ecumenical Review,* 26:1 (Jan. 1974), pp. 88-99. Two interesting analyses of the ecumenical effort in development have been subjects of doctoral dissertations. Karl-Heinz Dejung, 'Die Ökumenische Bewegung im Entwicklungskonflikt, 1910-1968' (Evangelische-Theologischen Fakultät, Universität zu Heidelberg, 1972); and Karl-Heinrich Rudersdorf, 'Entwicklungsförderung und Christliche Kirchen. Entstehung und Entwicklung des Konzepts der Entwicklungsförderung im Weltrat der Kirchen' (Philosophischen Fakultät, Freien Universität Berlin, 1973).

[154] See *The Economist,* reporting the 1973 meeting of the World Council Central Committee: 'Nor, unfortunately, does one, albeit sincere, attempt at political evenhandedness restore to the World Council the credibility which it started to lose a few years ago [sic] through its ever deeper and, in the view of its critics, ever more reckless intervention in social and political issues at the expense of its more traditional religious concerns'. 1 Sept. 1973, p. 30.

[155] For an incisive study and analysis of the role of the churches in development today which confirms the above analysis, *Line and Plummet* (1968), a study for SASP by Dr Richard Dickinson, cannot be too highly recommended. He looks frankly—one might say almost pessimistically—at the liabilities and assets of the churches in promoting development, and at the types of influence which the churches can hope to exert in this field.

[156] Carol J. Lancaster, 'The Politics of the Powerless, Pressures in the United Nations for Economic Development 1945-1965' (unpublished Ph.D. thesis, Univ. of London, 1972), p. 291.

CHAPTER 4: DISARMAMENT BEDEVILLED

[1] Arthur Nussbaum, *A Concise History of the Law of Nations* (1947), p. 25.

[2] Hudson, pp. 7ff.

[3] See ibid., ch. 9, for this story in detail.

[4] WCC, *The World Council of Churches: Its Process of Formation*, pp. 71ff.

[5] Visser 't Hooft, ed., *The First Assembly*, pp. 88-99.

[6] Quoted in CCIA, *Annual Report 1949/50*, pp. 26-7.

[7] WCC, Central Committee, *Minutes 1950*, pp. 91-2.

[8] It also quoted the part of the Statement which recommended that 'Governments must press individually and through the United Nations for a just settlement and conciliation.' 17 July 1950.

[9] WCC, Central Committee, *Minutes 1950*, pp. 93-4.

[10] CCIA, *Annual Report 1950/51*, p. 27.

[11] Ibid., 1951/52, p. 27.

[12] Ibid.

[13] CCIA, Executive Committee, Minutes 1952.

[14] Visser 't Hooft, ed., *The Evanston Report*, pp. 133ff.

[15] Ibid., pp. 146-8.

[16] CCIA, *Annual Report 1954/55*, p. 34; *Scotsman*, 19 May 1954.

[17] John Spanier and Joseph Nogee, *The Politics of Disarmament: Study in Soviet-American Gamesmanship* (1962), p. 88; see also Philip Noel-Baker, *The Arms Race* (1962), ch. 2; John Strachey, *On the Prevention of War* (1942), p. 157.

[18] WCC, Central Committee, *Minutes 1955*, pp. 51-2, 118-20.

[19] See, among others, Hedley Bull, *The Control of the Arms Race* (1961), and David V. Edwards, *Arms Control in International Politics* (1969).

[20] *New York Times*, 18 Feb. 1956.

[21] WCC, Division of Studies, *The Responsible Society in National and International Affairs: the Arnoldshain Report 1956* contains the complete record of the conference.

[22] CCIA, Executive Committee, Minutes 1956, pp. 6-7 and Annex V.

[23] The text is recorded in WCC, Central Committee, *Minutes 1957*, pp. 114-15.

[24] Ibid., pp. 62-3.

[25] CCIA, *Annual Report 1957/58*, pp. 27-8.

[26] CCIA, Executive Committee, Minutes 1958, Annex III.

[27] The CCIA statement is recorded in WCC, Central Committee, *Minutes 1958*, p. 126. The Central Committee's resolution, ibid., pp. 56, 127. *The Times* of 25 Aug. 1958 reported Dr Weizsäcker's statement.

[28] The Executive Committee Statement is reproduced in WCC, Central Committee, *Minutes 1959*, pp. 189-90.

[29] Ibid., pp. 82-3.

[30] Ibid., 1960.

[31] CCIA, *Annual Report 1959/60*, pp. 35-7.

[32] CCIA, Executive Committee, Minutes 1960, Annex 4. This minute was also adopted by the Central Committee.

[33] CCIA, *Annual Report 1961/62*, pp. 33-5.

[34] Memorandum from O. F. Nolde to K. G. Grubb, 27 Sept. 1961.

[35] Visser 't Hooft, ed., *The New Delhi Report*, p. 97.

[36] Ibid., pp. 107-8.

[37] Ibid., pp. 280-4.

[38] CCIA, *Annual Report 1961/62*, pp. 33-5.

[39] For the Statement of the Consultation, see WCC, Central Committee, *Minutes 1962*, pp. 81-2.

[40] Ibid., pp. 17, 74, 93-5.

[41] Ibid., 1963, pp. 10-11, 38, 83-4.

[42] CCIA, *Annual Report 1963/64*, pp. 32-3.

[43] CCIA, Executive Committee, Minutes 1964, Annex I.

[44] WCC, Central Committee, *Minutes 1965*, p. 42.

[45] CCIA, Executive Committee, Minutes 1965, pp. 11-12.

[46] WCC, Central Committee, *Minutes 1966*, pp. 67-8.

[47] World Conference on Church and Society, *Official Report* (1967), pp. 122-52.

[48] CCIA, *Annual Report 1966/67*, pp. 33-4.

[49] CCIA, *Background Documentation on Disarmament and Related Questions* (mimeograph), p. 56.

[50] CCIA, Executive Committee, Minutes 1957, Annexure 6.

[51] For this report, see Goodall, ed., *The Uppsala Report, 1968*, pp. 57-73.

[52] CCIA, *Annual Report 1969/70*, pp. 27-32, includes the full report of the Consultation. See also WCC, Central Committee, *Minutes 1969*, p. 42.

[53] WCC, Central Committee, *Minutes 1972*, pp. 145-6.

[54] United Nations, Secretariat, Dept. of Social and Economic Affairs, 'Disarmament and Development. Report of the Group of Experts on the Economic and Social Consequences of Disarmament', E.73.IX.1.

[55] The Visegrade document is reproduced in full in CCIA, *The Churches in International Affairs* (1974), pp. 147-50.

[56] *The Churches in International Affairs*, p. 186.

[57] Richard M. Fagley, 'The First Twenty Years in Outline', in CCIA, Executive Committee, Minutes 1966, Annex 1.

CHAPTER 5: THE CHRISTIAN CONSTITUENCY

[1] CCIA, *Annual Report 1968/69*, p. 6.

[2] For descriptions of other international interest groups see Keohane and Nye, eds.; international interest groups limited to a geographical region are described in Jean Meynaud and Dusan Sidjanski, *Les Groupes de pression dans la Communauté européenne*, 2 vols. (1969).

[3] For definitions of the term 'political interest group' and discussion of the characteristics of such groups, see *inter alia* Graham Wootton, *Interest Groups* (1970), ch. 1; and Gabriel A. Almond and G. Bingham Powell, Jr, *Comparative Politics: a Developmental Approach* (1966), chs. 4 and 5.

[4] For examples of British pressure group activities, see W. J. M. Mackenzie, 'Pressure Groups in British Government', *British Journal of Sociology*, 6:2 (1955), pp. 133-48. Harry Eckstein, 'The Politics of the British Medical Association', *Political Quarterly*, 26:4 (1955), pp. 345-59. For an international comparative treatment, see H. W. Ehrmann, ed., *Interest Groups on Four Continents* (1958).

[5] Wootton, p. 83.

[6] Ibid., chs. 3 and 4.

[7] For an interesting application of these two models to American government as well as an explanation of the theory, see Thomas R. Dye and L. Harmon Ziegler, *The Irony of Democracy* (1971). For more general discussion of élites, see T. B. Bottomore, *Elites and Society* (1966).

[8] Wootton, pp. 97ff.

[9] Arnold Wolfers, 'The Actors in World Politics', in idem, ed., *Discord and Collaboration: Essays on International Politics* (1962), p. 23.

[10] For a discussion of the importance of the concept of role, see Talcott Parsons, *The Social System* (1951), and Edgar Borgatta, 'Role-Playing Specification, Personality and Performance', *Sociometry*, vol. 24 (1961), pp. 218-33.

[11] This interesting concept is found in Julius Stone, *Social Dimensions of Law and Justice* (1966), pp. 116-18, 796-8.

[12] CCIA, *Annual Report 1968/69*, p. 6.

[13] *New York Times,* 18 July 1954.

[14] *The Guardian,* 14 May 1962. He is Principal of the Syrian Orthodox Theological Seminary in Kerala, India.

[15] *The Times,* 4 July 1949.

[16] *Neues Deutschland,* 7 Aug. 1956.

[17] *The Manchester Guardian,* 26 Aug. 1958.

[18] *The Guardian,* 5 July 1968.

[19] *Christian Science Monitor,* 3 Jan. 1953; *The Guardian,* 30 Nov. 1961.

[20] *New York Herald Tribune,* 19 Aug. 1954.

[21] *The Times,* 20 Aug. 1954.

[22] *New York Times,* 21 Aug. 1954.

[23] *The Times,* 24 Nov. 1961.

[24] WCC, Central Committee, *Minutes 1962,* p. 7.

[25] *The Times,* 29 Aug. 1963.

[26] *Frankfurter Allgemeine Zeitung,* 11 July 1968.

[27] Dr Jürgen Winterhagen, Executive Secretary of the Berlin Ecumenical Committee, 'Ueberwindung falscher Fronten', *Der Tagesspiegel,* 6 Jan. 1957.

[28] Walter Van Kirk, 'Pilgrimage to Amsterdam', *Christian Science Monitor,* 20 Aug. 1948.

[29] *Neues Deutschland* and *Der Tagesspiegel,* 14 Jan. 1950.

[30] *New York Times,* 5 Aug. 1956.

[31] *Frankfurter Allgemeine Zeitung,* 11 July 1969.

[32] *The Times,* 18 and 22 Feb. 1966.

[33] *Daily Telegraph,* 6 Aug. 1951.

[34] Three categories of NGOs are recognized by ECOSOC. Category I (formerly Category A) includes only those organizations which have a basic interest in all of ECOSOC's activities; among these are international business and trade union federations. They have formal opportunity to comment orally or in writing or in both ways. Category II (formerly Category B), of which there are more than 100, need have special competence in only a few of its activities. They may comment in writing only. Finally there is a Register of NGOs not in continuous consultative relationship with ECOSOC. Christian modesty and the meagre resources of the CCIA in 1947 had caused application for Category B status only. However, in view of its limitless boundaries as the Christian conscience, and the wide scope of its other activities, the CCIA applied for Category I status in 1969 during an ECOSOC review of its relationships with NGOs. Mr Aldron-Ramsey of Tanzania opposed Category I status for any religious body and proposed Category II status for the CCIA. He was seconded by Mr Nasinovsky, who, however, spoke quite favourably of the world-wide activities of the CCIA. By a vote of 6-0 with 6 abstentions, the CCIA was granted, and accepted, Category II status. (CCIA, *Annual Report 1968/69,* p. 29.)

[35] The first incident is noted in the CCIA correspondence files. The second is reported in CCIA, 'Report on the Tenth Conference of the FAO, October-November 1959' (mimeograph).

[36] 21 Apr. 1970.

[37] 'Friede zwischen den Kirchen', *Frankfurter Allgemeine Zeitung,* 23 Sept. 1966.

[38] *New York Herald Tribune,* 23 Aug. 1948; *The Times,* 4 Sept. 1948.

[39] 5 Aug. 1954.

[40] 18 Aug. 1958.

[41] 29 Aug. 1959 (and it was now called *The Guardian*).

[42] 6 and 23 Dec. 1961.

[43] In both cases 28 Aug. 1948.

[44] 27 Mar. 1951.

[45] 27 and 28 Aug. 1958.

[46] 17 July 1950.

[47] Reported in *The Scotsman*, 19 May 1954.

[48] 3 Sept. 1954 (author's translation).

[49] See, *inter alia*, *Neues Deutschland*, 4 Aug. 1956; the *Daily Worker* (London), 6 Aug. 1957, 12 Feb. 1959, 24 Aug. 1959, as examples.

[50] CCIA, *Annual Report 1968/69*, p. 32.

[51] *Report of the Structure Committee to the Central Committee* (Geneva, WCC, 1970), p. 19.

[52] CCIA, *Annual Report 1968/69*, p. 6.

[53] WCC, 'Conference on International Affairs, Cambridge, August 4th to 7th 1946', Paper III: 'The Churches and the United Nations' (typescript).

[54] Visser 't Hooft, ed., *The First Assembly*, p. 10.

EPILOGUE

[1] For a detailed report of WCC activities from 1968 to 1975, see David Johnson, ed., *Uppsala to Nairobi* (New York, Friendship Press, 1975).

[2] A. H. van den Heuvel, 'Ecumenical Diary', *Ecumenical Review*, 28:1 (Jan. 1976), p. 97.

[3] 'Protest by Briton as World Church Assembly Opens', *The Times*, 24 Nov. 1975.

[4] 'Facts about the Fifth Assembly', *Target*, 22 Nov. 1975.

[5] David M. Gill, 'The Fifth Assembly As (Some) Participants Saw It' (Geneva, WCC, 1976, mimeo), p. 5.

[6] van den Heuval, p. 99.

[7] 'World Church Council Elects 2 Women', *New York Times*, 7 Dec. 1975.

[8] 'Western Delegates Walk Out in WCC Protest', *The Times*, 3 Dec. 1975.

[9] *The Times*, 6 Dec. 1975.

[10] *Guardian* and *The Times*, 8 Dec. 1975.

[11] 'Bischof Class ist nicht gekommen', *Frankfurter Allgemeine Zeitung*, 24 Nov. 1975.

[12] Reports available to the author were not necessarily in final, edited form. All Nairobi reports may be found in the official report of the Assembly—David M. Paton, ed., *Breaking Barriers: Nairobi 1975* (London, SPCK, 1976).

[13] Gerard Kemp, '£128,000 Church Aid for African "Freedom Groups"', *Daily Telegraph*, 19 Nov. 1975, and Christopher Dobson, 'Churches' Crisis of Cash and Marxism', ibid., 23 Nov. 1975.

[14] Religionsfreiheit in Russland nur "angeblich" verletzt', *Frankfurter Allgemeine Zeitung*, 11 Dec. 1975; *The Times*, 10 Dec. 1975.

[15] Roger Mehl, 'Après la clôture de l'assemblée mondiale de Nairobi', *Le Monde*, 21/22 Dec. 1975.

[16] This article appears in full, along with other addresses to the Assembly, in *Ecumenical Review*, 28:1 (Jan. 1976), pp. 66-79.

[17] Dr Fagley's prescription for the role of the churches in the matter of disarmament: see the last paragraph of chapter 4 above.

[18] 'Ökumenischer Rat vermeidet Polarisierung', *Frankfurter Allgemeine Zeitung*, 2 Dec. 1975.

[19] 'Kämpferische Spiritualität in Nairobi, *Frankfurter Allgemeine Zeitung*, 25 Nov. 1975.

Select Bibliography

1. DOCUMENTS

Commission of the Churches on International Affairs. 'Background Documentation on Disarmament and Related Questions.' Mimeograph.
— Minutes 1948, 1954, 1961, 1968. Mimeograph.
— Enlarged Executive Committee. Minutes 1952. Mimeograph.
— Executive Committee. Minutes 1948-72. Mimeograph.
— — 'Report on the Tenth Conference of the FAO, October-November 1959'. Mimeograph.
Fagley, Richard M. 'The First Twenty Years in Outline', in CCIA, Executive Committee, Minutes 1966, Annex I. Mimeograph.
'Minutes of the Conference on the Situation in Korea at the Aldine Club, New York, October 11, 1912.' Typescript.
Report on the Memorial of the Churches for Peace Presented to the Conference at The Hague, 25th June, 1907. [London, privately printed, 1907.]
World Council of Churches. 'Conference on International Affairs, Cambridge, August 4th-7th 1946.' Typescript.
— Central Committee. 'Report on the World Council of Churches Sponsored Consultation on Racism Held in Notting Hill, London, May 19-24 1969 to the Central Committee Meeting in August 1969.' Mimeograph.
— — 'Withdrawal of Investments from Southern Africa.' Mimeograph. (Document 2A for Central Committee meeting at Geneva, 27-29 Aug. 1973.)

2. BOOKS AND ARTICLES

Abrecht, Paul. *The Churches and Rapid Social Change.* New York, Doubleday, 1961.
Adler, Elisabeth. *A Small Beginning: an Assessment of the First Five Years of the Programme to Combat Racism.* Geneva, WCC, 1974.
All Africa Conference of Churches. *Consultation Digest: a summary of Reports and Addresses . . . Inter-church Aid Consultation, Enugu, Eastern Nigeria, 4-9 January 1956.* Geneva, WCC, 1967.
Almond, Gabriel A. and G. Bingham Powell, Jr. *Comparative Politics: a Developmental Approach.* Boston, Mass., Little, Brown, 1966.
Ankrah, Kodwo E. 'Sudan: the Church and Peace'. *Africa,* no. 9 (May 1972), pp. 58-63.
Baldwin, James. 'White Racism or World Community.' *Ecumenical Review,* 20:40 (Oct. 1968).
Banks, Michael. 'Systems Analysis and the Study of Regions.' *International Studies Quarterly,* 13:4 (Dec. 1969).
Bauer, Fr Gerhard, ed. *Towards a Theology of Development: an Annotated Bibliography.* Geneva, Committee on Society, Development and Peace, 1970.
Beaujeu-Garnier, J. *Geography of Population.* New York, St Martin's Press, 1966.

Bell, George K. A., ed. *The Stockholm Conference, 1925.* London, OUP, 1926.

Bennett, John C., ed. *Christian Ethics in a Changing World.* Geneva, WCC, 1966.

Berger, Peter L. and Richard John Neuhaus. *Movement and Revolution.* New York, Doubleday, 1970.

Bhagwati, Jagdish. *The Economics of Underdeveloped Countries.* New York, McGraw-Hill, 1966.

Bock, Paul. 'Ecumenical Reconstruction in Europe.' Unpublished MST thesis, Yale Divinity School, 1957.

Borgatta, Edgar. 'Role-Playing Specification, Personality and Performance.' *Sociometry,* vol. 24 (1961), pp. 218-33.

Bottomore, T. B. *Elites and Society.* Harmondsworth, Penguin, 1966.

Bull, Hedley. *The Control of the Arms Race.* London, Weidenfeld & Nicholson, 1961.

Carnegie Endowment for International Peace, Division of International Law. *The Proceedings of the Hague Peace Conferences, the Conference of 1907,* vol 1 : *Plenary Meetings of the Conference.* New York, OUP, 1920.

Commission of the Churches on International Affairs. *Annual Report, 1947/48–1971/72.*

Committee on Society, Development and Peace. *World Development: Challenge to the Churches. The Conference on World Co-operation for Development, Beirut, Lebanon, April 21-27, 1968.* Geneva, 1968.

— *In Search of a Theology of Development: Papers from a Consultation on Theology and Development held by Sodepax in Cartigny, Switzerland, November 1969.* Geneva, Ecumenical Centre, 1970.

— *Partnership or Privilege? An Ecumenical Reaction to the Second Development Decade,* and *A Supplement.* Geneva, 1970.

— *Picking up the Pieces.* Geneva, 1971.

Cook, Robert, C. *Human Fertility: the Modern Dilemma.* New York, William Sloan Association, 1951.

Counter Information Services (CIS). *Business as Usual: International Banking in South Africa.* London, CIS for WCC, 1974.

Dejung, Karl-Heinz. 'Die Ökumenische Bewegung im Entwicklungskonflikt, 1910-1968.' Dissertation, Evangelisch-Theologischen Fakultät, Univ. of Heidelberg, 1972.

Deutsch, Karl. *The Analysis of International Relations.* Englewood Cliffs, NJ, Prentice-Hall, 1968.

Dickinson, Richard. *Line and Plummet. The Churches and Development.* Geneva, WCC, 1968.

Dye, Thomas R. and L. Harmon Ziegler. *The Irony of Democracy.* Belmont, Calif., Wadsworth, 1971.

Eckstein, Harry. 'The Politics of the British Medical Association.' *Political Quarterly,* 26:4 (1955).

Edwards, David V. *Arms Control in International Politics.* New York, Holt, Rinehart & Winston, 1969.

Ehrlich, Paul R. *The Population Bomb.* Rev. edn. New York, Ballantine, 1971.

Ehrmann, H. W., ed. *Interest Groups on Four Continents.* Pittsburgh, Pa, Univ. of Pittsburgh Press, 1958.

Elliott, Charles. *The Development Debate.* London, SCM Press, 1971.

Enke, Stephen. 'Agricultural Innovation and Community Development', in Lewis P. Fickett, Jr, ed., *Problems of the Developing Nations.* New York, Thomas Y. Crowell, 1966.

Fagley, Richard. *The Population Explosion and Christian Responsibility*. New York, OUP, 1960.

Francis, Roy, ed. *The Population Ahead*. Minneapolis, Univ. of Minnesota Press, 1958.

Garn, Stanley M. and Carleton S. Coon. 'On the Number of Races of Mankind'. *American Anthropologist*, 57:5 (1955).

Goodall, Norman. 'The Challenge of the Pretoria Conference'. *Ecumenical Review*, 6:4 (July 1954).

— ed. *The Uppsala Report 1968*. Geneva, WCC, 1968.

Grubb, Kenneth. *Crypts of Power: an Autobiography*. London, Hodder & Stoughton, 1971.

Gruber, Pamela H., ed. *Fetters of Injustice: Report of an Ecumenical Consultation on Ecumenical Assistance to Development Projects, 26-31 January, Montreux, Switzerland*. Geneva, WCC, 1970.

Hatt, Paul K., ed. *World Population and Future Resources*. New York, American Books, 1952.

Heilbroner, Robert L. 'The Engineering of Development', in Lewis P. Fickett, Jr, ed., *Problems of the Developing Nations*. New York, Thomas Y. Crowell, 1966.

Hudson, Darril. *The Ecumenical Movement in World Affairs*. London, Weidenfeld & Nicolson, 1969.

Judge, Anthony J. N. 'Visualization of the Organizational Network—the UIA as an International Data Bank', in *Union of International Associations 1910–1970: Past, Present, Future*. Brussels, UIA, 1970. (Documents no. 17.)

Karefa-Smart, Rena. 'Africa Asks Questions of the West'. *Ecumenical Review*, 10:1 (Oct. 1957).

Keohane, Robert O. and Joseph S. Nye, Jr, eds. *Transnational Relations and World Politics*. Cambridge, Mass., Harvard UP, 1972.

Lancaster, Carol J. 'The Politics of the Powerless, Pressure in the United Nations for Economic Development 1945-1965'. Unpublished Ph.D. thesis, Univ. of London, 1972.

Mackenzie, W. J. M. 'Pressure Groups in British Government'. *British Journal of Sociology*, 6:2 (1955).

Meynaud, Jean. *Groupes de Pression*. Lausanne, Etudes de Science Politique, 1961.

— and Dusan Sidjanski. *Les Groupes de Pression dans la Communauté Européenne*. 2 vols. Montreal, Univ. of Montreal, 1969.

Mikesell, Raymond F. *The Economics of Foreign Aid*. Chicago, Aldine, 1968.

Miles, Edward. 'Organizations and Integration in International Systems'. *International Studies Quarterly*, 12:2 (June 1968).

Moberly, Walter and others. *The Churches Survey Their Task*. London, Allen & Unwin, 1937.

Moltmann, Jürgen. 'Racism and the Right to Resist'. *Study Encounter*, 8:1 (1971).

National Council of Churches, Corporate Information Center. *The Frankfurt Documents: Secret Bank Loans to the South African Government*. New York, 1973.

Noel-Baker, Philip. *The Arms Race*. Dobbs Ferry, NY, Oceana, 1962.

Nolde, O. Frederick. *The Churches and the Nations*. Philadelphia, Pa, Fortress Press, 1970.

Nussbaum, Arthur. *A Concise History of the Law of Nations*. New York, Macmillan, 1947.

Oldham, J. H. *The Oxford Conference*. Chicago, Ill., Willett, Clark, 1937.

Osborn, Frederick. *Population: an International Dilemma.* New York, Population Council, 1958.

Paddock, William and Paul. *Famine, 1975!* Boston, Mass., Little, Brown, 1967.

Paton, David M., ed., *Breaking Barriers: Nairobi 1975.* London, SPCK, 1976.

Parsons, Talcott. *The Social System.* Glencoe, Ill., Free Press, 1951.

Peace and the Churches. London, Cassell [1908].

Pincus, John. *Trade, Aid and Development: the Rich and Poor Nations.* New York, McGraw-Hill, 1967.

Randall, Peter, ed. *Power, Privilege and Poverty.* Johannesburg, SPRO-CAS, 1972.

Rian, Edwin H., ed. *Christianity and World Revolution.* New York, Harper & Row, 1963.

Rouse, Ruth and Stephen C. Neill, eds. *A History of the Ecumenical Movement 1517–1948,* 2nd edn. London, SPCK, 1967.

Rudersdorf, Karl-Heinrich. 'Entwicklungsförderung und christliche Kirchen. Entstehung und Entwicklung des Konzepts der Entwicklungsförderung im Weltrat der Kirchen'. Dissertation, Philosophy Faculty, Free University of Berlin, 1973.

Siegmund-Schultze, F., ed. *Friendly Relations Between Great Britain and Germany.* Berlin, privately printed, 1910.

Söderblom, Nathan. *Christian Fellowship.* New York, F. H. Revell, 1923.

Spanier, John and Joseph Nogee. *The Politics of Disarmament: Study in Soviet-American Gamesmanship.* New York, Praeger, 1962.

Stebbins, Richard P. *The United States in World Affairs, 1950.* New York, Council on Foreign Relations, 1951.

Stone, Julius. *Social Dimensions of Law and Justice.* Stanford, Calif., Stanford UP, 1966.

Strachey, John. *On the Prevention of War.* London, Macmillan, 1942.

Union of International Associations. *Yearbook of International Organizations.* Brussels, UIA, 1974.

Visser 't Hooft, W. A. *The Ten Formative Years, 1938–1948: Report on the Activities of the World Council of Churches during its Period of Formation.* Geneva, WCC, 1948.

— *Christianity, Race and South African People. Report: an Ecumenical Visit.* New York, National Council of Churches of Christ in USA, 1952.

— 'A Visit to South African Churches in April and May 1952'. *Ecumenical Review,* 5:2 (Jan. 1953).

— *The Evanston Report.* New York, Harper, 1955.

— ed. *The First Assembly of the World Council of Churches: the Official Report.* New York, Harper & Bros, 1949. (This is vol. 5 of WCC, *Man's Disorder and God's Design.* Harper & Bros, 1949.)

— ed. *The New Delhi Report.* New York, Association Press, 1962.

de Vries, Egbert. *Man in Rapid Social Change.* New York, Doubleday, 1961.

Wilson, Bryan. *Religion in Secular Society, a Sociological Comment.* London, Watts, 1966.

Wolfers, Arnold. 'The Actors in World Politics', in Arnold Wolfers, ed. *Discord and Collaboration: Essays on International Politics.* Baltimore, Md, Johns Hopkins Press, 1962.

Wootton, Graham. *Interest Groups.* Englewood Cliffs, NJ, Prentice-Hall, 1970.

World Alliance for Promoting International Friendship Through the

Churches. *The Churches and International Friendship, Report of the Conference held at Constance, August 1914.* London, 1914.

World Conference on Church and Society. *Official Report.* Geneva, WCC, 1967.

World Council of Churches. *The World Council of Churches, Its Process of Formation: Minutes and Reports of the Meeting of the Provisional Committee of the World Council of Churches held at Geneva from Feb. 21st to 23rd, 1946; the Constitutional Documents of the . . . and an Introduction by W. A. Visser 't Hooft.* Geneva, 1946.

—— *Statements of the World Council of Churches on Social Questions.* 2nd edn. Geneva, 1956.

—— *The Witness of the Churches Amidst Social Change in Asia.* Geneva, 1959.

—— *Mission in South Africa, April–December 1960.* Geneva, 1961.

—— *Ecumenical Statements on Race Relations.* Geneva, 1965.

—— Central Committee. *Minutes, 1948–74.*

—— —— *New Delhi to Uppsala, 1961–1968.* Geneva, 1968.

—— —— *Report of the Structure Committee to the Central Committee, Addis Ababa, January 1971.* Geneva, Oct. 1970.

—— —— *Uppsala to Nairobi.* Geneva, 1975.

—— Department on Church and Society. *Christians and Race Relations in Southern Africa.* Geneva, 1964.

—— —— *Dilemmas and Opportunities: Christian Action in Rapid Social Change, Report of an International Ecumenical Study Conference, Thessalonica, Greece, July 25–August 2, 1959.* Geneva, 1959.

—— Division of Studies. *The Responsible Society in National and International Affairs: the Arnoldshain Report 1956.* Geneva, 1956.

—— Programme to Combat Racism. *The Cunene Dam Scheme and the Struggle for the Liberation of Southern Africa.* Geneva, 1972.

—— —— *Time to Withdraw: Investments in Southern Africa.* Geneva, 1973.

—— Second Assembly. *International Affairs—Christians in the Struggle for World Community.* New York, Harper, 1954.

Index